THE COMPLETE HANDBOOK OF BLOCK SCHEDULING

THE COMPLETE HANDBOOK OF BLOCK SCHEDULING

*Success for Students and Teachers through
Efficient Use of Time and Human Resources*

Thomas L. Shortt, Ed.D.
Yvonne V. Thayer, Ed.D.

A complete how-to for secondary school principals on alternative scheduling—including a CD that features master schedules, lesson plans, informational materials, surveys, and assessment tools

TECHNOS Press of the Agency for Instructional Technology
Bloomington, Indiana
www.technos.net

$39.95US
Published by TECHNOS Press of the Agency for Instructional Technology
Box A, Bloomington, IN 47402-0120
Internet: www.technos.net

CD-ROM
With printable, downloadable, and editable materials
Includes html and Microsoft® Word documents
Macintosh® and Windows® compatible
Includes Netscape Navigator® for Windows® 95/98/NT and Mac OS®
Usable with Netscape® or Internet Explorer®

AIT Customer Service 1-800-457-4509
Internet: www.ait.net

First Edition

ISBN 0-7842-0874-3

Library of Congress Catalog Card Number: 99-65522

CAROL BENTHAL-BINGLEY, B2 Design, *Cover Designer*
AMY BOND, TECHNOS Press Coordinator, *Publication Coordinator*
VANESSA DENNEN, quirkalot productions, *CD Programmer*
KARLA DUNN, AIT Marketing Specialist, *Text Designer & Compositor*
CAROLE NOVAK, Manager of TECHNOS Press, *Editor*
MICHAEL F. SULLIVAN, Executive Director, Agency for Instructional Technology, *Publisher*
STEPHANIE ZAISER, AIT's The Learning Odyssey Assistant Editor, *Assistant Editor*

Printed by Maple-Vail Book Manufacturing Group of The Maple Press Company, York, Pennsylvania, USA

TABLE OF CONTENTS

Staff development
Satisfying our education customers
Looking back . . .

CHAPTER 4—HOW WILL TEACHERS, STUDENTS, AND ADMINISTRATORS BENEFIT FROM A BLOCK SCHEDULING FRAMEWORK? 33

Looking ahead in this chapter . . .
Teachers
Students
Administration
Instruction
Comparison of alternating day, semester, and embedded block schedule models
The underlying principles and anticipated outcomes of block scheduling
Identifying measurable outcomes
Optimal use of time, skills, and energy
The planning cycle for block scheduling
Looking back . . .

CHAPTER 5—HOW DO YOU BUILD A SOLID FOUNDATION FOR BLOCK SCHEDULING? 47

Looking ahead in this chapter . . .
Building support for change
What is school restructuring?
How do principals engage teachers in change?
What is a school study team?
What is the selection process for? What are the responsibilities of a study team?
The role of the principal
Implementing the change process
Increasing the knowledge base
Who are the members of the school study team and action teams?
The school study team leader
Action teams
  The curriculum and instruction action team
  The public relations/communication action team
  The staff development action team
School study team membership
  Students
  Private/business sector of the community
  Professional community
  Special interest groups
  Others
  Faculty and staff
  Central office staff
  Support staff

What are the responsibilities of a school study team?
What restructuring possibilities should the study team explore?
Student issues
Instructional issues
Teacher issues
Administrative issues
Organizational issues
Timeline
Public relations/communication plan
Plan for all budgeting considerations
Plan for all staffing needs
Looking back . . .

CHAPTER 6—HOW DOES A SCHOOL STUDY TEAM DEVELOP STRATEGIES TO GET STARTED?   69

Looking ahead in this chapter . . .
What are the administrative issues that the study team should consider?
Creating a grassroots initiative
Determining the length of the school day
Examining the issues of time and learning
Creating more instructional time per class
Using homework to extend learning
Offering more courses
Improving the school climate
Steps to starting the change process
Using a network to gather resources
Collecting data
Preparing to conduct school visitations or surveying identified schools for information
Deciding who will visit schools
Preparing for the visit
Questions most frequently asked by customers considering a block scheduling format
Questions and responses regarding block scheduling typically asked during school visitations
Collecting data via surveys
Looking back . . .

CHAPTER 7—WHAT ORGANIZATIONAL ISSUES MUST BE ADDRESSED?   99

Looking ahead in this chapter . . .
Organizational issues
Review and study the schedule options
Investigate budgetary considerations
Consider the future financial impact
Establish the goals of a restructured day
Establish strategies to meet new objectives
Identify an action team to collect sample schedules

CHAPTER 8—WHAT LESSONS HAVE WE LEARNED FROM MIDDLE SCHOOL SCHEDULING?   137

CHAPTER 9—HOW DOES THE INSTRUCTIONAL PROGRAM CHANGE WHEN THE STAFF EXAMINES THE USE OF TIME?   151

CHAPTER 10—HOW DOES STAFF DEVELOPMENT LEAD TO IMPROVED INSTRUCTION?   189

CHAPTER 11—HOW DO WE BUILD A MASTER SCHEDULE?   209

IF the 1980s are remembered for anything in education, it is the attention given during those years to making schools more effective. As we began to use "restructuring" as our catch-all term for changing schools, we saw school leaders turn their ears toward the voices of the authors of *A Nation At Risk,* to John Goodlad and Madeleine Hunter, and to the many others who talked about what schools needed to do to be better. Among the topics of conversation that school reformers encouraged was that of time for learning. Some called for longer school days and school years, and others suggested looking seriously at what was occurring during the time that we had.

In the decade of the '80s, little was said about restructuring time. Yet the notion of restructuring in education goes far beyond changing staffing patterns, designing middle-level education, or training teachers in technology. Those things that we did in the name of restructuring were only part of a picture of school reform that might improve student achievement—the ultimate goal any of us should have had for restructuring.

Beginning in 1990, some of us thought seriously about how time was being used in our schools. We knew there was a lot of wasted time in class— unproductive time that did not engage students in learning. We knew that many teachers lectured too much and made no attempt to connect what they were doing each day to a larger context of learning. We knew that students had changed and were continuing to change and that their expectations for school were very low. We also knew that the environment surrounding education was becoming less tolerant of mediocrity. Greater numbers of parents expected their children to prepare for college while universities published data showing that a shocking number of students required remedial classes. Employers became actively interested in education, fearing that the unskilled applicants knocking on their doors were going to continue to expect jobs in a workplace that was technically oriented. Taxpayers sounded the alarm on growing education

costs, putting administrators in the middle of a battle for resources between crumbling infrastructure and weakening academic performance.

As the tension increased between implementing reform measures and adopting a back-to-basics philosophy, some school leaders began thinking about what could be done to really change what was happening in classrooms. One of those people was Tom Shortt, who was serving as a planning principal after spending several years in senior management in industry. A decade earlier, Tom had conducted research on time in classrooms and was convinced that time could be utilized better than what he had seen in school after school. Given the opportunity to open a new high school, Tom developed a block schedule for Atlee High School in Hanover County, Virginia, which was the first in a public school in Virginia and would serve as a model for the state and, later, the nation. Within two years, 33 high schools in Virginia were using a block schedule, among them the high school in the Gloucester County Schools division where Yvonne Thayer was assistant superintendent for instruction services.

In the years that have followed, we have worked with school leaders throughout our state, in other states, and in other countries to understand the advantages of block scheduling and the possibilities it has for helping to strengthen a school program. We have tried to answer the nitty-gritty questions about how to make this schedule work, as well as questions related to the larger issues of changing schools and changing teacher behavior. Additionally, we have tried to be visionary and suggest actions school leaders can take to avoid problems with block scheduling now and in the future. It has become crystal clear to us after numerous presentations and workshops that school principals and teachers need help with block scheduling. They need assistance from the day they begin thinking about a different way of using time, through the planning and implementation phase of block scheduling, to the staff development that continues several years into the scheduling change.

This book is our answer to the hundreds of questions that have risen about block scheduling. We hope the book provides more than simple answers, because we have intentionally made it comprehensive, dealing with all of the issues we found facing us, but trying to provide assistance that an administrator, in particular, needs. We have included in this book many sample schedules—student schedules, teacher schedules, bell schedules, and master schedules—for various types of block schedules. An administrator should be able to use this book to think about issues, plan comprehensively, and find resources in the book that will help him or her get started. Included are case studies and anecdotes that give the reader real examples of experiences we have had that have brought us to our consensual thinking about scheduling and using time.

Embedded throughout this book is a model for change that we believe any school leader can use. Although the book is about block scheduling, it serves a second purpose—that of showing administrators the change process based on our experiences of what worked in our schools. We admit up front that we both have been engulfed in Total Quality for a decade, and we believe completely in process improvement in schools using the tenets and practices of Quality espoused by W. Edwards Deming, Joseph Juran, and Tom Peters. We are not in the least apologetic about this bias. Our experience of working in educational organizations at the local, state, and national levels, and Tom's experience in business, has grounded our beliefs. Our work as change agents in block-scheduled schools is based on our belief that people will rise to the challenge of change, if emphasis is put on improving the system while supporting those who must make the system work. We believe that leadership is key to successful change—during the exploration and planning stage, during implementation, and continuing toward institutionalization.

Our book is presented in 13 chapters. While written as a sequential look at a school's change to block scheduling, each chapter stands alone. We believe that a school leader, teacher, parent, or community member could read a chapter independent of the others to obtain specific information. We know this structure is important, because often we find ourselves too busy to read several chapters leading up to the information we need for a meeting the next day. We also recognize that many folks are in process with block scheduling and may be interested in some parts of the book more than others. In addition, readers will find a wealth of information on the accompanying CD, produced by the Agency for Instructional Technology, to assist them in preparing for, implementing, and evaluating block scheduling in their schools.

The first chapter of this book establishes the context by exploring the current educational setting. It asks the question: "Will America's educators face up to change?" because we know it is easier to avoid addressing the tough questions facing America's schools. We try to get readers thinking about why we need to change. This is followed by a chapter that defines block scheduling. There are a number of types of block schedules being used and talked about, so we define them and talk about how each block works. We also introduce the notion of value-added time in Chapter 2, helping the reader understand the ultimate goal we have for block scheduling—improving how time is used in the classroom.

Chapter 3 presents a review of literature related to time and block scheduling. This leads to the chapter that discusses the benefits of block scheduling. After looking at the advantages for all users of school time, a comparison is made of various scheduling models, helping the reader understand the principles that undergird the whole notion. A planning cycle is first introduced in Chapter 4.

Chapter 5 helps the administrator get started by introducing the school study team that acts as a school improvement team. Here we discuss the make-up of the team and how action teams support the work that must be done in the planning phase. The next chapter suggests the actions in which the teams engage. Steps for beginning the change process include surveying and gathering data. Sample survey forms and letters that teams can use are included on the accompanying CD. A major portion of this chapter is devoted to listing and answering commonly asked questions about block scheduling.

Chapter 7 looks at organizational issues, including those that impact the school budget. The bulk of the chapter presents schedules for alternate day, semester, and other block schedules—and even more are presented on the CD. This comprehensive look at scheduling should answer questions that administrators, in particular, might have about the day-to-day organization of the block.

We leave the high school at this point to review what has been learned about scheduling at the middle school level. Middle school philosophy has encouraged teaming and arranging schedules that support interdisciplinary studies. Chapter 8 offers background, schedules, and supportive documents from middle schools (as does the CD). This chapter is intended to provide background information for the high school administrative staff and can help middle school administrators look at scheduling options that match the middle school philosophy.

Chapter 9 focuses on the instructional program. Perhaps the most critical part of this effort, instructional strategies and curriculum issues, are addressed in this section. To help teachers understand what classrooms look like in block scheduling, we provide sample lesson plans from practicing classroom teachers on block schedules representing various subject areas. (See the CD for more sample plans.) This chapter is followed by a look at staff development. We believe that nothing is more important than good staff development in preparing and supporting teachers through the change process. Chapter 10 suggests the specific training that a principal and planning team will consider.

Chapter 11 is designed to help the principal build the schedule after having looked at many models and having considered the issues for his/her school. Master schedules are constructed to help the reader work through this process of design, and concerns about student and teacher loads are addressed. The accompanying CD provides more examples.

Chapter 12 is designed to help the leader assess success with block scheduling by planning what is to be measured and what data is to be collected. Using the Quality planning process and tools that assist in managing and displaying data, the reader learns how to measure that which is important so that s/he can demonstrate effectiveness to customers of the school and continually improve that which has begun.

The final chapter, 13, allows us to explore briefly the future of block scheduling, given the changes we see occurring in the school business and our society. We consider the social, political, economic, technological, and cultural changes that are impacting our schools. We conclude our book with our hope for the future of block scheduling and our expectation that schools will continue to change rather dramatically in the next decade. We hope the reader leaves the book with the understanding that creative scheduling is not a one-time episode but will become one of the decisions that will be made on a regular basis as student needs evolve in our technological society.

We offer this book to our many friends in the profession who work hard every day to bring the best to the youth of this country. We thank you for thinking seriously about change and trust that your motives center on providing greater opportunities for students to learn, grow, and contribute to our world. Our work as educators is too important to trivialize this effort as another passing fad. We hope that the questions raised by this book and the ideas presented will serve as benchmarks for those who have not begun the journey toward changing how time is used. For those on the journey with us, we hope this book is helpful in evaluating where we are and what our next steps must be . . .

Continually to improve our education system. ❏

—T. S. and Y. T.

About the Use of this Book

Since this book has been designed to be used by educators who have previously implemented a block schedule format or by educators who are currently considering a block schedule format, we have given much thought to its format. After much consideration of the many formats that are on the market, we choose to present this book in a HANDBOOK format that we think will be most useful to you—the educator, teacher, building principal, district superintendent, central office administrator, curriculum specialist, supervisor—or if you are just interested in improving teaching and learning. The book has been divided into 13 specific chapters based on suggestions from seminars that we have conducted and input that we have received from educators throughout the country.

As a result, any one of the 13 chapters may be used independently. We propose that you skim the table of contents and find the chapter that will best suit your particular needs at any given point when considering school reform. Whether the issues that you are facing deal with a grassroots initiative to gain support for designing and implementing a block schedule, or refining the block schedule that you previously implemented, there is a chapter that will assist you in finding solutions as you consider different ways of increasing student achievement through a focus on teaching and learning.

We believe the change process that is described throughout this handbook is applicable to most initiatives that require a major change throughout the school. Basing decisions on data, involving faculty and community, using goals to guide actions, providing staff development, and monitoring success are all steps that lead to renewal, restructuring, and school improvement. ❑

We utilized the experiences of many educators as we conceptualized this book. We thank everyone who has spoken to us at a conference; called, written, or e-mailed us with information; or shared documents with us during the last eight years.

The authors acknowledge the following colleagues and friends for their substantial contributions to this book.

Carole Novak, for her understanding, support, and patience

The **students (especially), teachers, staff, and community** of Atlee High School in Hanover County, Va., from 1991–94, who worked so hard and showed the commitment to change needed to implement Virginia's first block schedule

Jean King, principal at Gloucester High School in Gloucester County, Va.

Dot Jones, Special Education Services in Henrico County, Va.

Phyllis Ayers, Virginia Department of Education, Richmond

Patricia Bailey, math teacher, Atlee High School, Hanover County, Va.

Wayne Mallard, C.D. Hylton High School, Prince William County, Va.

Sara Jo Williams, director of Guidance and Counseling, Atlee High School, Hanover County, Va.

Phyllis Martin, Virginia Department of Education, Richmond

Randy Barrack, executive director of the Virginia Association of Secondary School Principals, Richmond, Va.

James Bryant and *David Claxton,* physical education professors at Western Carolina University in Cullowhee, N.C., for their physical education lesson plan

Dr. Berkley Clear, principal of Abingdon High School in Abingdon, Va., for the short block information

Dr. Joy Colbert, director of the Institute for Connecting Science Research to the Classroom in the College of Human Resources and Education at Virginia Tech in Blacksburg, Va.

Karen Collins, former chair of the mathematics department at Atlee High School in Hanover County, Va., for the framework for institutional change

James Dalton and *George Saddler,* music teachers at Atlee High School in Hanover County, Va., for their comments on the impact of the block schedule on their music program

Luther W. Fennell, principal of Edison High School in Fairfax County, Va., for the embedded schedule information

Wayne D. Flint, principal of Parry McClure High School in Buena Vista, Va., for the E-X-C-E-L program information

Karen Flowe, chair of the English department at Gloucester High School in Gloucester County, Va., for her STIR© (Stimulation-Involvement-Response) 1996 process information

Jan Gaffney, principal at La Quinta High School in La Quinta, Calif., for the combination schedule information

Gloucester High School teachers, for sharing their lesson plans in their teaching fields:
>   *Sheila Austin,* chair of the science department
>   *Melissa Baldwin,* English
>   *Jo Ann Coogan,* French
>   *Jim Eccleston,* government and history
>   *Lora Price,* former chair of the foreign language department
>   *Carolyn Smith,* Advanced Placement Biology
>   *David Sutton,* mathematics

Patricia Griffin, principal, and *Tina P. Lenhart,* faculty planning council, at Princess Anne High School in Virginia Beach, Va., for the case study and staff development report card

David Hottenstein, principal of Hatboro-Horsham High School in Horsham, Penn., for the 4x4 intensive schedule

Dorothy Katauskas, principal of Strath Haven High School in Wallingford, Penn., for the Strath Haven 80-80-20 block schedule information

Dr. Marian B. Stephens, former principal of Osbourn High School in Manassas, Va., for the staff development information

David Stouffer, principal of W. Marshall Sellman School in Cincinnati, Ohio, for the 50-50-50-30 block schedule with intersession information

Dr. W.A. "Tony" Valentino, former principal of Stonewall Jackson Middle School in Mechanicsville, Va., for the block master schedules

A special thanks to Gordon Cawelti and Lynn Canady, who are change agents in the true sense of the word.

A very special thanks goes to one of our teachers, the late Edwards Deming, who helped us understand the meaning of quality in public education.

DEDICATION

Yvonne's: For David and Susie Vest, my very best teachers.

Tom's: To Hobert and Ruth Shortt, my first and best teachers, and to Lee I, Lee II, and Ann. I learn from you, I admire you, and I love you. Especially to Patty, because without her support my involvement in this project would not have happened.

CHAPTER 1

Will America's Educators Face Up to Change?

*T**he biggest infrastructure challenge for this country in the next decade is not the billions needed for railroads, highways, and energy. It is the American school system, from kindergarten through the Ph.D. program and the postgraduate education of adults. And it requires something far scarcer than money—thinking and risk-taking.*

—Peter Drucker

LOOKING AHEAD IN THIS CHAPTER . . .

Only those educators who learn to love change as much as we have disliked change in the past—or at least accept it and welcome it without resistance—will survive the present call of the public for higher expectations and accountability of student performance. Regardless of educators' beliefs about the level of expectations in classrooms and the accountability we feel in communities, the concern expressed throughout the country regarding the performance of American students on internationally compared assessments and the diminished workforce preparedness of graduating seniors imposes great pressure to raise student achievement. Not since the Sputnik challenge of the late 1950s have America's schools been asked to produce better thinking and better prepared students. Unlike the former challenge, today's educators are not being asked to raise performance standards to create more scientists, mathematicians, and engineers. Today's challenge is to strengthen the education of all students while promoting the notion of lifelong learning in order to maintain a strong country that is competitive globally and that depends on American citizens as its workers and leaders.

The structure of the schools impacts the teaching-learning process. The infrastructure of a school—which includes climate, governance, technology, training, time, and human resources—can be shaped in many ways to impact the school philosophy, goals, curriculum, instructional process, and student outcomes. We believe that our final product, student achievement, is largely determined by two factors: human resources and time. Schools depend on human resources to implement changes that could have either positive or negative effects on students. These resources come in many forms. Teachers and administrators are the most obvious, but community members, including school board members, business partners, and parents offer a variety of resources that help schools work. The variety of skills and level of information shared by these individuals can assist teachers and administrators in the awesome task of educating youth.

The second factor, time, determines the amount of exposure to instruction that a student will have. The amount of time designated for learning and the way time is used to enhance the learning process is believed to impact strongly the quantity of concepts and skills introduced to students that build a knowledge base of content and processes. If time in classrooms is sufficient, and if it is "on task," the classroom structure enables student learning.

Linked together, human resources and time are two factors that vary greatly, but they are factors over which we as administrators have much control. To become proactive and deal with the reality of these factors is difficult. It calls for changing some of the procedures and behaviors that are currently a part of the high school. Change is hard, and it is difficult for many administrators to admit that schools aren't working—that the way we are currently doing schooling is not working because all students are not achieving and many are achieving at unacceptably low levels.

The question asked by many of our external customers—the larger community that receives our students upon graduation—is, "Will educators face up to needed change and the consequences of that change?"

WHY IS CHANGE NECESSARY?

In response to pressure from customers, providers of all kinds of services are doing what manufacturers did in the 1980s and early 1990s. They are seeking new and creative methods of providing a quality product—or in this case, a quality service—at a fair price. Providers of services include school systems. Administrators throughout the country are reviewing current scheduling practices as one way of generating the results that are viewed as quality services by their customers. Because of the call for higher academic expectations from all customers—parents, employers, colleges and universities, politicians, and students—educators in school systems are identifying different ways of engaging all students in learning that will prepare them for productive futures. Some high schools and middle schools have abandoned the traditional approach of scheduling instructional time and have initiated different methods of restructuring time so that students and teachers have larger blocks of uninterrupted time that can be used to engage students in active learning.

Change is always a reactive process. It is a response to an idea, a situation, or an occurrence. Sometimes change is initiated to drive a new idea forward, to create a better situation, or to stimulate new thinking. More often change is initiated as a response to a process that is no longer working well. This is the case with schools. Although we measure student success in a variety of ways while the student is in school, the ultimate test of success is found in the student's ability to succeed in his post-high school experience. A number of indicators tell us that students are not doing as well as they should

---

CASE IN POINT

While Tom was working with a group of principals that were trying to come to a consensus about which scheduling configuration the schools would use, two of the administrators became involved in a heated "discussion" about change. One of the participants was very interested in moving to the block scheduling concept while the other principal was satisfied with his school's current schedule. The satisfied principal asked, "Why do we need to change? I have always done it this way. It was this way when I was in school here, and it worked for me as a student."

The response from the dissenting principal was more of a challenge than an answer. "Have you looked at your data to determine if you need to change and to determine if there is a need for improvement? My bet is that you have not and that the indicators for success in your school are flat. Satisfactory, but no continuing improvement!" There was no further discussion of this issue. The responding principal had made his point.

---

when they leave high school. Some students continue working in student jobs (such as fast food), which offer limited opportunities for full-time or management positions. Graduates have problems acquiring primary jobs—those jobs that offer the worker a future and provide an income that will support the American dream. Many students who apply for jobs do not have the technical, academic, and interpersonal skills required for the multi-task, team-oriented workplace. In addition, employers tell us that the high school diploma has lost its credibility and only represents attendance of high school. Companies spend millions of dollars annually training employees in basic skills they believe schools should teach. A large number of the students who begin college never finish, and many of those who attend must complete remedial coursework before being allowed to enroll in credit-bearing classes. Of those completing college, many graduates have difficulty securing jobs in their fields. And on it goes. In addition to the reports of how American students do in comparison with youth from other nations, there is evidence daily that our students leave schools unequipped for the society of the new millennium.

CAN AMERICA'S EDUCATORS MAKE IT WITHOUT CHANGE?

Change is a part of history. Even King Arthur recognized that the only thing constant is change itself. As perfect as Camelot was, he realized that it, too, had to face the inevitable force of change. As he watched his beloved Camelot fall, he declared that nothing stays the same.

There are many educators refusing to believe that change is an attribute of the educational process. Just as students change as they mature, they reflect different learning styles that require teachers to change their methodologies from year to year, class to class, student to student. Just as students change during adolescence, their environments impact on learning, and their changing needs and the experiences that they bring to the learning situation call for greater teacher flexibility. Just as students change as they become more self-directed in their learning, the policies, regulations, and statutes that govern the schools extend and limit the learning situation from year to year, requiring teachers to make adjustments and set new priorities. For those educators who lean back and take an "ain't it awful" view of their changing students, and for those teachers who really believe they can use the same lecture notes year after year, change must be introduced to them not as something that is probable but as something that is inevitable. And for those educators who tire of sameness and love change—love the challenge of moving forward to find what is possible—change becomes the catalyst for continuous improvement.

We can move ahead in time and predict the reaction of another famous literary character, Rip Van Winkle. As he awakens from his long mythical sleep, he perhaps would recognize the American tradition that we know as the high school classroom because it has changed so little in the past century. The culture of the school—that is, the way things are done in the school—is strong, predictable, and resistant to change. As we have worked in schools across the nation, we have found that high schools are remarkably similar. Rural, suburban, and urban classrooms in various regions of the United States are alike. It appears all of the teachers were trained in the same institution. In fact, they were. Our teachers come into the schools from universities, teacher preparation programs, industry, and the military and are acculturated immediately. The institution of schooling perpetuates itself well by issuing its own rewards to those who blend into the school. Those who are different—who try new approaches or challenge the system—meet resistance from administrators and other teachers. The culture always wins. Does change ever occur in schools? Of course, but the culture of a school changes only when the leaders of the organization demonstrate commitment to the change and help establish new norms of behavior. This kind of change doesn't occur frequently, but when it does it is permanent, and the new norms become the new "way we do things around here."

HOW DO WE EFFECT CHANGE?

Although you are willing to look at various opportunities for restructuring, the questions remain: *How do we restructure? How do we know when it is time to change what we are doing?*

Joseph Juran (1989), one of the leaders in the quality management movement, instructs leaders that they cannot identify change strategies without first using a planning process to establish goals and identify systems that will yield quality products. The first step is to initiate a planning process that requires a needs assessment to determine where your school is and what needs to be done to improve student performance. Several questions may help guide the principal's initial thinking about what needs to be done.

- Is there a need for restructuring based on the data I've collected? What is the purpose of reorganizing time?

- How do I identify organizational goals that support the needed restructuring?

- How do I identify strategies for initiating the goals that will ensure success?

- How will I measure the effectiveness of a change, to know whether the change has garnered good results?

HOW CAN WE MAKE CHANGE EASIER?

The mere thought of change may generate a mournful lament of "Change! Change! Who wants Change? Things are hard enough as they are!" Tom Peters (1994, p. 3) suggests that we must move beyond change. Change should become a part of our nature as much as breathing.

> Change. Change. Change. We must learn to deal with it, thrive on it. That's today's relentless refrain. But it's incorrect. Astoundingly, we must move beyond change and embrace nothing less than the literal abandonment of the conventions that brought us to this point. ERADICATE "change" from your vocabulary. Substitute "abandonment" or "revolution" instead.

In other words, change must become the norm. It must be internalized and become second nature to leaders. It must become second nature to find new and creative ways of doing business and to increase productivity for customers. When change becomes the norm in the culture of the school,

teachers and administrators understand continuous improvement to be a philosophy that guides their review of curriculum, teaching practices, and learning results. Regular corrections are made to a system that can produce better learners.

Peters (p. 45) poses another question that educators should answer in considering the commitment that change requires:

> **Question:** Why are companies putting themselves through all this radical (not to mention agonizing) change? **Answer:** Because customers are demanding quick, customized solutions to their problems, and smart companies are reinventing themselves to meet their demands.

For educators, the answer is and should be that we cannot afford not to change. Why? Because of the accountability factor that our customers are demanding in terms of higher test scores, increased attendance, reduced dropouts, and increased community involvement. As the principal in the previous Case in Point lamented, "Are you satisfied with flat indicators?" Can American educators continue to accept their students' leaving school without a diploma, leaving school with a diploma that doesn't mean very much, or leaving school clearly unprepared for the challenges awaiting them?

> . . . [I]n the school, efficient management of the budget is vital; yet a great school is never characterized by the remark, "It has a good budget." The superb school is superb only by virtue of its success in developing its ultimate customer: the student (Peters & Austin, 1985, p. 5).

WHAT IS CHANGE?

Michael Fullan (1991) describes change in educational practices as new materials, new behaviors/practices, and new beliefs/understanding. He suggests that there are patterns of change from which lessons can be learned. These patterns include the following (Fullan, 1995):

- Being able to work with polar opposites

- Pushing for change at the same time as allowing self-learning to unfold

- Being prepared for a journey of uncertainty

- Seeing problems as sources of creative resolution

- Having a vision but not being blinded by it

- Valuing the individual and the group

- Incorporating centralizing and decentralizing forces

- Being internally cohesive but externally oriented

- Valuing personal change as the route to system change

- Being self-conscious about the nature of change and the change process

It is important to note that educators acting as change agents must pay attention to the expertise that will allow successful change to occur. Without expertise and knowledge of the change process itself, a leader is not likely to effect desired change.

HOW DO EDUCATORS CREATE AN ORGANIZATIONAL CLIMATE CONDUCIVE TO CREATIVITY AND CHANGE?

On the basis of the restructuring that we have witnessed and experienced, change is uncomfortable and creates a high level of anxiety among teachers and staff. Some teachers have considered change such a traumatic experience that they have left the educational profession to seek other opportunities that provided a more stable climate. Others have remained and have adjusted over a period of time. During this adjustment period, the school administrator (and teacher-leaders) can facilitate the length of adjustment by providing support in the way of training, listening, and feedback. It becomes imperative at some point, however, to articulate the expectations of the principal to the faculty and staff. All who work in the school must understand that the change under way is moving forward and that you, as principal, expect everyone to support the effort and adjust to the changes being made. You must give people time to learn and adjust, but you must be clear that by an identified time—maybe one year, maybe two years—you expect everyone to be participating to make the change work. At the con-

clusion of the identified time, it is appropriate to reflect your expectations in the performance evaluation process. Currently this process is one of the few mechanisms principals have for recognizing effort and achievement. Clearly, any change that becomes the focus of the school should be rewarded.

CAN TEACHERS CHANGE?

As we gather more and more data related to the use of time, it becomes apparent that the most challenging issue regarding block scheduling may be changing teacher attitudes and classroom behaviors, teaching methods, and practices. This has also been an issue of concern in Canada.

CASE IN POINT

An outstanding veteran math teacher approached Tom during the summer prior to the implementation of the block schedule in his school. She informed him that she was very "nervous" about the anticipated change and was considering retirement. Realizing that her colleagues in the math department were very verbal and supportive of change, she confided in him that she did not want to be an inhibitor of the change that was taking place. She informed him that she had had many anxious moments since the decision had been made to develop a block schedule and that it was affecting her health.

Realizing the contribution that this teacher had made to the school and community and her potential contributions yet to be made, Tom and the teacher developed a plan that would allow her to keep in touch with him on a daily basis until she felt comfortable. She would be the one who would determine when the "hand holding" (as she called it) would end. This period lasted about six weeks.

To this day, she continues to provide outstanding math instruction. Just letting teachers know that you—the lead change agent—share similar anxieties will ease tensions and allow you as principal to provide support and reassurance.

Some teachers have made very little adjustments in their teaching methods in the longer period while others have made major curricular and methodological changes. Those that have made adjustments appear to be far more successful in making the learning experience more rewarding for students. It appears necessary to exchange some of the content normally covered in the past for a more in-depth study of major themes and skills to extract the greatest benefit from full-credit semestering (King, Warren, Bryans, & Pirie, 1977, p. 45).

Some of the data that we are collecting confirm these previous findings. The majority of the complaints that Tom received as principal of a high school using block scheduling came from parents and students who were concerned about "too much teacher talk." Our observations of classrooms in block scheduled schools confirm that there is indeed a great deal of "teacher talk" continuing, especially during the first couple of years on the new schedule. Teachers in all content areas need to change teaching strategies from a talk or lecture mode to an activities-oriented format that stresses active learning. Many teachers immediately recognize the need to change, and some teachers make the transition smoothly. Others need support, and some need a directive to incorporate new methodologies. Further, teachers need help in redesigning their instructional program. The decision to eliminate some course material in lieu of in-depth study of selected material does not come easily. With the current emphasis on standards in most states, teachers are confused about teaching to standards while implementing active student learning. The complexity of the change process soon becomes overwhelming, and teachers look to the principal or another educational leader to give them guidance.

Will teachers face the changes in practice that make the block schedule work?

IS YOUR SCHOOL COMMUNITY READY FOR CHANGE?

In order to relieve some of the anxiety associated with change, there are certain factors that should be considered before any major restructuring initiative becomes a part of the school's plan for improvement.

You—the change agent—must consider the readiness of your school and community for change. Readiness factors include the professional maturity of the faculty and staff. Do members of the organization understand the concept that is being considered? Is the total school-community ready and willing to embrace change? Customers must be provided answers to these and many more questions if change is to occur. Lack of information and poor communication are barriers to change. It is the responsibility of educators to move forward and deal with the many opportunities that are available to make a difference for those students in their care. Change that will provide opportunities for students and will make a significant difference in preparation for their future must be initiated by leaders, not managers or supervisors.[1]

---

[1] The words leader and leadership will be used throughout this book instead of managers or supervisors. Deming (1986) states that we must use the term leadership instead of supervision, because leadership is that which is needed for organizational survival.

CASE IN POINT

Yvonne has worked with faculties who are adjusting to the block schedule. Listening to their concerns after a year of teaching in 90-minute blocks, she has found that teachers respond to help with teaching strategies and lesson design if the staff development leader approaches change openly and honestly. After a summer workshop on teaching strategies in the block, a teacher thanked her for listening to the faculty's problems, acknowledging their legitimacy, and adjusting the workshop design to address the faculty's issues. The workshop objectives were met, but, just as important, the teachers learned they were not alone as they struggled with something new and adjusted to change. Although the principal made it quite clear to the faculty that they were not going to spend staff development time complaining, the faculty was given the opportunity to voice legitimate concerns and ask important questions that needed answers.

WHY IS CHANGE NEEDED FOR SCHOOL RESTRUCTURING?

When deciding to change, always do it for the right reasons. Too many times change in education is considered for all of the wrong reasons.

When Tom is asked by colleagues why he chose a block schedule, he shares the change process he experienced. The first task was to tie the change to the mission of the school. Would this change further the mission (i.e.: help the faculty accomplish their mission)? After analyzing the school's broad mission, the faculty formulated goals to change the instructional school day and to examine how time might be best used. Their initial attempt looked like this:

GOAL FOR CHANGE

To accomplish the stated mission of our school, we will attempt to restructure the traditional school day schedule by allowing for longer blocks of instructional time that will provide a climate that will allow opportunities for teachers to teach and students to learn.

The next step in the beginning of the process was for the team to brainstorm reasons for longer instructional blocks of time. Possibilities included the following:

WHY CHANGE TO LONGER INSTRUCTIONAL BLOCKS?

Longer blocks of time allow opportunities for students to:

- Have a longer period of time to enhance learning
- Increase their depth of understanding of content
- Become engaged in more hands-on activities
- Receive individual attention
- Develop personal relationships with teachers and other students
- Use technology and a variety of community resources in the learning process
- Participate in special courses such as alternative programs for at-risk students

Although the final draft of the measurable objectives for change in the school differed slightly, Tom continued to focus on the school's mission statement and how this change would impact student achievement.

Under a traditional schedule, time allocations for instruction during the school day are restrictive, rigid, and segmented. The time schedule for the school day should be flexible, supportive, and organized around the learning needs of the students rather than around facilities use, lunch, or other activities.

Teaching in the present setting creates authoritative instruction that is single-strategy and lecture-dominated. It would seem reasonable to assume that students in high schools that use a more traditional approach to scheduling are more passive consumers of knowledge and are dependent learners.

For decades school systems have worked to improve student performance. Both educators and students have worked hard to make the current system better with marginal results and great frustration. It is becoming obvious to many school officials and parents that the present system can achieve only minimal results. The world is being transformed by a technological revolution and the development of a global economy. It is time for a fundamental change in restructuring the school day, one that will encourage a different way of teaching and learning and one that will take advantage of technology, prepare students for a different workplace, and reflect the kind of thinking that is moving the United States forward in an unpredictable world.

WHO WINS WHEN SCHOOLS ARE RESTRUCTURED?

Over the last decade, a considerable body of research suggests school restructuring as a means of producing more effective teaching. Consequently, educators have implemented powerful instructional methodologies and techniques with sophistication and consistency. Although successful, many of these reforms created increased demands on teachers' time without reorganizing the school day to optimize teaching and planning time.

By using alternative block scheduling, teachers teach fewer classes per day, work with approximately half as many students per day or per semester, and have a longer planning period. Our experience has shown that teachers who teach fewer classes, have longer planning periods, and spend more time with their students each day can perform more effectively.

While the advantages of block scheduling are important to teachers, students are the real winners. A major objective of any school is to provide a school climate that fosters optimum learning experiences for all students. To provide such experiences, efforts to improve school climates must center on the most fundamental flaws identified within a school community. One such flaw that must be addressed is a different way of scheduling classes to provide large blocks of time that will afford students meaningful learning experiences (Goodlad, 1984).

At present, traditional schools are characterized by classes that change frequently, and classes are characterized by practices whereby large amounts of information are presented to students who rarely have enough time to internalize the information and make connections for further applications. The traditional 55-minute transition schedule focuses on passive learning, fragmented instruction, and disrupted concentration. Bells ringing, lockers slamming, crowds shuffling through hallways, and group dynamics adjusting may contribute to the social aspect of the student's school experience, but they do little to contribute to student-teacher interaction. They are just a few ways student-teacher contact time is lost.

LOOKING BACK . . .

The schedule can be either a solution to problems related to the delivery of instruction or a major cause of the problem. A schedule is a much greater resource than merely a means of moving teachers and students to various locations during selected periods of time. Using Thomas Edison's oath of persistence—"There is a way to do it better. Find it!"—educators are broadening the paradigm of traditional education to find the most efficient and effective methods of allocating resources. Optimizing resources creates maximum learning experiences and empowers all students to reach their potential. Block scheduling is an innovative approach and a proven resource to achieve academic integrity through differentiated learning and teaching. Block scheduling removes the major barrier to flexible teaching and permits the developing technologies of learning to become the norm in classrooms.

Block scheduling may be the impetus we need to transform classroom teaching: engaging students in activities that rely on research skills; collaborative learning; the ability to analyze, synthesize, and evaluate information; and the utility of using world-wide databases. Block scheduling may facilitate student learning by giving students time to learn. ❑

Chapter 2

What Is Block Scheduling?

*O*ne particularly antiquated tradition [in high schools] is the continued use of a daily schedule that requires students to spend between 45 and 55 minutes in seven or eight separate classes. Critics believe that this approach to scheduling lies at the root of many of the problems in high schools, including a fragmented curriculum, superficial coverage of material, inhibition of the development of analytic and problem-solving skills, suppression of the enjoyment of learning, and weak teacher-student relationships.

—Key High School Reform Strategies for the New American High Schools

LOOKING AHEAD IN THIS CHAPTER . . .

It is necessary to define block scheduling to understand the focus of this book. A definition of block scheduling will provide a foundation upon which to build a knowledge base that insures the reader's understanding of the concept. It is important for the school administrator and the planning team to realize that there is more than one block scheduling configuration, and the choice of one model over another may be critical to the success of the use of time in their school.

SCHEDULING TRENDS

There is no one perfect way to organize either a block schedule or a traditional 55-minute class period. Many administrators who are considering implementing block scheduling fail to realize that there are various types of schedule configurations that are designed to use the allotted instructional time of a school day effectively and efficiently. We often discuss the pros and cons of block scheduling with those interested in the use of time and learning. From these discussions, we realize that the greatest threat to the success of the block scheduling format is the misperception that there is only one type of block scheduling. Many educators refer to block scheduling as the 4x4 (four-by-four), or semester, block schedule. There are, in fact, many variations of the block, and it is important to understand that any school that is considering a new format can conceivably design a specific schedule that is a match for its particular curriculum and students. While it may seem more efficient to use a schedule that is modeled from another school's schedule, it may be better to design a schedule specifically for your school. A specifically designed schedule may not take on the characteristics of any existing block schedule that other teachers, students, or administrators have experienced.

BLOCK SCHEDULING DEFINED

The most common schedules used in high schools (other than the traditional single period schedule) include:

■ **Alternating Day**—also known as the A-B, Alternating Week, the Atlee Model, and the Alternating Ten-Day Cycle. Courses are offered on alternating school days for the entire school year. Usually there are three 90-plus-minute blocks of time and one 50-plus-minute block of time on any given day of a school year (usually 180 days per year).

■ **Semester Block**—also known as the Full-Credit Semester Timetable in Canada, the 4x4, the Block 4, and Semester Blocking. Courses are offered on consecutive days for 90 school days. Usually there are four 90-minute (more or less) blocks of time in any given day for a semester (usually 90 days, or half of the school year).

■ **Embedded Schedule**—also known as mixed, combination, and hybrid schedule. These schedules usually offer a combination of the alternating day, semester, and the traditional single period schedule.

■ **Block with Intersession**—a schedule that provides a short intersession of 10, 15, or 30 days of instruction for some specific purpose. The intersession is placed at a time within the school calendar year that meets the needs of a particular school. These models schedule the intersession between semesters or during the last 10, 15, or 30 school days of the year. It could also be placed at the beginning of the school year.

It should be noted that for the most part, the definitions of block scheduling and semestering timetabling (as used in the Canadian provinces) are congruent. There is little information from the available Canadian studies relative to other types of block scheduling (such as alternating day and combinations of alternating day and semester block schedule).

DIFFERENCES IN BLOCK SCHEDULES

The major difference in the alternating day block schedule and the semester block is that on the alternating day (A-B) block, students are engaged in the same courses over an entire school year, generally 180 instructional days. On the semester (4x4) block, the students take one-half of a whole year's course of study in a semester. That is, the student takes fewer courses, usually four, and completes the courses in 90 days. At the end of the semester, students enroll in new classes. The combination or embedded schedules offer characteristics of the traditional schedule, the alternating day block and the semester block. An example of such a schedule is one that offers blocked classes of 90 minutes for all but one period. The traditional 50-minute period offers six, seven, or eight classes that are taught daily for the length of the school year. The intersession can take on the appearance of both the alternating day and the semester block while adding its own characteristics.

EXAMINING SCHEDULES

H. R. Traverso (1984) examined various schedules defined as alternative scheduling models and concluded that there are many models that can address the issues and questions that administrators have in dealing with the daily operation of a school. These issues include (a) which schedule to use and (b) how to implement successfully a schedule that will allow maximum opportunities for student success. Traverso felt that the model selected should be designed to offer students opportunities to meet goals and objectives that are unattainable under the traditional five-period, six-period, or seven-period day model.

Later H. P. Traverso (1991) listed several schools where alternative scheduling models have been implemented. It appears that states in the southeast United States have the heaviest concentration of block scheduling as it is defined in this book. States in which block scheduling appears to be most concentrated include Kentucky, North Carolina, Virginia, and Georgia. Kentucky reported that 75 to 80 percent of its high schools used some form of alternative scheduling in 1998–99 (Kentucky Department of Education, 1999). In North Carolina, approximately 74 percent of the high schools used some type of block scheduling during the 1997–98 school year (North Carolina Department of Public Instruction, 1999). During the 1998–99 school year, approximately 68 percent of Virginia's high schools used a block scheduling configuration (Virginia Department of Education, 1997). (See Figure 1.) During the same period, 31 percent of high schools in Georgia had implemented block scheduling (Georgia Department of Education, 1997).

FIGURE 1
Types of Schedules Used in Virginia Public High Schools, 1998–99

CONFIGURATION	NUMBER OF SCHOOLS	PERCENTAGE
A-B	102	34.7
4x4	93	31.6
Other Block	5	1.7
Single Period	94	32.0

In a national study of 3,380 high schools that had restructured, Cawelti (1994) found that one-fourth of these schools had fully or partially implemented block scheduling. Another 15 percent of the schools surveyed planned to implement some form of block scheduling for the next school year. Sufficient data are available to suggest that alternative scheduling is widespread throughout the United States.

It is interesting to note that only one high school in Virginia was using any block scheduling configuration as recently as the 1991–92 school year. That school was Atlee High School in Hanover County, Virginia. The increase in the number of schools using block scheduling since then is impressive. Similar patterns have been noted in neighboring Southern states.

HOW BLOCK SCHEDULING WORKS

In their work with schools on scheduling since the early 1960s, Canady and Rettig (1995) reported that there are many ways that the school day can be scheduled. They have made observations and collected data from schools across the country, and they have found that many of the alternative block scheduling models have been implemented and that administrators, teachers, and students are beginning to report positive results. These schedules are working because the increase in class time provides opportunities for teachers to use a variety of teaching methods that respond to multiple learning styles in the classroom. Success is probable when teachers use time differently to respond to the ways students learn when teachers utilize the best practices from research that address adolescent learning. Canady and Rettig also report that they have not seen evidence sufficient to indicate that block scheduling has had any negative effects on student achievement.

Policymakers in some states believe that a change must be made in the way allocated instructional time is used. Policymakers in Kentucky have decided that the way the school day is organized should be reassessed. For instance, the Kentucky Education Reform Act KRS 158.6451 (4) states that ". . . The curriculum framework shall identify . . . alternative ways of using school time" (p. 294). The purpose of this mandate is to force schools to look at different ways of using instructional time. The school day should be organized around the curricular needs of students rather than courses, units, or facilities schedules. We believe the education leaders in Kentucky stated it well when they wrote: "As schools and districts look at new ways of doing business, it is essential to look at the way allocated instructional time is used" (Kentucky Department of Education, 1999).

In a 1994 report released by the National Education Commission on Time and Learning, entitled *Prisoners of Time*, the following observation was made:

> For over the past 150 years American public schools have held time constant and let learning vary. The rule, only rarely voiced, is simple: learn what you can in the time we make available. It should surprise no one that some bright, hard-working students do reasonably well. Everyone else, from the typical student to the dropout, runs into trouble (p. 7).

Cawelti (1994) in *High School Restructuring: A National Study* summarized the restructuring of high schools from a national perspective. He identified five major components of restructuring. Within each component, he identified elements that would provide opportunities for focusing on the restructuring of high schools. Block scheduling was identified as one of these elements that respondents indicated would allow restructuring to occur. Cawelti asserts that the major value of block scheduling "is to enable teachers to use a variety of teaching activities in these extended periods, and to greatly reduce the number of students seen by teachers in their classes each day" (p. 23).

INCREASING VALUE-ADDED TIME DURING THE SCHOOL YEAR

School administrators should give serious consideration to the way the instructional time in a school day is used by examining scheduling options for the school. The following questions should be discussed among the administrative team before a final decision is made about the yearly schedule.

- Is the present use of allotted instructional time efficient and effective for learning?

- Is adequate time provided for student learning?

- Is there a need to increase the length of the school day or school year for instructional purposes?

- If one of the goals for implementing block scheduling is to guarantee customers (i.e., students, teachers, and parents) that increased learning opportunities for students will be provided, what will insure that the allocated instructional time gained from restructuring the school day is used for instructional purposes?

As you move toward making a decision to study the block schedule format for your school, we suggest that you gather usable data by analyzing the use of instructional time in your current schedule format. The goal for the principal is to determine how much time is used well in a school day and how much time is lost. What is occurring that is adding value to the student's classroom experience? We call this *value-added time*—time that is composed of activities and experiences that contribute to the educational experience. An example of value-added time would be a field trip to a chemical laboratory that would be integrated with a unit of study in chemistry or a related vocational experience. The opposite of value-added time is ***non-value-added time***—time that does not contribute to learning and may detract from it. Non-value-added experiences include taking class time to deal with tardy students or watching a video that is unrelated to the class study.

Consider the following scenario based on the assumption that in the 180-day school year, the length of each course is 55 minutes and that there is a five-minute break between classes. Teachers teach five classes each day, and the allotted instructional time is divided into seven blocks of equal length. If you add the total time used for class changes in a school day, 30 minutes of instructional time are lost daily. Based on an analysis of the data of a study on teacher classroom behaviors, Shortt (1986) noted that an average of approximately eight minutes per block of time in a seven-period day was used for pre-instruction (beginning of class) activities that were non-value added or non-instructional related activities. This adds up to 56 minutes of non-value-added time per seven-period day. In the same study, students were found to engage in post-instruction (end of class) non-instructional activities approximately nine minutes per time period in a seven-period day. That adds up to 63 minutes of non-value-added time per day.

If you add up the amount of non-value-added instructional time per seven-period day, students are unengaged intellectually for approximately 149 minutes per seven periods. This non-value-added time does not include other types of disruption that occur on a regular basis at any school.

$$30 + 56 + 63 = 149$$
Class Changes + Pre-Instruction + Post-Instruction = Time Lost
149 Minutes x 180 Days = 447 Hours of Time Lost Per Year

Using these numbers, we believe any principal can argue that in a 180-day school year, approximately 447 hours of non-value-added instructional time could and should be used more effectively.

Let's compare the way time is used on a four-block day. Students change classes only three times a day, so the total amount of non-value-added class-changing time for any given day is 15 minutes. For pre-instruction time, the non-value-added time is 32 minutes per day. For post-instruction activities, the non-value-added time adds up to approximately 36 minutes per day. The total non-value-added time for the four-block day is 83 minutes. **The total difference of the non-value-added time between the traditional seven-period schedule and the four-period block schedule becomes approximately 66 minutes per day, or 198 hours per year.** This means that 66 minutes of time is available every day for value-added activities. In a year's time, a faculty has an opportunity to provide 198 hours of additional instructional time to the students on the block schedule.

The numbers in Figure 2 are based on the assumption that each student takes seven classes per day in a seven-period day and that students in a four-block day are taking four classes. The results could vary based on factors such as the number of transition minutes between classes, the number of classes that a student takes, and the length of the school year. The formula for determining the amount of value-added time that a block schedule can add to the school year is relatively easy to follow. Applying this formula to the allotted instructional time in your school may provide some fuel for change.

John Carroll (1963) noted in his research that the amount of learning that occurs in a classroom is congruent with the amount of time provided for learning. Wiley and Harnischferger (1982) concluded

that five extra minutes a day added up to three full days of instruction a year. If time makes a difference in student achievement gains, it is safe to assume that the additional value-added instructional time created by a more creative use of allotted instructional time will impact student achievement.

LOOKING BACK . . .

Is more time for instruction better? Or is that which happens in the classroom during the time allocated for instruction the critical variable that makes a difference in a student's educational experience? We suggest this is an issue relative to both elements. There must be sufficient time allotted for learning. But time—whatever the amount in minutes—must be used efficiently and effectively.

Since the emergence of national educational reports in the mid-1980s, educators and policymakers have argued over the merit of increasing the school day or the school year. Some have said that we should make good use of the time we have rather than increasing it. The block schedule provides you with a way to make better use of the time you already have. Remember, of all the resources you call upon each day in a school, time is the resource you have control over. Do you have the will to change how you look at time?

As we continue to look at the use of time, we will examine many different block schedules. Plugging your courses into these schedules is the easy part of change. The harder part is making the decision to look for better ways to serve students and

FIGURE 2
Comparison of Non-Value-Added Time on Seven-Period Schedule and Four-Period (Block) Schedule

	CLASS CHANGE TRANSITION TIME	PRE-INSTRUCTION TIME	POST-INSTRUCTION TIME	MINUTES NON-VALUE-ADDED TIME PER DAY	HOURS NON-VALUE-ADDED TIME PER YEAR
7 Period	30 minutes	56 minutes	63 minutes	149 minutes	447 hours
Block (A-B or 4x4)	15 minutes	32 minutes	36 minutes	83 minutes	249 hours
Difference or Time Saved or Value-Added Time	15 minutes	24 minutes	27 minutes	66 minutes	198 hours

leading teachers and the community in the process of change. The challenges you have as instructional leader are: to understand the different models of scheduling being used, to analyze the strengths of each schedule, to identify the major needs in your school, and to lead decision makers through a process that will yield a schedule for your school that maximizes learning, increases achievement, and provides opportunities for all students in the school population. ❑

CHAPTER 3

How Does Research Support Block Scheduling?

*T**he manager is a copy; the leader is an original. The manager maintains; the leader develops . . .The manager has a short-range view; the leader has a long-range perspective . . .The manager imitates; the leader originates.*

—Warren Bennis, 1989

LOOKING AHEAD IN THIS CHAPTER . . .

What do the literature and research say about time and learning? Are we using time in the most effective manner for instruction? We must answer these and many other questions if we want to maximize our instructional time to provide the best possible education for students. Are we satisfied with the status quo? Must we look at ways we can change the learning environment as it currently exists in order to avoid the challenges that may change education as we know it? Time is one of the structural dimensions that currently are undergoing change that will allow a change in the learning environment. Will this change in the learning environment continue to occur without our identification of certain support systems that must be in place? If never-ending improvement does not provide enough focus for change, then perhaps we need to identify foci that

will "hurl" us into the evaluation and change mode. If we are to change the way we go about teaching and learning, then we must look at the way we are currently doing business in education.

In 1991 (pp. 661 & 665), Kennedy identified five research findings that would indicate that we have serious problems in education. Four of the five cited here, we think, could be addressed by implementing block scheduling.

The first finding indicates that when we compare American students with their international peers, the American students fall behind in skills that call for higher order thinking. "Our students are not doing well at thinking, analyzing, predicting, estimating, or problem solving," she writes. The second finding indicates that textbooks are not requiring students to think. The author states that current texts offer no analysis and post no challenging questions. One of the primary reasons that many principals have changed to block scheduling is to provide teachers opportunities to teach content in depth and avoid the superficial skimming of knowledge that is taking place in classrooms. Her third finding supports the need for this effort, which indicates that "teachers teach most content for exposure, not for understanding." Kennedy confirms the perceptions that teachers are not providing opportunities for students to become creative learners. Her fourth finding states that "teachers tend to avoid thought-provoking work and activities and stick to predictable outcomes."

Kennedy sums up these four findings by stating that our current system of education ". . . provides very little intellectually stimulating work for students and that it tends to produce students who are not capable of intellectual work." According to the author, the implications of these findings are that we continue to do things the way things have been done. We must find a way out of what she refers to as the ". . . vicious circle of mediocre practice . . . ." As we look at these findings, we must look at other research to determine if block scheduling is part of the answer to breaking out of these mediocre practices. Perhaps administrators have not been providing teachers an opportunity to break out of this cycle because of a non-flexible scheduling of classes the way it has always been done. Perhaps block scheduling is the answer to part of the puzzle.

EFFICIENT USE OF TIME

Some principals are not quite sure how to begin the change process. How do we begin thinking about getting better as a school? One initiative that will likely provide a focus for change is an analysis of the use of daily instructional time. Such analyses often reveal that part of the school day is not value-added time.

"Value-added" is a term associated with organizational development as it relates to quality improvement. As it relates to schools, we think of value-added tasks as those that make a contribution in educating the student in the way or to the standard that the school has determined.

Value-added also applies to the use of time. Value-added time reflects activities and experiences that contribute to the educational experience. Most simply, non-value-added time is time that is wasted at school. It may be used for something viewed as necessary to someone in the school organization, but it is time that is not contributing positively to the educational process. Value-added time is composed of actions that, if they were eliminated, their contributions to education would be missed. Non-value-added time includes those actions that, if they were eliminated, may be missed by an individual or a group, but they are not critical to the customers of the school—the students, the parents, and the community.

A principal's analysis of the use of daily instructional time becomes an exercise in identifying value-added and non-value-added time during the school day. The results of such a study will challenge the principal to act to use non-value-added time more efficiently—to serve the external customers of the school better. As this analysis is made, the principal must also focus on the school's ability to serve internal customers effectively. Internal customers are those people involved in the school's educational process but who serve each other in the process as they work together to educate students. Teachers, support staff, and administrators are all internal customers at one time or another. The principal must determine what processes are in place in a school that may take time away from instruction but are vital to the operation of the school (the serving of lunch being a good example).

After the principal has studied the use of time and determined that it can be improved, s/he must articulate what needs to be changed, and those changes must be stated positively as measurable objectives. We cannot state too strongly how important it is to state objectives in measurable terms. Objectives that can't be measured are of no value to a leader. Only those objectives that can be measured can be used to improve a school continuously.

When the objectives have been developed, the principal then asks the obvious questions: Does the current school schedule allow the staff to reach the objectives and maximize the use of time? Would a block schedule optimize the resources of time, skills, and energy in a more efficient manner than the traditional scheduling approach that is now practiced? Would a block schedule facilitate adding value to the school day?

DEMAND FOR ACCOUNTABILITY

Peter Drucker (1982, p. 139), the preeminent business and management writer of our time, insists that the battle cry for the nineties

> . . . will be the demand for performance and accountability. For 30 years employers have been hiring graduates for their degrees rather than their capabilities; employment, pay, and often even promotion have depended on one's diploma. Now many major employers are beginning to demand more than the completion of school.

Drucker gets at the heart of the change issue:

> Students and parents, too, will demand greater accountability from schools on all levels. Indeed, with teaching jobs remaining scarce, the customers of education—parents, students, school boards—will have the upper hand no matter how militantly teachers unionize. It will be increasingly common to bring lawsuits against school districts and colleges for awarding degrees without imparting the skills that presumably go along with them.

He continues to provide a futuristic view of expectations of educators:

> Demand for education is actually going up, not down. What is going down, and fairly fast, is demand for traditional education in traditional schools.

Ten years later, Drucker sends another message to educators:

> The advent of the knowledge society has far-ranging implications for education. Schools will change more in the next 30 years than they have since the invention of the printed book. One reason is modern learning theory. We know how people learn, and that learning is not at all the same thing as teaching. . . . [T]he new learning tools are child-friendly, as anyone with a computer-using eight- or nine-year-old child will know. By the age of eleven most chil-

> dren . . . begin to be bored with the computer; for them it is just a tool. But up to that age, children treat computers as extensions of themselves. The advent of such powerful tools alone will force the schools to change (Drucker, 1992, p. 335).

If we as educators are to meet the demands of our customers—in most circumstances without additional funding—how are we going to meet this challenge? Drucker has been right. The demand for accountability has increased over the past two decades, and the public wants to know why America's students don't seem to perform as well as those in other countries. Concurrently, employers have asked students to come to them literate in the basic skills of communications, mathematics, and scientific methodology, while demonstrating strong interpersonal skills and a good work ethic. The demand to include technology in the curriculum is being driven by employers' expectations, software availability, and student readiness. It seems to educators that the needs are endless. One way educators can begin to meet the needs of customers is to use efficiently the resources that we currently have: time and human resources. To do that we must look at the way we schedule the school day.

CURRENT RESEARCH

Although many principals appear to focus on the administrative tasks that accompany the principalship more than on the instructional duties, administrative decisions should be driven by an understanding of instruction. This is particularly true when thinking about using time differently in schools. If the purpose of instituting block scheduling is to enhance learning opportunities for students, then the principal must be prepared to answer those questions that will emerge about the impact of the new schedule on learning. The principal will be well served to become knowledgeable about learning theory and some of the research that applies to time and learning. If a teacher asks the principal if a student can learn as well in a compacted amount of time, s/he must be prepared to answer this question. When a teacher asks (and she will) about the loss of information when a student does not take a subject for a semester and a summer, the principal should be able to respond, both from the perspective of schools that have experienced the block schedule and from expectations based on educational research.

The debate exists over student retention of information from certain courses (especially math and foreign languages) if the sequence of courses is interrupted by a long break in instruction. Some block models do not create the "learning gap," while others do. Some teachers see this as a problem, and others do not. The literature review on the retention of learning issue provides a picture that is not clear but does begin to identify the problem.

In a paper prepared for publication in the NASSP *Bulletin*[1], Kramer (1996) conducted a literature review on block scheduling, primarily for the purpose of answering questions posed by mathematics teachers. Kramer looked at block scheduling practices over the past 25 years—particularly as they relate to mathematics—in Canada as well as in the United States. Additionally, he interviewed teachers using a block schedule. We believe Kramer's synthesis of the research and his findings are extremely helpful to educators seeking information. Although conflicting or inconsistent information was found in the literature, Kramer (1997, pp. 79-80) suggests the following to reflect current experience with block scheduling (comments will indicate if the finding applies only to A-B or 4x4 schedule).

- School atmosphere may become calmer with **either** type of schedule. It is unclear whether there will be any change in student attendance. Student behavior may improve, and students may have a more positive attitude toward school.

- Dropout rates may decrease in **4x4**.

- Some **4x4** schools have maintained achievement while reducing allocated classroom time. Doing so may require extra planning time and staff development.

- Achievement has decreased in some schools that implemented an intensive block schedule without increasing planning time or staff development. Failure rates may decrease.

- Little information is available about student achievement under the **A-B** schedule.

- It may be possible to study topics in more depth on **either** block schedule. There may be more time for group work, investigations of complex problems, and other participatory activities. Lecturing may be less effective in holding student interest. Faculty may need to modify the curriculum to accommodate the new schedule.

- Less classroom time is used for administrative tasks on **either** block schedule. Absences may be more disruptive to student learning than they are under a traditional schedule.

- On the **4x4**, students may forget some mathematics material during gaps in sequential instruction, but this forgetting probably has little impact on performance in the next sequential math course. Weak evidence indicates that students may have a higher engagement rate than under a traditional schedule.

- On the **A-B**, students may complete less homework.

Many of the concerns expressed about block scheduling appear to come from mathematics educators. Interestingly, a principal in Central Texas implemented a modified block schedule for the expressed purpose of assisting students who were having difficulty with Algebra I. After initial success, followed by increased failure rates in some algebra classes, a study was conducted to analyze the academic impact of this block scheduling plan[2].

---

[1] Kramer's paper was published as two articles in the NASSP *Bulletin*, "What We Know About Block Scheduling and Its Effects on Math Instruction," Part I and Part II, February and March, 1997.

[2] A pilot program targeting Algebra I was implemented during the 1993–94 school year. The Algebra I block was defined as a two-period block lasting for 120 minutes. The block class was a slower version of the traditional class. Comparisons were made to traditional, one-hour algebra classes. We believe that this comparison has limited value, as slowing down algebra by adding class time creates a different kind of course, one more similar to a two-part algebra class (Algebra I, Part I, and Algebra I, Part II, being one example). Only two teachers taught the block class.

Skrobarcek and her research team (1997) reported the following results from a review of failure and absentee rates as well as teacher and student perceptions of the situation.

- Overall, teachers of the Algebra I block class had higher failure rates than the teachers of traditional classes.

- More absences were reported in block classes than in traditional classes.

- Students felt they learned more under the block format because it was easier to concentrate, they understood the lessons better, and they felt less stressed and rushed. Most students said they had a wide variety of learning activities. The most consistently mentioned positive aspect of the block class was time to complete homework, to receive further explanation, and to ask additional questions.

- Teachers said that the time saved on administrative, start-up, and close-down activities benefited the teaching process. They had more time to communicate with students, to individualize instruction, and to evaluate performance.

- They noted that they gave less homework and that using diverse teaching methods was helpful on the block schedule. They thought that students were both more interested and often bored in the block.

We suggest that principals should continue to review the research publications on block schedules. There are many lessons to be learned, and most publications that review the process offer suggestions for implementation (for example, R.D. Cunningham & Nogle, 1996; Schoenstein, 1995; Shortt & Thayer, 1995). Our goal is to lay a foundation in the relationship between time and learning (1) to help a principal prepare his/her study of block scheduling, and (2) to develop the context from which we work with schools and upon which the remainder of this book will be developed.

TIME AND LEARNING: THE QUEST FOR THE IDEAL SCHEDULE

The quest for the ideal secondary school schedule reaches as far back as the 1890s.

The ultimate arrangement of time, rooms, teachers, students, and curriculum has been a consistent issue to successive generations of reformers and visionaries. The pursuit is still important to a number of educators today (H. P. Traverso, 1991, p. 1).

The search continues for the best use of time in schools. Common sense would seem to lead us to increase allotted instructional time when attempting to increase student achievement. However, the debate continues over how this should be accomplished. Many advocate extending the school day or school year. Beginning with national reports of the mid-1980s, American educators have been accused of teaching too little—180 days a year—while German and Japanese schools exceed 200 days per year. But before we initiate a longer day or year, let's examine the way teachers currently spend their instructional day in the United States as well as abroad.

The Organization for Economic Cooperation and Development (OECD) recently compared the use of allotted instructional time between teachers in the United States and teachers in foreign countries. (See Figure 3.) They found that American teachers spend more time teaching than do their counterparts in other countries, even those with longer school years.

The non-instructional time of American teachers is used to secure materials, telephone parents, prepare for the next class, review student assignments, monitor the cafeteria, and attend to personal needs. By contrast, teachers from other countries have 15 to 20 hours per week outside the traditional classroom to meet with parents, plan as teams, review current teaching research, and attend professional meetings. In general, if American teachers do these activities, they are done outside the regular instructional day. Apparently, American schools have allocated enough total time for instruction, compared to the amount of time allocated in Japan and Germany, but are we using the allocated time in the most efficient way? The differences must be inside the time structure—how the time is used. How do teachers and students spend their class time?

FIGURE 3
Comparison of Teaching Hours Per Year Among Five Countries

COUNTRY	UPPER SECONDARY	LOWER SECONDARY	PRIMARY
Sweden	528	576	624
Italy	612	612	748
Germany	673	761	790
New Zealand	813	8976	790
United States	1019	1042	1093

Source: *Organization for Economic Cooperation and Development (OECD)*

SCHEDULING PRACTICES THAT INCREASE EFFICIENT USE OF TIME TO ENHANCE STUDENT ACHIEVEMENT

The alternative uses of scheduling practices are relatively new to the masses in the United States. As a result, there is very little research available in this country to guide the decision-making process for those who choose to stray from the traditional five-, six-, or seven-period day of 45- to 55-minute blocks of time. Researchers in Canada have been collecting data on "block time tabling" at least since the 1960s. However, there have been few empirical studies in Canada that assess the impact of block scheduling on student performance.

Most available studies have addressed pupil-parent-teacher satisfaction with schedule alterations resulting from organizational structures. An ERIC search revealed 13 studies directly related to block scheduling in Canada. Only two of these studies addressed the issue of block time tabling and its impact on student performance. Ross (1977) conducted one of the pivotal Canadian studies of time-table innovation which focused on the effects of semestering on a variety of variables, including student grades. In 1986, Raphel, Wahlstrom, and McLean investigated student achievement in mathematics as it related to block time tabling. They examined the results of the Second International Mathematics Study in relation to

> . . . claims of advocates of the semestered secondary school. While teachers in semestered Ontario schools reported greater vari-

ety in their teaching approaches, fewer hours of course instruction were reported. Analyses revealed that students enrolled in semestered Grade 12 and 13 mathematics classes demonstrated significantly lower achievement than their non-semestered school peers with no difference in attitudes . . . . [The authors also noted that] achievement differences in biology and chemistry tended to favor students enrolled in non-semestered classes (pp. 180-183).

There are still many questions that need to be asked regarding this research, such as: What is the teachers' experience? What training is provided to teachers in all subjects? Is the time-on-task issue related to the schedule? Or is it that there is less time to teach the same content?

The block schedule that was implemented at Atlee High School in Hanover County, Virginia, in 1991 actually increased instructional time (approximately 160 hours of instruction per class per year) in comparison to the average class time of less than 150 hours that existed in other schools in the same district and in schools throughout Virginia. While some teachers used additional time to expand their curricula, other teachers covered less subject matter than they had when class time was less. After the first year of teaching in the block schedule, teachers developed pacing guides and adjusted lesson plans to cover the required curriculum. Many teachers reported that they increased the amount of content covered during the school year.

In an analysis of an evaluation brief from the North Carolina Department of Education, Rettig (1997) observes that finally there is a large-scale study in the United States which suggests that, at the very least, block scheduling does not hurt student achievement. At best, blocked schools (4x4) seem to outperform non-blocked schools when controls are applied to adjust scores for the differences in student populations. The authors of the study noted that a broad generalization about the impact of block scheduling should not be made from these data, however.

In a summary of the 1996 North Carolina Department of Public Instruction study, "Blocked Scheduled High School Achievement: Comparison of 1995 End-of-Course Test Scores for Blocked and Non-Blocked Schools," the agency acknowledged that the study focused only on schools using the 4x4 semester schedule and did not consider variations that may exist in non-4x4 blocked schools (such as the A-B blocked schools). Additional studies have been completed in North Carolina, and the results are worth considering as we study block scheduling.

In the report, "Block Scheduling in North Carolina: Implementation, Teaching, and Impact Issues—An Executive Summary" (1997), key findings are summarized and recommendations are made based on the 1997 survey of principals, teachers, and students. These findings indicate that ". . . test scores in five required subjects, adjusted for parent education level and performance before moving to a block schedule [4x4] show few statistically significant differences between block and non-blocked schools" (p. i). The issues that surround these findings and that must be considered are basically two. First, what is the significance of the adjustment for parent education, and should it be considered when analyzing student outcomes related to block scheduling? Second, if schools on the A-B schedule were disaggregated from the non-blocked schools included in the data, would there be different findings?

Otherwise, the North Carolina study is consistent with the findings in Virginia. Both studies indicate that principals are the most positive about block scheduling, followed by teachers and then students. According to the North Carolina study, students with average or above average grade point averages (GPAs) are significantly more satisfied with block scheduling than students with lower GPAs and students enrolled in Advanced Placement courses. Still, students and teachers find block scheduling to be as good or better than the traditional schedule for all types of students.

Additional findings related to types of courses indicate ". . . that there is general agreement that math, foreign languages, and AP courses, as well as music, are less successful in the block schedule [4x4] than other courses" (p. ii, 1997). Instructional practices considered traditional are still being reported as the most frequently used teaching methods. Professional activities that are considered most essential are pacing guides, visits to other schools that are using block scheduling management of classroom instructional time, curriculum alignment, and discipline-specific planning.

Among the recommendations that were made in the summary are: align key reform goals; involve the staff and school community in understanding and planning block scheduling; and ensure rigorous standards with appropriate instruction and high expectations for all students. Perhaps one recommendation that we must pay attention to is to explore all scheduling alternatives. Combination schedules that will address the particular needs of a school and certain students in the school should be given careful consideration.

STUDENT ACHIEVEMENT

In our current political climate, accountability for educators has become the buzz word. "In this age of accountability, the ultimate test of any reform effort is a positive change in student achievement" (Shortt & Thayer, 1998, p. 78). Identifying indicators that impact student academic achievement and collecting data on resulting outcomes are critical if we are to determine the value of block scheduling. In an effort to collect appropriate data related to student achievement, the Virginia Department of Education conducted an extensive survey on block scheduling in 1997. The authors analyzed the survey results. One of the major findings related to the flexible use of time to meet the needs of students who are not willing or cannot adjust to learning in the traditional classroom setting. We found that the flexibility of the block schedule allowed non-traditional learning situations for these students. As the climate improves, the opportunity to learn increases for students who previously had difficulty in the classroom, students who can effect a negative impact on learning for other students.

Other data support the notion that a positive learning climate included less unsupervised movement of students within the school, a decline in discipline referrals to the administrative offices, improved teacher morale, and a noted increase in teacher attendance. Teachers indicated that they witnessed fewer fights, that there was an increase of focus on staff development, and there were opportunities to teach content in depth. Teachers and principals agreed that block scheduling had a positive impact on at-risk students. Seventy-one percent of the teachers responding to the survey indicated that they preferred block scheduling over the traditional schedule with 13 percent indicating that they had no preference. Only 16 percent indicated that they preferred the traditional single-period schedule.

The Virginia data indicate that generally administrators, teachers, and students are satisfied with block scheduling. All of these findings are important in making decisions related to block scheduling but may not warrant your changing to a block schedule without additional data to support increased student achievement. The results of the Virginia study indicate that 99 percent of responding teachers and 95 percent of responding administrators perceived block scheduling as having a positive impact on standardized test scores.

In the executive summary of the Virginia study on block scheduling, *Block Scheduling in Virginia: Implementation, Teaching, and Impact Issues*, it was noted that principals gave several reasons for changing to a block schedule.

- To provide more appropriate instruction to meet the needs of all students that will increase student achievement

- To offer in-depth learning

- To increase interaction between students and teachers

- To encourage teachers to use different instructional strategies to meet the needs of students with a variety of learning styles

- To offer opportunities for students to take more courses

The reasons cited by principals for not changing to block scheduling included:

- Traditional scheduling works well.

- There is concern about student learning in large blocks of time, especially in mathematics and foreign languages.

- Some performing arts courses would be impacted negatively.

- Instructional quality is already excellent.

- Actual instructional time would decrease.

- There would be a negative impact on Advanced Placement (AP) test scores.

The survey found that effective, inclusive planning and continuing teacher in-service training are critical to the success of block scheduling. Teachers indicated that it was helpful to have staff development in cooperative learning strategies, pacing of instruction, time management within the classroom, visits with teachers in schools using a block schedule, and planning lessons that teach conceptually rather than by discreet skills. Administrators indicated that they were observing changes within the classroom that included more cooperative learning, use of a greater variety of teaching strategies, more in-depth coverage of content, more class discussion, less lecturing, more individualized instruction, and more problem-solving activities.

As we consider the data related to all block scheduled schools in Virginia, scheduling practices do not appear to have significant disadvantages for students enrolled in AP courses, mathematics, foreign languages, performing arts, and vocational courses. When the data are disaggregated by schedule (A-B, 4x4, and single period), there are indications that students are more successful in the A-B schedule. When the data were analyzed by instructional practices, block scheduling appeared to lead to a number of positive changes in instructional practices of teachers, such as:

- Greater use of community resources

- More class discussion

- More emphasis on problem-solving skills

- Increase in technology use.

Eighty percent of teachers and about 70 percent of students agreed that students had become more involved learners and active participants in the teaching-learning process.

A review of performance indicators and survey data in Virginia suggests that block scheduling enhances student academic achievement. These indicators include mean grade point average, number of students on the honor roll/principal list, student attendance, teacher attendance, student tardies, discipline referrals, parental contacts, dropout rates, SAT math and verbal scores, as well as other standardized test scores.

Findings related to the academic level of students indicated that 80 percent of administrators view block scheduling as achieving a positive impact on the academic achievement of average-ability students, and 76 percent of administrators view block scheduling as achieving a positive impact on the behavior of these same students. Both teachers and administrators were more likely to indicate that block scheduling had a negative impact on students of low ability. Results of academic achievement differ when the data are disaggregated by type of schedule. A majority of teachers, administrators, and students indicated that block scheduling had a positive impact on the academic achievement of AP students (variable A-B schedule). Fifty-three percent of teachers indicated that block scheduling had a positive impact on limited English-proficient students.

While teachers were almost evenly divided regarding the impact of block scheduling on at-risk students, 75 percent of administrators saw block scheduling as having a positive impact on the academic achievement of students at risk. Sixty-two percent of the administrators agreed that block scheduling tends to lead to more rigorous courses. Generally, administrators and teachers tend to rate block scheduling positive for average and above-average students.

Although teachers, administrators, and students generally agreed that block scheduling had a positive impact on mean GPA and honor roll, students' level of perceptions were lower than that of administrators and teachers. When asked to indicate the impact of block scheduling on their performance on SAT verbal and math scores, students indicated that block scheduling had a very high level of impact on SAT verbal scores, but they did not see much impact on SAT math scores.

Students and teachers in Virginia found the block schedule to be as good as or better than the traditional schedule for all types of students. The survey found that students, teachers, and administrators generally agreed that block scheduling improved the quality of instruction. Students said that they learned more in class and had stronger relations with teachers, which led to increased student achievement. Additionally, students noted that the block schedule allowed teachers to give more individualized instruction to students, allowed students to complete instructional activities in one block, allowed students to concentrate on tasks and complete more homework, and allowed teachers more flexibility in meeting individual student needs.

One of the variables that Rettig has analyzed relative to student performance in the 4x4 (semester) model is that of parent education as a proxy for income. He warns us to be aware of income differences among schools on various schedules.

> I have observed, and this study confirms, that more affluent, suburban schools, who traditionally score well on standardized examinations have not been the first to implement block schedules, especially the 4x4. More rural, less traditionally high achieving schools have been the first to implement the 4x4 in search for an improved [instructional] delivery model. To compare achievement across such groups of schools without controlling for income is an unfair comparison (Rettig, 1997).

We have observed that in Virginia, North Carolina, and Maryland some of the first schools to implement a mixture of block scheduling configurations were affluent, suburban schools. In Virginia, both Atlee High School—the first school on a block schedule—and Osburne High School are affluent, suburban schools. Both use a form of the A-B schedule. In North Carolina, Ashboro High School (4x4) is affluent and in the suburbs, and in Maryland, Governor Thomas Johnson High School (4x4) is an affluent school. We suggest that these are variables that should be considered but that there are important issues to consider as we look at how block scheduling impacts student achievement. While the authors of the North Carolina study agree that schools cannot change student socioeconomic status, they can address variables such as instructional strategies and homework. One implication is that ". . . effectively using the 90-minute class period and completing more homework in blocked schools may result in even better performance in . . . tests" (North Carolina Department of Public Instruction, 1996).

While teaching in a block of approximately one hour and 45 minutes, Tom found that when he used instructional time to assign homework and to model homework examples, the students completed more homework outside of class, and the quality of their homework was better than in classes previously taught on a traditional schedule.

The North Carolina study did not address the issue of retention of information. This is a critical area worth continued investigation. We should collect data to support or reject certain assumptions that are being made regarding students' retention of information when using a block schedule. It will be important to study the 4x4 separately from the A-B schedule, since retention of information is a common concern for those using the 4x4.

STANDARDIZED TEST SCORES

To begin to answer some of the questions about time and learning as it applies to schools on block schedules, we conducted a study of student achievement in all Virginia high schools over a two-year period. Our goal was to determine if there were differences in gains made in reading and mathematics at the eleventh-grade level on norm-referenced tests among schools on traditional, alternate day, and semester schedules. Virginia had about 60 percent of high schools on a block schedule at the time of this study. Virginia is a highly diverse state, with rural, urban, and suburban schools, which made it fertile ground to begin studying student achievement as related to the use of time.

When analyzing standardized test results from all public high schools in Virginia, results from 1996 and 1997 showed that students in schools on the A-B schedule made greater gains than students in schools on the 4x4 or the single-period schedule in reading and mathematics. Results also indicated that students in schools on the 4x4 had higher gains than students in traditional schedules.

Baseline data from the 1998 Virginia end-of-course tests in English, mathematics, history, and science found that with the exception of science, more students in A-B schools scored at or above the state average than did students on the 4x4 and the traditional single-period schedules. Schools on the single-period schedule performed better in science than those on either block schedule.

NO HARM: IS IT GOOD ENOUGH?

Is the finding that block scheduling does not do any harm reason enough to initiate change to the degree needed to make block scheduling work? Should we not be looking for improvement in student achievement? Is status quo good enough?

USE OF TIME IN THE CLASSROOM

We argue that, based upon the literature reviewed and our observations in many schools, there must be sufficient time for instruction, but that the time allotted must also be used efficiently within the teaching block. Murphy (1992) indicates that higher levels of student learning are generally correlated to academic learning time. We believe that block scheduling allows opportunities for extended academic learning time, if teachers plan their teaching objectives around active student engagement. If an analysis of academic learning time is conducted, and all of the potential ways that instructional time is lost (because of class changes, pre- and post-instruction responsibilities, etc.) are calculated, it becomes clear that moving to a block schedule will save time in schools. Academic learning time increases because more efficient use of time is made, and non-value-added time (number of class changes) is diminished.

How teachers use instructional time in the classroom should be a major concern to change agents. The 1983 report of the National Commission on Excellence in Education (p. 29) recommended ". . . more effective use of existing school day, a longer school day or a lengthened school year." The Task Force on Education for Economic Growth (1983, p. 38) urged all states to ". . . increase both the duration and the intensity of academic learning time." The issue of increased instructional time for students was also addressed in *A Place Called School* (Goodlad, 1984). If the goal surrounded by time is to provide a quality education, Goodlad warns, "Increasing the days and hours in school settings will in fact be counterproductive unless there is, simultaneously, marked improvement in how the time is used" (p. 183). In a review of literature on educational reform, Blai's (1986) findings indicate that there is a high correlation between the amount of time that a student spends in the classroom and student achievement. He concludes that in general, educational researchers ". . . agree that the amount of time that one is exposed to instruction and the time engaged in learning bear a relation to what is learned" (p. 38).

Traditionally, schedules were developed around lunch, facility usage, and other non-instructional variables. As a matter of fact, ". . . it has been repeatedly reported in the literature that the traditional schedule did not support many of the changes that needed to be made in high schools across the country; in fact, it was often lamented that 'the schedule was the problem'" (Canady & Rettig, 1995, p. 4).

Based on present scheduling trends, the schedule of the 1990s and the new millenium appears to be some variation of the block schedule. This schedule—of which there are many variations—divides the allotted instructional time within the school day into fewer classes per day but longer blocks of time that will provide teachers more time to teach concepts and students longer periods of time to concentrate on a particular subject. Because the block scheduling concept (as defined in this book) is rela-

tively new in the United States, or at least some models of it are new, and since there has been very little data kept by schools that have implemented some form of block scheduling, there are still many questions to be answered.

Based on our personal experiences and a review of the literature of Stallings (1980), Karweit (1985), Goodlad (1984), Levin (1986), and the National Education Commission on Time and Learning

---

CASE IN POINT

Workshop participants always assume that we will try to convince them to develop a block schedule. While we do promote the concept and want administrators in particular to understand the value of alternative forms of scheduling, we do not automatically tell every educator that a block schedule is for him or her. Yvonne visited a high school in Alabama that in many aspects is a model school. The atmosphere of the school is positive, there is no differentiation between academic and career-bound students, most students complete an academic program, and student achievement is high. Teachers work hard teaching six classes a day and have a positive attitude. Every student takes seven courses each year, including four years each of English, math, science, and social studies. The school had slowly explored block scheduling and asked Yvonne what she thought. Her comments to the administration were that they should study the concept because organizing to provide common planning time for teams of teachers would be helpful. But her major concern was that they should protect what they have that is working well and not jump into a new schedule merely because neighboring districts are doing so.

School teams should always set goals that the time structure of the school can support. Why do many schools with problems choose a block schedule? They are looking for solutions to their problems. Why do many schools that are getting along well choose a block schedule? They are innovative and can see the possibilities for the future. Why are *you* studying the block schedule?

(1994), it appears reasonable to assume that student success depends upon a combination of the amount of time allotted for instruction and the way the time is used in the classroom. Therefore, providing additional time alone will not guarantee increased student achievement. Other evidence offered by these researchers indicates that other variables—such as climate, subjects taught, nature of student population, organization of instruction, and other opportunities to learn—affect student achievement. Levin (1983, pp. 29–30) emphasizes this point with the following comment: "What is done with the time is probably more important in affecting student achievement than mechanical increases in the length of the school day or the school year, or class time spent on particular subjects." As members of the National Education Commission on Time and Learning (1994, p. 7) observed, "Despite the obsession with time, little attention is paid to how it is used: in 42 states examined by the commission, only 41 percent of secondary school time must be spent on core academic subjects."

If the use of academic time and students' exposure to content is a variable that we must consider when making choices regarding certain block scheduling models, perhaps a review of literature related to opportunity to learn (OTL) should be considered. In a study on opportunity to learn conducted by Wang that investigated the relationship between students' opportunity to learn and their science achievement, he found that ". . . OTL variables were significant predictors of both written and hands-on test scores even after students' general ability level, ethnicity, and gender were controlled" (Wang, 1998, p. 137). Wang indicates that "content exposure was the most significant predictor of students' test scores, and quality of instructional delivery was the most significant predictor of the hands-on test scores" (p. 137). Reviewing other studies on opportunity to learn will provide direction for choosing schedule configurations that do not reduce the amount of instructional time.

In the National Association of Secondary School Principals' 1996 publication, *Breaking Ranks: Changing an American Institution*, one of the major recommendations for the high school of the 21st century is the call for high schools to use allotted instructional time in more flexible ways. Hopes are that such flexible use of time will allow appropriate use of allotted time to provide more opportunities for teachers, students, and administrators and better services for customers.

ADVANCED PLACEMENT COURSES

Advanced Placement examinations are offered across 32 subjects in May of each year. These AP courses are available to students in schools throughout the United States as well as other countries. The exams are administered by the College Board and graded by external evaluators. Students' scores range from 1 to 5. Certain colleges and universities offer college-level credit for a predetermined level of performance on the test.

The two issues that surround AP and block scheduling are related to the 4x4 semester schedule. The first of the two major issues focuses on students completing an AP course four to five months before the examination is administered. In such cases, retention of information becomes an issue. The time lapse between the completion of coursework as early as December and the administration of the exam in May could affect student performance, resulting in a lower score than a student would have had if s/he were enrolled in the course at the time of the testing.

The second issue addresses the instructional time issue. Students enrolled in second-semester AP courses have less time to complete the prescribed content than do students enrolled in the A-B or single period schedule. The second semester generally ends well after the AP examinations are administered in May. Thus, students do not have the same amount of instructional time (or opportunity to learn the content) as students who have been enrolled in the course for the entire year. Although some schools on the 4x4 schedule are addressing the issue in various ways, there are still many concerns related to the 4x4 block schedule and the AP examination issue.

In a 1998 report from the Educational Testing Services (ETS)—in "Research Notes: Block Schedules and Student Performance on AP Examinations"—Smith and Camara reported the results of a comprehensive analysis of AP examination scores. It analyzed the scores of students on semester schedules and those of students on a year-long schedule, and the impact of scheduling practices on student achievement on AP examinations in ". . . the four highest volume AP Examinations (U.S. History, English Literature, Biology, and Calculus AB)" (1998, p.2). The authors concluded from their findings ". . . that students, on average, obtain higher AP grades when instruction is given over the entire year [A-B or single-period day schedules] rather than in a semesterized block schedule format. These results are consistent across the four AP examinations and are found on 15 of the 16 comparisons between year-long and semester block courses" (p. 9). Other data from this report indicate that students who take the examination immediately following instruction may obtain higher AP examination grades, and there is some evidence that indicates ". . . that students obtain higher AP grades when more time is devoted to instruction" (p 10).

As educators have adopted block schedules, comments have been voiced concerning the need for AP testing at times of the year other than the traditional spring date. In September 1996, the College Board issued a statement based on information gathered through questionnaires, telephone surveys, open forums with AP teachers, and an analysis of student performance. After examining the various types of schedule scenarios, the investigators determined that only the 4x4 creates a need for a January examination. At this time, AP staff recommends that no action be taken to develop January exams. Studies will continue each year to determine if a January exam is warranted. The College Board gave five reasons for not recommending further action at this time (1996, p. 1):

1. The potential volume, even in 1999, is too small. In the latest survey of examinees, with 69 percent reporting, only 1.5 percent (about 8,500) reported that they took a yearlong AP course offered only in the fall. There were only five examinations for yearlong courses in which over 500 students said that they took a course offered only in the fall. The schools that indicated they used intensive (4x4) semester block scheduling for AP courses had only 8,150 examinations both semesters.

2. The cost of each January examination, assuming a continued modest growth in volume, would be about $200. Those surveyed indicated that this cost should be assumed only by students who benefit from the January administration but the cost should be about the same for the two administrations. Both goals cannot be accomplished at the same time while maintaining quality.

3. Students who completed yearlong courses offered only in the fall or only in the spring tended to perform poorly on AP examinations in 1995 and 1996. Of the 13 examinations in which there were 100 or more semester intensive block schedule students, those who took the course over a full year averaged higher scores in 77 percent of (20 of the 26) cases. In calculus, history, and the sciences, mean grades for block schedule students were about 0.6 (about half a standard deviation) lower than the mean for students who took the course over the full year.

4. In several surveys and meetings, AP teachers, coordinators, readers, and test development committee members overwhelmingly opposed both semester block scheduling and January examinations. The opposition appeared to be the strongest among teachers in block scheduling schools.

5. With January examinations, it would be more difficult to maintain quality of service and validity. There is particular concern about the test development and the reading process.

STAFF DEVELOPMENT

One observation from the research that is consistent as block scheduling evolves is the need for ongoing staff development. Teacher development must be planned; and pieces of it must be implemented before, during, and after the implementation of block scheduling. Teachers have reported, for example, that teacher-directed learning is difficult to sustain over extended periods of time (Styles & Cavanagh, 1974). Principals are often too busy to attend to staff development during the early years of the block schedule, and district staff development coordinators may not be totally in touch with the goals and initiatives of individual schools. In both the North Carolina and the Virginia studies teacher staff development is listed as critical to the success of block scheduling.

Staff development is composed of two parts: education and training. The literature on adult education is helpful in discriminating the differences between the two. Education refers to changing one's mindset or perspective on an issue, being able to view issues critically, and being able to take action on something new that is learned (Brookfield, 1986; Mezirow, 1991). Training is best thought of in relation to skills. Teachers need education to help them understand the evolving nature of schools and the value of using time differently. Teachers need training in pedagogical skills—methods that support active learning—to implement the block schedule effectively. Unfortunately, many school leaders focus only on training and promote staff development that offers workshops in cooperative learning, working with manipulatives, or even developing better lesson plans without doing the education groundwork that makes the training meaningful and relevant to the teacher.

SATISFYING OUR EDUCATION CUSTOMERS

In spite of reported positive results, block scheduling is not always embraced by school communities.

CASE IN POINT

In 1990, the School Committee members at Masconomet High School in Topsfield, Massachusetts, decided to terminate its Renaissance Program, a form of the Copernican Plan schedule. Although the program was terminated, it is important to note that favorable interim reports were in hand and that a careful study of the elimination of the program was due more to the political problems than the success of the program (Carroll, 1994).

Because there are some concerns from prospective change agents, it is extremely important to know why certain restructuring initiatives have not been successful. There are many reasons that have been cited in the literature, including those that are strictly political.

Another reason for the lack of success with block scheduling appears to be lack of ownership. In a major study to determine the effects of a mode of secondary school organization called full-credit semestering in Ontario, King and associates (1977) found that the way in which innovations were implemented was more important for student and staff satisfaction than the effects of the actual organizational changes.

CASE IN POINT

A school that used block scheduling for a significant period of time began experiencing a decline in the goals that had been defined when implementing the block schedule. The decline in student achievement was rather dramatic. Many teachers began blaming the scheduling configuration that was being used in the school.

The question to be answered was which variables had changed over the period of time from the beginning of the decline of performance. Some of the variables to consider might include a significant change in student population, change in measuring devices, shift in socio-economic status, change in policy that impacts identified goals, policy changes in measurements in student achievement, and leadership.

After investigating variables, the only significant change found in the school was the principalship. Now we must decide if the issue of the decline in the identifiable measurable objectives and teacher dissatisfaction is a block scheduling issue, or if the current results are a product of other variables. Using a subtest for faculty, the results indicated that there was a high dissatisfaction among teachers and support staff with the school, not with the block scheduling.

The staff and students in those schools in which the teachers and some students shared in the decision to introduce the new organizational mode and help in its implementation tended to be more supportive of the changes and consequently more satisfied with them than in those schools where the decision to change was made unilaterally (p. iii).

As block scheduling evolves, there will be success and failures. It is important to determine the causes for success as well as the causes for failure. As we look at the reasons for failure, we use the following questions to start our investigation.

- Is the reason for failure a result of the schedule failing to provide opportunities for student success, or do other variables not associated with the schedule have a negative impact?

- Is the reason for failure related to teacher satisfaction or dissatisfaction with the school environment?

King et al. (1977) suggest that if teachers are satisfied with their school, the organization of the school is not a major variable in their level of satisfaction. If dissatisfaction occurs, it may be the result of another major variable such as leadership.

LOOKING BACK . . .

Why all of the focus on literature and research in a "how-to" book? Simple: These issues are some of the most challenging that educators must first consider when trying to change a tradition that is older than most of the buildings that house the students. Time and learning and the need for change are some of the most challenging issues that a change agent will face when studying the restructuring of high schools. We have only touched on the issues that relate to changing a school to a new schedule. Principals are well served by reviewing literature on school culture, leadership, and the change process. All provide the school leader with helpful information about the influences in a school that maintain the status quo or move the organization forward. Principals reviewing these topics will learn that they are the key players in changing a school, not because of position or power but because of the opportunities they have daily to create a shared vision for the school, to help faculty learn, to reward initiative, and to keep the school focused on that which is important.

As one can determine from a review of the literature, findings on allotted instructional time and learning appear to be mixed. But there is a consistent thread throughout. There must be allotted time for instruction. How this time is used is critical for learning to take place. Will we be the change agents or will we be changed? The opportunities are there for building leaders to seize and move schools to the next millennium. **Just do it!** ❏

How Will Teachers, Students, and Administrators Benefit from a Block Scheduling Framework?

*A*lmost all youngsters—and apparently oldsters as well—are capable of attaining the same standards within a reasonable period of time. All but a few babies, for instance, learn to walk by the age of two and to talk by the age of three. But no two get there quite the same way, as parents have known for eons.

So too at higher levels. Some children learn best by rote, in structured environments with high certainty and strict discipline. Others thrive in the less-structured permissive atmosphere of a progressive school. . . . Some students need prescribed daily doses of information; others need challenge, the "broad picture," and a high degree of responsibility for the design of their own work. But for too long, educators have insisted that there is one best way to teach and learn, even though they have disagreed about what the way is.

—Peter Drucker

LOOKING AHEAD IN THIS CHAPTER . . .

Maybe time constraints have created the non-flexible teaching strategies. Maybe they have created situations where lecture is best. Could it also be that the reason elementary school teachers use such a diverse menu of teaching strategies is that they have students for longer periods of time, so they are able to be more flexible in their choice of methodologies? A basic change in the way time is scheduled could bring about opportunities for teachers at the middle and secondary levels to meet more completely the needs of individual students.

Based on our observations—as principal of a high school that implemented a block schedule that is still in use eight years later and as assistant superintendent over a high school that is in the fifth year of block scheduling—we offer the following ideas for consideration. These ideas should stimulate thought and allow initial talks and exploration of block scheduling to begin. These are the initial ways that the school's customers—both the primary customer (the student) and internal customers[1]—will be served by implementing a block schedule format.

TEACHERS

- Teachers and students have more quality time together, which creates an atmosphere conducive to bonding. Developing a rapport between teachers and students translates into maximized learning. Students also have more opportunities to remain with cohort or support groups.

- Teachers are more effective in evaluating student needs, progress, and achievement. Working with fewer classes and fewer students in a day, they are able to focus more on individual students and personalized instruction. Teachers have more time to identify and respond individually to student performance, use various teaching strategies that match student learning styles, and address individual needs by facilitating developmental, remedial, or accelerated programs of study. Students actively participate in and accept responsibility for their own level of academic achievement.

- Teachers are able to present a thorough presentation of a concept, theory, or new skill followed by practical applications and feedback exercises in the same block of time. This method allows for connections to be made between concepts and applications, helping students understand the real-world value of the material they are studying.

- Teachers are able to facilitate learning activities that utilize the classroom as a laboratory for learning and conducting research. Teachers can conduct lessons that are less procedural and more problem-oriented, helping students utilize the knowledge gained in other classes to augment what they are currently learning. Time is available to plan, develop, and share project work, emphasizing research skills and higher order thinking—skills valued in today's workplace as well as in college classrooms.

STUDENTS

- Students are better prepared to complete homework practice assignments correctly because there is enough time for teachers to provide guided practice in the classroom before making extended learning assignments. This practice does not suggest that all extended learning should be completed in the classroom. It requires efficient use of the time allotted for instruction so that the extended learning experience for the student will be productive and meaningful.

- Students have fewer subjects upon which to focus in a single day (three or four as opposed to six or seven). Students deal with varying requirements of fewer teachers daily and have fewer interactions that can be highly stressful for some students. Reducing the number of courses taken in one day may also reduce the quantity of homework, which can mean higher quality practice and better preparation for class.

- Students have more time to complete laboratory sessions in science, computer applications, technology education, consumer science, art, music, and writing, as well as to apply skills in interactive activities. In classes and labs that require preparation, set-up, takedown, and clean up, it is not uncommon to hear testimony from teachers and students that class time used for routine tasks is significantly reduced, thereby leaving more time for instruction.

[1]Internal customers are those whose work is passed to them from within the organization. For example, geometry teachers are customers of algebra teachers, ninth-grade English teachers are customers of middle school teachers, and all classroom teachers are customers of guidance counselors. The notion of internal customers is relevant in systems change because it is important that each person who works in the system understands how what s/he does affects others in the school. External customers include parents, employers, and community members. Students are the primary customers of the school and are viewed by some as the product that is shaped. They represent the work of the school to external customers.

■ Students particularly like the student activity period, which is used for co-curricular activities and extra help time for academics. Co-curricular activities include assemblies, club meetings, pep rallies, career counseling, and academic development. It is a good time to bring groups of students with common interests together for seminars. The time gives students equal access to co-curricular activities, and it is not uncommon for schools to report that student participation increases in these and other developmental activities after the block scheduling format is implemented. The time is also useful for making up missed work and participating in extra help sessions. Students enjoy being able to access teachers during the school day, rather than depending on after-school tutoring.

■ In-hand data indicate that one of the major strengths of the block schedule is the flexible use of the schedule to reduce the dropout rate for at-risk students and provide more opportunities for dropouts to return to school and complete educational requirements for graduation.

■ Accessibility of course options for students provides greater scheduling flexibility and increases opportunities for electives. In order to satisfy expanded graduation requirements in some school districts and some states, students take more courses in the core subject areas. Under the traditional schedule, students are forced to eliminate electives, thus reducing enrollment in technical education courses, art, music, and other electives. The increased number of courses that students are allowed to take increases elective opportunities.

■ If a student is failing a course, s/he does not have to remain in the class for an entire year—the course can be repeated the following semester, regardless of the type of block scheduling that is used. There is also more flexibility for alternative education programs, dual enrollment, and work-based learning experiences. These options offer students an opportunity to remain on grade level with age-appropriate peers.

ADMINISTRATION

■ Fewer class changes reduce disruption of instruction, and less unsupervised time minimizes discipline referrals. There is a reduction in the number of times students can be late to class because of fewer class changes during a single day. We argue that any building administrator who has the responsibility of student behavior on a day-to-day basis will testify that the fewer class changes and class interruptions that allow students to congregate in the hallways, commons areas, or other unsupervised areas, the fewer behavioral problems that will have to be dealt with. Block scheduling also decreases the number of discipline referrals from classroom teachers because many times disagreements that start in the hallway are carried into the classroom.

- Block scheduling is utilized to provide a school climate conducive to academic excellence for students and professional maturity for faculty and staff. A healthier and more inviting school climate exists, one in which the school community practices values that are guided by respect for others. A positive school climate increases accountability and responsibility for teachers and students.

- Block scheduling promotes greater parent involvement and positive school-home relationships because of the more frequent interaction between teachers and students and the longer periods of planning time that teachers have to contact parents. Contacts need not be cut short by a teacher hurrying back to class.

INSTRUCTION

- Expanded time and flexible periods for academic instruction provide better opportunities to connect curricula with hands-on activities, real-world applications, and interdisciplinary problems and projects.

- Longer periods for academic instruction provide opportunities to utilize available resources such as libraries, computer centers, laboratories, field trips, study groups, guest speakers, personalized tutoring via technology, learning centers, and more opportunities to participate in worldwide technology initiatives.

- Programmatic changes include increased course offerings, integration of curriculum, a more appropriate environment for student achievement, and increased opportunities for professional development for teachers and administrators. Student opportunities to connect with the private sector to expand courses for hands-on experiences are possible when the block-scheduling format is the norm.

- Block scheduling provides flexibility, which is conducive to utilizing technology as an instructional support tool for heterogeneous student grouping. Through individualized instruction, technology encourages exploration of concepts by correcting careless mistakes so that students can discover for themselves theorems, rules, etc. In a traditional schedule, concepts are often lost because of the fragmented instructional periods of development. Block scheduling coupled with technology optimizes the learning experience.

- A larger block of instructional time allows teachers the opportunity to utilize a variety of creative and innovative instructional strategies. A variety of teaching-learning activities emphasizes higher-level active learning and accommodates different learning and teaching opportunities that include the following.

Cooperative Learning	Teaching Partners
Individualized Instruction	Discussions, Analysis, Debate
Mastery Learning	Re-teach and Re-test Opportunities
Critical Thinking Techniques	Student-Student Partners
Case Studies	Independent Student Research
Virtual Reality Field Trips	Padiea Model (Socratic Seminars)
Virtual Reality Classrooms	

- Teachers concentrate on fewer students per day and shift gears only three or four times a day, instead of five or six changes. There is a reduction in the number of times teachers have to take attendance and focus on other clerical duties, thus allowing additional time for instruction. A teacher's daily schedule, focus, and responsibilities are less fragmented, so there should be more opportunities for improved instruction and additional student learning.

- Teachers have longer blocks of instructional planning periods to accomplish significantly more planning, collaboration, and tutoring without interruption. Increased planning time provides opportunities that enhance teaching-learning effectiveness. Block scheduling requires the use of time management skills by both students and teachers, so accountability for both groups is increased. Examples of time management plans are provided in Chapter 9.

COMPARISON OF ALTERNATING DAY, SEMESTER, AND EMBEDDED BLOCK SCHEDULE MODELS

To further determine ways in which block scheduling can be of benefit to all customers, one only needs to examine a comparison between the current schedule being used and the schedules being considered. This analysis will also serve to provide information for the school study team (defined in Chapter 5) as it goes about the task of recommending a schedule match with the needs of the school. Consider the following analysis.

GOALS	ALTERNATING DAY (A-B)	SEMESTER (4X4)	COMBINATION (EMBEDDED)
Opportunities for additional courses	Increase depends on the number of courses you are currently offering students	Increase depends on the number of courses you are currently offering students	Increase depends on the number of courses you are currently offering students
Optimal use of time, space, and human resources • course load	Teachers teach 5 courses per year	Teachers teach 6 courses per year	Both
• itinerant teachers	More efficient use of itinerant teachers	No appreciable change	More efficient use of itinerant teachers
• space	More efficient use of space	More efficient use of space	More efficient use of space
• work-based learning	Opportunities for students to receive in-depth training related to career goals because time is organized for students to some degree	Opportunities for students to receive in-depth training related to career goals because time is organized for students to some degree	Opportunities for students to receive in-depth training related to career goals because time is organized for students to some degree
• remedial summer school	Summer school still needed to some degree for remediation purposes	Opportunities to eliminate summer school for remediation purposes	Opportunities to eliminate summer school
Flexible use of allotted instructional time and schedule	Repeat courses if enrollment is sufficient No provisions for dropouts to return at mid-year	Repeat courses if enrollment is sufficient Opportunity for dropouts to return second semester	Repeat courses if enrollment is sufficient Opportunity for dropouts to return second semester

GOALS	ALTERNATING DAY (A-B)	SEMESTER (4X4)	COMBINATION (EMBEDDED)
	No mid-year graduation for at-risk or accelerated students	Possibility for mid-year graduation for at-risk or accelerated students	Possibility for mid-year graduation
	Transfer students handled in traditional manner	Develop a support system for transfer students	Transfer students handled in traditional manner
	90+ minute classes, 135-162 instructional hours per year	85+ minute classes, 127.5+ instructional hours per year	Increase depends on combination
	Flexible use of time to schedule at-risk students for success in out-of-school career-related opportunities	Limited flexibility	Flexible use of time to schedule at-risk students for success in out-of-school career-related opportunities
Calmer learning environment	Four class changes per day	Four class changes per day	Four class changes per day
Reduce teacher stress as related to number of classes and students taught per day or per year	Longer planning period	Longer planning period	Longer planning period
	Responsible for 5 class preparations per year	Responsible for 6 class preparations per year	Depends on combination
	Responsible for maximum of 150 students concurrently per year (50-75 daily)	Responsible for 75 students concurrently (150 students per year)	Depends on combination
Reduce student stress as related to learning • classes per day	Students responsible for maximum of 4 classes per day	Students responsible for maximum of 4 classes per day	Students responsible for maximum of 4 classes per day
• academics and electives	Provisions for balancing academics and electives on a daily basis	Provisions for balancing academics and electives each semester	Both
• time management	Students accountable for managing time as related to schedules	Same schedule each day	Both
• absences	One-day lapse before returning to class when student absent	Returns to class on day immediately following absence	Both

GOALS	ALTERNATING DAY (A-B)	SEMESTER (4X4)	COMBINATION (EMBEDDED)
• homework	Students have 2 nights to prepare for homework assignments	Homework preparation for same courses each night	Both
• concept attainment	Students have longer period of time for understanding concepts; not limited to 90 days	Understanding concepts limited to 90 days or repeat	Both
Opportunities to build a positive teacher-student relationship that will provide opportunities to enhance student learning	Longer block of time provides opportunities for teachers and students to work as a team, as partners, and individually for the purpose of learning	Longer block of time provides opportunities for teachers and students to work as a team, as partners, and individually for the purpose of learning	Longer block of time provides opportunities for teachers and students to work as a team, as partners, and individually for the purpose of learning
Improve opportunities for teaching and learning • partners in learning	Students become active consumers/partners in learning	Students become active consumers/partners in learning	Students become active consumers/partners in learning
• in-class time	Increased in-class instructional time	Increased in-class instructional time	Increased in-class instructional time
• continuity of instruction	Reduced continuity on a daily schedule due to alternate days of class	Reduced continuity for a sequence of courses due to potential lapse of semester or year before next level of course	Depends on combination of schedule selected
• regular reinforcement	Concerns over not meeting each day for reinforcement purposes in area of foreign languages	Not applicable	Some of these concerns are eliminated
• sequential learning	Not applicable	Concern over lapsed time between sequential courses, (e.g.: foreign language, music, math)	Allows opportunities to address such concerns
• curriculum	Curriculum development necessary	Curriculum development necessary	Curriculum development necessary

Comparison of 6 Single-Period Blocks per Year to 7 or 8 90-Plus-Minute Blocks per Year

GOALS	6 SINGLE-PERIOD BLOCKS PER YEAR	7 BLOCKS PER YEAR	8 BLOCKS PER YEAR
Opportunities for additional student courses	Minimum number of courses per year (6)	1 additional course per year	2 additional courses per year
Optimum use of time, energy, and human resources • classes taught	Teachers responsible for 5 instructional classes per year	Teachers responsible for 5 instructional classes per year	Teachers responsible for 6 instructional classes per year
• balanced schedule	Not applicable	Provides a balance of daily schedule for teachers and students	Provides a balance of semester schedule for students and teachers
• summer school	Summer school still needed	Summer school needed for remediation	Possible elimination of summer school for remediation purposes
• financial impact	Not applicable	No change in cost of textbooks—traditional text being used less	Mixed reports on financial savings due to need for fewer texts
Provide greater scheduling flexibility	No repeat of courses allowed within the school year	Limited opportunity to repeat courses at the end of the 1st semester	Opportunity to repeat failed courses 2nd semester
	No provisions for dropouts to return at end of 1st semester without special consideration	No provisions for dropouts to return at end of 1st semester without special consideration	Opportunity for dropouts to return 2nd semester
	Provides very little flexible use of schedule to meet special student needs	Provides optimum use of schedule to meet special student needs	Provides very little flexible use of schedule to meet special student needs
	No difference in the way technology is presented or learned	Sufficient time in each block to use a variety of instructional methods and provide opportunities for students to be involved in an international classroom inside as well as outside the school building	Sufficient time in each block to use a variety of instructional methods and provide opportunities for students to be involved in an international classroom inside as well as outside the school building
	No difference	Allows flexible use of time for interdisciplinary/team teaching because of larger pieces of time; especially effective at grade 9	Allows flexible use of time for interdisciplinary/team teaching because of larger pieces of time; especially effective at grade 9

GOALS	6 SINGLE-PERIOD BLOCKS PER YEAR	7 BLOCKS PER YEAR	8 BLOCKS PER YEAR
	150 hours of allotted instructional time per class per year	150+ hours of allotted instructional time per class per year	Depends on time-related variables
Fewer class changes provide a less disruptive school climate	No change	Fewer tardies because of fewer class changes	Fewer tardies because of fewer class changes
	No change	Fewer discipline referrals because of optimum supervision of students	Fewer discipline referrals because of optimum supervision of students
	5 class changes per day	3 class changes per day	3 class changes per day
Reduced student stress related to academic demands	Students responsible for 6 classes yearly/daily	Students responsible for maximum of 4 classes daily—7 yearly	Provides for balancing semester academic course offerings
	Responsible for teaching 5 classes daily	Responsible for teaching 2–3 classes daily	Responsible for teaching 3 classes daily
	Responsible for a maximum of 150 students daily/yearly maximum of 150 yearly	Responsible for a maximum of 50–75 students daily—a maximum of 150 yearly	Responsible for 75 students daily—a maximum of 150 yearly
Increased student understanding of content and opportunities for application of learned content	Classes are lecture dominated and students are passive consumers of information	Students and teachers are partners in a learning environment that is dominated by active student participation as active consumers of information	Students and teachers are partners in a learning environment that is dominated by active student participation as active consumers of information
	A variety of teaching methodology limited by time	Longer blocks of time allow for teaching strategies that provide opportunities to meet students' individual learning styles	Longer blocks of time allow for teaching strategies that provide opportunities to meet students' individual learning styles
	Not applicable	Some concern for not having first-year foreign language meet on daily basis for reinforcement purposes	Concern over lapsed time between sequential- and skill-related courses (e.g.: foreign lang., music, math)
Opportunities to build a positive teacher-student relationship that will provide opportunities to enhance student learning	Restricted by allotted instructional time for each class	Opportunities to identify learning styles and provide individualized instruction	Opportunities to identify learning styles and provide individualized instruction

Note: An embedded (combination) schedule will provide opportunities provided by neither alternating day nor semester block.

THE UNDERLYING PRINCIPLES AND ANTICIPATED OUTCOMES OF BLOCK SCHEDULING

As change occurs in education, there are underlying principles founded in sound educational reasoning which often drive the change. These principles are accompanied by measurable outcomes that provide a method for both formative and summative evaluations of the change.

The following are sound reasons to implement block scheduling as a change mechanism.

■ Block scheduling is part of a vision to improve school climate, create an environment that promotes positive relationships, and create professional renewal among teacher and administrative staff.

■ Block scheduling provides opportunities for cognitive coaching and reflective teaching practices that enhance positive restructuring.

■ Block scheduling provides opportunities for stakeholders to align curriculum, instruction, and assessment with desired student outcomes.

■ Block scheduling is used as a framework to encourage school-based action research, which allows stakeholders to determine needed professional staff development and the opportunity to refine other educational practices that are identified as inhibitors of change.

■ Block scheduling provides a framework that addresses time for planning, time for learning, and time for teaching.

■ Block scheduling provides opportunities for cross-team networking for academic departments, interdisciplinary teams, and student teaming.

■ Block scheduling is used for problem solving related to acceleration, attendance, discipline, academic scheduling, and at-risk students.

■ Block scheduling provides a framework that provides time for stakeholder collaboration to make the "big picture" a reality.

■ Block scheduling provides teachers an opportunity to become a part of the leadership team.

■ BOTTOM LINE: Block scheduling contributes to the success of students and teachers.

IDENTIFYING MEASURABLE OUTCOMES

Change must be managed by understanding the change process and by considering research data that have been designed to determine the effectiveness of a particular change process. Student performance on several quantitative measures—including summative examinations—is analyzed in comparison to past performance. Other qualitative data—based on measurable outcomes—are gathered and analyzed to provide a glimpse of teacher, student, and parent satisfaction with the new arrangement.

These outcomes, identified at the beginning of the change process, are evaluated on an ongoing basis. The effectiveness of the outcomes is based on regular monthly, semester, and annual "quality checks." These measurements or checks are used to assess the most recent available school data. When Tom was principal at Atlee High School, his school improvement team (see Chapter 5) identified the measurable outcomes to determine the progress and success of the block-scheduling format (see Figure 4).

There are many other outcomes unique to individual schools. The study committee team is a good resource to assist in identifying outcomes for a particular school.

OPTIMAL USE OF TIME, SKILLS, AND ENERGY

A schedule can be viewed as a resource in itself; it is the schedule that permits the effective and efficient utilization of people, space, time, and other resources in an organization. Block scheduling reflects time as a valuable resource to optimize quality production and performance—an imperative for success in the 21st century. We believe that the primary objective of block scheduling is to restructure existing resources for the most efficient and effective method of delivering quality instruction to a group of students. We offer the following questions to stimulate thinking.

Does block scheduling:

• Optimize the resources of time, skills, and energy?

• Promote greater parent and student involvement?

- Dropout rates for students will be lower, as measured by the number of annual dropouts.

- Fewer students will need remediation, as measured by the number of students who advance to the next grade level and the number of students who pass all classes.

- More students will continue to higher education for academic and technical training, as measured by the number of students who enroll in two- and four-year colleges, universities, and specialty schools within four years after entering ninth grade.

- Students' academic achievement will increase, as measured by standardized test scores.

- More students will enroll in Advanced Placement and dual-credit courses, as measured by actual yearly enrollment.

- Students will take advantage of job counseling and placement services, as measured by the number of students who receive career counseling while in high school and job placement during high school or within one year after leaving high school.

- Discipline referrals will decline, as measured by the number of discipline referrals submitted to administrative offices for resolution.

- Achievement and success of special populations in school and the workplace will increase, as measured by the number of special population students who receive on-site job training while in school and job placement after leaving high school.

- Graduation rate will increase, as measured by the number of students who graduate within four years of entering ninth grade.

- Student attendance will increase, as measured by annual percentage of student attendance.

- Teachers will use a variety of instructional methodologies, as measured by surveys, observations, and student and teacher interviews.

- Provide opportunities for a variety of teaching/learning activities that emphasize active learning and higher order thinking skills, and accommodate a variety of student learning styles?

- Promote professional growth for faculty/staff?

- Facilitate greater personalization of student instruction?

- Provide for a more efficient use of facilities and human resources?

- Provide for more teacher planning time that leads to more effective teaching/learning experiences for teachers and students?

- Create opportunities for interdisciplinary teaching/learning for teachers and students?

- Provide opportunities for students to enroll in a wider variety of courses from the school's course of study?

- Encourage efficient time management by teachers and students?

- Provide a climate with an emphasis on increased responsible behavior?

- Increase student/teacher accountability?

Restructuring the traditional school day in a block schedule format is a flexible use of time, which provides an optimum learning opportunity for students at every ability level. Block scheduling actually increases instructional time within the school day. Less time devoted to class necessities—such as calling roll and starting and stopping class—provides additional time to communicate in more interactive instructional methodologies for student learning.

Restructuring of the school day to use a block scheduling format will not solve all programmatic or organizational problems. However, as Canady and Rettig (1995, p. 29) put it:

- A schedule can be viewed as a resource; it is the schedule that permits the effective utilization of people, space, time, and resources in an organization.

- A schedule can help solve problems related to the delivery of instruction; or a schedule can be a major source of problems.

- A schedule can facilitate the institutionalization of desired programs and instructional practices.

THE PLANNING CYCLE FOR BLOCK SCHEDULING

As we have implied throughout, a plan of action including a rationale for change must be in place to realize successful change. The process is never-ending and must be consistently monitored so the desired results will be accomplished. There are many models that can be used to plan and monitor change. The model that we have successfully used as a tool for change is the Shewhart Cycle as defined by Deming (1982, 1986, p. 88). We highly recommend the use of this cycle as **a procedure for any change** effort. It is sometimes known as the PLAN-DO-CHECK-ACT Cycle.[2]

- **Step 1: Plan**—What does the needs assessment tell us about how things are now? What do existing data report? What is the desired state we want to reach? What is the new process we want to put into place (e.g.: creating a new schedule), and what are the steps in that process? Or, what is the new product we want to produce (e.g.: new technology course or new curriculum guide), and what are the steps in producing that product? Does the school have the capability to create and deliver the new service/product? What changes should we make or what actions should be taken before we begin doing something different? Is taking the proposed action going to create new problems that will have to be solved? What communication should we plan with the public related to implementing change?

- **Step 2: Do**—Implement the new process that delivers the service or creates the product.

- **Step 3: Check (Study)**—Observe the effects of the change that were implemented and review the data on the process.

- **Step 4: Act**—Based on what the data reveal, improve the process by making changes that result in a better service/product.

At the conclusion of Step 4, the change agent repeats the process until s/he is satisfied with the results of the change.

> ### CASE IN POINT
>
> While working with a group of teachers in a workshop, Tom asked them why they wanted to change the schedule they were presently using. The following interpretation is an attempt to summarize their responses, which we think covers all the bases.
>
> *Common sense allows us to assume that the time schedule of the school day should be organized to meet the needs of students, not around courses, classes, units, and lessons, which are organized around activities' or facility's schedules. Instructional activities must have enough flexibility to demonstrate their learning in a variety of ways. Blocks of time must be devised to allow more flexible daily scheduling for students.*
>
> *Experience shows us that these larger blocks of time will provide teachers and students longer periods to be engaged in educational activities, additional time for team building, collaborative teaching opportunities, enrichment opportunities for all students, additional support for thematic teaching, and real opportunities for teacher-student dialogue. These larger blocks of time will create additional time for students to participate in field studies as well as independent studies, mentorships, apprenticeships, and real work opportunities for those students who choose to enter the work force after high school.*

---

[2]During the last years of Deming's life and work, he changed the cycle to PLAN-DO-STUDY-ACT, helping people understand that the CHECK part of the process was monitoring the process, not evaluating people; as well as using the results from what was learned to refine the process in the ACT stage.

LOOKING BACK . . .

As we move through the process of implementing block scheduling, we must address the issue of how we can successfully build a solid foundation for the future of block scheduling. The information shared in this chapter addresses the reasons for educators, parents, students, and community members to support block scheduling, as well as the outcomes they can expect. Additionally, it speaks to the differences of the schedules usually considered for alternative use of time.

As the building principal begins thinking seriously about the process of change—which includes involving stakeholders in the development of a new schedule—the Shewhart planning cycle offers him or her an excellent way to organize actions, including the gathering and use of data to make good decisions about change. ❑

How Do You Build a Solid Foundation for Block Scheduling?

*W*holesale involvement is necessary to engender the level of quality, service, and flexibility required by today's markets. . . . Intense communication is required to foster that involvement; we must:

- *Listen constantly, congregate, or share ideas/information and recognize achievement.*
- *Celebrate—informally and formally—the 'small wins' that are indicative of the solid day-to-day performance turned in by more than 90 percent of your work force.*

—Tom Peters

LOOKING AHEAD IN THIS CHAPTER . . .

Unprecedented information-sharing with, interaction with, and recognition of staff and community are required to induce the attitude change and horizontal communication necessary to foster widespread involvement in and commitment to change. Anyone who thinks that changing a school—which means expecting the behaviors in the school to change—is an easy task and merely requires a strong manager is naïve about the American high school. Totally resistant to change and resilient after failed efforts, the institution of schooling, its teachers, and its stakeholders will pose many barriers to the change agent who proposes block scheduling or

any other radical change in the school day. Change is hard but it is not impossible, and strong school leaders are changing high schools every day. The key is leadership and using the tools of change that have been proven in other arenas. Peters (1987, p. 304) thinks the key is communication, especially listening to members of the organization, and he advocates the following:

Develop formal and informal devices aimed at spurring intense, proactive listening— these should range from "chats with the chairman" to extensive formal surveys. Invest lavishly in regular get-togethers—at least bimonthly, for all hands, in each facility.

Support these with ancillary devices—such as weekly (or more frequently) newsletters, videos, or audios. Hold a minimum of five celebrity "events," small or large, each month; top this off with a minimum of ten thank-you notes per week for jobs—particularly small ones—well done.

Will building-level administrators encourage support systems for change? Implementing such systems means sharing responsibility for decision making, which entails sharing the power that accompanies that responsibility. Perhaps the most relevant problem related to change is the reluctance of the principal to embrace partnership—engaging partners from outside of the building and empowering them to act as true partners. There is a difference in verbalizing the need and support for building these systems and actually changing the process to include new systems. The change process includes sharing all information and power with customers. If the principal is not committed to this concept, the chance of success with change is not likely. Finding ways to include all impacted customers in the process is imperative.

Building a foundation and designing strategies for implementing the block schedule will often lead to the success or failure of the change effort. Ask yourself:

- Which stakeholders do I involve and to what extent do I empower these stakeholders to make decisions?

- Will stakeholders selected to serve on teams represent a broad-based constituency?

- Should they be involved in the change process from the beginning?

- Are there functional teams in place? Or will the change process provide new experiences for team members (as well as new experiences for the lead change agent, the building principal)?

- Will the role of the team and team members be defined before the study begins?

- Will team members be apprised of the many options available for restructuring the school day before making decisions?

- Will identifying special interest groups who need to be included in the change process foster ownership and consequently willing partners?

- What are action teams? What role will these teams play in the process?

- What student, instructional, teacher, and administrative issues will need to be addressed?

- What restructuring possibilities exist?

These questions will be addressed in this chapter, which is designed to help the building administrator understand the actions that build a support system for change in schools.

BUILDING SUPPORT FOR CHANGE

When planning for change, one of the important issues that a school administrator must examine is that of building a solid support system to embrace and foster change. In the case of block scheduling, the issue is one of building support for a change process that will result in re-engineering the allocation of instructional time, which will better serve students and teachers. Each building principal is accountable for examining the allocation of instructional time for students and determining the optimal use of available instructional time for instructional programs. It is with this underlying principle in mind that we must consider the options that are available for more efficient use of allocated instructional time.

The notion of re-engineering time is associated with school restructuring. To develop the context in which change should occur and, more specifically, to understand that the use of time is only one part of the restructuring process, it is helpful to review how we see school restructuring and where the use of time fits into a big picture.

WHAT IS SCHOOL RESTRUCTURING?

The term "restructuring" is commonly associated with the business community and suggests a rather negative picture of downsizing and doing more with less. Companies restructure their organizations to become more efficient, cut costs, and increase profits. In some cases, restructuring is done to save an organization that is sinking, giving it a second chance to rethink its mission and address systemic problems. Restructuring causes the processes through which an organization functions to change.

Why then do we restructure schools? Is it because they are inefficient, or that they are sinking? Educators have generally not felt the same urgency to change schools that a CEO may feel after his board of directors examines a disappointing financial report. However, school leaders, school boards, and some community members have voiced concerns about student achievement, high dropout rates, school violence, and a mismatch between the world of work and the preparation students receive in school. Educators are accountable to those groups for those outcomes. For these or other reasons, school leaders have attempted to improve schools by taking an aggressive approach to change that moves beyond adopting new textbooks or adding additional teachers. What we educators call restructuring is rarely a comprehensive restructuring of the school organization aimed at transformation of schooling. More frequently it is viewed as a change in:

- school organization (such as creating schools-within-schools) or

- curriculum (such as integrating the curriculum) or

- pedagogy (such as designing interdisciplinary teams) or

- governance (such as developing site-based management) or

- the technology of teaching (such as accessing databases for current information) or

- staff development (such as training with high tech companies) or

- the use of time (such as designing a block schedule)

Rarely is restructuring a radical change that includes most of the components of the school structure: governance, climate, empowerment, staff development, technology, human resources, funds, and time. However, true restructuring probably is best described as a change or at least a refinement of all of the components of the structure that surround the philosophy, goals, curriculum, instruction, stu-

dent assessment and program evaluation, and outcomes of education. (See Figure 5.) The purpose is to change what happens within that structure, and it is driven by a set of assumptions and beliefs that are rarely articulated but must be a part of the change agent's thinking. Restructuring puts into motion process changes that can transform a school. Maintaining the same types of resources that were previously available to a school, a transformed school uses resources differently to achieve different outcomes, thereby transforming the organization from how it functioned before and what it previously achieved to an organization that uses different processes to achieve a better end result.

Put in simple language, a transformed school uses its resources differently to create a school that produces better-prepared students.

At least three **assumptions** drive the transformation of schools:

1. Schools can be better.

2. The community will support the schools.

3. Teachers have the capacity to change.

The change agent will also hold a set beliefs or values which should be developed with teachers, becoming the shared values or guiding principles for the school. These beliefs must be unique to each school and cannot be copied from someone else's mission statement. Belief statements should be generated and discussed early in the planning process.

FIGURE 5
Transformed School

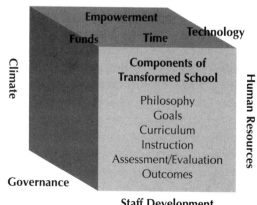

The following are *examples only* of **belief statements**:

- We want the best schools possible.

- Continuous improvement of the system is desirable.

- All students can be successful.

- Some practices are better than others.

We raise this discussion of restructuring to drive home the following points:

- Restructuring is comprehensive and, therefore, suggests systemic change and the interdependencies that are involved in changing a system.

- Using time differently is one part of changing the structure of school; by definition, solely changing time will not yield better educational outcomes without attention being given to other components of the school structure.

- Engaging in restructuring is a worthy effort, but only if the change agent continually keeps the effort focused on the vision—and that vision must converge on student outcomes: higher achievement, success for more students, or readiness for the 21st-century workplace.

HOW DO PRINCIPALS ENGAGE TEACHERS IN CHANGE?

Our experiences working with teachers and administrators, conducting training over the past decade, implementing change processes ourselves, reviewing literature, and interviewing staff developers about successful change efforts suggest a process that can be followed by a leader who is serious about creating change. We offer a brief description of a process we call Intentional Change to help lay the foundation for the remainder of this chapter.

Intentional Change is a collection of proactive steps that successful leaders follow to *create* change. It is not a blueprint that can be followed sequentially, because the human element of change requires leaders to set their course in conjunction with the maturity of staff, past experiences of staff, the culture of the school, and the urgency of the change process. However, Intentional Change may be help-

ful in designing a course of action and understanding why we propose the actions that follow throughout this book as we talk about implementing scheduling changes.

Intentional Change is a framework of change for schools moving toward the philosophy of continuous improvement. In order for change to occur, a visionary leader—a principal or other leader who knows where s/he is leading the organization—is imperative. This person must be able to articulate the change needed, state the purpose of the change and the outcome desired, and develop a shared vision for the school staff. In order to do this, the principal must understand the beliefs of the teachers. Observing a faculty's theories-in-use[1] (beliefs that are practiced, not merely espoused) gives the principal insight into the faculty's beliefs. Throughout this process of building a shared vision, building trust, and gaining commitment by staff, the principal must communicate honestly, involve the faculty in the change effort, and demonstrate personal commitment to the change process.

In order for change to occur successfully, the purpose of the change (espoused by the principal) must be clear. This means that the faculty will understand why this change has been undertaken and where it is supposed to lead. Change cannot be rushed or artificially placed into a timeline. Implementation of the change process, including the change in relationships and roles, will take time. Additionally, the process of educating faculty needs time and should not be rushed. The faculty should be highly involved in the change process and understand that change is a step-by-step process that is developed over time.

As the principal leads the faculty and community through the steps of change, it is helpful to provide teams with training in specific skills associated with organizational improvement. The training that we used and recommend is that commonly associ-

---

[1]For example, a teacher may espouse that all students can learn and will be successful in her class. However, her theory-in-use does not support what she says because she provides no extra help for students and expects some students to do poorly in her class. Her theory-in-use indicates that she does not believe all students will be successful in her class.

ated with Total Quality[2] and continuous improvement. The Quality culture allows school improvement to occur under the assumption that continuous improvement is desirable. This culture, unlike the traditional school culture, embodies the concepts of empowerment, teaming, shared decision making, and the use of data for decision making. These practices become the basis for training of teams that will design and lead ongoing improvements in the school.

Teacher training should be based on the Quality tools and skills needed for group processing and teaming. This content should be designed around proven practices from adult education.

- Motivate teachers who are participating in training.

- Show the relevance of training concepts to the world of the teacher.

- Include critical reflection[3] as a learning strategy during training.

- Engage teachers in dialogue so that they can voice and examine their assumptions.

- Integrate information about restructuring as part of the context for training.

More will be said on training in Chapter 10, which deals with staff development.

Having laid the foundation for change, we begin our work with the development of the school study team.

WHAT IS A SCHOOL STUDY TEAM?

A school study team is a group of educators and community members who study issues critical to determining the need for change in a school. In this particular change process, the study team will look at the issue of block scheduling, the present use of allocated instructional time, and the most efficient method of time to use. They will make a recommendation about the need for change if they determine there is such a need. Once all related data are gathered and analyzed, it is the responsibility of the study team to make recommendations to the principal regarding the use of instructional time.

This team will be actively involved in determining the school's direction in using allocated instructional time from the beginning of the process until the final decision is made. It has been our experience that many members of the study team will continue to be involved in the restructuring process of the school after the final decision regarding scheduling has been made and implementation is under way.

Some administrators have kept the study team intact beyond the recommendation stage. Since members of the team have ownership, they will continue to monitor the implementation process to ensure that there are no unanticipated barriers that impede the success of the project. Some team members become involved in other issues related to the school and serve in leadership roles for several years.

WHAT IS THE SELECTION PROCESS FOR? WHAT ARE THE RESPONSIBILITIES OF A STUDY TEAM?

There must be a beginning to any process. Therefore, the first step that the building administrator must take is to determine the way in which the study team will be selected, to identify the members of the study team, and to voice the responsibilities of the study team. The principal in charge of developing the change process must remember that a major focus of the study team is to ensure the integrity of the process and provide direction until the task has been completed. It will be advantageous for team members to remain active in the process throughout the initial implementation to ensure a successful transition of the project through the first year. Additional responsibilities of the study team include appointing action team members who will be responsible for collecting data and information relative to restructuring the school day and making recommendations to the study team during the change process.

---

[2] The concepts attributed to Quality are commonly associated with W. Edwards Deming and Joseph Juran. We use Total Quality here as the generic term used in organizational management to refer to the management philosophy that has been derived from the work of both men.

[3] Critical reflection is a practice in the adult education literature. It states the importance of having adults reflect critically upon new information they are learning, seeing both sides of issues, and placing the information into their own personal context and experiences before determining a position on the value of the information.

One of the most critical roles the principal will play in the change process is the selection of the study team. The principal should be an active participant in this selection process. A group of individuals that we will refer to as an action team, appointed by the principal, should convene to assemble a pool of potential team members. Members of the action team are individuals who have both the confidence of the principal and credibility within the school community. This team should represent a broad-based constituency.

Once the pool of potential candidates is identified, the principal may choose to do the following:

- Make the final decision regarding members of the study team.

- Appoint an action team to select the members of the study team.

- Empower existing teams within the school community to act as the study team. Such teams represent a broad-based constituency of a school community.

Existing teams are sometimes referred to as school improvement teams, school steering teams, faculty advisory teams, school leadership teams, or school councils. There is nothing wrong with using existing teams as long as the principal believes the team will be open to new ideas and will not let personal agendas color the thinking of the team during this important process.

The next step is to select a chair or team leader of the study team. Again the principal has options. S/he may empower the action team to select the chair, or the principal may choose to make the appointment. The appointment of the team chair is extremely critical to the change process. The person who assumes this role must be open minded, accepting of change, and willing to be an advocate for the decisions of the team. The relationship between the chairman and the principal is critical. The chairman must be "up front" with the principal at all times. If the process is not working well, the principal must hear it first from the chair rather than from a critic of the change process.

CASE IN POINT

The data collected by King et al. (1977) provide information on block scheduling practices that suggests that those schools in which staff members were directly involved in the implementation process were far more likely to be satisfied with the change when it was implemented.

Recently, when Tom was doing a presentation on block scheduling, a teacher in attendance made a statement and then asked a question. Her statement: "The school where I teach implemented block scheduling a year ago. We went back to the regular seven-period day this year because we had encountered so many problems and there was so much staff dissatisfaction."

Her question: "What can we do to ensure the success of such a schedule, if we decide to revisit the block schedule concept?" Tom's question to her: "What process did your school use when deciding what model of the block schedule you would use?"

She answered with the following statement: "My principal attended a conference on block scheduling the summer prior to implementing the schedule in our school. He said he liked what he had seen at the conference, and he returned to school and set about implementing the semester schedule concept for the upcoming school year. Although word leaked out concerning the schedule change, teachers were not officially notified until they returned for teacher workdays in August."

Consequently, the schedule was a flop.

This was a failure in the system and not the schedule. The principal failed to engage the faculty and community in thinking about change and in choosing a model that they would support and work hard to implement successfully. The principal had not become a change agent and had not led this school-community through the steps of change.

Both appointments to study team membership and the chair position are critical to the process. Consideration for membership on any team associated with this process should reflect the diversity of the school community.

THE ROLE OF THE PRINCIPAL

If this process is to be perceived as highly participatory, then why has the principal taken such an active leadership role in the initial stages of the process? There are two reasons for the initial assertive involvement of the principal: (1) S/he must be the visible initiator of change and must assume the responsibility of the lead change agent, and (2) s/he is held accountable by all customers for the final decisions. As stated earlier, the principal is the person who keeps everyone's eye on the vision, the goal, and an anticipated outcome. But at the same time, s/he cannot dismiss the daily duties of running the school and being responsible for everything that occurs in the school. The principal cannot let this or any other intended or unintended change occur without his or her involvement.

Although the change process is more likely to succeed if it is highly participatory, it is critical that highly skilled change agents be in positions that will allow the change process to occur.

IMPLEMENTING THE CHANGE PROCESS

Involvement of all customers cannot be superficial. If customers are asked to study the issue of change, they must be empowered to design the process and make recommendations that will be given appropriate consideration for implementation. Perhaps the most devastating blow to any change process is to have the results of the study team's recommendation announced before decisions have been made. This action will destroy the morale of all involved in the change process, and we have found that the change will likely not be successful.

It is critical to the long-term success of the project to involve representatives of all customers in the change process. The chances of success for change will increase with participation from all customers.

INCREASING THE KNOWLEDGE BASE

It is the responsibility of the school study team chair to provide training opportunities to members of the school study team to increase their knowledge base as well as to provide a base for making a more informed decision. This procedure will provide a support system that will enable team members to answer questions that customers may ask concerning the change process. Members of this team should be able to provide information to any member of the school community who wishes to be informed about the opportunities that block scheduling offers. Team members should seek opportunities to share the block-scheduling message with all members of the community. Opportunities for sharing the message include the following:

- Electronic systems such as Internet and World Wide Web home pages, public broadcasting (visual and audio), and print

- Informal conversations during community activities (shopping, attending extra- and co-curricular school activities)

- Meeting with service and civic organizations

- Telephone trees

- Local student support groups (PTA, athletic, academic, music boosters, and other special interest groups)

- Producing a video starring team members who will tell the story of block scheduling and answer the ten questions most frequently asked by customers about block scheduling.

WHO ARE THE MEMBERS OF THE SCHOOL STUDY TEAM AND ACTION TEAMS?

At Atlee High School, we used a team already in place, the school improvement team, to serve as our school study team. The Figure 6 graphic indicates the purpose of this team and suggests the constituency representation of various customer groups on the team.

The chances of a successful block scheduling initiative are greatly enhanced if representatives of all customer groups in the school community are actively involved in the decision-making process from the beginning. If customers are not empowered to make decisions, it is unlikely that the process will be successful.

FIGURE 6
School Improvement Team

School Study Committee
Purpose: To establish recommendations for use of instructional time

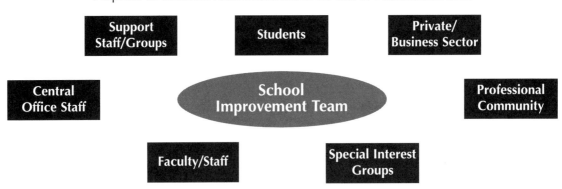

Initially the most important member of the school study team is the principal. The primary role of the principal is that of a facilitator, making sure that members of the school study team work within the identified parameters—including legal ones, those set by local and state education agencies, and the political boundaries of the school community. These policies and parameters will guide the team's formal and informal direction.

THE SCHOOL STUDY TEAM LEADER

If the chair of the school study team has not previously been appointed by the principal or by the action team, then the emerging informal leader might be considered for appointment. If not, we recommend that the team leader be elected by the school study team. Again, we reiterate that the chairman of the school study team is critical to the success of the process. The principal will serve as the informal leader. It is critical that the school study team leader be capable of taking the task at hand and moving forward because the principal has many other responsibilities for which s/he is accountable.

ACTION TEAMS

It would be impossible for the school study team to collect all of the necessary data and information needed for decision making. Perhaps one of the first tasks that the school study team should undertake is to appoint action teams to collect data and make recommendations to the full school study team.

Needed information could be divided into categorical issues. These issues should relate directly to restructuring for the most efficient use of time within a school day.

CASE IN POINT

Policies and parameters that the school study team had to resolve when Tom's school was in the process of exploring alternative schedule options included the length of the school day and the minimum requirements of 150 hours of instruction per Carnegie unit necessary for accreditation by the state. Consideration had to be given to the number of students and classes teachers could teach per year.

There were also informal agendas that had to be addressed because of local politics. Music and other fine arts programs in his school were highly visible and successful programs. Because of expectations of the school community, Tom had to give serious consideration to these programs when deciding on the scheduling format to be used. Many students in the school were enrolled in Advanced Placement courses—a hot issue with many of his local customers. He found it to be very difficult to recognize all of the local parameters with which he was dealing, but he left no stones unturned in attempting to identify them before they emerged unexpectedly.

CASE IN POINT

Tom was working with a school district that was considering implementing block scheduling in all of its high schools. His contact person was the assistant superintendent for instruction, who was very knowledgeable about the components of a successful change process. He had taken great care to empower the principals and their teams to study all options and eventually submit a recommendation for consideration to the district school board.

From time-to-time he would communicate with Tom about the progress of the process. Although he was somewhat apprehensive, he was excited about the possibilities that block scheduling would offer students and teachers. The assistant superintendent frequently reported that the process was going well, and he was sure that each school would make a recommendation to implement some form of block scheduling.

Approximately two months before the teams from each school were to report their recommendations to the local school board, Tom received a phone call from him. He could tell from the moment that they began talking that something was wrong. Within minutes, he informed Tom that an overzealous school board member, in a conversation with a member of the local news media, had announced that all high schools would implement the block schedule during the next school year. Although he had tried to convince the principals that a decision had not been made and that this was only one school board member talking, the principals were not buying it. They were asking him why they and the team members had even bothered to expend time and energy to make the effort to study the block scheduling issue. He assured Tom that block scheduling was not likely to happen any time soon in his school district.

Again, the system had failed—not block scheduling—because the process for successfully implementing change was not followed and trusted.

Figure 7 illustrates the purpose of the action team and some of the issues that action teams must deal with when considering the block schedule. Each major issue should be assigned to an action team whose sole purpose is to develop strategies to deal with the identified issue. An action team will include the same representation that is included on the school study team, but membership will be smaller. This team will probably be constituted for a much shorter period of time than the school study team.

Action teams play a very important role in the process. Since it would be impossible for one team of 20 to 25 people to address all related change process issues, the school study team should appoint action teams that will study specific issues and bring recommendations or information back to the school study team. This procedure will enable members of the school study team to make more informed decisions. This is also a great platform from which to get more customers involved in the process. Our experience has shown that these action teams operate efficiently in groups of eight to twelve people and should be chaired by members of the school study team.

Issues addressed by action teams usually pertain to the assessment of the impact of change on various aspects of the school's operation that include the following: student issues, instructional issues, teacher issues, organizational issues, and administrative issues. Each issue is critical to the success of

FIGURE 7
Action Teams

Purpose: To establish strategies that will ensure the accomplishment of identified objectives

STUDENT ISSUES

TEACHER ISSUES

INSTRUCTIONAL ISSUES

ORGANIZATIONAL ISSUES

ADMINISTRATIVE ISSUES

any block schedule format that is being considered for restructuring purposes. Because of the critical nature of these issues, perhaps one of the first responsibilities of the school study team should be to appoint action teams to address each of these areas. (These issues are addressed later in this chapter.)

Consider the following examples of action teams:

■ The Curriculum and Instruction (C&I) Action Team

As a component of the school study team, the curriculum and instruction action team is composed of students, faculty, staff, parents, and special interest groups within the community. The chairman of this team should be a member of the school study team. Other team members may be from the school study team, or they may be other customers within the school community.

This team is involved in an ongoing process to provide data, case studies, or other related sources for collecting additional information for the school study team. This information should be relative to curriculum and instruction and how it will be impacted by a block schedule format.

The action team provides recommendations to resolve problems and issues. The results of the action of this team will provide students with an environment that will support student achievement.

Because instruction is the major focus of the school day, we recommend that the C&I action team be responsible for the completion phase of the project. All components of the project would be reviewed by the C&I action team to determine if recommended changes are supportive of and directed toward student success. The functions of this team are similar to a quality control team found in industry and in some progressive school districts that have implemented the quality process.

■ The Public Relations/Communication (PR/C) Action Team

The public relations/communication action team is responsible for devising a plan to communicate the recommended change to all customers. This plan is designed in the format of a comprehensive public relations plan. The plan includes input from faculty, staff, students, parents, the superintendent, and the general school community (all customers). This process is never-ending, and appropriate communications should be provided to all customers throughout the process. This plan includes reasons for the change, weekly up-dates on the progress of the change process, and anticipated quality outcomes. An evaluation/assessment process is also included. It can be used to collect data from all customers within the school community and to provide contacts for customer questions or input.

■ The Staff Development (SD) Action Team

The staff development action team is responsible for designing an appropriate staff development plan that provides in-service opportunities for all students, faculty, and staff. These opportunities include activities designed to address identified issues related to teaching and learning in longer blocks of time. In conjunction with the PR/C action team, the SD action team should provide frequent updates on planned training opportunities available prior to the implementation of the effort.

SCHOOL STUDY TEAM MEMBERSHIP

The composition of the School Study Team should include representatives of all customer groups as well as those who are supplying the instructional program. If any customer or supplier group feels omitted from the process, then you will have an adversarial relationship to make right. If you discover that a group has been overlooked, do not hesitate to add representatives after the process has started. Members of the school study team will include representatives from the following customer groups:

■ Students

A diverse student component is one of the first considerations that a selection team should make when assembling the school study team. The student members should represent all factions of the student population. Student members should include student leaders, students who have learning disabilities, students who are not the best academic students, students who have attendance and behavioral problems, and students whom teachers do not want in their classes. In many instances, these students often have some of the most innovative ideas about how their particular problems can be solved through the efficient use of time and resources. If a team that is already in place is identified as the school study team, some revision may be necessary to ensure the diversity needed for the success of the process.

■ Private/business sector of the community

This sector of the school community is not often involved in decision making at the building level, but its members are frequently major players in the budget decision-making process within the larger community. Many members of this community have a clear understanding of the efficient use of available resources, including time. Expertise from these partners can influence big picture decisions that affect the day-to-day operations of the overall learning and teaching process. Members of this group will also offer suggestions regarding courses students need to take in order to be successful in the workplace and what types of co-op, apprenticeships, mentorships, and job placements opportunities are available.

■ Professional community

The professional community includes members of legal, medical, college, and university communities as well as other professional groups. Members of these groups will provide information that addresses such issues as the advantages of longer blocks of time and how these blocks of time can enhance the learning process for students interested in related careers. Many of these partners have expertise that can be shared in the form of mentorships and apprenticeships, as well as serving as resources for research in science courses, business, and English courses. These partners can also provide suggestions on the length of the block and how time can be most efficiently utilized for mentorships or apprenticeships. Generally, this input should bring about a change in the way courses are taught and a degree of credibility to students who are planning to pursue a career in related professions.

■ Special interest groups

Special interest groups, such as advocates for students with disabilities, gifted students, or music programs, bring an entirely different perspective to the concept of block scheduling. You will listen to them now, or you will listen to them later. They have legitimate concerns, and these concerns must be addressed in order for block scheduling to be a success. Special groups with other concerns include customers who are interested in such topics as: student attention span, individual assistance plans, acceleration, Advanced Placement courses, early graduation, dual enrollment. The list is endless. Other special interest groups that should be involved from the beginning on the school study team or action teams include parent/teacher/student organizations and music, athletic, academic, and vocational education support groups. They all have opinions about what the schedule should be. The inclusion of these groups will help the school study team avoid facing what would be major barriers that prevent moving the process of change to conclusion. In many instances, the objections of these groups are from lack of understanding of the purpose of change.

■ Others

There are many other members of a community who are unique to each school and should be

---

CASE IN POINT

The school improvement team debated the issue of how they would address the use of toilet facilities, since students, accustomed to a break every 55 minutes, would now break every 104 minutes. One of the team members, a student with a learning disability, presented a very workable plan to the group. With some additional input from other team members, the plan was implemented and was very successful in preventing potential problems and is still in use today. The quality of this plan—submitted by a student—increased the credibility of including students on action teams.

included in the school study team's membership. We found, for instance, senior citizens, the local chamber of commerce, and the real estate community to be very supportive of our efforts. They served as valuable resources in the planning and implementation phases as well as the evaluation phase.

Members of the school study team also will include representatives from the following supplier groups:

■ **Faculty and staff**

The selection of teachers for a team should be considered very carefully. A teacher with many years of experience has quite a different view about the way time should be spent during the school day than does a beginning teacher who has not experienced a full complement of changes that have passed through the education profession. In most cases, beginning teachers do not have the maturity around teaching or an understanding of the related methodology that more experienced teachers have. Therefore, younger teachers have a different perception of the use of instructional time and how that time is scheduled for students than do the more experienced teachers.

The beginning teacher's bag of instructional tricks is not so full as that of the more experienced teacher; however, what is in the bag is sometimes highly desirable. In some instances, it is more diffi-

cult for the beginning teacher to adjust to the larger block of time than it is for the experienced teacher. At the same time, the beginning teacher is more likely to be receptive to change than the experienced teacher and may very well become one of the most ardent supporters of the schedule change. Our recommendation: Include teachers with a range of teaching experiences on the study team. The more input, the greater the chance for success.

It is also important to include naysayers on a school study team. Experience has shown that many naysayers do not understand the proposed change and are protecting their turf. Once they have an opportunity to explore the change concept and have a greater knowledge of the anticipated outcome, they may become active supporters for change. Indeed, naysayers that are won over carry a great deal of weight in convincing other teachers to change. Remember, there are many teachers who will consider a change in scheduling a very traumatic, job-threatening change.

Teachers within the school who represent unions and other professional groups should also be included. Becoming a part of the process affords these members an opportunity to be in the loop of information. Additionally, the information that they share with their particular organization will be accurate, not unclear information that has passed through many interpretations from the original source.

We recommend that the school study team also include faculty members who are proponents of block scheduling and believe it is the only way to use allocated instructional time. These school study team members are often the risk-takers and may be willing to pilot pieces of the block schedule.

■ Central office staff

Members of the central office administrative and instructional staff should also be included. These members have experiences and pieces of information that will make the process goal more obtainable. Also, they manage resources that you may need to access later.

■ Support staff

Do not forget the school custodial staff, cafeteria staff, and bus drivers, all of whom are partners as well as parents. They come in contact with more members of the school community than any one teacher or administrator does.

WHAT ARE THE RESPONSIBILITIES OF A SCHOOL STUDY TEAM?

The school study team's functions are many, but the two major functions of Tom's school study team were to (1) identify the change(s) that is/are needed, and (2) identify key strategies to support the change process and ensure successful outcomes of the change.

Time is an important factor in considering this change. Members of the school study team must consider issues related to assigning instructional time to a different format that is more student and teacher friendly. If the school study team is successful in selecting the best schedule match for the school, some measurable results will be immediately noticeable.

WHAT RESTRUCTURING POSSIBILITIES SHOULD THE STUDY TEAM EXPLORE?

Although the school study team's primary agenda is studying the issue of effective allocation of time, the team must also be aware of related issues, such as concern for transfer students or a high number of Advanced Placement offerings that may impact the change process. Such issues and how they interrelate with the task at hand need not become barriers. These issues are frequently difficult to identify, but they must be addressed as key components in the process. They must be kept on the table at all times for team members to study. The list of possible issues to consider is ever expanding, but any one of these issues could determine which scheduling format the team recommends.

CASE IN POINT

One of the indicators for success that Atlee's school study team selected was:

Discipline referrals will decline as measured by the number of discipline referrals submitted to administrative offices for resolution.

By the end of the first semester, the number of discipline referrals had declined by 14 percent on block days as compared with the number of discipline referrals on days that all seven class periods met. Immediate improvement was easy to measure for this indicator of success. The rationale for this improvement is: When a school has three class changes per day (block), as opposed to six class changes (traditional seven-period day), students do not change classes as often and, therefore, are not left unsupervised as frequently. Thus, there is measured improvement in an identified indicator for success.

■ Student issues

Is the type of schedule more student friendly or more teacher friendly? In other words:

- Will the type of block schedule that a school adopts be of more benefit to students? Or will it be of more benefit to teachers?

- Will instructional time for students decrease, while teachers' planning time increases? How will less teacher-student contact time affect student success?

- Will a different type of schedule allow students to take required courses as well as courses in which they have a special interest, such as music, art, Advanced Placement, or vocational program offerings?

- Will providing opportunities for students to take more courses add to the total number of units required for graduation? Should students take more courses?

- Will class sizes increase if a certain type of schedule is selected?

- Will students have an opportunity to balance academic courses with electives?

- Will homework and student planning time for other activities become issues?

- To what extent will additional student responsibilities become a major issue? (e.g.: what courses to take, what extra- or co-curricular activities to eliminate in order to take additional courses)

- Will increased student responsibilities, such as forced choice selection, become a major issue?

- Do students have the means or necessary skills to make these forced choices? (such as a fourth year of foreign language or an Advanced Placement class instead of music or art) Can a student take both?

- Will the change in the amount of homework create issues with which the administration, faculty, and especially students and parents must deal?

- Will a change in schedule affect student attendance policy?

- What about student study halls and lunches?

- Will training be provided for students in areas such as how to prepare for a larger block of time, how to be active participants in class, and how to manage time effectively?

These are only a few issues that an action team will need to address before making recommendations to the school study team.

CASE IN POINT

Question: What if a high percentage of students in a school district are transfer students? Could this issue have an impact on whether the school study team decides to recommend the alternating day (A-B) block scheduling, the semester plan, the trimester plan, or just leave the schedule as it is?

Question: Could the debate surrounding the inclusion of certain electives such as music and Advanced Placement courses be the issue that is the determining factor in what schedule is recommended? Some schools have chosen to implement the alternating day (A-B) schedule to eliminate controversy regarding the negative issues relating to music and Advanced Placement offerings.

An analysis of recent data collected on schools in Virginia indicates that only a small percentage of schools that have implemented the semester model of block schedule are urban/suburban schools. These schools have voiced concerns about transfer students and the ability to provide these students with a quality program of studies. Advanced Placement offerings also are cited as a major concern when recommending a schedule. As a result, many schools with these demographics chose the alternating day or a combination of schedules. Many of the rural schools in Virginia have chosen the semester model. Generally, these schools have fewer students and do not have a large number of transfer students.

■ Instructional issues

One of the major issues with longer blocks of time was how teachers would adjust instructional strategies they had been using. If longer blocks of time are to be the centerpiece of restructuring, the allocated instructional time of the school day, adjustments in current strategies, and development of new strategies are critical to teacher success. It is the responsibility of the school study team to address all related instructional issues.

Changes in teaching behaviors and instruction must be measured after the schedule change has occurred. The school study team must be willing and ready to make recommendations for ways to measure these changes or lack of changes so that an ongoing improvement process will be in place. This will ensure success for students and teachers. If success is to occur, the following questions must be addressed by action teams:

- What new skills will teachers need in order to teach effectively in a larger block of time?

- Will instruction include skill-based activities as well as content-based activities?

- Will teachers be willing to use varied teaching methodologies in larger blocks of time?

- Will principals be willing to use collected data related to student performance and teacher behaviors to identify improvement plans that will increase student achievement?

- Will instruction be student-centered and hands-on? Or will it remain teacher-centered, passive learning with business as usual once the doors to the classroom are closed?

- Will the content of the curriculum be covered if the new schedule does decrease the amount of allocated instructional time per credit?

- Will the selected schedule allow for an integrated curriculum and flexible instructional delivery?

■ Teacher issues

Teacher issues that the school study team must find answers for are many. The success of the

---

CASE IN POINT

At the end of the academic year, Tom and Yvonne both surveyed and interviewed students, parents, and faculty regarding their perceptions of the strengths and weaknesses of block scheduling. The one thread consistent throughout the data from these surveys was that teachers must change the way they teach. As one teacher summarized the teaching situation: "It ain't teaching as usual. Lecturing for a[n] entire class just doesn't get it anymore." As a result, we used the data from our surveys to provide input for our strategic plan for staff development.

---

change will, in part, be attributed to how effectively these issues are dealt with. Teachers are critical players in the success of the change process. The following questions suggest the kind of issues that must be addressed relative to teacher behaviors in the classroom:

- Will the total number of courses increase or decrease on a yearly basis? On a semester basis?

- Will teachers be required to teach more courses per year, if certain schedules are selected?

- What impact will this have on accreditation standards and bargaining agreements with professional organizations?

- Will these changes meet accreditation standards set by accrediting agencies throughout the country? Contractual variables with unions? Local education authorities? Is a waiver necessary or even possible?

- Will the number of students taught on a yearly or semester basis increase or decrease? If there is an increase, will this issue create problems with accreditation agencies or unions or other customers?

- Will the amount of teacher planning time change? If so, will the change meet contractual requirements? Will teachers teach more courses per year or more minutes per year?

- Staff development issues are important and must be addressed. Are there funds for staff development? Will teachers be required to participate in staff development? If so, will teacher availability be a factor?

■ **Administrative issues**

One action team must focus on administrative issues that are vital to the success of the change process. Although many of these issues are related to instruction, facilities, and available resources as well as other issues that must have administrative approval, our experience is that budgetary considerations are of top priority.

- Will the schedule that is chosen need additional staff, training, or teaching materials? Will these needs increase budget requirements? If so, are there other sources of money that can be tapped?

- Is this a grassroots model? Or will the school study team be limited in its direction by an overriding top-down model of decision making?

- Will there be different issues related to scheduling courses and facilities? If you offer more science courses, will you need more labs? Will student course options be limited by available classroom space?

- Will attendance, tardy polices, etc., need revision?

CASE IN POINT

Some forms of the semester schedule require teachers to teach six courses a year as opposed to the five a year that a teacher has under the traditional schedule arrangement. This generally means that a teacher will teach three courses a semester. Our observation is that teachers generally prefer to teach three courses per semester as a trade-off for teaching fewer students per semester, although the number of students taught per year generally increases. If this is a characteristic of the schedule that you choose, will re-negotiations with teacher organizations/unions or special permission from the local school board be in order?

- Will special accommodations for certain students need to be revised/restructured (e.g.: physically handicapped students, music or art students)? Will this call for additional funding?

Again, there are many other issues unique in each school that must be answered by the school study team or assigned to action teams for recommendations.

■ **Organizational issues**

Organizational issues that the school study team must consider are often left to the discretion of the building administrator. In many instances, these issues deal with a local educational agency regulation, a state regulation, or a contractual issue with a union or local school board. Generally, these issues can be negotiated or renegotiated so that it is possible for schools or school districts to change to the recommended schedule. This is another reason why it is so important that change be a grassroots effort.

Organizational issues that must be given consideration when looking at a scheduling change are as follows:

- *The length of the school day.* Will the length of the school day or the school year need to be extended to meet the number of required instructional hours per unit when a class does not meet the amount of time required for a specific subject by a state agency, a local educational agency, or other accrediting agencies? If the length of the school day is changed, will this affect in a negative way the transportation system? And will there be additional responsibilities for faculty? Will an increase in responsibilities violate contractual agreements?

- *Length of each instructional period.* Will the length of the instructional period change the way you do business? We think it will. Although there will be fewer class changes during a school day, some schools have found it necessary to increase the length of these changes. This has created a need for additional supervision in hallways, common areas, cafeterias, and other areas that are traditionally unsupervised. A critical issue that arises from a lengthened class is the student use of toilet facilities, perhaps because of poorly developed policies regarding when students would be allowed to use those facilities. This issue was the number one complaint from students and parents when Atlee first implemented block scheduling. There are many students who will take advantage of the lengthened class time as an excuse to use the toilet facilities more frequently than in a traditional schedule. They will cite longer classes as an excuse for not getting to the restroom as often as needed. It is important for administrators and teachers to remember that there are students who have legitimate problems, some health-related, and do need to use toilet facilities more frequently than others. The 90-plus-minute block of time creates a situation that magnifies such problems. Teachers at Atlee first addressed the issue with the entire class and then the issue was handled on an individual basis.

Tom found that this problem could not be ignored, and that it would not go away without some intervention and direction by the principal. His suggestion: Address it upfront by bringing together an action team from your school study team and empowering them to deal with the issue before it becomes a stumbling block to the positive aspects of changing the schedule.

• *Number of course offerings per year or per semester.* The number of course offerings per semester or per year depends on the schedule that you choose.

■ Timeline

Develop and follow a timeline for planning and implementing block scheduling. This task should be one of the school study team's initial activities. Schools frequently allow too little time for studying block scheduling and the consequences or benefits to students. In many instances, it is not the schedule that fails but the lack of process planning and customer understanding.

An action team is responsible for tracking its own timeline. The action team holds regular meetings to determine the progress of the school study team and make necessary adjustments. The timeline

---

CASE IN POINT

In Tom's school, teachers chose to address the issue of restroom breaks class by class. The administration kept a list of students who visited the toilet facility during the instructional period. Teachers were provided the names of students who visited the toilet facilities during the instructional period more than five times in a five-day period. Teachers analyzed the list and handled these students on an individual basis. Other teachers chose to provide a short toilet break during transition from one instructional activity to another. This break usually occurred without disturbance to other classes in progress.

---

should be flexible so that it can be altered at any time. It is posted so that all customers will be able to track the progress of the process and provide productive feedback.

■ Public relations/communication plan

Our experience in both education and industry leads us to believe that many projects fail due to a lack of communication. All customers must understand the reason for change, the process to be used, and the expected results. The project will be in jeopardy from the start if a public relations plan (or communication plan) is not designed and implemented. The reason is obvious: Customers do not clearly understand the concept of the project or why change is necessary unless they are informed by the change agents. Rumors and misinterpretations will misguide the support of a project. Consequently, opportunities that existed were never given a chance to mature. Again, the failure was not the project concept but an important part of the process—communication.

When making a decision concerning the reorganization of the instructional time of the school day, a strategic plan must be established for communication or public relations that will keep all customers informed. Some strategies that can be used for such a plan include sending memos to all customers informing them that the school is considering

The semester block schedule will allow students to choose four courses per semester for a total of eight per year. Other alternative block scheduling models will offer students the opportunities to take a maximum of six, seven, eight, or nine courses. Although we were on a seven-period, alternating-day block schedule, we found that many students opted to take the 0 block (early morning), which enabled them to take as many as eight courses per year. This schedule required changing the way faculty and students were assigned. An example of our change, the traditional way that a teacher's instructional day was organized, is explained in the following scenario.

If a faculty member chose to teach in the early morning block, this meant that the faculty member started his/her contract day an hour earlier than other faculty members. Thus, his/her contract day ended an hour earlier than other faculty members. Students who chose the early morning courses also had the option of leaving an hour before other students. Thus, you no longer have a neat little package of a school day that allows everyone to begin his/her day at the same time and end at the same time. The traditional communication process must be re-engineered because many students and faculty are not there at the end of the last block to hear announcements or attend faculty meetings. The traditional faculty meeting at the end of the day must be rethought, and a different way of communicating and providing information must be considered. Our suggestion for eliminating such barriers to restructuring is to use the team approach to problem solving. Empower members of your school study team to recommend strategies for a solution. Teachers who were assigned to 0 block knew up-front that there would be certain staff meetings that they would be required to attend at the end of the regular contract day. Initially there were some complaints about staying the additional hour. An action team recommended that a schedule of required meetings be given to all faculty at the beginning of the school year so that necessary arrangements could be made for those faculty members who were assigned to a 0 block. A partner faculty member was assigned to each of these faculty members and was responsible for updating them on any subsequent information inadvertently missed.

---

alternatives to the present bell schedule, and identifying a person(s) who is knowledgeable in the change process to respond expeditiously on a daily basis to questions from customers. This person will be the person to lead the action team on public relations. Consider the following strategies for keeping customers informed.

- Actively seek speaking engagements at civic, professional, volunteer, and parent and/or student organizations as well as other audiences that will listen to your story related to the merits of what you hope to accomplish by implementing block scheduling.

- Schedule weekly or monthly information releases on the merits of block scheduling to the news media. Make sure that these releases are available to all customers. Develop a rapport with the person(s) assigned to cover your school or the area that your school is located in. If some-

one is not assigned to your school area, then call the source of the news in your area and inform them that you have a story to tell. Also use other available resources to tell the story, such as student newspapers and networks that are used to disseminate student information (e.g.: homework hotlines and school information networks).

- Utilize technology such as the World Wide Web to tell your story and receive feedback.

- Remember that an effective public relations program will make the difference in the success or failure of the change process.

■ Plan for all budgeting considerations

When a school is planning a change from a traditional approach to scheduling students with a more creative use of instructional time, there may be additional budgeting issues to consider. This is perhaps one of the most important issues that a school study team will evaluate. If an increase in teaching personnel is needed in order to implement the type of schedule that has been recommended, additional funds will need to be encumbered. If there are no additional funds, we suggest that the study team look at an alternative schedule rather than abandoning the change.

If the school study team has recommended moving to a seven- or eight-period day from a five- or six-period day, will budgetary considerations be an issue that will need to be resolved?

- Is funding readily available? Or are there other funding sources within the budget that might be used for additional personnel, staff development, instructional materials, and other anticipated needs? What about unforeseen emergency needs?

- If funding does not come from the traditional sources, are there alternative sources of revenue that might be found? Are additional personnel available from non-traditional sources? (e.g.: an engineer from an engineering firm to teach an advanced math course, a chemist from a

research and development division of a company to teach a class on chemistry)

Lack of additional funding or limited funding may have a considerable impact on the schedule model selected.

■ Plan for all staffing needs

The use of human resources could perhaps be one of the most controversial issues that an administrator will deal with when changing schedules. If teachers or other staff members perceive that individual responsibilities are going to increase or that positions will be cut, these perceptions will generally become barriers to any change that is being considered. These perceptions must be addressed

---

CASE IN POINT

Tom discovered the timeline to be invaluable as his faculty proceeded toward their goal of implementing the block schedule. They found that by posting the timeline in various areas where it would be noticed by all customers, there was lots of activity in those areas by interested customers. General comments were made to various team members concerning the progress of the process. The visibility of the timeline also created a sense of urgency for team members to complete their assigned tasks on the assigned dates.

Since many schools are using longer periods of time for study before implementing—some as many as two years—the focus that a timeline provides is even more critical. The timeline can be a road map to the success of the change process.

CASE IN POINT

Early in the information stage of the change process, Tom's school identified many strategies for customers' input. One strategy was for committee members to accept as many speaking engagements as schedules would allow. After providing information to the audience, there were always opportunities for questions.

During one of the questioning sessions, a parent posed a question to Tom about the lack of the efficient use of time. Her question dealt with the alternating day block scheduling. She was concerned that students would get only four credits a year and that they would be required to attend school only three days on A week and two days on B week. Her interpretation of the information that she had received was that students would be required to attend school only five out of every ten days. Since she had children in the ninth and tenth grades and neither had jobs, nor did she want them to work, she was concerned about a lack of supervision on their days out of school. It took just a few minutes to explain that students could take as many as eight courses in a school year and that they would be attending school each day of the week. She was much relieved, and the school had another supporter of block scheduling.

early in the process and appropriate information communicated to all customers. We suggest that the following questions regarding change be addressed as soon as possible. Hopefully, the information that is communicated to customers will alleviate negative perceptions or misinterpretations of the intent of change, and thus these perceptions will not be barriers to the change process.

- Will the current staff meet the requirements of a restructured bell schedule?

- Can human resources be realigned so that they may be used more efficiently?

- Will additional staff members be needed for supervision during breaks, lunch, study blocks, or in-school suspension?

- Will an expanded course offering and students taking more courses require more staff? If not in the first year of the implementation, will the increase in cost come in future years?

- Will there be a need to have more supervision, since students in some schedules will have more freedom to move through the building and the grounds of the school while teachers are assigned to more instructionally related activities such as tutoring, make-up work, and other related responsibilities?

- Will class size increase, and thus teachers teach more students per day? Per year? Per semester?

- Will there be a reduction in the number of staff needed, because teachers will be teaching more classes per year?

- Will there be a need for additional staff in the food services department, since more students will be taking more courses and in some instances there will be more lunch periods needed?

Based on the schedule selected for a school, staffing needs can change drastically. These changes must be considered as well as the impact that change will have on the selected schedule.

LOOKING BACK . . .

Remember, when planning for change:

- Involve representatives from a wide constituency.

- Develop formal and informal communication channels for distributing information and receiving feedback from customers.

- Build a solid foundation through involvement of all customers for support of change.

- Identify key partners in the change process and empower them to make meaningful decisions.

- Identify and address all key issues that might provide barriers to the process of change.

- Build a school study team and action teams that are diverse.

- Study all possibilities before deciding on a match for your school community.

- Give careful consideration to budgetary matters.

- Develop a public relations/communication plan. TELL YOUR STORY!   ❏

Chapter 5 Appendix on CD

❏ Communications plan for implementing block scheduling Menchville High School, Newport News, Virginia

- Informational Paper: New Kids on the Block (word version)

- Trifold Brochure: New Class on the Block (word version)

How Does a School Study Team Develop Strategies to Get Started?

*I*t is not the critic that counts, not the man who points out how the strong man stumbles or where the doer of deeds could have done them better. The credit belongs to the man who is actually in the arena, whose face is marred by dust, and sweat, and blood; who strives valiantly, who errs and comes short again and again because there is no effort without error and shortcomings; but who actually tries to do the deed, who knows the great devotion; who spends himself in worthy causes, who at best knows in the end the high achievement of triumph and who at worst, if he fails while daring greatly knows his place shall never be with those timid and cold souls who know neither victory nor defeat.

—Theodore Roosevelt

LOOKING AHEAD IN THIS CHAPTER . . .

This chapter will address administrative strategies for getting the change process started. We will look at issues that must be addressed in this grassroots initiative. These issues include the involvement of all customers and determining the length of the school day, the length of each block, the course of study, and the improvement of school climate. Other issues that we will address include how to prepare a school study team to visit schools and what to look for when collecting data that will be used in the implementation process. (See Chapter 5 for the discussion of how to design a study team.) We will

examine a list of the questions most frequently asked by teams visiting schools that have implemented the block schedule. Possible answers—supported by research when appropriate—will be provided. Actual surveys—used by experienced block scheduled schools to collect data—are included for study team consideration. Budgetary considerations as well as other factors to consider when selecting the best schedule match for your school are addressed. To summarize, this chapter will address actions critical to the grassroots initiative that **must occur** for block scheduling to be successful.

We are totally committed to involving the school's faculty and staff and the school community in the process of changing a school. Not only have we found success in using this process, we also have found consistently that school leaders who attempted change without this involvement were doomed to failure. Therefore, we take a firm stand: The school administrator must know his/her community and involve all members of it in understanding why change is sought and what is likely to occur if change is made. While there may be no one way to approach parents and community members, giving them a voice and finding a productive role for them, as well as using their expertise, should be on the principal's task list. Community support will both ease the transition of change and assist the administrator and faculty with unanticipated barriers that someone is likely to construct on the road to school improvement.

WHAT ARE THE ADMINISTRATIVE ISSUES THAT THE STUDY TEAM SHOULD CONSIDER?

Restructuring the school day involves more than a principal acting alone to rearrange time requirements of students and teachers. It requires research and discovery, trial and error, opinions of a diverse population of a school community, and the external pressures and forces of special-interest groups at work within a school community. Restructuring the school day requires a bold response from teachers, parents, students, and community leaders to move structure, practices, and relationships beyond tradition to systemic change. Strategies for getting started are carefully planned to serve as the catalyst that brings all customers together in a collegial and collaborative endeavor. These strategies generally fall into five major categories which can (and should) be adjusted to meet the needs of the individual school community: administrative, organizational, instructional, teacher-related, and student-related. This chapter will focus on issues that we define as **administrative**.

While the study committee is involved in the process of determining the schedule to be used, the administrative team of the school must exercise leadership options in providing logistical information and direction. Administrative issues that must be considered include:

- Instructional focus

- Budgetary considerations

- Decision making

- Grassroots initiative (that is: bottom up).

There are many strategies that administrators can use when taking advantage of this opportunity. This section provides suggestions that can assist administrators in facing up to change and serving as the main change agent in the school.

CREATING A GRASSROOTS INITIATIVE

The first task of the school study team is to define what a "grassroots initiative" means. Then they must identify the issues that will lead to student success in the form of increased achievement when implementing the new schedule.

One strategy is consistent, as we receive feedback from schools that have implemented block scheduling: The more involvement of **all** customers, the more successful the implementation of the block. Once a plan is conceived and begins to take shape, the study team should take the plan to customers to garner as much support as possible. An effort should be made to present the proposed schedule to the entire school community.

Strategies to inform the community might include:

- Presentations to students and parents of the middle and elementary schools that feed into the high school

- Briefings to all students and parents that attend the school

- Periodic reports to the superintendent and the local school board, keeping them informed so that they will be knowledgeable of the process as it evolves

- Regularly scheduled discussions with teachers so that they will also be knowledgeable

- Presentations to community groups, including civic organizations such as the Chamber of Commerce, Rotary, and Business Women; service organizations and church groups, such as the

The summer prior to the opening of Tom's school and prior to the first year implementing the block schedule, a plan to inform students and parents was developed. Tom's faculty selected a week in late summer to provide orientation and information on the block schedule to all of their students. To get more parents, as well as students, involved, they provided opportunities for students to pick up schedules and textbooks and pay applicable fees prior to the beginning of school.

The parent organization (PTA) held the annual school opening celebration in conjunction with "Back-to-School Night." This event—held on school grounds—was considered a major community event and was well attended. Getting the message to the community was a grassroots initiative and was the result of a community effort that involved thousands of hours from parent and community volunteers.

In order to better manage the process, the students in each grade level were scheduled to obtain course schedules and textbooks on a particular evening. The following schedule was used: Monday: 12th grade; Tuesday: 11th grade; Wednesday: 10th grade; Thursday: 9th grade. Specified hours on Friday (6:30 a.m.–7:30 p.m.) were set for students and parents who were not able to attend during the evening sessions earlier in the week. These evening sessions were held from 5:00 p.m. to 9:30 p.m., and a specified schedule was followed throughout the evening. As each student, parent, or guardian entered the designated area of the building, there were trained students, parents, and faculty guides, as well as signs, that informed those attending of the process for the evening.

The first step was to pay applicable fees. The second step was to attend a session on block scheduling conducted by various members of the staff. At the conclusion of this 30-minute session, students were given their schedules and proceeded to pick up books and locker assignments.

Although several tasks were accomplished during the prescribed time frame, the major purpose was to provide students and parents an orientation to block scheduling. After teachers returned from the summer break and before students returned to school, an evening was scheduled for students and parents to visit and actually participate in a shortened version of the bell schedule that the students would follow during the upcoming school year.

This process proved very successful, and each year the faculty continued to refine and use it. Other benefits were derived from this strategy. Teachers were relieved of the burden of collecting fees and distributing textbooks on the first day of school. On that day, the emphasis was on instruction, not administrative details. This set the tone for the academic year.

Ministerial Association and Jaycees; retired citizens groups; economic development groups; and any others that will listen to your story (most groups are looking for good programs for their meetings)

- Involvement of all segments of the school community in the process

- Invitations to members of the school community to become active members of the process by joining the study team, by visiting schools that are on non-traditional schedules, by reviewing and studying different scheduling options that are available, and by actively participating

in the selection of the best possible option for the school.

DETERMINING THE LENGTH OF THE SCHOOL DAY

Before implementing the block schedule chosen for your school, the planning team should give consideration to and investigate the impact of standards for required instructional contact hours established by local education, state, federal, or accreditation agencies. In other words, determine the benchmarks established by these agencies as well as other customers of the school for the use of time. In order to comply with these standards, will it be necessary to lengthen the instructional day? If lengthening the instructional day is necessary, will this be in violation of teacher agreements or union contracts? What financial considerations will be necessary to implement such a schedule? Can you lengthen the school day without additional funding and resources? Obviously, the principal will become familiar with districtwide needs or requirements that relate to these questions and will work with offices such as personnel and transportation to reach definitive decisions relating to time changes.

There may be barriers to overcome, but if we continue to search for ways to reshape the restrictive paradigms that we often see in education, we will find strategies that will allow us to use allocated instructional time more effectively.

EXAMINING THE ISSUES OF TIME AND LEARNING

If a school team decides to implement a block schedule model that offers students opportunities to select and enroll in more courses, will these additional course offerings be offered at the expense of a decline in allocated instructional time per block? If this is the situation, will this decision negatively impact student achievement or other indicators that measure the success of our education system? There is an ongoing debate regarding the relationship between the amount of time it takes to teach or learn any given concept and the courses that should be offered in a secondary school program. Will a decision regarding a decrease in allocated instructional time for each block create a barrier to imple-

---

CASE IN POINT

As Tom prepared to implement block scheduling in his school, the planning team considered expanding the school day in order to provide remediation and acceleration courses during the fifth/extended block. The plan for this block was for identified students to meet from 3:45 p.m. to 5:45 p.m., Monday–Thursday. Teacher issues had been solved by implementing a flexible schedule that would provide opportunities for certain teachers, on a volunteer basis, to begin their school day at a non-traditional time (e.g.: 10:15 a.m. instead of 8:15 a.m.) and complete their day at a non-traditional time (e.g.: 5:45 p.m. instead of 3:45 p.m.).

The issue that had not been considered was the transportation situation. Buses that transported students were also used to transport elementary and middle school students. Bus schedules had been determined based on the amount of time it would take the buses to complete their routes and make connections with other buses at each school. Although Atlee was unable to provide the extended school day experience to all students because of the transportation issue, the school was able to offer some transportation by connecting with activity bus schedules. As a result, many hours of instruction were provided for students who took advantage of the additional opportunities. It proved to be very beneficial for those who participated.

Yvonne's school dealt with extended time for learning by building an activity period into the school schedule, so that each day every student had an opportunity for reteaching, tutoring, test-taking, or individual teacher contact. This period proved to work well where teachers structured it to work. Some teachers, such as those in the math department, developed an after-school extra help program that gave students an additional opportunity for learning. Again, the school activity buses were critical in providing the transportation that made after-school academic support work in a rural community.

In both cases, we were expanding the use of our physical facilities for instructional purposes beyond the traditional day. Needless to say, this was a positive public relations move that was very endearing to many of our external customers. We also recommend that this practice be extended into the evening hours, giving faculty the option to report at non-traditional times (as late as needed to complete contractual hours) and provide instructional services to students who might better succeed in a non-traditional environment. Based on our experiences, we argue that this is an alternative that deserves further consideration as we think beyond the "way that it has always been done."

menting the block schedule, even though additional courses are offered via this plan?

There is much in educational literature that addresses the issues surrounding time and learning. The landmark study, *A Nation At Risk: The Imperative for Educational Reform*, prepared by the National Commission on Excellence in Education (1983), concluded

> . . . that declines in educational performance are in large part the result of disturbing inadequacies in the way the educational process itself is often conducted. The findings that follow, culled from a much more extensive list, reflect four important aspects of the educational process: content, expectations, time, and teaching (p. 18).

These findings by the Commission could have an impact on the future success of block scheduling. Although it is common sense to assume that much has been done to address the findings of the Commission's report since it was released, there is still a need to address some issues. We see the block scheduling initiative as one strategy for addressing not only the time issue but also concerns regarding expectations, curriculum, and teaching addressed in the Commission's report.

The following indicators are what we perceive to be block scheduling issues that are related to the Commission's findings. These indicators should be given serious consideration by study team members as they work to find the best possible schedule match for your school:

- Curriculum offerings based on the most efficient use of money, time, and human resources

- Expectations of customers

- Prioritizing curriculum offerings when limited resources force hard decisions.

Each of these issues will have an impact on how time is used during the school day. In fact, they will determine if there is truly a need for an extension of the school day to increase instructional time, or if a more efficient use of the time available could be the answer. It is critical that all issues related to the extension of the school day be explored. The most prevailing question is whether or not the block scheduling concept can assist in a more efficient use of time so that extension of the school day will not be necessary. It is important to note that some schools have reported that the issue of time has been the barrier that has impeded and/or prohibited the implementation of the block scheduling process.

CREATING MORE INSTRUCTIONAL TIME PER CLASS

Perhaps the most important finding of the Commission related to the block scheduling concept was the evidence regarding time. According to the Commission, time is ineffectively used to further the academic expectations of students in American schools (Commission on Excellence in Education, *Nation at Risk*, 1983, pp. 21–22). Evidence presented by the Commission pertaining to the study of time in high schools revealed that the school week in the United States ". . . provided students only 17 hours of academic instruction during the week, and the average school provided about 22 [hours]."

A body of literature supports the concept that there is a positive correlation between student achievement and the amount of instructional contact hours (Blai, 1986). Depending on the block schedule format chosen, allocated instructional time may increase or decrease. If the alternating day (A-B) schedule is implemented and all variables such as length of school day and number of courses offered remain constant, then allocated instructional time increases. On the other hand, when implementing the semester block, if the same variables are considered, the amount of allocated instructional time will decrease. This decrease is due to offering additional course opportunities for students (eight courses a year instead of seven) without extending the school day. Of course, there are strategies that can be suggested by the study team that will address the issue of maintaining a benchmark for instructional contact time for teachers and students.

USING HOMEWORK TO EXTEND LEARNING

Homework is an expected component of schooling, and it can be highly effective in the learning process. It can also be ineffective and redundant. How can it be used to benchmark instructional time? Homework was a major concern with students, teachers, and parents when developing the block schedule, and we found it surfaced as an issue for debate after we implemented the block. How much homework is necessary when a class is meeting for longer periods of time? Is it reasonable to expect twice as much homework nightly in a class on a semester block? Is there anything wrong with allocating some class time for homework completion? Is it appropriate to expect students to complete homework when some students deal with survival issues outside the school walls?

According to the findings of the Commission, homework is an area of concern as well as a resource that we should consider when extending instructional time. The Commission noted that ". . . homework for high school seniors has decreased (two-thirds report less than one hour a night) and grades have risen as average student achievement has been declining" (Commission on Excellence in Education, 1983, p. 20). This is definitely an action team issue.

We as educators must use the issue of time to address the concerns of the critics of schools as they are evident in the following testimony from the Commission: ". . . the public has no patience with undemanding and superfluous high school offerings . . . . The citizen is dismayed at a steady 15-year decline in industrial productivity, as one great industry after another falls to world competition" (Commission on Excellence in Education, 1983, p. 18). If we educators are to rebut these accusations leveled at our lack of productivity, then we must begin to seek strategies that will provide opportunities to use most effectively the one common denominator that is available to all—time.

OFFERING MORE COURSES

Depending on the block schedule format that is implemented, the availability and number of student course offerings change. The study team must decide if offering more courses is an important objective for implementing the block schedule, and if so, what impact an increase in course offerings will have on physical facilities, instructional supplies, and human resources.

There are some block schedule models that provide students the opportunity to take up to two additional courses per year, but many of the block schedule models that provide opportunities for additional courses may have a financial impact. This financial impact could create a barrier that would stall or even halt the implementation of the block schedule process.

Is offering more courses one of the primary objectives for transitioning to a block schedule format? It appears that many customers feel that we have expanded our curriculum beyond its intent. The Commission on Excellence in Education reports that "[t]his curricular smorgasbord, combined with extensive student choice, explains a great deal about where we find ourselves today.... Twenty-five percent of the credits earned by general track high school students are in physical and health education, work experience outside the school, remedial English and mathematics, and personal service and development courses, such as training for adulthood and marriage" (pp. 18–19).

If we are concerned about the long-term success of block scheduling, we must consider additional evidence reported by the Commission:

CASE IN POINT

Osbourne High School in Massassas, Virginia, elected to implement an eight-block alternating day (A-B) schedule. The principal and the planning team believed that it was important to maintain at least the current benchmark for instructional contact hours. They were committed to providing a format that would offer students more course selections, eight instead of six per year; fewer class changes; a calmer school climate; and instruction that is student-centered.

Results: The instructional school day was extended by 43 minutes, thus offering students the opportunity to take two additional classes per year. Students were not the only benefactors of the extended day. Teachers were also provided a 90-plus-minute planning period each day. Each class met in excess of 90 minutes on alternating days and in excess of the 150 instructional hours required per year for state accreditation. By all accounts and feedback that we've received, the program has enjoyed a great deal of success.

Secondary school curricula have been homogenized, diluted, and diffused to the point that they no longer have a central purpose. In effect, we have cafeteria-style curriculum in which the appetizers and desserts can easily be mistaken for the main courses. Students have migrated from vocational and college preparatory programs to "general track" courses in large numbers. The proportion of students taking a general program of study has increased from 12 percent in 1964 to 43 percent in 1979" (p. 18).

If block scheduling is to be successful in providing opportunities for student success (defined as higher student achievement), then we must have solutions to the many concerns that are being brought about by change, especially change in the way we use time.

IMPROVING THE SCHOOL CLIMATE

Because of fewer class changes, there is a calmer school environment on a block schedule. Optimum student supervision is possible because students are in classes during a larger part of the school day. During our combined 55 years in education, we have observed that most disciplinary problems are created during non-class time; i.e.: before school, during lunch, and during class changes. By eliminating a number of class changes, it is feasible that there will be a decline in the number of discipline incidents. This is what school administrators on the block schedule report. They see a decrease in the number of discipline referrals. We suggest that a more positive school climate created through a reduction in student behavioral problems will lead to a more positive teaching and learning environment. It is reasonable to assume that a positive school climate will correlate to higher student achievement.

We advise the study team to examine anecdotal cases on school climate, research from the literature, and other data available. Determine the relative importance of climate improvement to your overall school improvement plan. For some schools, climate change is extremely important. As principal, Tom found that it was advantageous to develop a plan immediately to measure the results of a more posi-

---

CASE IN POINT

The original schedule that Tom designed at Atlee High School in the fall of 1991 offered the alternating day format, Monday–Thursday. On Friday of each week, the school followed a seven-period format. All classes met for a shorter block of time one day per week. During the first semester, the perception of the faculty and staff was that they had many more discipline referrals on Fridays—when they were changing classes six times—as opposed to the other days, when classes changed only three times a day.

This was a consideration when the faculty changed the schedule to include Friday in the alternating day format. Once the transition was made, Tom compared second semester and first semester data related to disciplinary referrals. The faculty's perceptions were correct. They discovered that they had 14 percent more discipline referrals on Friday during the first semester than they had on all of the other four days of the week combined!

---

tive climate and keep all customers informed of progress. Because they were able to show positive gains early in the implementation process, this strategy helped Tom's staff gain momentum as well as customer support for the block schedule format. Yvonne found that when her school board asked for a report on the success of block scheduling during the first year (when there was little achievement data available), the data on the learning environment was persuasive enough to convince the school board that the question need not be asked again.

STEPS TO STARTING THE CHANGE PROCESS

■ Using a network to gather resources

A proven strategy that administrators can generally rely on when facing change is networking. School leaders throughout the country have experienced or are experiencing the change process. Therefore, there are many opportunities for networking electronically, at conferences, or at informal gatherings of colleagues. Information collected from networking will assist administrators in identifying resources that will direct the block scheduling implementation process.

Although professional networking is perhaps one of the strategies most often used for collecting data to support a change process, there are many other sources for collecting information that will ensure a more informed decision-making process.

■ Collecting data

The most frequently used method to ensure a more informed decision-making process is to visit schools that have implemented block scheduling and collect data from surveys, either self-designed or created by other schools. These surveys are designed to collect data about the block scheduling experience in schools that had previously implemented block scheduling as well as from schools in the implementation process. Information collected from surveys include reasons for considering a schedule change as well as the problems encountered throughout the process. Regardless of the method that a school study team chooses for collecting information, the change process requires a lot of work and preparation.

■ Preparing to conduct school visitations or surveying identified schools for information

Through networking, administrators have access to schools throughout the country that have successfully implemented various models of block scheduling. Before determining which school(s) the study team will visit, there are several issues that the team must consider.

Deciding who will visit schools. In his experience as principal of a school that hosted more than 2,500 visitors over a three-year period, Tom found that there was a combination of groups that visited schools. All were looking for answers that would assist them in the process of implementing block scheduling. These groups ranged from the principal on a scouting mission to teams that included administrators, students, parents, school board members, members of the business commu-

nity, and teachers. Follow-up data collected from visits indicated that the schools most successful in implementing the block schedule were represented by visiting groups that were broad based, prepared for the visit, and knew the right questions to ask and whom to ask. Many of the most successful visiting schools sent more than one group to visit the same school, and each group was, most frequently, composed of a broad cross section of the school community.

We believe that the visiting group should represent the school community, as should the study team. Teams should include students, faculty, parents, central office staff, members of the professional community, school board members, leaders in parent organizations (such as booster clubs and PTAs), and other customers who might be productive in assisting the team with a smooth implementation process.

For those who propose that it is a bad idea to release teachers from teaching responsibilities to make these visits, we suggest that this is some of the best staff development teachers can receive. Visiting a school, watching teachers in action, talking with peers, and reflecting on their own practice provides teachers with information and stimulation that is

> ### CASE IN POINT
>
> During the second year on the block schedule, Tom had the opportunity to present Atlee's model of the alternating day block schedule to a group of middle and secondary school principals. At the conclusion of the presentation, a principal approached him and wanted to discuss the advantages of rearranging allocated instructional time. About three weeks after the conversation, Tom received a call from the principal asking if it would be possible to send a "scout" team of teachers to visit his school and talk with staff members about the block schedule. Six teachers and the principal made the first visit. Before her school made the final decision, each member of the principal's faculty had visited Atlee and "shadowed" a teacher for a day. For them, the decision to move to block scheduling was easy.

often lacking in in-service training. Treating teachers as professionals—letting them out of the building and valuing their opinions and suggestions—builds support for the change the principal seeks. If seeing a picture is worth a thousand words, then visiting peers and observing something new in practice is worth several textbooks and a couple of graduate courses.

Preparing for the visit. Once members of the visitation team are identified by the school study team, preparation for the visit should be completed prior to selecting schools to visit. During this preparation, the team should analyze the demographics and logistics of potential sites to visit.

Several factors should be given consideration when selecting a school to visit: school community population, socioeconomic influences, and location

(urban, suburban, inner city, or rural). Other factors to consider include number of transfer students, funding, and student transportation. Even the compatibility of the schools' visions and strategic plans are worth considering. It is important that these factors compare favorably with the sites that the school study team will visit. Would a team find much value in visiting an urban school with high military mobility if they represent a rural school from a community with a static population?

Sufficient preparation for the visit is vital if the visiting team is to optimize the limited time they have been allotted to interact with students and members of the faculty and staff. Before the scheduled visit, contact the host school and prepare the building administrator for any special or unusual requests that your team may have. In our experience hosting visitors, our team of teachers was much better prepared to provide helpful information when visitors forwarded questions or special requests in advance of the visit. If the teams are not prepared, the visit can be a waste of time for both visitors and hosts.

Special requests from visiting teams may include the following:

- Allowing students from visiting schools to shadow students from the host school

- Allowing teachers from visiting schools to shadow teachers from the host school

- Having parents from the school community available to speak with members of the visiting team

- Having members of the school board available to talk with visitors

- Sending all members (or as many as possible) of the faculty of the visiting school to shadow fac-

ulty of the host school for a day (in small groups). This is very beneficial, if arrangements can be made with the host school. It creates a support system over a period of time that will be helpful during the implementation phase of block scheduling. The faculty and staff of the host school serve as resources to answer questions or address concerns of members of the visiting school throughout the implementation year and beyond.

■ Reviewing questions most frequently asked by customers considering a block scheduling format

Another source of information that administrators and the study team will likely rely upon will be the answers to questions that have been asked by teams or individuals who have "lived" the journey of scheduling change. Before visiting a school or in the early stages of planning strategies for change, consider questions that must be answered prior to making a decision regarding the change. The study team may discover that there are too many questions that cannot be answered and choose not to proceed with the change process. As the team prepares for the visit to a host school or the study team considers the issues that must be addressed, the following questions could serve as the focus for interaction among team members and the host school. These questions—collected over a three-year period—were the most frequently asked by visitors to Atlee. We offer responses to these questions based on our experience as planners for change to block scheduling. These answers can be supplemented with the growing body of research that uses data to address some of these questions.

Questions regarding block scheduling typically asked during school visitations—and responses

QUESTION: *How do you incorporate the various segments of your instructional program into a block schedule (i.e.: technical education, work study, marketing, physical education, co-curricular, activities/clubs, Advanced Placement courses, interdisciplinary offerings)?*

RESPONSE: The flexibility of block scheduling is conducive to providing these types of services for students. Vocational/technical education, work study, and marketing programs are handled on an individual basis and continue to allow teachers opportunities to provide successful learning experiences for our students. You may find that it is necessary to revisit the curriculum and program design of technical programs and collapse some courses to fit into the block model. However, this is something you will want to do anyway with all of your program areas.

We experienced no negative implications, and in many instances, the flexibility of block scheduling allowed all partners to be more flexible in planning programs. If a school chooses to implement a semester schedule, it is important to provide a two-semester opportunity for students enrolled in co-op programs that require students to report for work on a daily basis.

Scheduling Advanced Placement courses, honors courses, music, physical education, and other elective courses created no major problems because courses were based on a year-long schedule. The major focus in these classes as well as other class offerings was training teachers to use the larger blocks of time effectively. If a school has implemented a semester schedule, there are some concerns related to AP classes, mathematics, foreign languages, and music, as well as courses requiring testing at the end of the traditional academic year.

A student activity period of approximately 30 minutes was built into the schedule each Friday in Tom's school. As a result, data from surveys indicated that there was an increase in the number of students who participated in co-curricular activities. Atlee also experienced growth in the number of interdisciplinary offerings. Teachers indicated that there was more planning time and flexibility in the design of curriculum and teaching strategies because of the longer block of time.

QUESTION: *When are homeroom tasks handled (i.e.: Student Government Association voting, collection of personal data, etc.)? What do you see as the advantages or disadvantages of a designated homeroom?*

RESPONSE: Each school should decide the issue related to homeroom. Atlee did not have homeroom because, in the faculty's opinion, it was not the most efficient use of allocated instructional time. Time was allocated in the first block to allow teachers to take care of activities that are normally addressed in traditional homerooms. Models of block scheduling that have a study block scheduled during the day handle traditional homeroom activities during that time. For example, at Yvonne's school the study block was held daily, and activities directed to all students, such as viewing CNN, were conducted during that time. If, however, homeroom is a separate activity, there is another bell and additional unsupervised time as well as a loss of instructional time.

QUESTION: *Is the list of electives shortened in any way because of time?*

RESPONSE: Although neither of us added an additional block of instruction, we observed that students chose to take additional classes instead of early dismissal. Schools on a 4x4 block schedule may actually add electives, depending on the requirements for graduation and the school's philosophy

---

CASE IN POINT

We considered the alternating day (A-B) block schedule that we implemented to be what was referred to as "student friendly." The reason for this perception was that it provided opportunities to build the schedule around the needs of students and not build the needs of students around the schedule. A student enrolled in a co-op work study program was employed at a local business on a part-time basis. She began her job each day at the end of Block 3. Her co-op teacher received a call from her employer informing the teacher that the student had an opportunity to receive a promotion in her job, but the student would need to work more hours. Because the schedule was "student friendly," the staff was able to schedule four classes on A days, and she reported to work for a full day on B days. In addition to the four academic credits that she received, she also received credit for on-the-job training, which was part of the work-based learning curriculum. She continued this schedule until she graduated.

regarding early dismissal and early graduation. However, decisions about electives and course offerings should not be driven by the schedule. The schedule should facilitate earlier decisions regarding curriculum and course offerings. Changes in electives, for example, should follow discussions about program standards, courses that support career pathways, emerging needs in the workplace, and preparation for college.

QUESTION: *Does block scheduling affect class size?*

RESPONSE: This depends on the type of schedule that a school decides to implement. If you are on a traditional six-period schedule, and your school decides to implement the semester block schedule, there will be an increase in the number of faculty needed and an increase in the number of students per class if additional faculty are not hired. We have received reports from schools that there has been a slight increase in class size if additional faculty are not employed. We experienced no change in class size because some financial parameters restricted the number of faculty that we had available. We knew from the beginning of this process that we would be limited to the human resources that were currently assigned based on student enrollment, and there would be no money available to hire additional faculty. Some hard decisions had to be made.

We caution about telling teachers that their class sizes will be reduced on a block schedule unless you are certain this will occur. We have visited teachers who expected small classes on the block and actually had larger numbers of students with the new schedule. Naturally their disappointment did nothing to help their adjustment to the block schedule.

QUESTION: *Is the time between classes extended? How long? Problems? Suggestions?*

RESPONSE: Time for transition between classes was not increased from the previously allocated amount of time. It is important to keep non-value-added time to a minimum. We found students to be very responsive and generally to be in class on time. The time needed for class change should be a reflection of the size of the school facilities, not the school schedule.

QUESTION: *How are discipline problems handled for in-school suspension and out-of-school suspension?*

RESPONSE: Block scheduling does not affect the way that ISS and OSS are handled. Because of the flexible use of time, Atlee was able to do more intervention; therefore, discipline became a way to correct student behavior rather than a form of punishment. In general, because students are more directly supervised due to fewer class changes, Tom's staff expected and subsequently experienced a decline in discipline incidents. The block schedule plan should facilitate improvements in responsible student behavior for the following reasons.

- Teachers and students enjoy a more personalized relationship.

- Students succeed more often.

- The entire student body changes classes only three times during the school day instead of the traditional six changes.

QUESTION: *How many preparations does each teacher have?*

RESPONSE: Our goal in both schools was to limit teacher preparations to no more than two per year. Two preparations per year would be a possibility due to the alternate day schedule. Traditionally, teachers are responsible for five classes per year. Many schools that have implemented the semester block model have reported that as a result, teachers have only two preparations per semester. Of course, the number of teacher preparations will vary with the type of block schedule implemented, the size of the school, and the extent of program offerings.

QUESTION: *How do you actually formulate the schedules for all students? Do you have a specific computer program to help? What is it?*

RESPONSE: Scheduling depends on the type of block schedule that you choose. If the schedule is an alternating day schedule, there is no change in the way scheduling is processed. You simply schedule classes 1–7 for each student. Schedule classes 1, 3, and 7 on B (or odd) days and classes 2, 4, and 6 on A (or even) days. Block 5 is a 55-minute class that meets each day (singleton or study block). There are several commercial software programs that can be used for scheduling.

If a school is using a semester block, then students are scheduled for eight blocks at the beginning of the year. Four blocks are assigned each semester. Often a member of the central office computer programming staff is available to write a computer program that will fit the scheduling needs of schools that are implementing the block format. Some schools have reported scheduling each student at the beginning of each semester. According to feedback we have received from schools using the semester schedule, the most successful practice is to schedule all classes at the beginning of the year, rather than scheduling them at the beginning of each semester. Sometimes problems occur with students getting the classes they need when schools schedule by semester. This could also create a major personnel problem because of the time needed during the first semester to schedule students for the second semester.

Some schools have reported doing schedules by hand after generating a conflict matrix by computer. Private companies are providing these services. Selecting a firm will depend on the section of the country in which your school is located.

QUESTION: *How do you deal with student absences? Make-up work?*

RESPONSE: Make every effort to impress upon students that each instructional period is equivalent to two days of instruction on a traditional schedule. Many students indicated that they made a special effort to attend school, and the attendance data at Atlee supported this observation. Data from other schools also reported that attendance was better. Over a three-year period, Atlee's student attendance averaged approximately 96 percent.

Students became more accountable for following up with their make-up work. As a rule, we did not extend time for make-up work. We helped students understand the school policy: Make-up work was due the second class meeting after the student returned to school, unless other arrangements were made with the teacher. Therefore, make-up work was not an issue created by block scheduling. In

schools with a study block, the schedule can facilitate making up work quickly because all students have access to all teachers during the school day.

QUESTION: *How much staff development did you provide or would you recommend before the change to block scheduling? What would be the estimated cost? How long before implementation of block scheduling would you begin in-service teacher training? What topics would you recommend be covered in depth?*

RESPONSE: Based on feedback that we have received from teachers over the past eight years, staff development is the single most critical issue that impacts the success of block scheduling. All needed staff development cannot be provided prior to the implementation of block scheduling. Training must be an ongoing effort. The cost incurred depends on the amount of staff development that actually takes place. We recommend a long-term staff development plan with an accompanying budget. (See Chapter 10 for additional comments on staff development.)

QUESTION: *Which teaching techniques or strategies have you found to be most helpful? How were they presented to your faculty?*

RESPONSE: The most helpful strategies initially were classroom time management and cooperative learning. They were presented in staff development workshops and were attended on a voluntary basis. All but a few of both faculties with which we worked were trained in cooperative learning. Yvonne trained all of her faculty in quality management techniques for two purposes: understanding teamwork and learning how to analyze and present data.

QUESTION: *How did you present your plan to the community, teachers, and students? How did you handle negative criticism, such as: "Why should we change?" or "Why fix something that's not broken?"*

RESPONSE: Atlee's study team developed a public relations plan. They took every opportunity to tell their story to the community. They listened to anyone who responded either positively or negatively. They concentrated on the many opportunities that this schedule would provide for students.

Yvonne's school used the study team to gain support from parent groups and the school board, as well as the faculty and students. Presentations were made by teachers so that the idea of block scheduling didn't appear to belong solely to the principal (which it didn't). The study team focused on improving student achievement and making the classroom more conducive to active student learning.

QUESTION: *Why did you go with block rather than modular or some other type of flexible scheduling?*

RESPONSE: Atlee's study team looked at many types of schedules, including the semester timetable that is used in Canada, the trimester, and the Copernican model, as well as variations of the schedule they selected. After a careful analysis of the opportunities that each schedule offered the student population, the staff chose the alternating day schedule. It was the best choice for the school community.

QUESTION: *For administration, faculty, and students: What did you think of the concept of flexible scheduling before implementation, and how do you feel about it now?*

RESPONSE: Both faculties were very apprehensive about issues that we may not have anticipated and the problems that might be caused by these issues. The problems never occurred. We had done our homework and were well prepared to deal with any issues that might have been a problem. The key to the success of change is preparation.

After the first week of school, Tom felt that his staff had made a decision that would provide many positive learning opportunities for students. The first year after implementing the block schedule, 96 percent of the faculty indicated that they would not want to return to a traditional schedule. Three years after implementation, data collected via their annual survey indicated that only one faculty member desired a return to a traditional scheduling format.

QUESTION: *Does block scheduling improve learning for all students?*

RESPONSE: Our observation is that block scheduling provides opportunities to improve achievement for all students. It provides time for specialized instruction for all students. Of course, teachers must take advantage of the opportunity they have to redesign how they teach to use to the fullest the longer blocks of instructional time. We equate more specialized instruction to improved learning, and we are now beginning to review data from schools that have been on the block several years to determine achievement gains.

QUESTION: *Will block scheduling lower student/teacher ratios if no money is spent to hire more teachers? In general, what were the financial ramifications of a block schedule? Do costs increase more for a block schedule than for a seven-period day?*

RESPONSE: Increase in financial responsibilities depends on the type of block scheduling that you choose. If you move to alternating day from a seven-period traditional schedule, there is no additional cost with the exception of staff development. If you are on a seven-period day, and you choose a semester block, there is a possibility that there will be a need for a funding increase to support the additional classes (because teachers continue to teach only six periods). If your school is on a six-period day schedule, and you move to a semester block, there will be an increase in financial commitment.

QUESTION: *We have been told a block schedule is easier on teachers and students. True in your opinion?*

RESPONSE: Teachers on the alternate day (A-B) are still responsible for five blocks of instruction over a year. However, on any given day, a teacher will not teach more than three classes, which means that s/he would teach only two classes the next day. If a school is using a semester format, normally teachers are responsible for teaching three of the four blocks each semester, which equates to six blocks a year. We both found that more planning was needed during the first year of implementation, but during the second year the time for planning changed somewhat. During the first year, the teacher must adjust lesson design to the 90-minute block. Also, during the first year decisions have to be made about different instructional strategies. During year two, the planning emphasis shifts from day-to-day survival on the block to the bigger picture of conceptual learning.

After becoming accustomed to the 90-minute block, the teacher can begin thinking more about interdisciplinary instruction, teaming with other teachers, and redesigning the curriculum to reflect conceptual frameworks. Teachers are able to plan more student projects that require greater amounts of in-class time, as well as take advantage of technology available in the school. On the block schedule—A-B or 4x4—teachers have a longer planning block, which seems to work well.

QUESTION: *Our Advanced Placement teachers have decided that they cannot teach the required AP material in less than one school year. Therefore, two of the eight available course slots will be taken up by each AP course a student takes. Do you know other schools that have arranged AP courses in this way under a semester schedule? How does that arrangement work? We think this limits the AP students in their choice of electives and may lead to changing AP courses to one term instead of two (the entire year). Are there problems involved in scheduling that prevent students from being scheduled into AP or other advanced course offerings?*

RESPONSE: There are many questions yet to be answered concerning Advanced Placement courses offered in a block schedule. If a school uses the alternating day format, there are no problems created by the schedule. If a school uses the semester format, there are several concerns that must be addressed. If students are scheduled to take AP classes the first semester but tests are not administered until the Spring, student performance may be affected to some degree. If the student takes the course in the Spring, s/he will not cover as much content as students on other schedules before the test is administered.

Also, the number of AP classes may be limited per semester because of the "overload" of academic classes in one semester. Some schools using the semester have reported limiting the number of AP classes that students take to two per semester.

Our suggestion would be for each school to evaluate individual situations regarding the role that AP offerings play in the school's program of studies. This should include the number of students presently taking AP classes and the percentage of students attending college after high school graduation. Students should be encouraged to balance their courses when planning their four-year program of studies.

Review and practice sessions could be established prior to the examination for the student who completes an AP course during the first term. Look at these issues as opportunities to improve learning for students.

QUESTION: *What effect does block scheduling have on music and art? Will classes in the fine arts be affected?*

RESPONSE: Parents and students will need to consider carefully the number of blocks devoted to any particular subject area. We experienced very few concerns relative to music and art in the alternating day schedule. Some adjustments were made in the way teachers instruct students because of the longer blocks of time. However, this is true in most classes.

Schools on the semester block have reported some problems sustaining enrollment in performing arts programs. Students may choose to take music one semester but other courses the following semester (even though music is available). This scenario creates two concerns. First, many music teachers perceive the need to keep students in a sequential program of music throughout the year to build their skills. These teachers express concern about music students who take a semester and then are off a semester before they are again involved in formal instruction. The second concern expressed by parents and students is that deans of admission at competitive colleges and universities will not look favorably on students who elect to stay in the music program each semester and accumulate eight credits of music in a four-year high school program. If a student takes another music elective, such as performing choir or jazz band, s/he could show up to 16 credits on a transcript over a four-year period. This is an issue that should be given careful consideration.

Visual arts instructors in our schools have reported only positive experiences for their classes. The extended instructional time gives more flexibility and time to do, as one teacher put it, ". . . meaningful art projects at a level of qualtiy that I have never witnessed in my teaching career."

QUESTION: *Mathematics and foreign language teachers are very concerned about teaching in a block scheduling format. Do they have a legitimate concern? Are there data on the effects of the long gaps between sequential classes (e.g.: Algebra I and Algebra II or Latin I and Latin II)? Will the study of foreign language be affected by the block schedule?*

RESPONSE: Some block scheduling formats have been implemented where these concerns are not an issue. The A-B schedule is the most well known.

These concerns must be dealt with if a school is implementing a semester schedule. There are reported concerns of sequencing of mathematics, music, and foreign languages for schools in the United States and Canada that use the semester format. Issues center around the retention of information over long periods of time for students who take the second or third course in a sequence after having been away from the subject for different lengths of time with varying degrees of retention. Data collected from some Canadian schools report that the semester scheduling format has created additional work for teachers and students, and that standardized test scores are declining in some disciplines when compared with schools using a year-long schedule (King et al., 1977).

Teachers of music report that students are choosing not to continue with their music program each semester. These student choices can create a problem with continuity when students are preparing for performances and developing or refining technical skills.

The semester schedule may create gaps in sequencing in such courses as mathematics and foreign languages. Students and parents are encouraged to consider carefully when they elect to take foreign language and math courses. Once a student begins a sequence in mathematics or foreign language, s/he will have the opportunity and be encouraged to complete the sequence of courses in consecutive terms. Bottoms and Creech found that career-bound students who are taking mathematics their senior year in school perform better than students who are not taking mathematics (1997).

The block scheduling plan allows students not only to accelerate the number of courses completed but also to defer beginning a foreign language until later in high school. This might be especially important if a student plans to attend college and wants or needs to include a foreign language in his/her college or career plans.

Sequencing is not a problem with the A-B schedule. Mathematics teachers at Atlee were the most vocal supporters of the alternating day format because they reported that they had opportunities to teach concepts rather than chapters. Tom observed their teaching changing from lecturing and board work to student-teacher interaction, technology-based, and hands-on or practical applications of concepts. After the first year of block scheduling, math teachers reported covering up to six weeks more material than previously taught under the traditional 55-minute schedule.

At this time there is little research on this topic. Some publications report this problem and provide pieces of information that help to identify it. There are Canadian studies that compare achievement in math for students on a semester timetable with that of students who use a yearlong schedule (Raphel, Walstrom and McLean, 1986). Canadian research also addresses perceptions regarding the teaching of foreign language in the block timetable (King et al., 1978). The school study team should address this issue before making a decision about a new schedule.

QUESTION: *Why is there a wave of interest in block scheduling? Is this a nationwide trend or mainly limited to the Southeastern states?*

RESPONSE: Experimenting with alternative ways of using allocated instructional time is not new to public education. Decision makers in Canada have been using some form of what they refer to as block time tabling as early as the 1960s. There are many public and private schools throughout this country that have been using alternative forms of block scheduling since the 1980s and earlier. Although the use of block scheduling appears to be concentrated at this time in the southeastern United States and particularly in Virginia and North Carolina, there is use of block scheduling throughout this country and foreign countries.

QUESTION: *Why have some schools gone to block scheduling and then abandoned it? For how long did they try it?*

RESPONSE: There are incidents of schools that have tried block scheduling and then returned to the traditional schedule. There are many reasons why schools change back to the previous schedule. There are also schools that started with the alternating day schedule and then changed to the semester format, and vice-versa. The school board of a large school district in Virginia approved two schools to pilot the alternating day schedule and two schools to pilot the semester schedule. After a year of piloting, the school board made a decision based on public hearings involving all interested customers, that all high schools in the school district would use the alternating day format.

Each school that has switched from one schedule to another has reasons for making these changes. We suggest that, if a thorough analysis of the school's needs had been made prior to making the final decision, changes might not have been necessary. Compared to the number of schools that have moved to a block scheduling format, the number that have elected to move back to their previously used schedule is few.

QUESTION: *Are there any different approaches to scheduling in schools other than the semester or alternating day block?*

RESPONSE: Many schools are using some variation of the pure semester or alternating day schedule, and some schools are using a combination of these schedules. We have been in communication with schools that are using the trimester schedule, as well as some form of the Copernican Model. Schedules are as varied as the schools that use them. Each school that is considering a change in present scheduling practices should complete a needs assessment and develop a schedule that will meet those needs.

QUESTION: *Do you know of any data that support claims of better learning under block schedules?*

RESPONSE: There are many schools that have reported that more students are making better grades as determined by indicators such as honor roll, principal's list, and dean's list. Based on data that have been collected from schools in the United States and Canada, there are perceptions by parents

and teachers that students are learning more and are performing more effectively on tests and other types of assessment instruments. New data are being collected on an ongoing basis that will provide us with some answers very soon. (See Chapter 3 for additional data.)

QUESTION: *Is block scheduling basically a schedule for students who won't do homework?*

RESPONSE: We have found block scheduling to be an efficient and flexible use of time that provides teachers an opportunity to meet the needs of **all** students.

QUESTION: *How can a math, science, or foreign language teacher accomplish as much work when a student has one-half as much homework (18 weeks of homework nights versus 36 weeks of homework nights)?*

RESPONSE: There is a need for teachers to rethink homework in terms of quality rather than quantity. Teachers and students in Canada report that there is not as much homework required on the block schedule (King et al., 1977). Apparently there is more in-depth study of a subject, although there are reports that less material is covered in the semester block. Again, this is not an issue if a school chooses to use the alternating day block schedule.

When and where homework is being done is a major concern to parents and administrators. In some schools students have reported that teachers are giving actual class time to complete homework assignments. This generally occurs when teachers do not plan and/or when teachers have not received staff development to enhance their use of various teaching strategies that can be integrated into instruction for the entire class period. If this is a problem area, we suggest conducting an assessment of the teaching staff to determine staff development needs, followed by sufficient opportunities for development.

QUESTION: *What percentage of teachers can effectively use 90-plus minutes of class time?*

RESPONSE: There are many teachers who have taught in long blocks of time throughout their careers. Teachers who teach summer school and vocational teachers as well as teachers of special needs students are some who teach in blocks that exceed the traditional 55-minute block. However, for most teachers, it is a change in the **way** they teach, so staff development is required. Veteran teachers may have less difficulty with the larger blocks than beginning teachers because they can pull from the many teaching strategies they have developed over the years. Additionally, they can use strategies they had wanted to use but didn't have sufficient instructional time to employ. Experienced teachers report having time to cover material and teach concepts that they had not had time to teach in the past. Beginning teachers will need more assistance and direction in developing plans of instruction in order to be effective in longer blocks of time. On the other hand, the advantage of working with beginning teachers is that you don't have to break down existing mindsets of how teaching has to be done.

QUESTION: *If we want our schools to be used as a recruiting tool by local industry to attract the best and brightest employees (especially scientists and engineers), how would we want to structure our school?*

RESPONSE: This is exactly the reason that you want to include members of the professional community and the private-sector community as part of your study team. We found the professional and private-sector community very supportive of the block scheduling format for various reasons. Each customer has different needs, and block scheduling provided opportunities to address many positive suggestions when we were preparing to face the process of change.

QUESTION: *How will the block schedule affect student learning?*

RESPONSE: Teachers using the alternate day schedule have reported that students cover slightly more material; but, more important, they appear to learn content with more depth and understanding. Because of added instructional time, we have witnessed more time on task, more engaged learning time, and much higher student success ratios. There are more opportunities for students to be successful, which results in less need for remediation.

Teachers who are teaching in schools that are using the semester block schedule have reported that they have not covered as much material in a semester as they had in year-long courses, but they are covering material in more depth. The central question becomes: Is it more important to cover material, or to understand the material covered?

QUESTION: *Besides measurable learning and high success ratios, what are other significant benefits for students?*

RESPONSE: Tom observed a degree of interaction occurring between students, teachers, and parents that had not occurred before block scheduling. Teachers reported that this increased interaction was a result of teaching fewer students each day and being able to spend more time with them and getting to know them better. As a consequence, teachers understood student learning styles better and felt more comfortable interacting with students and parents. This appeared to lead to more frequent interaction with parents and resulted in a higher rate of success for students.

QUESTION: *How will the sequence of courses be determined?*

RESPONSE: If a school is using the alternating day schedule, sequencing of courses is not affected. Sequencing is an issue on the semester block. Each department must carefully review its curriculum and develop a recommended sequence of courses. Much attention must be paid to the experience of other schools that have changed to the semester system. Parents and students must be made aware of these recommendations and must be encouraged to consider long-range planning when developing student schedules.

QUESTION: *Can a student repeat a course in the second semester if the student is not successful during the first semester?*

RESPONSE: Some schools offer the option of repeating courses at the end of the semester. These options depend on different variables, such as school policy, course of study, and the choice of block schedule implemented. If a school uses the semester block, students schedule all eight blocks at the beginning of the year. The possibilities of a student repeating a course the second term depends on the number of students requesting the course, the flexibility of the student's schedule, and the availability of teachers and teaching stations. Students who attend schools that are on the alternating day plan can repeat certain subjects if there are sufficient numbers to warrant offering a repeat course.

QUESTION: *Can students graduate early when a school implements a block schedule?*

RESPONSE: Many school districts have a policy related to early graduation. The possibility for early graduation is enhanced when students have the option to take eight classes per year, as opposed to six or seven per year. Requests for early graduation are generally considered on an individual basis. At this stage in the block scheduling restructuring process, we have had no reports that this has been an issue. We are familiar with one school with a high-risk student population that adopted the 4x4 with the expressed intent of moving students out of the school early (i.e.: completing their academic program) into career training and work opportunities.

QUESTION: *How will lunch be conducted with the block schedule?*

RESPONSE: The number of lunch sections that a school offers depends upon the number of students in school and the seating capacity of the eating area. The best scenario is to offer lunch periods without splitting instructional blocks. Generally, this can be done when you offer no more than two lunch blocks. If there are more than two lunch blocks, alternative plans must be used. This is a task that an action team can address.

There are many creative solutions implemented by schools. Albemarle High School in Charlottesville, Virginia; Thomas Jefferson School for Science and Technology in Fairfax, Virginia; and Franklin County High School in Rocky Mount, VA, provide an hour for all students to eat during the same block of time. Princess Anne High School in Virginia Beach, Virginia, implemented the alternat-

ing day (A-B) schedule. All students attend the first three instructional blocks of the day. Students who schedule a fourth block have a 10-minute break for a snack (vending machine type) and then attend the fourth block. Those who elect not to take the fourth block leave school. There is no official lunch period.

Other schools are using the "food court" approach. A food court provides different menu selections at multiple serving stations: Station 1: salads; Station 2: pizza; Station 3: traditional selections. This will create opportunities to serve more students in a shorter period of time. Again, each school has its own unique variables that must be dealt with when making these decisions.

CASE IN POINT

If a school chooses the alternating day block schedule, the following process can be used to offer students who are having difficulties achieving the opportunity to repeat courses.

This plan was submitted by members of the faculty at Atlee High School. Opportunities for repeating classes were limited to English, first-year foreign languages, and mathematics. Other course options could be added. When scheduling teachers for teaching assignments, pair teachers who teach classes that are offered for repeat purposes during the same block. At the end of the semester, students who need to repeat a particular course will be assigned to one teacher, and those who need to accelerate will be assigned to the paired teacher. The teachers involved will pre-determine which teacher will teach which class at the beginning of the school year. The next semester, teachers will switch assignments. This method of regrouping for instruction is used commonly in elementary schools, allowing teachers and students to focus on meeting needs of students during the school year.

At the end of the school term, a student can either take the second semester of the course by entering summer school or by electing to take it the first semester of the next school term. Each option depends on the availability of teachers and students needing remediation or acceleration.

QUESTION: *What effect will the block schedule have on overall student attendance?*

RESPONSE: Tom's school showed an improvement in attendance. Students were aware that if they missed a day, it was the equivalent of missing two traditional days. Student and teacher attendance increased each year they were on block scheduling. Many factors contribute to poor student attendance. Out-of-school suspension and students' not succeeding in the classroom are only two. Because of the flexibility of the block schedule, Atlee was able to implement a system that would allow faculty to keep in touch with those students who were at risk for high absenteeism and dropping out of school.

Consider the following scenario: A student is suspended from school and falls behind in his/her school work during suspension. As a consequence, the student becomes frustrated and embarrassed because s/he cannot succeed in class. Subsequently, the student becomes a discipline problem and (usually) is suspended again or begins missing school on a regular basis. This affects student attendance, and attendance is correlated with student achievement. Next step: Dropout, if s/he is old enough. This is a cycle in which many students are trapped.

QUESTION: *What effect will the new plan have on the dropout rate?*

RESPONSE: Because of the flexibility of block scheduling, Atlee was able to tailor many individual programs for students, and each year we experienced a decline in dropouts. From 1992 to 1995, Atlee High School had no dropouts. The Case in Point on page 89 addresses the flexibility of the block schedule when providing opportunities for students to stay in school.

QUESTION: *Do you anticipate changes in the approach you now take to student progress/school/home/communications?*

RESPONSE: Yes, detailed report cards will continue to be issued at more frequent intervals because of the amount of material being covered and the fewer times that a class meets. There are other ways of keeping the lines of communication open. Electronic voice mail—a communication system that automatically dials a student's home phone—can provide information as well as a pre-recorded message to customers who call regarding school assignments, major tests, grading periods, homework assignments, school functions, and other related activities. This process has received a great deal of support from parents. Parent visitations are also scheduled at appropriate times during the school term to collect input and provide feedback. Teachers have also reported that because of longer planning periods, they have had more time to communicate with parents.

QUESTION: *How would the block schedule affect transfer students?*

RESPONSE: If your school is on a alternating day (A-B) schedule, transfer students will continue to use the schedule that they bring with them. At this point, there have been no major problems with the transfer issue on the alternating day (A-B) schedule.

If you are using a semester schedule format, students who enroll during mid-year will be scheduled individually into courses that most closely match their needs. Schools should have a number of resources which make flexible scheduling possible. We have had reported incidents that students have been granted credits without meeting all of the course objectives, and that students lost credits because they transferred from a six- or seven- period day schedule to a four-course semester schedule, which limited students to enrolling in a maximum of four courses.

There are still many unanswered questions concerning transfer students and the quality of instructional programs offered when they transfer from a non-semester schedule. This is an issue that must receive a lot of thought and attention if you are contemplating going to the semester block. It could be the barrier that stops change.

QUESTION: *What is an academic resource center?*

RESPONSE: This center is known by several names, such as, the advancement center, the study center, and the transfer center. Regardless of the name, the purpose is to provide transfer students a support system until they can catch up in course work when they transfer from schools that have a different schedule than the receiving school.

These centers are staffed in many different ways. Some schools assign teachers to this center as a part of their regular teaching assignment. Some schools use student mentors and parent volunteers, and some teachers are assigned to these students in lieu of study hall or duty periods. It is important to staff the center with individuals who have content expertise such as math, science, foreign language, English, and other areas where a school perceives a need. Some schools also use these labs for students who have not been successful in class because of absenteeism or who are in need of additional academic support.

QUESTION: *Will exams be given?*

RESPONSE: Exams will be given. The 90-plus-minute block provides sufficient time for examina-

tions. Before block scheduling was implemented, eight school days (four each semester) were devoted to examinations in Tom's district. Under the block schedule, only two days are devoted to examinations, and no bell schedules need to be changed. This is a net saving of six instructional days. Some schools that implemented the semester block in Canada reported eliminating exams, although that turned out to be an unpopular decision with many parents and teachers.

QUESTION: *What will become of courses that have, in the past, been offered for only one semester?*

RESPONSE: All courses that are currently one semester have been reviewed and evaluated. In many cases, these courses could be re-designed and offered as one-credit courses that would occupy one block of time. In some block scheduling models, half-credit courses as well as semester courses are still offered.

QUESTION: *What effect will the block schedule plan have on elective courses?*

RESPONSE: By providing students with 32 choices in a four-year period, the semester block schedule provides opportunities for elective courses to be added to a student's schedule. Because of these opportunities, semester block scheduling should have a positive impact on certain electives.

This impact depends on the number of blocks a student can take in a year. If a school is moving from a six-period traditional day to a seven block, then student opportunities for electives increase. In our schools, electives increased because we eliminated study halls and increased elective offerings, such as photo journalism, oceanography, geology, foreign languages, the Academy of Finance, music, visual arts, and theater.

QUESTION: *How will special education students be affected by this plan?*

RESPONSE: Members of the special education faculty work closely with students and parents to develop Individual Educational Programs (IEPs), which will continue to meet student needs for spe-cial education services. Teachers of students with special needs reported that the longer blocks of time allowed more opportunities for individual instruc-tion as well as other instructional strategies that enhance success of students with learning disabili-ties. For teachers working collaboratively to provide inclusion opportunities, the longer block provides time for a student to work in the regular program and with his or her special needs teacher. Many of these teachers have already been teaching in longer blocks of time because of the needs of their stu-dents. This was supported by information we re-ceived when compiling data from our annual survey.

QUESTION: *Are there likely to be changes in the atten-dance policy?*

RESPONSE: Some changes are expected if pres-ent policy is tied into the traditional use of instruc-tional time. If your policy only allows X days per year before losing credit or reporting for truancy, then policymakers will need to keep in mind that whether you are on the alternating day (A-B) or semester block schedule, each instructional period is equivalent to two traditional instructional periods.

CASE IN POINT

Tom received a call from a division superintendent asking for a recommendation for the following situa-tion: A student had transferred to a high school in his district at the end of the first semester. The school the student transferred from was on a semester schedule, and the school transferred to was on a tradi-tional seven-period 55-minute day schedule. The transferring student needed seven Carnegie units to graduate and was taking only three the first semester, but he was scheduled to take four the second semester. Since the school he had transferred to was at the midpoint of the year, any new course in which he would enroll would be halfway finished, leaving him at a disadvantage. What was the superintend-ent to do? Since the superintendent was committed to providing all students an opportunity for a quality education, the student was provided a tutor in the four courses that he needed for graduation, at a cost to the school district.

Will all superintendents and principals be willing to go to this extent if there are large numbers of trans-fer students? A former student recently called to discuss a pending interview with a principal who was a proponent of the alternating day schedule (A-B). During the conversation, she told Tom that she was teaching in a school that was on the semester block. Although the conversation was related to the alter-nating day block and increasing her knowledge base to prepare for her interview, they also discussed the semester block. When Tom asked her how she enjoyed teaching in the semester block, she shared with him that providing appropriate learning opportunities for transfer students was a major problem, and regardless of the plan they implemented to deal with the issue, they were never sure that students were the winners.

An action team should address this issue and make recommendations for a solution.

QUESTION: *Is block scheduling simply a matter of changing the schedule to 90-minute classes and having classes meet for 90 days instead of 180?*

RESPONSE: Block schedule is more than a matter of scheduling. It is a **new way of doing business.** It is a more efficient use and application of time. It provides teachers and students opportunities related to teaching and learning not possible under a traditional scheduling model. **If the purpose of changing schedules is simply to double the amount of time that a student spends in a class each day, then don't change.**

It should also provide opportunities for creative curriculum development, creative ways of teaching that are prohibited in a shorter block of time, and the flexible use of time to assist students that have non-traditional problems.

QUESTION: *Are 90-minute classes too long and boring?*

RESPONSE: If teachers continue to teach in the traditional sense to which students and teachers have become accustomed, the classes could be very long and boring. But a part of the strategic planning of block scheduling should be to assist teachers in discovering and using new and different teaching strategies.

We observed that many teachers who had used the traditional lecture method were beginning to look for new teaching strategies that would bring about more positive student achievement. As a teacher of English in the block schedule, Tom found that it was impossible to teach in the traditional method and still be an effective teacher. He had to find a variety of teaching methods that would meet his students' needs. With the assistance of the students, Tom developed a classroom time management plan that called for at least four different teaching strategies per class period, with a certain amount of time allocated for each strategy. If used efficiently, large blocks of time can be used to make classes student friendly and exciting learning centers for active learners.

CASE IN POINT

The attendance policy in the school district where Tom served as principal denied credit to students for a course in which they had missed 20 days of classes per year. After changing to the alternating day (A-B) block schedule, policymakers had to adjust those numbers because students only met half as many times as they met on a traditional schedule of 55 minutes per day. The policy was changed to reflect a denial of credit after missing 10 days in a class. The situation would be very similar when moving to a semester schedule.

QUESTION: *Is block scheduling beneficial to both the college-bound and the vocational/technical student?*

RESPONSE: A block schedule provides long blocks of time for vocational/technical classes and, at the same time, more course opportunities for all students. With a variety of teaching methods and more active participation, students of all types are more likely to stay focused on learning. Also, in a block schedule, teachers have fewer students each day and can provide more individual help. Many vocational/technical teachers have been using block scheduling for years.

QUESTION: *How does block scheduling affect the serious student taking difficult courses?*

RESPONSE: We assume the question refers to students who enroll in Advanced Placement, International Baccalaureate, and advanced course offerings. These students will be able to focus on fewer classes a day. Of course, this is true for all students. For those students who are more focused on AP and advanced or upper-level classes, it is important to balance their academic load. This will necessitate a more collaborative effort between parents, students, and guidance counselors in planning a student's four-year program and course sequence. It is not always advantageous for some students to take seven or eight AP courses in a year, because such a schedule could create an unnecessary stress situation for some students.

CASE IN POINT

A student had just returned from school after giving birth. As she was leaving school at the end of the first day, Tom had an opportunity to talk with her. When he asked her how things were, she immediately responded that she might have to drop out of school because she needed to work. Financially, she could not afford to have someone babysit. Since she was the sole source of income, she needed to work more than she needed to come to school. He asked her to meet with him the next day.

Tom and the student met with her guidance counselor the next day, evaluated her situation, and discovered that she needed only two classes to graduate. Because of the flexibility of the alternating day (A-B) schedule, she was able to take two classes on alternating days and be out of school by 12:15 p.m. each day that she attended. This meant that she was available to work each afternoon on the days that she attended school, and five out of every ten days she was available to work a full day.

For those critics who would suggest that she was only in school every other day, and therrefore wasn't a full-time student, we simply respond by pointing out her options: Take two courses and graduate, which she did; or drop out of school, which she didn't. The schedule should be designed to meet the needs of the students, not those of the perimeter players.

We would also need to ask these questions: Is there an advantage in allowing students to take eight classes over the course of a school year? If the opportunity is there, do students take advantage of this opportunity?

According to some of the research in Canada and the feedback that we have received from schools that have been on the semester plan for two or more years, students in the last two years of school are not taking advantage of the eight-period day to take more classes. Based on the studies of semester schedules in Canada, students average five classes per year during their high school careers (King et al, 1978).

QUESTION: *How does block scheduling impact a student-athlete's eligibility?*

RESPONSE: Student-athletes must meet eligibility requirements. Meeting these requirements sometimes calls for a revision that can occur only with the cooperation of the athletics governing agency and the school. If a school is using an alternating day schedule, this is not an issue. If a school chooses a semester type of block schedule, then there are differences that must be settled.

Both Virginia and North Carolina agencies that govern athletic competition revised their policies to accommodate athletes in schools that changed to a semester schedule. Sometimes a problem with athletic eligibility is created when a student transfers from a semester school to a school with a traditional schedule or an alternating day (A-B) schedule.

QUESTION: *Are there any yearlong classes?*

RESPONSE: In the alternating day schedule, block 3 is a yearlong block that meets every day. If a school uses the alternating (A-B) schedule, most of the classes are yearlong courses. There are some schools that are using a combination of schedules that allow some semester course offerings as well as some yearlong courses. More and more schools that are implementing block scheduling are offering a combination of semester and year-long courses.

QUESTION: *What is the role of parents in the block schedule?*

RESPONSE: If a school uses a participatory process from the beginning of the restructuring process, parents are major players. They will continue to be a part of the restructuring process, and they will be valuable allies as administrators deal with the many issues that will need to be addressed as the block scheduling concept matures. Parents can serve as barometers of the restructuring process.

QUESTION: *How does the block schedule affect the coordination of audio/visual equipment and other instructional aids that are limited in numbers? The use of the library or media center?*

RESPONSE: Tom observed an increase in the use of audio/visual equipment as well as an increase in the use of the library. This is what Atlee's study team had anticipated, and they were excited that it was occurring.

The increased demand for instructional materials required a reorganization of procedures for the use of this equipment. A collaborative effort between the instructional staff and the library staff provided a system that was implemented to help meet the demands for instructional equipment, the use of the library, and computer labs. This system depends on the amount of equipment a school has, the seating capacity of the library, and the number of computer labs or the electronic configuration of a school.

The plan could call for the library center to consign equipment to instructional pods or departments for assignment. If allowed, an action team could develop alternatives to the traditional "check-out" method, which equates to exciting learning and teaching opportunities for students and teachers.

QUESTION: *How does the block schedule affect the tardy policy?*

RESPONSE: First, because of the decrease in the number of times a class changes, it is safe to assume that there will be a decrease in the number of tardies reported. Second, as is the case with absenteeism, any policy regarding tardies must take into account that a block schedule class is equivalent to two traditional classes.

One strategy that encouraged students to be in class on time, regardless of the schedule configuration, was to begin class with an instructional activity that required students' active involvement, such as a pop quiz. Remember that any delay in getting class started or any unnecessary interruptions are non-value-added time.

Since many schools experience a degree of frustration with tardiness to class, we recommend that an action team be assembled to deal with this particular situation. We discovered that involving students in the problem-solving process provided successful strategies for decreasing tardies as well as absenteeism. Since change is occurring, this would be an opportunity to change other policies to provide additional advantages for instruction and learning.

QUESTION: *How does the block schedule affect assistance for teachers having trouble with the transition from teaching in a 55-minute block to a 90-plus-minute block?*

RESPONSE: At Atlee, it was assumed that some teachers would experience difficulties in the transition process. There are certain safety nets that can be put in place to provide a support system for teachers who are experiencing difficulties. First, the concept of teacher as facilitator was infused throughout staff development opportunities to provide different teaching strategies to all staff before implementing the block schedule.

CASE IN POINT

The policy established by the Virginia High School League, the governing agency that determines eligibility for athletes enrolled in Virginia high schools, states that a student must pass five subjects to be eligible to participate in sports in schools that are in competition with other member schools. When high schools in Virginia began implementing the semester schedule, the Virginia High School League adapted the academic requirements to accommodate the students who were in a semester situation. It was revised to read that students in a semester school would be required to pass three classes out of a possible four that students might elect to take.

The problem: A student who is taking three classes and is enrolled in a semester school transfers to a non-semester school in January of the school year. Since the student is now enrolled in a school that is on an alternating day schedule or traditional schedule and the first semester is coming to a close, where is the student placed? S/he has almost completed three courses in which s/he is enrolled and has no background that would support success in two new courses at this time. Which eligibility rule applies?

Next, a teacher support program was put in place. This type of program includes assigning teacher partners. We assigned teachers who felt comfortable with teaching in longer periods of time with teachers who were apprehensive about success in longer blocks of time. Department chairs identified those who needed assistance and prescribed helpful resources, and identified other teachers with experience in specific areas who were available to provide assistance.

QUESTION: *Is there a need for additional supervision during breaks?*

RESPONSE: The need for supervision depends on the type of schedule that a school implements. If a school has implemented an alternating day block schedule, and the class change time is limited to time needed to safely move from one class to the next, there is no need for increased supervision. There should be less need for supervision because of the fewer number of class changes.

If additional breaks are given to students or existing breaks are extended, additional personnel to provide supervision may be needed. To answer this question for a specific school, information regarding the size of the school and the number and length of breaks would need to be taken into consideration. Remember, when considering breaks, one of the goals for implementing the block schedule should be to increase value-added time for instructional purposes.

QUESTION: *Is there a need for a "trial" block schedule the year before implementing the block schedule on a permanent basis?*

RESPONSE: There have been reported incidents of "trial" scheduling on a modified basis. Our recommendation is to implement the block schedule in full. If you implement the schedule on a two-day a week, a six-week period, a semester or another form of an experimental schedule, a school community does not experience the total impact of block scheduling. This will provide the opponents of block scheduling an opportunity to select the non-essential components of the schedule as reasons for not implementing on a permanent basis.

We are aware of schools that tried a six-week mock schedule and some schools that tried a two-day-a-week "trial" schedule and never implemented it on a permanent basis because some members of the school community who had not been provided adequate information about the block schedule had negative perceptions.

CASE IN POINT

Approximately six weeks into the first year of implementing the block schedule, the chairman of the Atlee math instructional team identified a number of math teachers who were experiencing difficulties due to the longer blocks of time. After a meeting to discuss the problem, all members of the math instructional team agreed to the following plan.

Teachers were paired and assigned responsibilities for the remainder of the school term, subject to revision if initial assignments and pairings did not match the skills and personalities of the participants. These responsibilities included gathering instructional materials as well as creative strategies used in teaching mathematics specific to their assigned content area (such as algebra, geometry, trigonometry, calculus, as well as other math-related areas). This plan also included meeting on a weekly basis during lunch to share information and lesson plans.

This resulted in more than just sharing materials. The math team became a cohesive unit of instructional personnel, and many innovative teaching strategies and techniques came from this group of dedicated teachers. They were convinced that there was not a problem related to instruction in the block schedule for which they could not find an answer. Needless to say, their actions made the responsibilities of the school administrator a lot easier.

Bottom line: Student expectations increased, math below the Algebra I level was not offered, more students enrolled in upper-level math courses, and student achievement increased as measured by an increase on standardized test scores.

Remember, change is difficult, and it takes time to realize its benefits. You will not benefit from a change to block scheduling in six weeks, a semester, or a year. There must be a commitment to long-term change. To implement a change that is as major as restructuring the allocated instructional time of a school day, the change agents need to be totally committed.

QUESTION: *If we choose a block schedule that has an extended study block included in the schedule, is student attendance required during these study blocks?*

RESPONSE: Again, we must remember that one of the goals for implementing a block schedule is to **increase** the effective use of **value-added** time. In our opinion, all students should be required to attend these study blocks and take advantage of the many instructional opportunities that are available. These blocks can be used for research, individual tutoring with teachers, re-testing, and make-up work for students, as well as for teacher meetings to plan and discuss instructional strategies. Staff development opportunities could also be made available for teachers during this block. These blocks will also provide additional time to contact parents on a more frequent basis. All of these activities lead to value-added time and a higher level of student achievement.

QUESTION: *Do instructional leaders, such as department chairmen, have release time to provide leadership?*

RESPONSE: If at all possible, instructional leaders should have release time to provide assistance to teachers and administrators in planning and training. Providing release time for teacher instructional leaders was one of the most important decisions that we made when implementing the block schedule. Teacher instructional leaders were vital in the success that we enjoyed with block scheduling.

If there are problems in providing release time, administrators must look at innovative ways to create release time. The problem that occurs most often is a shortage of personnel. In many instances, schools do not have personnel to provide this form of leadership. Action teams can come up with many creative ways to provide release time for instructional leaders.

QUESTION: *Does block scheduling have long-range implications on any school restructuring factors other than use of instructional time?*

RESPONSE: Tom recently had a conversation with an architect who was designing a new secondary school for a large urban school district. He had encountered the term "block scheduling" in his first planning meeting with the school planning team. His question to Tom was how to make a school "block schedule friendly." They discussed his concerns for some time, and by the conclusion of the discussion, he had decided that there were several ways that classrooms and excess space could be altered to meet the needs of both students and faculty who were learning and teaching in large blocks of time.

Tom receives frequent inquiries from division superintendents about potential candidates for secondary school principalships. One of the questions often asked is, "Does s/he know anything about block scheduling?" Yes, block scheduling is impacting more components of the school community than just the way time is used. Block scheduling is a process for breaking old paradigms.

CASE IN POINT

During the first year of implementing the block schedule at Atlee High School, we were able to provide release time for instructional team leaders. When we were making teacher assignments for the second year, it was obvious, based on the number of students who were registering for classes, that enrollment in certain classes had increased. Students were staying in school and electing to take more classes.

The following question came from an instructional action team meeting: Since we were on an alternating day, would it be possible for administrators to teach a class? With four administrators, this would free up four instructional periods for teacher instructional leaders. Each administrator, including the principal, taught one class during that school year. One can only imagine what that did for the morale of the school community.

QUESTION: *What arrangements did you make for visitors who wanted to learn about block scheduling?*

RESPONSE: Over a period of three years, Atlee hosted many visitors from throughout the United States and foreign countries that were interested in observing first-hand a change in how we had restructured the allocated instructional time in our school. During the second and third years, requests were so numerous that we had to limit the number of days visitors were allowed because we perceived that the frequent disruptions had begun to interfere with instruction. We instituted a procedure that would provide the most efficient use of our day as well as the visitors' time. Unless there were special requests, we limited visits to two hours. These two hours were very structured and used efficiently.

The first 30 minutes of the visit, administration and guidance provided a general overview of the schedule and our rationale for selecting the type of schedule that we had chosen. We answered as many questions as possible during the allocated time. If visitors had questions that were unique to their school, we answered them individually before the visitors left or provided a written response that we forwarded to them at their school.

During the second 30 minutes, a teacher panel presented the block schedule from the teachers' perspective. They presented the strengths and the areas that needed improvement. There was also time for questions to the teachers.

The beginning of the second hour, a student panel presented the students' views of the block schedule. This panel was composed of a diverse group that included students who were enrolled in AP classes, students who had learning disabilities, students who participated in extra-curricular as well as co-curricular activities, and students who were enrolled in co-op and vocational education programs. A member of the faculty or administrative team was always present with students during their presentation and the question-and-answer period.

The last 30 minutes of the visit was scheduled around one of the lunch blocks, and visitors were offered the opportunity to have lunch with students, faculty, or administration. They were encouraged to ask questions and visit classrooms that had been pre-selected with the cooperation of the teachers.

Visitors always wanted to return to their school with a packet of information. We included in this packet the following materials:

- Decision-making process

- Master schedule

- Implementation strategies

- Staff development opportunities

- Comparative data of before and after and each year's measurements of our goals

- Sample lesson plans

CASE IN POINT

During a student question-answer session, students were discussing the advantages of block scheduling. A visiting teacher interrupted a student panel member who was giving his opinions about block scheduling. Her question was preceded by the following comment: "All of you students appear to be above-average students and are taking advanced courses. What happens to students who are below average, or might have learning disabilities and are in a 'slower track'?"

Since our school was as heterogeneously grouped as a school with a diverse population can be, the students looked at each other then at Tom to respond. After he explained that Atlee did not "group" according to the teacher's definition and that any student in school had a number of options that s/he could choose from the school's course of study, a student with a learning disability shared his experiences with the group. He shared with them that he was identified as learning disabled, but because classes were longer, he was able to take many regular classes such as Spanish III and advanced math courses because he could receive a great deal of individual help. Another student in the group explained that she was in a co-op program and worked for her only source of income every afternoon.

Leave it to the students to come up with the appropriate response.

- List of faculty members that were willing to continue distance dialogue

- Student planning book and calendar

COLLECTING DATA VIA SURVEYS

If a school's study committee cannot make a site visit to a school that has implemented a block schedule, another strategy for gathering information is the use of surveys. Collecting data can range from a very formal research design to an informal design that addresses the issues that are important only to the members of your study team.

If the study committee decides to use the survey method as an alternative or as a part of the data collection in preparation for selecting a block scheduling model, there are two choices that we recommend in selecting surveys to be used. One choice is to develop a survey that meets the particular needs of a school. The second choice is to use a survey that has been previously developed by other schools.

The accompanying CD provides a sample survey/questionnaire which might be considered if this method is chosen. The survey would begin with a cover letter to the building administrator explaining the purpose of the survey. When developing the survey(s), it is very important to remember that the demographic match with your school is critical in the decision-making process.

Examples of appropriate surveys are also included on the accompanying CD. They will indicate only some of the questions that need to be answered before making an informed decision regarding block scheduling. There are many other concerns unique to each administrator and to each situation that need to be addressed. Additional questions can be formulated to gather needed information to assist in making an informed decision on block scheduling.

LOOKING BACK . . .

Pre-determining strategies for implementing block scheduling are critical to the success of the process. An active school study team will take advantage of the many opportunities to involve all customers in

CASE IN POINT

One of the first schools to use semester block scheduling in the Southeastern United States was a large rural school of approximately 2,000 students. The school has used the block schedule since the fall of 1992, and by all reports the schedule is considered a success.

School administrators from across the United States visited the school and proceeded to implement the semester block model. Many of these schools have successfully used this model, and students continue to reap the benefits. However, there were schools that were just as large but with quite different demographically—for instance, urban/suburban versus rural—that visited the school and implemented the model. As a result, many problems have occurred because the semester was not a good match for certain schools, and some have abandoned the semester block but have successfully implemented other models of the block schedule. More and more urban/suburban schools are using some form of the alternating day (A-B) block schedule because it meets their needs and is supportive of their student population.

restructuring how time is used for instructional purposes during the school day. They will seek many strategies that will ensure a smooth transition to a scheduling alternative that will match the specific needs of your school. Members of the team will assist the administrator as s/he leads the change process. The study team will seek opportunities for networking with other schools, individuals, and other study teams that have been or currently are involved in the restructuring process. Data gathered by the team should be pertinent to the mission of the school and should be gathered from as many resources as possible. This strategy will provide a great deal of information from diverse experiences, which will be most helpful when providing feedback/information to a diverse school community. ❏

Chapter 6 Appendix on CD

❑ Surveys to assist in adoption decision
- Cover Letter to Principal (word version)
- Information-gathering Surveys
  - Administrator Survey (word version)
  - Descriptive Survey (word version)

What Organizational Issues Must Be Addressed?

*N*ever tell people how to do things. Tell them what to do, and they will surprise you with their ingenuity.

—General George Patton

LOOKING AHEAD IN THIS CHAPTER . . .

Perhaps the most critical decision in the reform process is to determine the block schedule format that will be implemented. If the schedule selected does not match the needs of the school community, successful implementation is improbable. If issues surrounding the selected schedule are not appropriately addressed, it is likely that the change process will be delayed and possibly halted altogether. Issues critical to the process that will be addressed in this chapter include:

• Maximizing the time allotted during the instructional day for learning and teaching

• Using allotted instructional time for student learning

• Identifying and selecting appropriate curricula that will match the selected schedule format

• Ensuring that the schedule and related issues do not have a negative impact on the school climate.

Other organizational issues that will be considered include budgetary issues and the selection of a schedule based on the school's mission and goals for restructuring the school day. This chapter includes a variety of actual samples of school schedules that are currently in operation throughout the United States. *(See the accompanying CD for more samples and measurements of success.)*

Selecting a block schedule format provides administrators with the opportunity to move beyond the traditional scheduling paradigm and consider different schedules that allow curriculum to become the major driver of the instructional schedule, rather than physical facilities or other non-instructional issues. Scheduling becomes a problem-solving tool that allows administrators to schedule time, human resources, and physical facilities more efficiently.

ORGANIZATIONAL ISSUES

As we have already mentioned, the creation of action teams is an important part of the planning process for block scheduling. Perhaps the next action team to be identified is one that will focus on organizational issues. The focus of this team should be limited to issues that are related to the process of identifying a schedule. These issues include: (1) designing a grassroots initiative and reviewing actual scheduling possibilities; (2) strategies for identifying and implementing the block schedule; (3) length of the school day; (4) length of each block period; (5) number and quality of course offerings; and (6) the impact of block scheduling on school climate. Recommendations to the administration from the study team regarding these issues will vary depending on the mission/goals of any given school.

CASE IN POINT

An instructional leader in a school district that had an interest in implementing a block schedule shared the following information with Tom. Several schools in his district had implemented different block scheduling formats. He had been exploring the semester block but found that each time he attempted to discuss the issue with his staff, he was given different reasons or excuses why the semester block wouldn't work. The most frequent concern raised was the issue of transfer students and the number of students enrolled in Advanced Placement classes.

Tom's first question to him after he shared this information was, "What percentage of transfer students do you have each school year?" His response: "Approximately 18 percent."

The reason for the resistance was clear. The demographics of the schools in his area were totally different than in the rural schools he had visited. His schools served a military base, which accounted for the high percentage of transfer students. What could the instructional leader implement instead of a semester schedule? The schools in his district are now in the third year of the alternating day (A-B) schedule—a block schedule with less impact on transfer students—and he has reported that the schools have been very successful in meeting measurable goals.

It is critical that the study team consider **all** strategies for collecting data and use **all** available information in order to make the most appropriate schedule match for the school. If the principal and action team are not confident that they know how to collect or analyze data, we suggest three courses of action. The team can ask for a quick course in Total Quality training that will introduce them to the tools of data management and analysis. A second path is to call upon an experienced administrator who is strong in the use of data. S/he can guide the team as it proceeds to gather information and make sense of it. A third solution is to just delve in and learn together as a team. Make a list of the data available in your school (e.g.: assessment results, SAT scores, attendance rates, discipline referrals, and freshmen grades) and assign people to collect it. Also make a list of information needed that the team can solicit through surveys or interviews as well as data that can be provided by the district office. The study team must be informed and prepared to do the tasks we discuss in this chapter, which will impact the success of block schedule implementation.

REVIEW AND STUDY THE SCHEDULE OPTIONS

After the planning action teams have exhausted all avenues of collecting information to assist in making an informed decision, the study team begins the review process of analyzing all the data. When analyzing the findings, the team should consider issues that have previously been identified as critical to the implementation process. These issues should be investigated thoroughly by the study team before recommendations are made to the building-level administrator or his/her designee.

Identified issues that are critical to the success of the implementation include:

- *Number of transfer students.* Does the school have a plan for dealing with transfer students, especially in highly mobile localities?

- *Number of students enrolled in Advanced Placement classes.* Has the school provided a learning schedule that will encourage participation in AP courses and will support, not hinder, good performance on the spring AP exam?

- *Funding considerations when moving from a six- or seven-single period day to a seven- or eight-block schedule.* There may be a need for additional staff, instructional materials, and classroom space to provide teaching areas for additional course offerings because of additional classes offered to students. This could affect either the alternating day (A-B) or semester block schedule.

- *Need for staff development opportunities.* Has the school team recognized that the staff will need development activities in the months before and during the implementation of block scheduling? Is staff development recognized as an ongoing need that requires adequate planning and adequate resources?

- *Professional maturity of staff and any additional staff development needed to bring the staff to a maturity level required for a successful change.* A good source for additional information on this topic is John Goodlad's book, *A Place Called School*. Additionally, Ken Blanchard's situational leadership model may be helpful to principals whose teachers reflect different levels of professional maturity. Michael Fullan's work is also helpful in understanding change in schools.

- *Economic and social demographics.* The school will reflect the dynamics of demographics and how they are perceived and reflected by faculty.

- *Number of lunch blocks needed to meet the needs of the highest number of students who use the food services in a given day.* This would be based on available physical facilities and requires cooperation with your food services staff.

• *Political and community concerns with the potential to interrupt the successful change process.* What is important to your school community? And how has the planning team communicated the intent of change in relation to the community's identified needs?

• *Music offerings. This issue has the potential of completely halting the scheduling reform process.* Generally the music/performing arts program in a school district has high visibility. Parents of students who participate in these programs are very active, vocal, and well organized. We have had parents of students enrolled in these programs from California to New Hampshire and in between call and email us for feedback on the issue of block scheduling and performing arts. Generally, they are looking for information that will help them stop the process of change, since they believe a new schedule will negatively impact participation in band, orchestra, or chorus.

• *Foreign language offerings.* Does the schedule enhance the opportunity to develop a strong foundation in introductory foreign language courses? Are courses offered at the optimum time to continue learning the language? Does the block schedule imitate immersion?

• *Other considerations unique to a particular school community.* Transportation in rural communities drives many decisions. Transfer students in inner-city schools and curriculum issues in suburban schools cannot be ignored when considering changes in course offerings. Are there important school-related issues that your community cannot ignore when restructuring issues arise?

INVESTIGATE BUDGETARY CONSIDERATIONS

Budgetary items for consideration will depend on the type of schedule that a school chooses to implement. Based on our work with block scheduling, we project that moving from a six- or seven-period day schedule to a 4x4 format will increase the personnel budget approximately 6 to 11 percent. If you move from a five-period day to a six- or seven-period A-B block, there may be a need for additional funding.

Perhaps the major increase of funding will be the impact of teacher training. There should be an increase in allocated funds for teacher training, if moving to block scheduling. As we have stated throughout this book, teaching in a 90- to 110-minute block of time is quite different from teaching in a 45- to 55-minute block of time. It is important to align curriculum; develop materials to support teacher success; conduct workshops on developing teaching strategies and pacing guides; and provide in-service training, tuition assistance, and external consultants to assist teachers in preparing for the change. Consideration should be given to:

• Staff for additional course offerings

• Food services, if the new schedule impacts the number of students served and a possible change in demographics of service area

• Resource rooms for students transferring from non-block schools

- Additional instructional supplies needed to assist teachers in using various instructional techniques, i.e.: computers, software programs, graphing calculators, scientific probes

- Funds for additional staff development or a re-direction of current staff development funds to provide training that will ensure the success of the schedule

- Textbooks for additional course offerings

- The appropriation of funds, since additional funds may be needed beyond the first year of the schedule implementation (Many schools have implemented pieces of the funding allocations over a period of time.)

CONSIDER THE FUTURE FINANCIAL IMPACT

The long-range plan for implementing and evaluating block scheduling should be given careful consideration when planning for future budgets. Planners should consider the following questions:

- When students are offered the opportunity to take more classes, will they chose to do so?

- Will this increase the number of students taking elective courses, which will create a need for additional staff, and subsequently, an unanticipated increase in budget requirements?

If this could happen in a school district, then additional funding is necessary and should be factored into planning future budgets.

ESTABLISH THE GOALS OF A RESTRUCTURED DAY

When selecting the schedule that best matches your school's needs, the goals for restructuring your school should be given careful consideration. These goals should be developed by the stakeholders involved, such as the school improvement team or the school planning team.

What are the goals for restructuring the school schedule? And will these goals provide opportunities for measurable student success? Examples of appropriate measurable goals might include:

- To provide maximum educational opportunities for students in an environment that is conducive

---

CASE IN POINT

A school that wanted to implement a 4x4 block schedule recognized up front that the impact of the overall school budget would be a major concern. Since in any school, personnel accounts for the major portion of the budget, staffing the school was a major concern.

A prototype schedule was designed to determine the financial impact of the schedule on the budget. As a result of their trial run, they found the impact to be minimal. They conducted an audit of all course offerings and recommended that classes in which few students enrolled be eliminated and staff be used for other teaching assignments in the school. Thus, the cost increase was minimal.

The staff recommended the following teacher training budget to the school board for consideration: $6,000 for workshops/in-service training, including designing pacing guides and sample lesson plans; $3,000 for tuition assistance for conferences and graduate classes related to block scheduling issues.

Based on their proposal, the budget included an increase of $3,000. Other issues—such as increased cost for new textbooks, phased in over a period of two years—could actually be a savings. Of course, the size of the school, the staff, the stated objectives for block scheduling, and the textbook purchasing philosophy drive the budget. Cost is relevant to the amount of funds a school has available for training.

"When a man sits with a pretty girl for an hour, it seems like a minute. But let him sit on a hot stove for a minute, and it's longer than any hour. That's relativity." —*Albert Einstein*

---

to learning, as measured by sub-scores on school climate surveys.

- To increase student performance, as measured by scores on standardized test, grades, number of students receiving academic recognition, academic scholarships, academic monograms (letters), certain scores on Advanced Placement courses, recognition in National Merit

Scholarship programs, number of students enrolled in International Baccalaureate programs, etc. The indicators for success should be designed to meet the needs of a particular school.

- To offer more quality course selections, as measured by the additions to the school course of studies and the number of students enrolled in new course offerings.

- To improve student and faculty attendance, as measured by actual monthly/yearly attendance.

- To develop positive relationships among faculty and students, as measured by a sub-scale on schoolwide climate surveys.

- To reduce student discipline problems, as measured by the actual number of discipline referrals to administrative offices.

- To provide for applications of knowledge with an emphasis on active student participation, with success measured by teacher observation and student achievement on teacher-constructed tests and standardized test scores.

- To foster interdisciplinary teaching/learning, as measured by the increase in the number of interdisciplinary course offerings and students enrolled in these courses.

- To provide for flexible time formats to meet instructional needs of students, as measured by the number of dropouts, student attendance, and student success in class.

- To encourage better time management by faculty and students, as measured by the efficient use of time that includes maintaining time schedules, pacing courses, arranging time for homework, reducing tardies to school and to classes while keeping pace with a demanding course of study.

- And other measurable objectives that have been recommended or established by the study team or other stakeholders.

ESTABLISH STRATEGIES TO MEET NEW OBJECTIVES

Strategies that will be used to meet stated objectives should be considered before a final decision is made regarding the schedule that will be implemented. After all the objectives have been identified, the following questions should be answered:

- Is there a need to change the current schedule? To answer this question, you must perform a

---

CASE IN POINT

As schools move from a traditional 6- or 7-period day to an 8-period block, students are provided opportunities to increase the number of credits they earn before graduation. Earning additional credits provides students opportunities to graduate early and perhaps to leave school early each day because they can earn the number of credits needed for graduation by taking fewer courses per day. Many students are taking advantage of these opportunities, especially leaving school early each day. Because of this practice, some local school boards are concerned about the number of students who leave school early and do not take advantage of the opportunities to take additional courses. Consequently, they are putting strategies in place that require students to take more courses; i.e.: increasing the number of units for graduation or requiring students to take seven or eight courses per year.

Actions such as these must be anticipated when considering initial funding for block scheduling. They will impact the long-term success of student achievement in schools using a block schedule format where additional staff may be necessary to meet the demands of students taking additional required courses.

An innovative school district changed to the semester schedule in 1993, and students and teachers have experienced much success with the schedule. In the spring of 1996, the local school board voted to require all students to take eight credits per year. The only students who were allowed to leave school during the instructional day were those who were involved in work-based programs for which they were earning credit.

self-analysis. If you are thorough in your self-analysis, you may answer the second question.

• Are any of the identified objectives so controversial in nature that they might be viewed as inhibitors to change? If so, perhaps the objective should be eliminated or given consideration at a later stage of the process, after the schedule has met success in other areas.

• How are you planning to meet the stated objectives? Before you give your blessing to any objective, be sure that there are strategies planned that will ensure the success of the measurable goals as related to student achievement. **All change should be related to student achievement!**

If major issues must be addressed, such as additional funding or additional physical facilities, and the possibility of obtaining this type of support for restructuring is improbable, then consideration might be given to a different type of schedule. Do not force the implementation process. It is better to delay the implementation process for a year or two than never to have the opportunity to implement the schedule. Before a final decision is made, **all** issues must be addressed, regardless of the consequences. Trust the process that you have put in place.

Once major issues, such as budget implications, have been resolved and other unresolved issues are considered only minor, then a simple statement by the study team or the administrator in charge might be made to give assurance that there are no major barriers to meeting stated objectives. The following is an example of such a statement:

> We [our school] believe that we can accomplish our stated measurable objectives within the existing physical plant and without additional funding. Any funds available for the restructuring effort will be channeled into staff development and the purchase of instructional materials.

IDENTIFY AN ACTION TEAM TO COLLECT SAMPLE SCHEDULES

At this point in the process, an action team must be identified to gather what might be some of the most important data that will be used in determining the match for your school. The team should solicit samples of block schedules that are currently being used by other schools with demographics similar to those of your school. The primary responsibility of the action team is to collect sample schedules that might be considered as a model for your school. The following models are some of the "first wave" of schedules designed to meet time requirements for instruction in an efficient manner. There are as many ways of scheduling time for instruction as there are schools that need to reschedule time. Find a schedule that you can adapt or one that stimulates your thinking about more friendly instructional scheduling.

■ Sample block scheduling models

The following schedules are actually in use in schools throughout the United States and in some foreign countries. We have seen most of these schedules in action and have talked at length with the administrators who have implemented them. These are not the only models available, but we are confident that these schedules will work. These schedules were chosen because the school leaders utilized the process we have suggested: Establishing measurable goals, utilizing all available information, and learning from other schools.

THE ALTEE MODEL—SEVEN-CREDIT ALTERNATING DAY

In 1990, the planning team for Atlee High School's scheduling reform gave serious consideration to the following models:

- The Copernican Model—Two large blocks of time each day for 60 days and a singleton of approximately 60 minutes per day that would be embedded throughout the year for a total of seven courses per year for a total of 180 days. The singleton was put into the mix because of the political reality that students in our school district already had an opportunity to earn seven Carnegie units per year.

- Semestering (as used in certain Canadian provinces) or the 4x4 model (four courses per day for one semester or 90 days for a total of eight courses per year for a total of 180 days).

- The Trimester Model—Two 75-day sessions with a 30-day intersession that could be scheduled at the beginning of the school term, at the end of the school term, or at the end of the first 75 days of the school term.

After analyzing all the data, providing options to our customers, and listening to their concerns, we chose to implement the alternating day (A-B) schedule in the fall of 1991.

Implementation and revision

The first model was designed by the stakeholders in the school where Tom served as principal. The original model was a four-block alternating day schedule that met on the alternating days for four days a week. On Friday all classes met for a shorter length of time. This schedule was followed for only one semester (90 days) and was popular among many students and some faculty. Based on data and evaluations at the end of the semester, teachers perceived that Fridays were very disruptive when all classes met for approximately 50 minutes followed by an activity period. One veteran teacher told me: "We just don't have time to get anything done." Of course, the students had another perspective. "Fridays are fun. We don't have time to do anything

other than take a test, and then class is over." It appeared that all teachers were testing on Friday, and therefore all students were taking tests in each of their classes on the same day.

At the end of the first semester, Tom and his staff included Fridays in the alternating day scheme, and eight years later Atlee still uses the alternating day block schedule scheme.

Seven-credit alternating day (A-B) with all classes meeting on Friday (See Figures 8, 9, 10, and 11.)

Pros and cons for meeting all classes on Friday

- The Friday schedule was the traditional 50-minute format, and it was a schedule that both students and faculty were familiar with in the midst of a major reform process. It brought some measure of stability to the process.

- Because all classes met on Friday, teachers and students felt that this was a time to review, bring closure to the week's work, and prepare for the following week.

- Classes met for the traditional 50 minutes. Teachers expressed concerns about not having time to use instructional strategies similar to those used in the longer block of time.

- The majority of teachers were giving tests on Friday. This resulted in many students taking tests in each of their classes on the same day.

- Students perceived that Friday was a non-instructional day. As one student explained: "Not much happening. Not enough time to get much done. Just test and then rest."

Considerations in scheduling students in the seven-credit alternating day (A-B) schedule (See Figure 12.)

■ Students are scheduled for lunch either block IIa or IIb. They are not scheduled for both lunch blocks. Their assignment to lunch block usually

(Continued on page 110)

FIGURE 8
Sample Bell Schedules for Alternating Day (A-B) Block with All Classes Meeting on Friday

Monday–Thursday Bell Schedule

TIME	BLOCK	MINUTES
7:30–8:25	Early Morning	55—Each Day
8:30–10:30	Block I: Announcements, Etc.*	120—Alternating Days
10:34–12:15	Block II	101—Alternating Days
12:15–12:45	Lunch Block I	30—Each Day
12:20–1:15	Block III A	55—Each Day
1:15–1:45	Lunch Block II	30—Each Day
12:50–1:45	Block III B	55—Each Day
1:50–3:30	Block IV	100—Alternating Days
3:45–5:45	Extended Day Block**	120—Each Day: Structured Tutoring, Make-Up Work, Etc. Detention, Etc.

*Block I was extended for morning announcements and homeroom activities.
**The extended block is used for a variety of instructional activities as well as for "after-school detention," etc.

Friday Bell Schedule

TIME	BLOCK	MINUTES
7:30–8:20	Early Morning	50
8:25–9:15	Block I	50
9:20–10:10	Block II	50
10:15–11:05	Block III	50
11:10–12:00	Block IV A	50
11:10–11:40	Lunch Block I	30
11:45–12:35	Block IV B	50
12:05–12:35	Lunch Block II	30
12:35–1:25	Block V	50
1:30–2:20	Block VI	50
2:25–3:30	Block VII*	55

*Block VII meets for an additional five minutes. This provides an opportunity for schoolwide announcements.

FIGURE 9
Sample Student Schedule for Alternating Day (A-B) Block with All Classes Meeting on Friday

BLOCK	MONDAY	TUESDAY	WEDNESDAY	THURSDAY	FRIDAY
I	Music	Algebra	Music	Algebra	Music
II	Science	History	Science	History	Science
III a	French	French	French	French	French
III b	**Lunch**	**Lunch**	**Lunch**	**Lunch**	**Lunch**
IV	English	Accounting	English	Accounting	English
V	XXX	XXX	XXX	XXX	Algebra
VI	XXX	XXX	XXX	XXX	History
VII	XXX	XXX	XXX	XXX	Accounting

Student follows the same schedule for each week of the school year.

FIGURE 10
Sample Teacher Schedule for Alternating Day Seven-Credit (A-B) Schedule with All Classes Meeting on Friday

BLOCK	MONDAY	TUESDAY	WEDNESDAY	THURSDAY	FRIDAY
I	English 10	English 9	English 10	English 9	English 10
II	Planning	English 9	Planning	English 9	Planning
III	English 9	English 9	English 9	English 9	English 9
IV	English 10	Duty/Plan	English 10	Duty/Plan	English 10
V	XXX	XXX	XXX	XXX	English 9
VI	XXX	XXX	XXX	XXX	English 9
VII	XXX	XXX	XXX	XXX	Duty/Plan

Teachers have same schedule each week throughout the school year.

FIGURE 11
Seven-Credit Alternating Day (A-B) With a Singleton

Sample Bell Schedule Monday–Thursday

TIME	BLOCK	MINUTES
7:30–8:25	Early Morning	55—Each Day
8:30–10:30	Block I: Announcements, Etc.*	120—Alternating Days
10:34–12:15	Block II	101—Alternating Days
12:15–12:45	Lunch Block I	30—Each Day
12:20–1:15	Block III A	55—Each Day
1:15–1:45	Lunch Block II	30—Each Day
12:50–1:45	Block III B	55—Each Day
1:50–3:30	Block IV	100—Alternating Days
3:45–5:45	Extended Day Block**	120—Each Day: Structured Tutoring, Make-Up Work, Etc.; Detention, Etc.

*Block I is extended for morning announcements and homeroom activities.
**Extended day block is optional and can be used to address many issues that administrators and teachers must deal with on a daily basis.

Friday (Including an activities period)

TIME	BLOCK	MINUTES
7:30–8:25	Early Morning	55
8:30–10:20	Block I	110
10:25–11:56	Block II	91
11:56–12:26	Lunch Block I	30
12:01–12:52	Block III A	51
12:52–1:22	Lunch Block II	30
12:31–1:22	Block III B	51
1:27–1:55	Activities*	28
2:00–3:30	Block IV	90

*When the activity period is used for pep rallies or assemblies at the end of the day, students report to block IV at 1:27 p.m. Students will then be released at 2:55 p.m. to attend these activities that are scheduled to include the entire student body.

FIGURE 12
Seven-Credit Alternating Day (A-B) With a Singleton

Sample Student Schedule—A Week

BLOCK	MONDAY	TUESDAY	WEDNESDAY	THURSDAY	FRIDAY
I	Music	Algebra	Music	Algebra	Music
II	Science	History	Science	History	Science
III a	Lunch	Lunch	Lunch	Lunch	Lunch
III b	French	French	French	French	French
IV	English	Accounting	English	Accounting	English

Students will reverse schedules during the next week, which is B week. Courses taken on Monday, Wednesday, and Friday during A week will be taken on Tuesday and Thursday; courses taken on Tuesday and Thursday of A week will be taken on Monday, Wednesday, and Friday.

Sample Student Schedule—B Week

BLOCK	MONDAY	TUESDAY	WEDNESDAY	THURSDAY	FRIDAY
I	Algebra	Music	Algebra	Music	Algebra
II	History	Science	History	Science	History
II a	Lunch	Lunch	Lunch	Lunch	Lunch
III	French	French	French	French	French
II b	Lunch	Lunch	Lunch	Lunch	Lunch
IV	Accounting	English	Accounting	English	Accounting

depends on balancing the number of students in any given lunch block based on the physical facilities available for lunch. Once students have been assigned a lunch block, they will have the same lunch block for the entire school year, unless the circumstances dictate a change in a particular student's schedule.

■ Blocks I, II, and IV meet every other day for an extended period of time that averages approximately 1:47 minutes.

■ Block III meets daily for 55 minutes.

■ An activity period is scheduled for approximately 30 minutes each Friday. Time is deducted from each block to accommodate this special block of time. Activities and co-curricular activities such as make-up tests, tutoring, clubs, assemblies, pep rallies, school pictures, school ring sales, etc., are conducted before and after school and during this block. This block can be coupled with lunch to enhance the efficiency factor involving the use of time.

■ Two lunch blocks scheduled around block III are approximately 30 minutes each.

■ Teachers who do not have other duty assignments (i.e.: activity sponsor) are assigned to those classes attended by students who are not involved in planned activities during the activity block. These periods provide opportunities for students not involved in activities to receive counseling and tutoring, as well as time for make-up work.

- By enrolling in the 0 period (early-morning classes) and taking seven periods during the regular school schedule, a student can earn up to eight credits per year.

Considerations in scheduling teachers in the seven-credit alternating day (A-B) schedule (See figure 13.)

- Each teacher is scheduled for a total of five classes per year.

- There is a combination of schedules to which teachers are assigned. Some teachers will teach three classes on one day and two classes on alternating days. Some teachers choose to teach four classes one day and only one on alternating days.

- During a two-day cycle, it is possible for teachers to have a total of 160 minutes of planning time.

- Student instructional time is increased when using this schedule because of a more efficient use of allocated instructional time.

Variations of the seven-credit alternating block schedule

The schedule in Figure 14 is a slightly different approach to the alternating day (A-B) block scheme. It was implemented at Lee Davis High School and Patrick Henry High School (Hanover County, VA) in 1992, a year after Atlee implemented the alternating day (A-B) schedule. These two high schools are located in the same district as Atlee High School and are still using the schedule they implemented. Components of the alternating (A-B) schedule with a study block include using the study block for:

- student remediation

- student acceleration

- additional student choices for accountability for their own learning

- specified time for non-curriculum related events which historically detract from instructional time, such as school pictures, pep rallies, etc.

FIGURE 13
Sample Teacher Schedule: A Week—Seven-Credit Alternating Day (A-B)

BLOCK	MONDAY	TUESDAY	WEDNESDAY	THURSDAY	FRIDAY
I	English 10	English 9	English 10	English 9	English 10
II	Plan	English 9	Plan	English 9	Plan
III	English 9	English 9	English 9	English 9	English 9
IV	English 10	Duty/Plan	English 10	Duty/Plan	English 10

Sample Teacher Schedule: B Week—Seven-Credit Alternating Day (A-B)

BLOCK	MONDAY	TUESDAY	WEDNESDAY	THURSDAY	FRIDAY
I	English 9	English 10	English 9	English 10	English 9
II	English 9	Planning	English 9	Planning	English 9
III	English 9	English 9	English 9	English 9	English 9
IV	Duty/Plan	English 10	Duty/Plan	English 10	Duty/Plan

Gloucester High School in Gloucester, VA, developed a similar schedule and implemented it in 1993. (See Figure 15.) During the first three years, the 50-minute study period (called Extended Instructional Block, or EIB) was contiguous with the lunch period. Although EIB worked well for many students—especially those involved in a mastery program that required tutoring during the school day—the arrangement with lunch was problematic. Students moving throughout the building during their EIB were distracted by the lunch groups, and administrators had to closely monitor movement in the commons area of the building where students ate lunch. In 1996, the schedule was modified to maintain EIB but to move it to a different time of the day, the second instructional block of time. Also, the school decided to offer several singleton classes during the second block to allow students to take a seventh class in lieu of the study block. Gloucester has an A-B schedule with six 95-minute blocks. Classes are directly linked to the lunch block for which the students are assigned.

FIGURE 14
Sample Bell Schedules for Alternating Day (A-B) Seven-Credit Schedule with a Study Block

BLOCK	REGULAR	1:15 E.D.*	2:00 E.D.	1 HOUR LATE	2 HOURS LATE
0	7:30–8:25	7:30–8:25	7:30–8:25	XXX	XXX
1/2	8:35–10:05	8:35–9:20	8:35–9:35	9:35–10:45	10:35–11:20
3/4	10:10–11:50	9:25–10:20	9:40–10:50	10:50–12:10	11:25–12:35
5/6	11:55–1:55	10:25–12:25	10:55–12:55	12:15–2:15	12:40–2:40
Lunch 1	11:50–12:20	10:20–10:50	10:50–11:20	12:10–12:40	12:35–1:05
Lunch 2	12:25–12:55	10:55–11:25	11:25–11:55	12:45–1:15	1:10–1:40
Lunch 3	1:00–1:30	11:30–12:00	12:00–12:30	1:20–1:50	1:40–2:15
7/8	2:00–2:30	12:30–1:15	1:00–2:00	2:20–3:30	2:45–3:30
Extended Day	3:35–4:25	1:20–2:10	2:00–2:55	3:35–4:25	3:35–4:25

*E.D.: Early dismissal
Last 10 minutes of blocks 3/4 are for attendance and announcements.
Study block is block 7.
All blocks are 90 minutes in length on regular schedule.
Blocks 1/2, 3/4, 5/6, and 7/8 meet on alternating days. Block 1 meets on Monday, Wednesday, and Friday; Block 2 meets at the same time on Tuesday and Thursday. The schedules are reversed during the next week.

FIGURE 15
Alternate Bell Schedule for Alternating Day (A-B) Six-Credit Schedule with a Study Block

8:00–9:45	9:51–11:21	11:27–12:44	11:21–11:46	11:50–12:15	12:19–12:44	12:50–2:20
1st Block	2nd Block	Study Block or Singleton Class	1st Lunch— Science, Math Wing	2nd Lunch— Humanities Wing	3rd Lunch— Health, Fine Arts Wing	3rd Block

The importance of flexibility

The beginning and ending of the school day is often affected throughout the year, regardless of the schedule a school uses. Some days will begin later, and some days will end earlier (i.e.: late openings because of inclement weather and earlier closing because of teacher staff development). The schedule in Figure 14 addresses the issues of a regular schedule, an early dismissal at 1:15 p.m., and another at 2:00 p.m. There are also schedules that address the issue of one- and two-hour late openings. The schools involved start the regular school day at 8:30 a.m. and end the regular school day at 3:30 p.m. These times are within the confines of the school district's policy regarding the length of the school day.

Scheduling considerations when scheduling the alternating day (A-B) schedule with a study block

■ A schedule with a study block offers advantages in three areas:

- student remediation and/or acceleration

- additional student choice in his/her own learning

- specified time for non-curriculum related events, which historically has been taken from instructional time.

FIGURE 16
Student Schedule: A Week—Seven-Credit Alternating Day (A-B) Schedule with a Study Block

BLOCK	MONDAY	TUESDAY	WEDNESDAY	THURSDAY	FRIDAY
I	Algebra I	English	Algebra I	English	Algebra I
II	History	Biology	History	Biology	History
III a	Lunch	Lunch	Lunch	Lunch	Lunch
III b	Band	Spanish	Band	Spanish	Band
IV	Study Block	Health/P.E.	Study Block	Health/P.E.	Study Block

Students reverse the schedule during B week. A week classes that meet on Monday, Wednesday, and Friday meet on Tuesday and Thursday during B week. Classes that meet on Tuesday and Thursday during A week will meet on Monday, Wednesday, and Friday during B week.
(See accompanying CD for B week schedule for students.)

FIGURE 17
Teacher Schedule: A Week—Seven-Credit Alternating Day (A-B) Schedule with a Study Block

BLOCK	MONDAY	TUESDAY	WEDNESDAY	THURSDAY	FRIDAY
I	English 9	English 11	English 9	English 11	English 9
II	Plan	English 9	Plan	English 9	Plan
III	English 9	Plan	English 9	Plan	English 9
IV	English 11	Study Block	English 11	Study Block	English 11

Teacher schedules reverse during B week. Classes that meet on Monday, Wednesday, and Friday during A week will meet on Tuesday and Thursday during B week. Classes that meet on Tuesday and Thursday during A week will meet on Monday, Wednesday, and Friday during B week.

- Each student has a 90-minute study block each day that can be used for make-up work, tutoring, picture taking, ordering class rings, completing labs and other class projects, intramural competition, assemblies, homeroom activities, and club activities. All of these activities can be accomplished without interfering with instructional time.

- Lunch and study block are scheduled around block III.

- The study block can be scheduled at the end of the school day and can be used for early release of school teams who must travel for competition (e.g.: tennis teams, debate teams). This will allow team members to leave earlier than during the traditional schedule and to return home earlier, especially during exams and times when standardized tests are administered, such as AP examinations, achievement tests, SAT tests, etc.

- Classes taken by students on Monday, Wednesday, and Friday of A week will be taken on Tuesday and Thursday of B week; classes scheduled for students on Tuesday and Thursday of A week will be scheduled on Monday, Wednesday, and Friday of A week.

Eight-credit alternating day (A-B) block

Another creative alternative to the use of instructional time is to divide the school day into four equal learning/teaching blocks that meet on the alternating day format. Students have the option of taking a maximum of eight courses per year. Classes meet on alternating days for the entire

FIGURE 18
Sample Bell Schedule for Eight-Credit Alternating Day (A-B) Schedule

TIME	BLOCK	MINUTES
7:30–9:00	Block I	90
9:10–10:40	Block II	90
10:40–11:10	Lunch A	30
11:20–12:50	Block III	90
12:20–12:50	Lunch B	30
1:00–2:30	Block IV	90

school year. This configuration allows students to complete eight credits per year without administrators having to deal with many of the controversial organizational issues that surround the semester (4x4) block configuration, which also offers students an opportunity to earn eight credits per year. The schedule in Figure 18 is based on the assumption that school begins at 7:30 a.m. and ends at 2:30 p.m.

Scheduling considerations for students (See Figure 19.)

- During B week, classes that were taken on Monday, Wednesday, and Friday are taken on Tuesday and Thursday in the same block of time.

- Students are offered the opportunity to take eight 90-minute classes scheduled over a two-day period for the school year.

FIGURE 19
Sample Student Schedule: A Week—Eight-Credit Alternating Day (A-B) Schedule

BLOCK	MONDAY	TUESDAY	WEDNESDAY	THURSDAY	FRIDAY
I	Spanish	Art	Spanish	Art	Spanish
II	Phys. Ed.	English	Phys. Ed.	English	Phys. Ed.
III a	Lunch	Lunch	Lunch	Lunch	Lunch
III b	Algebra	History	Algebra	Algebra	Algebra
IV	Chemistry	Music	Chemistry	Music	Chemistry

- Students can earn up to eight course credits per year.

- Generally, students take the same classes for the entire school year.

- There are two lunch blocks scheduled around the third instructional block.

Scheduling considerations for teachers

- The teacher schedule is reversed during B week. Classes taught on Monday, Wednesday, and Friday of A week are taught on Tuesday and Thursday of B week. Classes taught on Tuesday and Thursday of B week are taught on Monday, Wednesday, and Friday of A week.

- Each day, classroom teachers are assigned three classes of 90 minutes each, a 90-minute planning period, and a 30-minute duty-free lunch period.

- Teachers are responsible for a total of six 90-minute classes over a two-day period.

- Lunch is scheduled before or after the third block, depending on a student's third or fourth block assignment.

- This schedule has proven to be very effective, but it should be noted that funding is needed for additional staffing to implement this schedule if moving from a six- or seven-period schedule to the eight-period alternating day block.

Conclusion

There are many versions of the alternating day schedule. If this is the schedule configuration that you think fits the need of your school community, research and network until you are sure that you have a schedule configuration that is in line with the needs of your school community. Tailor it to meet these needs as much as possible.

SEMESTER (4x4) BLOCK SCHEDULE

The semester (4x4) block also has many advantages over the traditional 55-minute schedule, as discussed throughout the remainder of this chapter. Again, the questions that must be answered relate to

the needs of a particular school or school division. Be thorough in your self-analysis and tailor the schedule to meet the needs of your community as much as possible. The models of the 4x4 in Figures 20 and 21 are for your consideration.

Scheduling considerations for students

- Classes meet each day for 90 minutes.

- Students have the option of taking four classes per semester.

- Students may choose to earn eight credits per year.

- Students usually generate a yearly schedule when choosing classes for the coming year rather than enrolling in classes at the beginning of each semester.

- There are generally two lunch blocks scheduled at the end of the second and third instructional blocks.

- Some scheduling choices are pre-determined by the administration because of policy related to sequencing and retention of information. These typically occur in mathematics, foreign languages, and music.

Student planning in the 4x4 block

It is critical for students to plan for their entire high school experience early in the cycle. This means planning at the eighth grade or sooner. The process must be a total effort between the student, his or her parent/guardian/student advocate, the counselor, and the teachers. A tentative plan mapping the direction of academic/career preparation for each student should be in place when the student enters high school. This will help eliminate glitches that may prevent students from being successful, as well as emphasize the importance of planning a meaningful high school program. The success of our students should be our top priority on paper as well as in personnel commitment. There are many combinations of plans that students might use when planning their high school careers. A plan for success is critical when a schedule such as the 4x4 offers so many options. Time management and course management become essential to all players involved in directing the student's success plan. Of course, the student and his/her parents should be most accountable for tracking the success plan for his/her future success. (See Figure 22 for an example of a four-year academic plan.)

Scheduling considerations for teachers

■ Each teacher is responsible for three 90-minute blocks each day.

■ Each teacher has one 90-minute planning block each day.

■ Each teacher teaches a total of six classes per year.

■ Each teacher's schedule for the second semester could depend on the requests of students.

COMBINATION SCHEDULES

Because of the controversy surrounding certain schedules in some school communities, administrators continue to search for a schedule that will meet the needs of all students within their school community and one that meets as little resistance as possible. One such schedule is the combination schedule. Although somewhat more complicated to understand and design, this schedule employs the best pieces of other block configurations (i.e.: alternating day (A-B), semester (4x4), and singleton blocks).

■ **The combination schedule in action**

An innovative scheduling approach is being used at La Quinta High School in La Quinta, California. Principal Jon Gaffney reported a great

FIGURE 20
Four-Credit Per Semester (4x4) Block Schedule Sample Bell Schedule with Lunch Schedules

STUDENTS WHO EAT FIRST LUNCH		STUDENTS WHO EAT SECOND LUNCH	
8:30–10:00	Block I (90 Min.)	XXX	XXX
10:05–11:35	Block II (90 Min.)	XXX	XXX
11:35–12:10	Lunch I	Block III (90 Min.)	11:40–1:10
12:15–1:45	Block III (90 Min.)	Lunch II	1:10–1:45
1:50–3:20	Block IV (90 Min.)	XXX	XXX

The same bell schedule is used first and second semester.

FIGURE 21
Four-Credit Per Semester (4x4) Block Schedule Sample Student Schedules

FIRST SEMESTER

BLOCK	I	II	III	IV
CLASS	Spanish I	Music	English II	Biology

SECOND SEMESTER

BLOCK	I	II	III	IV
CLASS	History	Geometry	Technology	Spanish II

FIGURE 22
Students Academic Career Success Plan For Grades 9–12

GRADE 9

TIME	SEMESTER 1	SEMESTER 2
8:30–10:00	Course 1 World History	Course 5 French 2
10:05–11:35	Course 2 Health/P.E. 9	Course 6 Fine Arts
11:40–1:10 12:15–1:45	Course 3—Geometry Lunch 11:35–12:10 Lunch 1:10–1:45	Course 7—Earth Science Lunch 11:35–12:10 Lunch 1:10–1:45
1:50–3:20	Course 4 English	Course 8 Journalism/Creative Writing

GRADE 10

TIME	SEMESTER 1	SEMESTER 2
8:30–10:00	Course 1 Computer Systems 1	Course 5 French 3
10:05–11:35	Course 2 Health/P.E. 10	Course 6 Fine Arts
11:40–1:10 12:15–1:45	Course 3—Algebra 3 / Trigonometry Lunch 11:35–12:10 Lunch 1:10–1:45	Course 7—Biology Lunch 11:35–12:10 Lunch 1:10–1:45
1:50–3:20	Course 4 English 10	Course 8 Journalism 2/Yearbook

GRADE 11

TIME	SEMESTER 1	SEMESTER 2
8:30–10:00	Course 1 Adv Tech (CAD)	Course 5 French 4
10:05–11:35	Course 2 English 11	Course 6 Biology 2
11:40–1:10 12:15–1:45	Course 3—AP Chemistry Lunch 11:35–12:10 Lunch 1:10–1:45	Course 7—Concepts in Chem/AP Review* Lunch 11:35–12:10 Lunch 1:10–1:45
1:50–3:20	Course 4 AP U.S. History	Course 8 Leaders in U.S. Hist./AP Review*

GRADE 12

TIME	SEMESTER 1	SEMESTER 2
8:30–10:00	Course 1 Psychology	Course 5 U.S. Government
10:05–11:35	Course 2 AP English	Course 6 Novel/AP Review*
11:40–1:10 12:15–1:45	Course 3 Physics Lunch 11:35–12:10 Lunch 1:10–1:45	Course 7 Calculus Lunch 11:35–12:10 Lunch 1:10–1:45
1:50–3:20	Course 4 Fine Arts	Course 8 Economics

* Companion course for AP (if student takes AP, he must take the companion course)
(See accompanying CD for sample teacher schedules by semester on the 4x4.)

deal of success in helping at-risk students through remediation during the intersession. He reported that ". . . we were able to reclaim a significant number of failing students. [Our data] show us that we need to adjust our remedial class methods in order to motivate the remaining 20 to 40 percent of students failing after the intersession."

Consider the 75-30-75 schedule formats in Figures 23 and 24.

Scheduling considerations

■ Teachers teach five classes during the 75-day session and 2.5 classes during the intersession.

■ Students have six opportunities for classes during the 75-day intersession.

■ Students have opportunities to take nine classes during a school year.

■ Because of the flexible use of time and human resources during the 30-day intersession, many opportunities exist that will permit time for staff development and team teaching as well as other creative teacher teaming opportunities. Teachers will be able to create blocks of time to be used for staff development as well as for tutoring and mentoring students.

Intersession for remediation

■ Students who failed classes were given an opportunity to retake the classes during the intersession.

FIGURE 23
75-30-75 Combination Schedule With Intersession

Bell Schedule—First 75 Instructional Days

BLOCK	MONDAY	TUESDAY	WEDNESDAY	THURSDAY	FRIDAY
I	8:00–8:55	8:00–8:55	8:00–9:53	8:00–9:53	8:00–8:55
II	9:01–10:01	9:01–10:01	9:53–10:08	9:53–10:08	9:01–10:08
III	10:07–11:02	10:07–11:02	10:08–12:06	10:08–12:06	10:07–11:02
IV	11:08–12:03	11:08–12:03	12:52–2:45	12:52–2:45	11:08–12:03
Lunch	12:03–12:43	12:03–12:43	12:06–12:46	12:06–12:46	12:03–12:43
V	12:49–1:44	12:49–1:44	12:46–2:45	12:46–2:45	12:49–1:44
VI	1:50–2:45	1:50–2:45	Block 1-3-5	Block 2-4-6	1:50–2:45

FIGURE 24
75-30-75 Combination Schedule with Intersession

Bell Schedule—30-Day Intersession

BLOCK	MONDAY	TUESDAY	WEDNESDAY	THURSDAY	FRIDAY
I	8:00–9:53	8:00–9:53	8:00–9:53	8:00–9:53	8:00–9:53
II	10:08–12:06	10:08–12:06	10:08–12:06	10:08–12:06	10:08–12:06
Lunch	12:06–12:46	12:06–12:46	12:06–12:46	12:06–12:46	12:06–12:46
III	12:52–2:45	12:52–2:45	12:52–2:45	12:52–2:45	12:52–2:45

Note: The second 75-day session follows the same schedule of the first 75 days. Teachers teach in tandems during the 30-day session.

- Of the students who failed classes and re-took the same class during the intersession, Gaffney (1997) reported the results in Figure 25.

Additional opportunities

- As a result of the success of this schedule, consideration is being given to offering future remediation classes on a variable credit system, much like a continuation school within a school. This concept takes one of the key components of successful alternative education programs and applies it to a comprehensive setting.

- Students who pass all classes have opportunities to select courses from a varied menu of electives as well as core courses.

- Core academic and elective courses are chosen by the more motivated students. Thus these classes are larger, while remedial classes are smaller and allow teachers time to provide more individual instruction for the students.

- The following process might be considered for the registration process for the intersession, if all students are involved in the intersession:

  • Students register using the arena registration process.

  • Seniors passing all classes register first, juniors second, etc.

  • Seniors failing one or more classes register second, juniors next, etc.

  • Students failing one or more classes are automatically scheduled into one or more remedial classes prior to the arena registration.

- Attendance was higher during the intersession than during the regular 75-day session.

80-80-20 block schedule with intersession

Another version of a schedule with an intersession, the 80-80-20 block schedule, has been implemented by Strath Haven High School in Wallingford, Pennsylvania. The first 160 days of this schedule can be implemented as an alternating day schedule or as a semester schedule format. The

FIGURE 25
Student Results of Intersession

COURSE	% OF REPEAT STUDENTS PASSING
English	75
Social Studies	88
Mathematics	54
Physical Education	61
Science	81
Computers	100
Foreign Language	87
Total % Passing	72

process for planning and implementing this schedule is very important because it is perceived as more different, even than the alternating day or the 4x4 schedule configuration. (See Figure 26.)

During the 20-day term, students will have exposure to a variety of offerings. These offerings could include interdisciplinary courses taught by a team of teachers during double blocks of time, extended field trips, or mentor programs that might be in an environment outside the traditional school building. This type of learning experience might be the only class that students are enrolled in for the 20 days. Remediation and acceleration programs can be provided. Students can be given opportunities to concentrate on one or two courses that a student needs to move to the next grade or level. Opportunities for acceleration will permit students to concentrate on areas of interest to earn credit to graduate early or to study an area of interest in depth. Other areas of opportunity for students include community service and senior projects. Again, these would be the only "courses" a student would enroll in during this 20-day session.

It is impossible to list all of the opportunities that may be offered students because of the variables that would be addressed. The key is to be flexible and use human resources (including teachers) to meet the needs of all students in your school.

DAILY SCHEDULE	FALL TERM 80 DAYS	WINTER TERM 80 DAYS	SPRING TERM 20 DAYS
Block I	Course 1	Course 5	Interdisciplinary Courses
Block II	Course 2	Course 6	Extended Field Trips, Mentors
Block III	Course 3	Course 7	Remediation, Acceleration
Block IV	Course 4	Course 8	Community Service, Senior Projects, Etc.

Length of each block depends on the length of the school day.

A student could be enrolled in technology class every day, all day for the 20 days. The same would be true for the senior project, work-based learning, and remediation or acceleration.

Considerations for the 20-day intersession

Some students will not follow the bell schedule at all. Certain students may be on an extended foreign language field trip. Music students may be involved in an extended performance tour, etc.

Scheduling considerations

■ The school must make a commitment to interdisciplinary teaching during the 20-day intersession.

■ Team teaching must be considered in order to use the allocated time efficiently during the 20-day intersession.

■ Communication to all customers is extremely important, since this is a new and different concept of providing services to students.

■ The school must address the issues of what to do with the 20 days. Before the schedule is presented to decision makers, a specific plan of action should be identified regarding classes that will be taught, constraints to the curriculum, the efficient use of human and physical resources, special student populations, etc.

■ Preparation must be made for an "overuse" of labs, learning centers, and media centers.

■ Plans must be made to deal with customer complaints of a decrease in instructional time.

■ Impact on Advanced Placement offerings/testing must be considered because instruction in all AP classes would have been completed before the AP testing dates.

■ Plans must be made as to how to deal with early graduation.

■ Additional human resource needs must be addressed.

■ Bell schedules and lunch schedules should be designed to meet the length of the instructional school day and the physical facilities that are available for food services. Be creative in using space other than the traditional areas used for food services. Also, consider creative ways of servicing students in the space available.

Areas of concern

Dorothy Katauskas, principal of Strath Haven High School, expressed concern in the following areas:

■ **Decrease in actual class time.** Loss of actual class time is offset by time gained from

FIGURE 27
Sample Student Schedule for the 80-80-20 Using the Alternating Day (A-B) Schedule

First 160 Days—A Week

BLOCK	MONDAY	TUESDAY	WEDNESDAY	THURSDAY	FRIDAY
I	English	Math	English	Math	English
II	History	Music	History	Music	History
III	Foreign Lang.	Foreign Lang.	Foreign Lang.	Foreign Lang.	Foreign Lang.
IV	Vocational Ed.	Science	Vocational Ed.	Science	Vocational Ed.

Alternate the days and courses for B Week.

FIGURE 28
Sample Student Schedules for the 80-80-20 Using the Semester Block Schedule

First 80 Days

BLOCK	MONDAY	TUESDAY	WEDNESDAY	THURSDAY	FRIDAY
1	English	English	English	English	English
II	Math	Math	Math	Math	Math
III	Music	Music	Music	Music	Music
IV	Vocational Ed.	Vocational Ed.	Vocational Ed.	Vocational Ed.	Vocational Ed.

Second 80 Days

BLOCK	MONDAY	TUESDAY	WEDNESDAY	THURSDAY	FRIDAY
I	Science	Science	Science	Science	Science
II	History	History	History	History	History
III	Foreign Lang.	Foreign Lang.	Foreign Lang.	Foreign Lang.	Foreign Lang.
IV	Art	Art	Art	Art	Art

FIGURE 29
Sample Student Schedule for the 20-Day Intersession—To Accompany Either the Alternating Day or Semester Block Configuration

BLOCK	MONDAY	TUESDAY	WEDNESDAY	THURSDAY	FRIDAY
I	Technology	Technology	Technology	Technology	Technology
II	Senior Project	Senior Project	Senior Project	Senior Project	Senior Project
III	Work-Based Learning (WBL)	Work-Based Learning (WBL)	Work-Based Learning (WBL)	Work-Based Learning (WBL)	Work-Based Learning (WBL)
IV	Research Project	Research Project	Research Project	Research Project	Research Project

fewer starts and stops. Adjustments to passing time and lunches can compensate for lost time. Educators may need to redesign the curriculum to redefine what students need to know, what is required for graduation, and how performance is to be assessed.

■ **Class absences.** Students miss more course content with each absence. Employ technology (modem, TV, computers) to reach students at home. More work is missed per class, but fewer classes are missed.

■ **Course sequencing.** Alternating terms may interrupt learning of sequential-based courses, such as science, math, and foreign language. Creative scheduling options may be used to include sequential terms if desired.

■ **Overload of reading as a result of intensified schedule.** Redesign curriculum requirements and/or schedule reading-intensive courses in alternate terms.

■ **Impact on AP curriculum.** Lobby for test reschedule. Teach AP courses over two terms.

■ **Premature graduation.** Establish graduation requirements in advance. Anticipate that some students may complete academic work yet lack the necessary maturity to leave high school. Work with area colleges and universities.

■ **Other Concerns.** There may be a need for additional resources and paraprofessionals. With

three separate registration periods per year, there will be increased administrative demands.

The planning process

Katauskas warns against underestimating the school community in the planning process. With the encouragement of her school board and superintendent, she investigated alternative scheduling concepts. She organized a task force consisting of action teams that she called independent research groups. These teams collected data and studied options for approximately a year. Then they recommended a

FIGURE 30
Sample Teacher Schedule for the 80-80-20—For Use With Either the Alternating Day or Semester Block Configuration

20-Day Intersession

BLOCK	MONDAY	TUESDAY	WEDNESDAY	THURSDAY	FRIDAY
I	Using Tech. for Research	Using Tech. for Research	Using Tech. for Research	Using Tech. for Research	Using Tech. for Research
II	English I Ext. (Remed. Course)	English I Ext. (Remed.)	English I Ext. (Remed.)	English I Ext. (Remed.)	English I Ext. (Remed.)
III	Multimedia Workshop	Multimedia Workshop	Multimedia Workshop	Multimedia Workshop	Multimedia Workshop
IV	Plan	Plan	Plan	Plan	Plan

75-75-30 schedule to the faculty. Teachers and students voted in favor of changing to block scheduling. However, because of public reaction from people not involved in the process, some compromises were made. The schedule was changed to an 80-80-20 schedule. Another compromise was that there would be a one-year pilot program scheduling only ninth graders into the new schedule. Tenth, eleventh, and twelfth graders were scheduled in the traditional schedule. Therefore, a dual schedule was prepared: one for students scheduled with the new format and one for the traditional scheduled students.

Katauskas listed the following planning cautions:

- Don't underestimate the customers.

- Consider the experience of the present teaching corps.

- Consider the need to redesign the curriculum (i.e.: reorganizing math instruction from teaching chapters to teaching concepts, etc.).

- Teachers will need to change the way they do business.

- Change marking periods to match the schedule so that customers will be informed.

- Keep the 20-day session focused on academics and not on courses of trivial interest.

- Consider how seniors will fit into the last 20-day session.

- Strath Haven is considering a senior experience for the final 20 days of the year. There are many possibilities, but some of the more attractive ones are mentoring, travel experiences (foreign languages), apprenticeships, extended field trips, research experiences at museums, hospitals, local governments, and local businesses.

(Thanks to Dorothy Katauskas, principal, and her staff from Strath Haven High School for permission to use the information on the Strath Haven 80-80-20 Block.)

COMBINATION SCHEDULES WITH EMBEDDED COURSES

For the purposes of meaningful explanation of the combination schedule, we use the term "embed-

ded." Certain issues relative to combination block scheduling should be given careful consideration by the action team before a final implementation decision is made. These issues include:

■ "Embedded" must be defined to meet the needs of your school. Embedded courses are those courses that will meet on alternating days or every day for a shorter period for the entire school year (180 days). Or, if you prefer, embedded classes can be defined as classes that meet each day for 90 minutes for a semester (90 days).

■ To distinguish the difference between embedded classes and the classes that are a part of the combination schedule, a system for identifying that difference must be put in place in order to minimize confusion when scheduling and communicating course offerings to students and parents. Edison High School in Fairfax County, Virginia, identifies embedded classes by a number system. Embedded classes that meet on block 1 day 1 (first block on Monday) would be identified as block 11; block 2 day 1 (second block on Monday) would be identified as block 21; block 3 day 1 (third block on Monday) would be identified as block 31; block 3 day 2 (block 3 on Tuesday) would be identified as block 32; and so on. In most instances, these blocks meet on alternating days for the entire year. Blocks that are not identified as embedded are referred to as 0 blocks and are identified by the block in which they meet; i.e.: block 1 would be identified as block 10, block 2 would be identified as block 20, block 3 would be identified as block 30, and block 4 would be identified as block 40. These classes meet each day for the semester.

■ Once embedded courses are defined, they must be identified. A decision must be made as to whether these courses will be identified on a permanent basis or if embedded courses will be defined each year. Some embedded courses are defined as those that meet on alternating days, or daily for shorter periods of time for the 180-day school year. Some suggested classes for this schedule might be certain music courses, ESL classes, some self-contained special education classes, AP courses, journalism courses that have the responsibility of the school yearbook and school newspaper, first level of foreign languages, first level of algebra, and other courses that require national/state level testing at a certain time within the school year that could have a negative impact on student performance. Certain students might also be given special consideration for enrollment in embedded courses rather than semester courses.

■ Reporting grades must be given careful consideration (an action team project) because of the various points during the year when grades must be reported, such as mid-term and end-of-the-year. Special consideration might be needed to satisfy customer needs (parents, students). Interim reports will be required for all students at the halfway point of the grading period. For students who are enrolled in non-embedded courses, it might be advisable to notify parents if grades fall below a previously identified standard (D). There should be conferences between teachers, administrators, parents, and students on final reporting dates, and these dates should be made available to all customers by various modes of communication. It is also important to identify and communicate the intent of interim reports. Interim reports generally serve as an indicator of performance in a course at the time that the report is issued.

■ For purposes of implementing the combination schedule with embedded courses, the school year is divided into two semesters: fall and spring. Each 180-day school year is divided into 90-day semesters. Students have the opportunity to enroll in four courses per semester, for a total of eight per year. Some of these courses meet on alternating days, and some meet each day of the semester or school year.

■ It is possible to have half-credit embedded courses that meet on alternating days for a semester. Students enrolling in these courses must take a companion course that will meet during the same block during the second semester. There might also be opportunities for students to enroll in semester embedded courses. If this occurs, students enrolled in these courses would receive credit at the end of 45 days. But it is necessary for students to select companion classes for the next 45 days, as well as for the following semester.

■ Students enrolled in yearlong embedded courses will receive credit at the end of the school year instead of receiving a half-credit at the end of the first semester, as do students enrolled in semester courses. This could also necessitate students' taking more than four courses in a given term but would not necessitate any student attending more than four classes in a given day.

■ When scheduling students, courses must be selected for the entire school year.

■ Students will select eight courses when building their schedule for the school year. Students and parents should give careful consideration to the schedule selected, since it will be difficult to change classes during the semester.

■ It is critical to identify and make appropriate schedule changes for students in the first week of the new semester. For instance, a senior who failed a required course needed for graduation— such as English 12—may need to repeat the course during the second semester.

■ A decision needs to be made concerning allowing students to repeat classes during the same school year. Issues that need to be addressed include teacher class load and class size. We suggest that a decision to allow students to repeat a course (with the exception of seniors who need courses to graduate) be delayed until after the first year of implementation.

■ Most of the faculty will be assigned to no more than three blocks per day or six blocks per year. Due to the embedded courses, some teachers could be assigned to more than three courses during a term but will not teach more than three blocks per day. If a teacher is assigned to only two blocks per term, the third assignment is the student resource room, achievement center, etc. (another action team task).

■ Eligibility for participating in certain extra/cocurricular activities must be addressed. A specific statement must be made to communicate standards to faculty, students, and parents. For example, a student enrolled in four courses must pass three of them, and a student enrolled in five courses must pass four to be eligible for participation.

■ Attendance is critical to student success because some classes are so highly concentrated. It is necessary to be specific concerning the consequences of absentees and tardies.

Scheduling issues when implementing the embedded schedule

In the spring of the preceding school term, students select eight courses for the coming school year. Scheduling conflicts are eliminated by the opening of school. However, administrators and counselors need to be flexible initially and consider certain schedule changes that may be needed at the opening of school for various reasons.

Figure 31 is an example of a student schedule with embedded classes; Figure 32 is for teachers..

Sample bell schedules

The bell schedule in Figure 33 can be used to implement the combination schedule with embedded courses. Included are modified schedules for inclement weather and other school functions that create a need for change in the daily school schedule.

(Thanks to Luther W. Fennell, principal of Edison High School, and his staff in Fairfax County, VA, for information on the embedded schedule, showcasing the flexibility that an administrator has in constructing a schedule.)

FIGURE 31
Embedded Schedule For Typical Student

BLOCK	MON	TUE	WED	THUR	FRI	X	MON	TUE	WED	THUR	FRI
I	AP Eng.	Calc.	AP Eng.	Calc.	AP Eng.	X	Calc.	AP Eng.	Calc.	AP Eng.	Calc.
II	Gov.	Gov.	Gov.	Gov.	Gov.	X	Acct.	Acct.	Act.	Acct.	Acct.
III	Band	Phys.	Band	Phys.S	Band	X	Phys.	Band	Phys.	Band	Phys.
IV	Span. 4	Span. 4	Span. 4	Span. 4	Span. 4	X	Span. 5	Span. 5	Span. 5	Span. 5	Span. 5

The accompanying CD provides three examples of student schedules using a combination schedule with embedded courses.

FIGURE 32
Embedded Schedule for Teacher—Combination Schedule with Embedded Courses

BLOCK	MONDAY	TUESDAY	WEDNESDAY	THURSDAY	FRIDAY
I	Algebra I	Algebra II	Algebra I	Algebra II	Algebra I
II	Geometry	Geometry	Geometry	Geometry	Geometry
III	Plan	Plan	Plan	Plan	Plan
IV	Geometry	Geometry	Geometry	Geometry	Geometry

In Block I, the teacher would teach Algebra I and Algebra II on alternating days for the entire school year.
In Blocks II and IV, the teacher would teach the same students the first semester and would change students and possibly course assignments the second semester.

FIGURE 33
Embedded Schedule Bell Schedule

REGULAR   **THREE-HOUR LATE OPENING**

Block 10,11/12	7:30–9:00	X	Block 10, 11/12	10:30–11:15
Block 20	9:07–10:37	X	Block 20	11:22–12:07
Block 30, 31/32	10:37–12:43	X	Block 30, 31/32	12:07–1:28

A Lunch	10:37–11:06	X	A Lunch	12:07–12:36
A Class	11:13–12:43	X	A Class	12:43–1:28
B Class	10:44–12:14	X	B Class	12:14–12:59
B Lunch	12:14–12:43	X	B Lunch	12:59–1:28

Block 40	12:50–2:20	X	Block 40	1:35–2:20

ONE-HOUR LATE OPENING   **PEP RALLY/ACTIVITY**

Block 10, 11/12	8:30–9:45	X	Block 10, 11/12	7:30–8:50
Block 20	9:52–11:07	X	Block 20	8:57–10:17
Block 30, 31/32	11:07–12:58	X	Block 30, 31/32	10:17–12:23

A Lunch	11:07–11:36	X	A Lunch	10:17–10:46
A Class	11:43–12:58	X	A Class	10:53–12:23
B Class	11:14–12:29	X	B Class	10:24–11:54
B Lunch	12:29–12:58	X	B Lunch	11:54–12:23

Block 40	1:05–2:20	X	Block 40 Pep Rally	12:30–1:40 1: 50–2:20

TWO-HOUR LATE OPENING

Block 10, 11/12	9:30–10:30
Block 20	10:37–11:37
Class A (30, 31/32)	11:44–12:44
Lunch A	11:37–12:06
Class B (30, 31/32)	12:13–1:13
Lunch B	12:44–1:13
Block 40	1:20–2:20

TECHNICAL EDUCATION AM SCHEDULE   **X**   **TECHNICAL EDUCATION PM SCHEDULE**

7:30–10:30	Vo-Tech Block I	X	7:30–10:30	Block 10,11/12
10:37–12:43	Block 30, 31/32	X	10:37–12:43	Block 20
10:37–11:06	A Lunch	X	10:37–11:06	Lunch
11:13–12:43	A Class	X	11:10–11:55	Study Block*
10:44–12:14	B Lunch	X	12:00–2:20	Vo-Tech Block II
12:14–12:43	B Class	X	XXX	XXX
12:50–2:20	Block 40	X	XXX	XXX

Study block in PM schedule can be used for a variety of purposes; e.g.: a singleton credit class that meets 50 minutes a day for the entire school year; travel to vo-tech center if the center is off grounds, a study block for tutoring purposes, etc.

COMBINATION SCHEDULES WITH COMPANION COURSES

The issue—Schedule for Advanced Placement offerings

Perhaps one of the "monsters" of the 4x4 block scheduling is the Advanced Placement course offering issue. When do we offer AP courses? When do we test AP students? How do we schedule AP courses? Will there be other testing dates for AP students? These are a few of the questions that have been asked when considering a block schedule format. We have answered some questions; we are still working on solutions for others; and for some, there will be no answer until there is enough data collected to give educators direction.

The questions we are really asking are:

- Will the retention gap make a difference on student test scores when the student takes the AP class first semester and does not take the test until the second semester?

- Can the appropriate curriculum be covered to prepare a student for an AP examination in 90 days?

First, let's eliminate the schedules where AP is not a major issue. If your schedule is an alternating (A-B) schedule, each course is offered on alternating days for the entire year. Therefore, AP should not be an issue. If you are using a combination schedule, and you choose to offer AP courses for the entire school year on an alternating day or every day format, AP should not be an issue.

Many teachers have expressed a concern that students taking certain math and foreign language courses need the daily reinforcement of the content. In this case, it may be necessary to offer a companion course, a course similar to the AP course in curriculum scope and content and offered on alternating days of an alternating day (A-B) block or during the following semester of the 4x4 block. (See Figure 34.)

If the schedule is a 4x4 schedule, the AP course can be offered during either the first 18-week instructional period or the second 18-week instructional period. When the class meets depends a great deal on the flexibility that an administrator has in constructing a schedule.

Combination/companion courses

What are some combination courses that could be offered as companion courses for AP classes? Certain courses may necessitate a yearlong course.

FIGURE 34
Combination/Companion Courses

AP COURSE	COMPANION COURSES	OTHER MATCHES
AP Biology	Research in Biology	Advanced Biology
AP Chemistry	Research in Chemistry	Chemistry II (Advanced)
AP Physics B/C	Research in Physics	Advanced Tech
AP French	French V	College-Level French
AP Spanish	Spanish V	College-Level Spanish
AP Latin	Latin V	Virgil
AP English	American Literature	Study of the Novel
AP U.S. History	AP European History	Contemoprary Issues in World History
AP Calculus	Calculus	Research Projects

Positive impacts of a companion course schedule

In our opinion, this way of scheduling AP courses has only positive impact. More time is allocated for AP courses, and students have an opportunity to study a course more in-depth. They are spending time in a course in which they are interested. If more time allocated to instruction is in fact a variable in student learning, then students should score higher on the AP examination—which is indicative of an increase in student achievement. Students will also have an opportunity to gain a broader and deeper knowledge of content that will increase their opportunity for success. (See Figure 35.)

Many subjects can be taught with companion courses, especially in subject areas where the concepts are difficult for students to process. This will provide additional time and a more in-depth understanding of the concept.

Although Advanced Placement courses are important, we must ask if we are allowing AP to drive our schedules. If so, we must then ask ourselves if this is a sound educational practice, when we consider the number of students in our schools who are not enrolled in AP classes.

Students have choices. Perhaps programs such as the International Baccalaureate Program or dual enrollment courses from local universities, colleges, or community colleges should be considered. These options are generally of similar quality as the AP curriculum, and in many instances they offer more flexibility.

SCHEDULES THAT COMBINE CORE COURSES WITH ELECTIVES

In a school that had a very effective but conservative and mature staff, the principal expressed concern about meeting the needs of his students, his school board, and his superintendent. But he and his staff were not ready to take on a full block schedule. As we discussed the situation, it was evident that the only solution to his dilemma was to rearrange instructional time. The question was: How do you add 10 additional instructional minutes to each of the identified core classes of English, science, social studies/history, and math? Additional core courses could be added to the core list as identified by the school or school division.

Considerations in constructing the schedule

There were several limitations that the principal had to consider.

- 150 hours of allocated instructional time were required for each of the core courses before a Carnegie unit would be granted.

FIGURE 35
Embedded AP Courses/Companion Courses in Alternating Day (A-B) Schedule

BLOCK	MONDAY	TUESDAY	WEDNESDAY	THURSDAY	FRIDAY
I	AP French AP Spanish AP Latin	French V Spanish Latin V	AP French AP Spanish AP Latin	French V Spanish V Latin V	AP French AP Spanish AP Latin
II	AP English AP U.S. History	American Novel U.S. History	AP English AP U.S. History	American Novel U.S. History	AP English AP U.S. History
III	AP Euro. Hist. AP Physics	AP Govern. AP Calculus	AP Euro. Hist. AP Physics	AP Govern. AP Calculus	AP Euro. Hist. AP Physics
IV	AP Chemistry AP Stats	AP Music AP Art	AP Chemistry AP Stats	AP Music AP Art	AP Chemistry AP Stats

- The school day or school year could not be extended to schedule the additional time.

- The current schedule was a traditional seven-period single period day.

- Students would need 23 Carnegie units for a regular diploma and 27 for an advanced diploma.

- Physical constraints of the building required three lunch blocks.

- An award-winning fine arts programs had very vocal group of parents.

- Classes had to be offered on a daily schedule for the entire school year.

- A strong vocational/technical program was in place.

- The transportation system (bus routes) had elementary, middle, and secondary school connections.

- The existing school day started at 8:14 a.m. and ended at 2:56 p.m.

- Some teachers were teaching more minutes than their colleagues.

Features of the schedule

The schedule that we developed included the following features:

- An opportunity to enroll in four core classes per day

- An opportunity to enroll in three or more electives per day

- An opportunity for seven or more Carnegie units per year

- Three core classes meet for 58 minutes per day.

- One core class is split because of lunch and meets for a total of 57 minutes.

- Non-core classes meet for 38 minutes each day. Non-traditional time is used to ensure that instructional objectives are met. Some non-core courses include:

  – Music—Have rehearsal/practice before and after school for competition, performance, independent practice, composition, etc.

  – Art—Use non-traditional school time for exhibits, continuation of projects, before- and after-school work, independent study/projects, etc.

  – Physical Education—Utilize time spent in interscholastic athletic competition, cheerleader, organized activities or independent teams/events not associated with the school (such as gymnastic training, dance, soccer, golf, independent studies, etc.).

  – Vocational or Technical Education—Give credit for skills learned in part-time job-related activities (either associated or not associated with the curriculum), preparation for contests and independent projects, time related to competitions, and before- and after-school related activities.

- Foreign languages should be considered a core subject for the purpose of this schedule configuration.

Considerations in scheduling students

■ Students enrolled in morning classes will complete the first period at the home school, periods 2 and 3 at the vo-tech school, a core course in periods 5 or 6, and an elective period 7 at the home school.

■ Students enrolled in afternoon vo-tech school will complete periods 1 and 2, A or 5 with electives 3 and 4. Vo-tech periods are scheduled 6 and 7.

■ Students not enrolled in vo-tech school have an opportunity to enroll in the following combinations:

  – four core courses and three electives

  – three core courses and four electives

  – two core courses and six electives

Benefits of the short block period

The short block periods created by the schedule can also be used in the following ways.

- To identify and re-engage students who need additional time to be successful in core classes required for graduation, work-related skills, performing skills, etc.

- To tutor students who need extra help

- To review for standardized tests, etc.

- To conduct activities unrelated to co-curricular activities (pep rallies, pictures, assembly, etc.)

- To make up work

After much conversation and thought, the schedule in Figure 36 was recommended.

THE TRIMESTER SCHEDULE—A SCHEDULE OF THE FUTURE

Regardless of the way instructional time is scheduled, there will be issues that must be addressed. Year in and year out, we continue to address the current 45- to 55-minute schedule that we use, remaining boxed in to traditional ways of using time. But we must continue to be risk takers and search for creative new methods of using allocated instructional time.

In considering the trimester schedule, as with any schedule, it is important to look at criteria for restructuring the allocated instructional time. As usual, we begin by assessing the advantages and disadvantages in the trimester format. This analysis should relate to the needs of your particular school.

Some advantages of a trimester schedule

- It increases student opportunities to take more courses.

- It provides extended time for teaching and learning.

- It reduces the number of courses that students must prepare for on a daily or weekly basis.

- It reduces the number of contact hours that a teacher is responsible for on a daily or weekly basis.

- It provides opportunities for students to re-enroll in classes for remediation.

- It eliminates many potential discipline problems. (Often, when students realize that they have no chance of passing a class, they create discipline problems in order to be removed from the class.)

- It provides opportunities to prepare for standardized tests during a regular school day.

Scheduling considerations

Many of the same concerns expressed by stakeholders who use other alternative schedules occur with the trimester schedule.

- Teachers will teach more classes.

- The need for library and laboratory space for computers, science, mathematics, and writing will increase.

- There could be a reduction in instructional time. This depends on the length of the current school day and the willingness of those involved to increase the length of the school day or school year.

- Intensive staff development will be necessary.

- Teachers will need to change their instructional strategies.

- The curriculum may change.

- There may be concerns about learning gaps and retention. Less material may be covered.

- There are concerns about AP classes and fine arts classes.

Trimester calendar (based on a 180-day school year)

The school year is divided into three semesters that are as equal as possible. Vacations, teacher workdays, and other breaks in the school year must be considered. These are generally unique to a particular school division.

Each semester usually consists of approximately 60 days with variations unique to individual school districts, such as the length of the instructional

FIGURE 36
Short Block Schedule: Sample Student Schedule with 4 Core and 3 Electives and Lunch 5A

PERIOD	MONDAY	TUESDAY	WEDNESDAY	THURSDAY	FRIDAY
1 8:14–9:12	Core	Core	Core	Core	Core
2 9:16–10:14	Core	Core	Core	Core	Core
3 10:20–10:58	Elective	Elective	Elective	Elective	Elective
4 11:02–11:40	Elective	Elective	Elective	Elective	Elective
5 11:44–12:41	Core	Core	Core	Core	Core
6 12:45–1:12	Lunch	Lunch	Lunch	Lunch	Lunch
7 1:16–2:14	Core	Core	Core	Core	Core
8 2:18–2:56	Elective	Elective	Elective	Elective	Elective
9	XXX	XXX	XXX	XXX	XXX
10	XXX	XXX	XXX	XXX	XXX

See the accompanying CD for short block schedule with additional lunch periods.

FIGURE 37
Short Block Schedule: Sample Student Schedule with 2 Core and 4 Electives

PERIOD	MONDAY	TUESDAY	WEDNESDAY	THURSDAY	FRIDAY
1 8:14–8:52	Elective	Elective	Elective	Elective	Elective
2 8:56–9:34	Elective	Elective	Elective	Elective	Elective
3 9:38–10:36	Core	Core	Core	Core	Core
4 10:42–11:40	Core	Core	Core	Core	Core
5 11:44–12:22	Elective	Elective	Elective	Elective	Elective
6 12:22–12:50	Lunch	Lunch	Lunch	Lunch	Lunch
7 12:54–1:32	Elective	Elective	Elective	Elective	Elective
8 1:36–2:14	Elective	Elective	Elective	Elective	Elective
9 2:18–2:56	Elective	Elective	Elective	Elective	Elective
10	XXX	XXX	XXX	XXX	XXX

FIGURE 38
Short Block Schedule: Sample Student Schedule with 9 Electives

PERIOD	MONDAY	TUESDAY	WEDNESDAY	THURSDAY	FRIDAY
1 8:14–8:52	Elective	Elective	Elective	Elective	Elective
2 8:56–9:34	Elective	Elective	Elective	Elective	Elective
3 9:38–10:16	Elective	Elective	Elective	Elective	Elective
4 10:20–10:58	Elective	Elective	Elective	Elective	Elective
5 11:02–11:40	Elective	Elective	Elective	Elective	Elective
6 11:44–12:22	Elective	Elective	Elective	Elective	Elective
7 12:22–12:50	Lunch	Lunch	Lunch	Lunch	Lunch
8 12:54–1:32	Elective	Elective	Elective	Elective	Elective
9 1:36–2:14	Elective	Elective	Elective	Elective	Elective
10 2:18–2:56	Elective	Elective	Elective	Elective	Elective

FIGURE 39
Short Block Schedule: Morning Vo-Tech Sample Student Schedule with 2 Core and 5 Electives

PERIOD	MONDAY	TUESDAY	WEDNESDAY	THURSDAY	FRIDAY
1 8:14–9:12	Elective	Elective	Elective	Elective	Elective
2 9:12–11:44	Vo-Tech	Vo-Tech	Vo-Tech	Vo-Tech	Vo-Tech
3 9:12–11:44	Vo-Tech	Vo-Tech	Vo-Tech	Vo-Tech	Vo-Tech
4 11:44–12:11	Lunch	Lunch	Lunch	Lunch	Lunch
5 12:15–1:12	Core	Core	Core	Core	Core
6 1:16–2:14	Core	Core	Core	Core	Core
7 2:18–2:56	Elective	Elective	Elective	Elective	Elective
8	XXX	XXX	XXX	XXX	XXX
9	XXX	XXX	XXX	XXX	XXX
10	XXX	XXX	XXX	XXX	XXX

Vo-tech students take period 1 at their home school, attend vo-tech, return for lunch, take core courses periods 5 and 6, and an elective period 7.

FIGURE 40

Short Block Schedule: Afternoon Vo-Tech Sample Student Schedule with 2 Core and 4 Electives

PERIOD	MONDAY	TUESDAY	WEDNESDAY	THURSDAY	FRIDAY
1 8:14–9:12	Core	Core	Core	Core	Core
2 9:16–10:14	Core	Core	Core	Core	Core
3 10:20–10:58	Elective	Elective	Elective	Elective	Elective
4 11:02–11:40	Elective	Elective	Elective	Elective	Elective
5 11:44–12:11	Lunch	Lunch	Lunch	Lunch	Lunch
6 12:11–2:56	Vo-Tech	Vo-Tech	Vo-Tech	Vo-Tech	Vo-Tech
7 12:11–2:56	Vo-Tech	Vo-Tech	Vo-Tech	Vo-Tech	Vo-Tech
8	XXX	XXX	XXX	XXX	XXX
9	XXX	XXX	XXX	XXX	XXX
10	XXX	XXX	XXX	XXX	XXX

Afternoon vo-tech students take core courses during periods 1 and 2. They take their electives during periods 3 and 4 at their home school, attend vo-tech, and end their school day there.
(Thanks to Dr. Berkley Clear, principal of Abingdon High School, Abingdon, VA)

school year, holiday breaks, and teacher workdays built into the school year.

Sample bell schedules

The length of each block depends on the length of the school day. Assume that we will offer only five course options for students because of the trimester schedule, and that the school day is in operation from 8:30 a.m. until 3:35 p.m. Remove 30 minutes for lunch, and this leaves a total of 6.5 hours for instruction and hall passing. Each block will be approximately 75 minutes long. A bell schedule may look like the one in Figure 41. (See Figures 42 and 43 for student and teacher sample schedules.)

Building a master schedule for the trimester is very simple and very similar to building a 4x4 semester schedule. Many of the same factors must be considered, such as sequencing and special programs. Many variations and variables should be considered when implementing the trimester schedule. If this is a schedule that interests you, you may first want to do a self-study, planning the necessary

staff development, sharing with all customers your plan and intent, and considering the mechanics of scheduling the trimester from your perspective.

E-X-C-E-L—EXTENDED CLASSES FOR ENHANCED LEARNING

Parry McClure High School in Buena Vista, Virginia, has been a leader in innovative ways to serve customers since 1973–74, when it first imple-

FIGURE 41

Trimester Calendar: Sample Bell Schedule

BLOCK	TIME
1	8:30–9:45
2	9:50–11:05
3	11:10–12:25
4 Lunch	12:25–12:55
5	1:00–2:15
6	2:20–3:35

FIGURE 42
Trimester Calendar: Sample Student Schedule for the Entire School Term

BLOCK	TIME	FALL	WINTER	SPRING
1	8:30–9:45	Science	Math	Phys. Ed.
2	9:50–11:05	English	English	English
3	11:10–12:25	Music	Music	Music
4 Lunch	12:25–12:55	Lunch	Lunch	Lunch
5	1:00–2:15	Math	Science	Math
6	2:20–3:35	Social Studies/History	Art	Science

FIGURE 43
Trimester Calendar: Sample Teacher Schedule for the Entire School Term

BLOCK	TIME	FALL	WINTER	SPRING
1	8:30–9:45	Teach	Teach	Teach
2	9:50–11:05	Plan	Teach	Teach
3	11:10–12:25	Teach	Plan	Teach
4 Lunch	12:25–12:55	Lunch	Lunch	Lunch
5	1:00–2:15	Teach	Plan	Teach
6	2:20–3:35	Teach	Teach	Plan

mented a fourth quarter that provided year-round schools for customers who wished to take advantage. Adding a summer quarter was not difficult since it was similar to summer school. This fourth quarter offers tuition-free opportunities for students who wish to enroll in school for remediation, enrichment, or acceleration purposes. Over 60 percent of Parry McClure students take part in this learning experience. Even without the fourth quarter, the schedule is indeed very interesting and worthy of investigation if you are looking for a different kind of schedule that is designed for students.

How does the schedule work?

The first three quarters of the 180 days are divided into 60 days each (similar to the Copernican model). During each 60-day quarter, the school day consists of one block that is 115 minutes long, one block that is 110 minutes, and two 45-minute blocks that are extensions of the morning classes. The fifth block of the day is used for teacher planning and student activities. A 36-minute lunch block is also a part of the school-day schedule, and 15 minutes are allowed for class change. This totals to 376 minutes, or 6 hours and 16 minutes per day.

The schedule allows 160 instructional clock hours for the first block, and 155 instructional clock hours for the second block. During each of the 60-day terms, the typical student will enroll in two subjects, which equates to six subjects per year. A typical student schedule may look like the one in Figure 44.

This schedule has many of the same advantages of other block schedules, but there are additional benefits.

- Students focus only on two subjects per quarter.

- More time is spent in class, so there is increased instructional time.

FIGURE 44
Sample Student Schedule for an EXCEL Block Format

DAILY SCHEDULE	QUARTER 1	QUARTER 2	QUARTER 3
Block 1 (120 Min.)	Algebra 1	Science	Health/P.E.
Block 2 (110 Min.)	Music	World History	English
Block 3 (Lunch 43 Min.)	Lunch	Lunch	Lunch
Block 4 (First Elective 45 Min.)	Music	World History	English
Block 5 (Second Elective 45 Min.)	Algebra 1	Science	Health/P.E.
Block 6 (Student Activity and Teacher Planning)			

FIGURE 45
Sample Calendar Year for Trimester Scheduling

TRIMESTER 1	TRIMESTER 2	TRIMESTER 3
Aug 28–30 Teacher Workdays	Dec 2 Teacher Workday	March 9–10 Teacher Workdays
Sep 4 1st Teaching Day for Trimester 1	Dec 5 1st Teaching Day of Trimester 2	March 13 1st Teaching Day of Trimester 3
Oct 17 End of Midterm Grading Period	Dec 8 Issue Report Cards for Trimester 1	March 15 Issue Reports for Trimester 2
Oct 24 Issue Midterm Report Cards	Dec 22—30 Winter Break	April 14–21 Spring Break
Nov 24–25 Fall Break	Jan 25 End of Midterm Grading Period	May 1 End of Midterm Grading Report
Dec 1 End of Trimester 1	Feb 1 Issue Midterm Report Cards	May 8 Issue Midterm Report Cards
	March 8 End of Trimester 2	June 13 End of Trimester 3

- Students who need additional assistance could receive as much as 240 clock hours of class.

- Students can accelerate by taking two additional courses per term or independent studies, as well as take three consecutive math or foreign language classes in one year.

Adjustments to dates and other specifics related to district policy can be made as necessary. The schedule in Figure 45 is just an example that can be adjusted to meet individual school or school district needs.

(Thanks to Wayne D. Flint, principal of Parry McClure High School in Buena Vista, VA.)

LOOKING BACK . . .

As we have stated many times: use scheduling as a problem-solving tool. Conduct an analysis of a perceived need in your school or school district.

Consider your customer base, and design strategies that will meet the needs of these customers. Remember there will be specific needs that special customers have. Look at all of the positives and the opportunities for challenges and determine what battles are worth fighting. Once the decision is made, move forward with the challenge. Be flexible, and don't be afraid to design and try a solution that is new—unique—to your school. But above all else, remember that what you are proposing is done in the best interest of student success. Keep the bar high and assist students as they reach for excellence.

If you as an educator are serious about reform, then do not fail to design an evaluation plan for this or any other reform effort that you chose to implement. This is the difference between current reform and reform of the past: **MEASUREMENT AND EVALUATION!**   ❏

Chapter 7 Appendix on CD

❏ Success Stories

- A Success Story from the Southeast: Using the Alternating Day (A-B) Block at Princess Anne High School, Virginia Beach, Virginia (word version)

- A Success Story from the North: Using the 4x4 Intensive Schedule at Hatboro-Horsham High School, Horsham, Pennsylvania

  - Success story (word version)
  - Regular Bell Schedule (word version)
  - Regular Bell Schedule with Minutes (word version)
  - A.M. Assembly Schedule (word version)
  - P.M. Assembly Schedule (word version)

What Lessons Have We Learned from Middle School Scheduling?

*T**he objective of the middle school schedule is instructional responsiveness.***

—Paul S. George and William M. Alexander, 1993

LOOKING AHEAD IN THIS CHAPTER . . .

Middle schools are continuing to look at restructuring the school day. Although the history of middle schools lends itself to more flexible use of instructional time, administrators are redefining instructional time to encourage greater student success. Strong middle schools, using the philosophy of continuous improvement, use data and feedback to revisit the initial way they designed the school to implement changes that improve the overall program.

THE RIGHT SCHEDULE

Just as in high school, there is a right schedule for a notable occasion, a particular curriculum situation, and a unique community/customer need at the middle school. The trick is to find or design the necessary schedule and follow the change process for implementation and evaluation. The principles for reform at the middle school are the same as those found at the high school, and the overriding concern must be creating the optimum learning situation for students. Some middle schools have created schedules with double planning periods so that teams have adequate time to function. Some schools change schedules two or three times a year to ensure equitable schedules for all middle school teams. Schools in the middle continue to address issues relative to providing the best possible learning and teaching climate for students.

OBSERVATIONS

When exploring the use of larger blocks of time in high schools, we found that many middle schools were already using some form of the block concept but that their use of time was still fragmented. We believe it could be used more effectively. What strategies were middle schools using that were different from those used in most high schools? Developing skills in language arts and mathematics appeared to be the norm. Teachers are usually organized in teams. These teams plan together, conference with parents, and design activities that incorporate skills and content from all subject areas. Some teams deliver instruction cooperatively, using team teaching or other interdisciplinary methods. Flexibility of administrators and teachers at the middle school appeared to increase as teachers changed schedules, teaching strategies, and in some cases students on a regular basis.

THE ACADEMIC EXPECTATIONS OF THE BLOCK SCHEDULE

If the expectations of all stakeholders in the school community are not related to higher academic expectations for students, why bother with change? With the assumption that all stakeholders support the goal of higher academic expectations for students, what must we do to ensure that higher standards are achieved?

■ Students will be engaged in learning for longer periods of uninterrupted time and will be able to focus on learning with more effective strategies.

■ The schedule reduces fragmentation of instruction and allows for group projects, research, and lab experiments to be completed in one period.

■ The schedule provides teachers more time to work on individual student needs within the class period.

■ The schedule can provide opportunities for extra help and extra time for learning.

■ Better use can be made of community resources and guest speakers within the classroom on a daily basis.

■ There are increased opportunities for interdisciplinary team teaching and planning.

■ There is increased opportunity to build a continuum of learning experiences that relate to life in the real world.

■ Students and teachers will have more time to engage in individual and group projects, presen-

tations, and other academic activities that need additional attention.

■ Teachers will have opportunities to collaborate with colleagues on a regular basis, to discuss student issues, to reduce teacher isolation, and to determine curriculum issues.

■ Teachers will have the opportunity to design an integrated curriculum that demonstrates a continuum of learning experiences built upon previous knowledge and linking it to the real world.

■ The schedule will support curriculum compacting so students can move beyond the curriculum to receive accelerated instruction.

■ There will be opportunities for teachers to use teaching strategies that will actively engage students in learning.

■ A variety of assessment strategies can be used in determining academic expectations because students have more time to demonstrate what they have learned.

■ There will be opportunities for teachers to plan collaboratively for inclusion or other strategies to accommodate the needs of all students.

SPECIAL EDUCATION

One of the questions we are frequently asked is, "How do special education students adjust to a block schedule?" One teacher recently asked this question during an information session and commented that it seemed to her that disabled students would have a hard time dealing with an alternate day schedule and with the longer blocks of instructional time.

Henrico County Public Schools near Richmond, Virginia, has all middle schools on a block schedule. Special education supervisor, Dr. Dorothy Carson Jones, advises that the block schedule has worked very well for special education students who are included in the regular classroom program. Teachers have commented that they are able to use instructional time better, completing topics and skill lessons that previously were carried over from one day until the next. Flexibility has been key. Middle level students have not had difficulty adjusting to the block schedule, and the school buildings are noticeably quieter (Jones, 1999).

This report confirms what we saw in our schools and suspected from other observations. Although many disabled students need consistency and structure, the block schedule does not pose a problem. The ability to be flexible with instruction serves these students well. If the block schedule has advantages for special students in the middle schools who are typically 10 to 13 years of age, it should not provide problems for older disabled students who are able to be mainstreamed into regular education at the high school level.

FLEXIBLE SCHEDULING

As we continue to explore options to make choices for students that will raise academic expectations at the middle level, we offer the following schedules as alternatives.

- 4x4 Semester Block

- Combination Schedule (consideration must be given to developmental skills, length of block)

- Alternating Day (A-B) Block

4 x 4 SEMESTER BLOCK

We are often asked about using the 4x4 (semester) block schedule at the middle school level, and we do not recommend this schedule at this level because of the developmental stage of middle-level-aged students. The 4x4 is based on the assumption that students can process information in a compacted format, attention being given to fewer subject areas at a given time. Completing some exploratory courses in a compacted time frame may work very well and should be considered when core courses require larger amounts of time. Using a semester approach may be too intense for 10 to12 year olds and certainly would limit the interdisciplinary learning opportunities that are a premise of the middle school program.

Middle schools encourage experiential learning and using projects as a way of developing skills with content that is learned. While a block format is perfect for this way of learning, we believe the 4x4 would inhibit some of these activities that develop in middle school classrooms over a period of time.

COMBINATION BLOCK

The combination block asks the faculty to agree on academic or learning priorities in the school curriculum. Students are assigned to core subjects on a daily schedule and electives on a rotating day basis. In other words, math is taught each day for 80 minutes, and physical education or other electives are taught for 100 minutes every other day. This provides opportunities for teachers and students to use time more efficiently as each teacher has a longer block of time (although some courses are taught more frequently and are allocated more instructional time overall). Students have time to "dress" for physical education and become engaged in an activity in 100-minute blocks.

- Students take no more than four core courses each day. The other blocks are for electives, counseling, and individual student work.

- Because students are in teams, blocks one and four can be designed in accordance with the students' needs. Just because there are two blocks does not mean that each subject is given equal time. These decisions are made by team members.

- The block assigned for exploratory courses or electives may be used for one elective on alternating days or for multiple electives over a two-day period with different time allocations for each elective.

The combination schedule is limited only by the imagination. The great flexibility in the use of allotted instructional time should provide more efficient use of time for teaching and learning. (See Figure 46.)

ALTERNATING DAY (A-B) BLOCK SCHEDULE FOR MIDDLE SCHOOLS

Now let's look at an alternating day (A-B) block master schedule. The advantages for students and teachers are many of the same previously noted for the combination schedule and the block schedules used at the high school level. Students take classes on alternating days. The amount of time allotted to each block depends on the content. Core courses are generally scheduled for more time than electives. (See Figures 47, 48, 49, and 50.)

FIGURE 46
Sample Combination Block Student Schedules for Grades 6, 7, and 8

Grade 6

BLOCK NO. AND BELL SCHEDULE	COURSE 1	COURSE 2
8:00–8:10	Home base	**XXX**
I—8:13–9:33	English	Reading
II—9:38–10:58	Math	**XXX**
III—11:03–12:23	Exploratory	**XXX**
IV—12:26–12:51	Lunch	**XXX**
V—12:55–1:23	Flex time	**XXX**
VI—1:28–2:48	Social Studies	Science
VII—2:50–3:00	Advisor/Advisee	**XXX**

Grade 7

BLOCK NO. AND BELL SCHEDULE	COURSE 1	COURSE 2
8:00–8:10	Home base	**XXX**
I—8:13–9:33	English	Reading
II—9:38–10:58	Exploratory	Exploratory
III—11:03–11:30	Lunch	**XXX**
IV—11:33–12:00	Flex time	Flex time
V—12:03–1:23	Science	Social Studies
VI—1:28–2:48	Math	**XXX**
VII—2:50–3:00	Advisor/Advisee	**XXX**

Grade 8

BLOCK NO. AND BELL SCHEDULE	COURSE 1	COURSE 2
8:00–8:10	Home base	**XXX**
I—8:13–9:33	Exploratory	Electives
II—9:38–10:58	Math	**XXX**
III—11:03–11:30	Flex time	Flex time
IV—11:33–12:00	Lunch	**XXX**
V—12:03–1:23	Science	Social Studies
VI—1:28–2:48	Math	Foreign Language
VII—2:50–3:00	Advisor/Advisee	**XXX**

CONSIDERATIONS IN DEVELOPING A MIDDLE SCHOOL BLOCK SCHEDULE

If your middle school schedule is currently using a form of block scheduling or a traditional schedule that has been in place for a number of years, perhaps a self-analysis is in order. Such an analysis might provide data that can be used as a vehicle for reconsidering your current school-day structure. The first question should address the flexibility of the current time arrangement. The schedule should be flexible enough to allow teachers opportunities to teach the curriculum and allow students opportunities to learn and be successful in an academic environment. This flexibility should allow teachers opportunities to change teaching strategies every 15 to 30 minutes. Occasionally, a middle-level teacher may engage students in an activity (such as a simulation) that consumes more than 30 minutes, but this should be infrequent. The nature of early adolescents is such that they require both structure and great flexibility in the classroom. Middle-level teachers should have the opportunity to flex the schedule as needed to provide learning activities that are engaging but on-target to meet the standards set for the curriculum.

DIVISION OF TIME

When considering the time issue relevant to the length of the block, rethink the idea of assigning each block the same amount of time. Consider scheduling the core areas into longer lengths of time than electives. Such issues are generally addressed in policies set forth by the local school or school division.

Data recently reported, including the results of the National Assessment of Educational Progress (NAEP) and the Third International Mathematics and Science Study (TIMSS), indicate that middle schools will need to change classroom practices and emphasis if American middle students are going to compare favorably academically with students of the same age from other nations (Cooney, 1998). Additionally, the standards movement in this country is creating a new emphasis on academic performance at all levels, including the middle level. Together, these events are driving middle school principals and teachers to examine the emphasis of their program and how time has been distributed in the schedule. As students continue to be tested in the core academic areas, educators may see a need to place greater emphasis on the core areas, thus increasing the amount of classroom time in these four areas and reducing the time in courses such as career exploration, physical education, and the arts.

As educators review the use of time in middle schools, it is not likely that we will abandon middle schools and return to the junior high school concept because we understand the value of offering small learning communities for pre-adolescents. The middle school concept has much to add to a child's educational experience. Decisions about how time is used as a part of that concept are, however, critical to the outcomes sought—a student well-prepared to move into the high school experience and to accept the challenges of a demanding high school curriculum.

CURRICULUM DELIVERY

Many strategies currently used in middle schools will be appropriate for use on the high school block schedule. Delivery methods such as interdisciplinary teams, team teaching, and sharing the same teaching space are often found in the middle school. As high schools move toward a more flexible use of instructional time, they need to look closer at these curriculum delivery methods.

In an **interdisciplinary team,** grade-level teachers share the same space and the same students in order to provide learning experiences in different content areas. Generally, a grade level is divided into teams of students and teachers. The number of teams and the number of students and teachers on a team depend on the size of the school, the number of faculty and staff, and the philosophy of the school or school district. For this delivery method to be successful, it is critical that member teachers of the team share **common planning time.** Activities that occur during these common planning blocks should include planning teaching methodologies, auditing student progress, conducting parent conferences, participating in specific staff development, and advising administrators of the progress of students as well as other information that will keep the administration in the know. Good news is always welcomed by administrators from any group—so share!

(Continued on page 146)

FIGURE 47

Sample Master Schedule for Even Days (Blocks 2, 4, 6, and 8) for Grade 6

GRADE 6	8:15–8:30	8:38–10:05	10:08–10:35	10:38–12:30	X	12:33–2:00	2:03–3:30
EVEN DAYS	HOME BASE	BLOCK 2	FLEX TIME	BLOCK 4	LUNCH	BLOCK 6	BLOCK 8
TEAM 6A	XXX	XXX	XXX	XXX	XXX	XXX	XXX
TEACH 1	101	Life Science	101	Language Arts/ Read 6	A	Life Science	Individual Plan
TEACH 2	102	Individual Plan	102	Language Arts/ Read 6	A	World Studies	World Studies
TEACH 3	103	Read/Math Tutorial	103	Language Arts/ Read 6	A	Math 6	Individual Plan
TEAM 6B	XXX	XXX	XXX	XXX	XXX	XXX	XXX
TEACH 4	104	Individual Plan	104	Language Arts/ Read 6	A	Life Science	Career Exploratory
TEACH 5	105	Math 6	105	Language Arts/ Read	A	Math 6	Individual Plan
TEACH 6	106	Read Tutorial	106	Language Arts/ Read 6	A	World Studies	Individual Plan
TEAM 6C	XXX	XXX	XXX	XXX	XXX	XXX	XXX
TEACH 7	107	Individual Plan	107	Language Arts/ Read 6	A	World Studies	Exploratory Cultural Studies
TEACH 8	108	Individual Plan	108	Language Arts/ Read 6	A	Life Science	Pre-Algebra
TEACH 9	109	Individual Plan	109	Language Arts/ Read 6	A	Math	Life Science
TEACH 10	NHB	Resource 6		Read 6	B	Math 6	Team
TEAM 6D	XXX	XXX	XXX	XXX	XXX	XXX	XXX
TEACH 11	111	Team	111	Language Arts/ Read 6	B	Life Science	Exploratory Computer
TEACH 12	112	Team	112	Language Arts/ Read	B	Math	World Studies
TEACH 13	113	Team	113	Language Arts/ Read 6	B	Pre-Algebra	Exploratory Keyboarding
TEACH 14	114	Team	114	Language Arts/ Read 6	B	World Studies	World Studies
TEAM 6E	XXX	XXX	XXX	XXX	XXX	XXX	XXX
TEACH 15	115	World Studies	115	Language Arts/ Read 6	B	World Studies	Team
TEACH 16	116	Science Research	116	Language Arts/ Read 6	B	Life Science	Team
TEACH 17	117	Read Tutorial	117	Language Arts/ Read 6	B	Math	Team

(See accompanying CD-ROM for A-B master schedule for odd days for grade 6.)

GRADE 7	8:15–8:35	8:38–10:05	10:08–10:35	10:38–12:05	X	12:08–2:00	2:03–3:30
EVEN DAYS	HOME BASE	BLOCK 2	FLEX TIME	BLOCK 4	LUNCH	BLOCK 6	BLOCK 8
TEAM 7F	XXX	XXX	XXX	XXX	XXX	XXX	XXX
TEACH 1	101	Math	101	Language Arts/ Read 7	D	American Studies	Individual Plan
TEACH 2	102	Physical Science	102	Individual Plan	D	Physical Science	Core
TEACH 3	103	Language Arts/ Read 7	103	Language Arts/ Read 7	D	Individual Plan	Core
TEACH 4	104	Individual Plan	104	American Studies	D	American Studies	Core
TEACH 5	105	Health/P.E. 7	105	Health/P.E. 7	C	Health/P.E. 7	Individual Plan
TEACH 6	106	Math 7	106	Individual Plan	D	Pre-Algebra	Core
TEAM 7G	XXX	XXX	XXX	XXX	XXX	XXX	XXX
TEACH 7	107	Language Arts/ Read 7	107	Team	D	Language Arts/ Read 7	Core
TEACH 8	108	Physical Science	108	Team	D	Physical Science	Core
TEACH 9	109	American Studies	109	Team	D	American Studies	Core
TEACH 10	110	Pre-Algebra	110	Team	C	Algebra I	Core
TEACH 11	111	Resource 7	111	Team	D	American Studies	Language Arts/ Read 7
TEACH 12	112	Health/ P.E. 6	112	Team	D	Health/ P.E. 7	Health/P.E. 6
TEAM 7H	XXX	XXX	XXX	XXX	XXX	XXX	XXX
TEACH 13	113	American Studies	113	American Studies	D	American Studies	Core
TEACH 14	114	Physical Science	114	Physical Science	D	Physical Science	Core
TEACH 15	115	Language Arts/ Read 7	115	Individual Plan	D	Language Arts/ Read 7	Core
TEACH 16	116	Algebra I	116	Pre-Algebra	D	Math 7	Core
TEACH 17	117	Health/P.E. 7	117	Health/P.E. 7	X	Individual Plan	Health/P.E. 6

(See accompanying CD for grade 7 A-B master schedule for odd days.)

GRADE 8	8:15–8:35	8:38–10:05	10:08–10:35	10:38–12:05	X	12:08–2:00	2:03–3:30
EVEN DAYS	**HOME BASE**	**BLOCK 2**	**FLEX TIME**	**BLOCK 4**	**LUNCH**	**BLOCK 6**	**BLOCK 8**
TEAM 8I	XXX	XXX	XXX	XXX	XXX	XXX	XXX
TEACH 1	101	Core	101	Individual Plan	E	Language Arts/ Read 8	Language Arts/ Read 8
TEACH 2	102	Health/P.E. 6	102	Health/P.E. 8	C	Health/P.E. 8	Individual Plan
TEACH 3	103	Core	103	Geometry	E	Individual Plan	Algebra I
TEACH 4	104	Core	104	Earth Science	E	Individual Plan	Earth Science
TEACH 5	105	Core	105	Citizenship	E	Individual Plan	Citizenship
TEACH 6	106	Individual Plan	106	Citizenship	E	Resource	Language Arts/ Read 8
TEAM 8J	XXX	XXX	XXX	XXX	XXX	XXX	XXX
TEACH 7	107	Citizenship	107	Citizenship	X	Citizenship	Team
TEACH 8	108	Individual Plan	108	Health/P.E. 8	C	Health/P.E. 8	Team
TEACH 9	109	Core	109	Read/Math Tutorial	E	Individual Plan	Team
TEACH 10	110	Core	110	Geometry	E	Read/Math Tutorial	Team
TEACH 11	111	Core	111	Citizenship	E	Citizenship	Team
TEACH 12	112	Core	112	Earth Science	X	Earth Science	Team
TEAM 8K	XXX	XXX	XXX	XXX	XXX	XXX	XXX
TEACH 13	113	Core	113	Language Arts/ Read 8	E	Team	Language Arts/ Read 8
TEACH 14	114	Core	114	Read/Math Tutorial	E	Team	
TEACH 15	115	Citizenship	115	Citizenship	E	Citizenship	Individual Plan
TEACH 16	116	Health/P.E. 8	116	Health/P.E. 8	C	Health/P.E. 8	Individual Plan
TEACH 17	117	Earth Science	117	Individual Plan	E	Science Research	Earth Science
TEACH 18	118	Math 8	118	Earth Science	E	Life Science	Team

(See accompanying CD for grade 8 A-B master schedule for odd days.)

FIGURE 50

Sample Master Schedule for Odd Days (Blocks 1, 3, 5, and 8) for Content Area Teachers

CONTENT AREAS	8:15–8:35	8:38–10:05	10:08–10:35	10:38–12:05	X	12:08–2:00	2:03–3:30
ODD DAYS	HOME BASE	BLOCK 1	FLEX TIME	BLOCK 3	LUNCH	BLOCK 5	BLOCK 7
FOREIGN LANGUAGE	XXX	XXX	XXX	XXX	XXX	XXX	XXX
TEACH 1	101	Individual Plan	101	Spanish I	D	Spanish II	Spanish I
TEACH 2	102	Exploratory 6	102	Individual Plan	XXX	French I	French II
TEACH 3	103	Spanish II	103	Spanish II	XXX	Individual PLAN	Spanish II
TEACH 4	XXX	German I	XXX	XXX	XXX	XXX	XXX
VOCATIONAL	XXX	XXX	XXX	XXX	XXX	XXX	XXX
TEACH 5	105	Individual Plan	105	Keyboarding	D	Keyboarding	Keyboarding
TEACH 6	106	Individual Plan	106	Agriculture Exploratory	C	Agriculture Exploratory	Agriculture Mechanics
TEACH 7	107	Exploratory 6	107	Individual Plan	C	Exploring Technology Systems	Technology Systems
TEACH 8	108	Exploratory 6	107	Teen Living	C	Team Leader/ Cafeteria	Life Management Skills
TEACH 9	XXX	Exploratory 6	XXX	Shared	XXX	Shared	Shared
ART/G&T/ MUSIC	XXX	XXX	XXX	XXX	XXX	XXX	XXX
TEACH 10	110	Team Plan/ Office Duty	110	Individual Plan	C	Exploratory Art	Art Alternate Day
TEACH 11	111	Individual Plan	111	Exploratory Art	C	Art 8	Art Alternate Day
TEACH 12	112	Individual Plan	112	G&T Seminar	XXX	Individual Plan	G&T Resource 6
TEACH 13	113	Individual Plan	113	Chorus 2	E	Chorus 3	Beginning Chorus 6
TEACH 12	XXX	Shared	XXX	Shared	XXX	String Ensemble	Beginning Strings 6
TEACH 14	114	Band 2	114	Team Plan/ Lunch Duty	E	Band 2	Beginning Band
SENIOR TEACHERS	XXX	XX	XXX	XXX	XXX	XXX	XXX
TEACH 15	XXX	Exploratory 6	XXX	XXX	XXX	XXX	XXX
LIBRARIAN	XXX	XXX	XXX	XXX	XXX	XXX	XXX
TEACH 16	XXX	Library	XXX	Library	XXX	Library	Library
TEACH 17	XXX	Exploratory 6	XXX	Library	XXX	Exploratory 6	Library

(See accompanying CD for the similar teacher schedule for even days.)

(Thanks to the staff at Stonewall Jackson Middle School in Brookland, VA, and Dr. Wade A. (Tony) Valentino, former principal, for sharing the preceding information.)

Tom was visiting a middle school during the exploratory stage of the block scheduling process. The school principal shared with him that she scheduled her core subjects in three large blocks daily and then alternated art and physical education on a rotating day basis. She needed a schedule that would allow her to offer her students more course opportunities. Students at various grade levels were scheduled in a variety of ways. Sixth- and seventh-grade students did not take a foreign language, while eighth graders had that option. At the eighth grade, students began what she called a transition to the high school approach of scheduling. They were offered the opportunity to take four core courses, which included Algebra I and a foreign language, for high school credit. She found that it was not always possible or even necessary to schedule all classes for the same amount of time in the same grades in the same building.

Another middle school strategy that has great potential at the high school level is referred to as **flex time** or **directed studies.** This is a block of time that provides opportunities for students and faculty to pursue academic support activities. These opportunities include additional band or chorus rehearsal during peak performance times, individual and small group tutoring or reteaching, make-up work, research and reading, exploring the library, group seminars/lectures with special guests, special programs, and career planning and advisement. The length of the block depends on the student population's needs, the building-level administration, and the philosophy of the school or school division.

ADVANTAGES TO STUDENTS

A block schedule produces the following advantages for students.

■ Fewer class preparations per day

■ Exposure to a variety of teaching and learning methods by teachers who have had special training to teach in large blocks of time

■ Fewer text and class resources to deal with on a daily basis

■ Increased opportunities for interaction with teachers (This should result in more personalized attention with faculty and higher academic achievement.)

■ Decrease in passing time, which equates to additional instructional time

■ Less stopping and starting of classes, which results in less fragmentation of instructional time

■ More time for teachers to evaluate student achievement effectively

The advantages depend on the school's philosophy and the willingness of all stakeholders to allow opportunities to occur. Manning and Saddlemier (1996, p. 339) list at least two middle-school practices that have potential to ". . . increase student academic achievement . . . and improve attitude toward school" at the secondary level. The first is an advisor-advisee program; the second is an interdisciplinary team approach to instruction. But they warn high school educators that before choosing one or both of these concepts for implementation, they "should ask themselves the following questions: considering the characteristics of our high school, which concepts hold the most promise for (1) improving academic achievement, (2) improving student behavior . . ." (Manning & Saddlemier, 1996, p. 339). They warn that the change process will not always be easy. Educators must be committed in time and persistence—and training will be necessary—but the effort will be worth it.

ADVISOR-ADVISEE PROGRAMS

Now that high school educators have shifted the paradigm for the use of instructional time, they may elect to use the new way of doing business to implement the advisor-advisee program. This flexible use of time has the potential to impact the overall climate of a school, which will impact student achievement. This concept has been used in middle schools for many years and has been reported to be very successful. The advisor-advisee program, sometimes called a teacher advisory, ensures that each student has at least one adult who knows him or her well and also that each student belongs to a small, interactive group. Advisory groups promote students' social, emotional, and moral growth while providing personal and academic guidance. To reduce the student-teacher ratio, all professional staff members serve as advisors. Although some descriptors recommend that these advisory sessions should be held daily and can be 25 to 40 minutes long, many schools implement this program with fewer meetings.

Advisories can focus on students' concerns and suggestions or can be based on "advisory plans" prepared by professional writers. Most high schools have guidance counselors and guidance programs that operate in accordance with district policy and/or accrediting associations. It should be noted that adding advisor-advisee programs to the high school guidance program neither negates nor undercuts the work of counseling professionals (Manning & Saddlemier, 1996, p. 339). One national reform effort, *High Schools That Work*, recommends advisor-advisee initiatives as a way of increasing career counseling services to secondary students (Southern Regional Education Board, 1994).

This type of strategy may be under the direction of the guidance director, but it must be a priority of the principal if the time allocated is to be used well. It creates the potential for a positive climate for student learning and increased student achievement. Such a program provides direction for academic and social success, especially for at-risk students who do not always encounter a positive role model on a daily basis. However, without commitment to this effort, the time allocated can be misused and unproductive for students. Let's look at the components needed to assure the success of this initiative.

■ Staff training

Just as with any new initiative, staff training for advisor teachers is vital if the advisor-advisee initiative is to succeed. The chair of the action team to prepare for this should be the director of guidance. This would send two messages to the faculty and staff: first, that this is a schoolwide effort; and second, that it is not a separate program that will undermine the guidance and counseling program in

the school. It is a program aimed at helping students meet high expectations and achieve at a higher level.

This action team assumes responsibility for placing students, designing activities related to curriculum, monitoring academic achievement, providing communication to parents and other customers, and other related issues. This action team also plans a variety of structured activities and small group activities throughout the school year to address academic goals and expectations related to careers as well as other issues that are important to students.

Each student remains with the same group and same advisor throughout the school year. Of course, there are always exceptions, and some students may need to change groups to find a proper fit. An evaluation of the program based on measurable indicators should be done at the end of each semester. It should be repeated at the end of the second year of implementation and annually after it has been refined.

CASE IN POINT

Advisor-advisee groups will meet on a weekly basis during a pre-established activity/study block period usually for 30 minutes. During this advisory period, the teacher serves as a facilitator and attempts to establish an environment where students can develop a network with a faculty member and other students so that they can explore possibilities and set goals and discuss academic or other school-related issues. Structured activities should be developed by the teacher and the advisees within the group. Topics such as course selection, study skills, SAT preparation, job interview skills, conflict resolution, and success in achieving rigorous academic expectations will be topics of discussion during these sessions. There are many advantages that cannot be measured that will emerge from these sessions, all hopefully improving the school climate that leads to student achievement. These programs should be evaluated on a regular basis to provide direction as well as to look at the strengths and weaknesses of such a program. The program should be revised according to the data collected from the assessment process.

■ **Planning for the implementation process**

If you believe the advisor-advisee program worthy of consideration, an action team should convene to determine if there is a need for such a program, and if so, to develop a plan that will include all involved customers in the process. The plan should enumerate the benefits to the students and the ways this program will enhance student academic achievement. The action team should consider the demographics of the community, the school structure

(K–12), and the missions of the school and school district before a recommendation is made. If the process is truly participative, the recommendation that is made to the administration may not be one with which you agree. These differences should be explored to ensure that they will not have a negative impact on the mission of the secondary schools as perceived by the customers of the secondary schools.

As in other programs, a public relations/communication plan should be designed under the direction of an action team. All information should be shared with customers as often as possible during the process. Parents will want to know that this program exists, especially as it relates to information about course content, academic and career pathways, and developing personal skills needed for success in school. The team must identify an evaluation plan related to student achievement early in the planning process. This will likely provide direction for the program and support the program as needed from dissenters. These data will determine if the program has in fact been worth the effort.

A critical piece of the process would be the ability of an action team convened to design a long-term plan of programs for the advisor-advisee program. The team chair should be a member of the school counseling/guidance team. Members of the team should include staff, teachers, social services, and other members of your school improvement team. Local issues that are controversial should be avoided as part of this program.

ADVISOR-ADVISEE AND THE USE OF BLOCK SCHEDULING

Because of a more efficient use of time, innovative programs using the block schedule are limited only by the imagination of the customers within a school community. One such program is called the advisor-advisee program. This program provides a format for interaction between students and faculty. Interactions between a school staff and students will hopefully create a positive school climate, which will provide opportunities for all students to increase student achievement and reduce potential student behavior problems. The purpose of the advisor-advisee program is not to replace an existing guidance/counseling program but to provide a format for students and teachers to approach solutions to student learning problems in a proactive manner. This program provides all students an opportunity to receive academic and career advice from a professional staff member.

Each faculty member will be assigned a manageable group of students (12 to 15) who are in the same age/grade level. A staff development program should be developed by present counselors in the school to help teachers deal with conflict resolution, group dynamics, and career orientation skills.

Consider the schedule in Figure 51 when using a seven-period day block scheduling format with an advisement block.

As usual, when using an alternating day (A-B) block, the schedule would rotate during the B week of the schedule. The amount of time spent with each student or by each teacher depends on the size of the school, the length of each block, the philosophy of the school, and the stated intent of the program.

Middle schools have often taken a step ahead of high schools with many of their programmatic and instructional decisions. Similarly, some middle schools have looked at block scheduling differently and presented new models that should be considered at the high school level, including the scheduling of an intersession with alternative course selections. For an interesting case study of W. Marshall Sellman School and its 50-50-50-30 block schedule, which features an intersession, see the accompanying CD.

The Sellman materials in the case study include the following:

- Description of the 50-50-50-30 model
- Timeline for implementing the plan
- Parent Information Sheet
- Frequently Asked Questions
- Letter to Parents
- Instructions for Registration
- Parent Evaluation Form and Results
- Volunteer Form
- Student Evaluation Form and Results
- Teacher Evaluation Form and Results
- Course offerings for the 30-day schedule
- Sellman traditional 90-90 schedule
- Sellman 75-75-30 block schedule
- Sellman 30-day intersession
- 30-day teacher schedule
- Sample course descriptions

OPPORTUNITIES OFFERED BY THE SELLMAN 50-50-50-30

Offerings many times, in any schedule, depend on the demographics of the community, the composition of

FIGURE 51
Seven-Period Day Alternating Block with an Advisor-Advisee Block

MON=A	TUE=B	WED=A	THUR=B	FRI=A
Block 1	Block 1	Block 1	Block 1	Block 1
Block 2	Block 2	Block 2	Block 2	Block 2
Study/Advisement Block 3	Advisement 9 and 10 Block 3	Block 3	Advisement 11 and 12 Block 3	Block 3
Block 4	Block 4	Block 4	Block 4	Block 4

Advisement meets only one day a month throughout the year.

the staff, and the school mission for including the intersession. A word of caution: Many times, the title of the course offering does not adequately reflect the content that is being taught. If the names of courses that teachers submit for the intersession tend to be controversial or counter to the school district's vision, give serious consideration to changing the name of the course, not necessarily the content. This is especially true in conservative communities. In many instances, a misunderstanding of the purpose of any realignment of time is a result of customers not being educated about the change taking place.

CAUTION! NO FRIVOLOUS OFFERINGS

If one of the objectives of finding more innovative ways for scheduling students is to increase student achievement—and it must be—then courses should be designed around the achievement standards of the school. They should be designed to meet the needs of students who require assistance to be successful (low achieving and at-risk students), students who are making it but need motivation to do even better, and students who need the challenge to move to newer heights in learning. With the current national attention to accountability that has driven new standards of performance in many states, it is critical that changes in schedules be tied to higher achievement of students in basic core courses, rather than being viewed as a strategy for making more time for the fun stuff.

LOOKING BACK . . .

Addressing organizational issues appropriately and in a timely manner will mean the difference in the success or failure of the schedule format that you have chosen. If you address the issues from this chapter and put in place a contingency plan for unanticipated issues, a win-win situation is created for all customers and students. ❏

Chapter 8 Appendix on CD

❏ Creative Scheduling at the Middle School Level

- Even- and Odd-day Schedules from Stonewall Jackson Middle School, Mechanicsville, Virginia
  - Sample Master Schedule for Even Days (Blocks 2/4/6/8)
  - Sample Master Schedule for Odd Days (Blocks 1/3/5/7)
- A Case Study of the Sellman 50-50-50-30 Block Schedule
  - Introduction to Case Study (word version)
  - Timeline (word version)
  - Materials and Forms from Sellman
  - Evaluation Results
  - Course Offerings (word version)
  - Sample Schedules
  - The Sellman 30-Day Intersession
  - Course Descriptions

How Does the Instructional Program Change When the Staff Examines the Use of Time?

*T*ime will no longer manage my students. My students will manage time.

—Linda Motley, 1996

One of the many positive products of block scheduling is the win-win situation created in the school's instructional program. Teachers and students win when block scheduling is implemented effectively. Teachers win because they have longer blocks of time to explore topics with students as well as to plan with peers. Students win because they have the time to be actively engaged in learning and can concentrate on one subject area for a longer period of time before moving to another area of study. Thus, it is important for teachers to understand why the "old way of teaching" must change. Planning for longer periods of time is critical to providing enhanced learning opportunities. Single-topic lessons must disappear as teachers move to teach units that integrate concepts. Teachers should continue to incorporate technology-based instruction so students have access to the most current research and information available.

Changes also occur in the way that classrooms are managed by teachers. Teachers provide opportunities for active student involvement, and the classroom climate becomes one of collaboration and mutual respect between teacher and student. Teachers provide immediate feedback on homework assignments as well as classroom assignments. Homework assignments must be judged on quality, not quantity, as has been past practice. For this change to occur in teaching and learning, teachers must define what "different" means as they implement the change process.

Staff development is critical to the success of the block schedule, and a plan must be tailored to meet the needs of the school in which the block schedule is being implemented. Teachers collaborate with colleagues to create ways that will allow teachers and students to become partners in learning.

Additionally, students need training as they become more accountable for their learning, management of time, and behavior. The role of the student changes as each becomes an active participant in the learning process, rather than a passive consumer.

IMPROVING INSTRUCTION

Many school administrators who have implemented a block schedule agree that the block scheduling format has a positive impact on many issues regarding students and teachers. One of the most important factors in the success of scheduling change is that of staff development. Staff development designed to change and improve teaching strategies is critical if students and teachers are to be successful in using longer blocks of instructional time more efficiently. For this reason, staff development will be discussed as an instructional issue.

"We can no longer teach the way we have been doing it," Karen Collins, a teacher at Atlee High School told a group of teachers who were visiting Tom's school. She continued: "The business of teaching is not business as usual, and the old way of teaching won't cut it, if you implement block scheduling."

It is common sense to assume that when instructional time is doubled, instructional practices will change. Based on comments from teachers and administrators over the past five years, this is not the case in many classrooms. In order for increased instructional time to benefit students, teachers must use a variety of teaching methods to sustain student interest.

Milton Goldberg, who was the executive editor of *A Nation at Risk* and executive editor of *Prisoners of Time*, frequently talked about change. He concluded that regardless of the changes that were made related to the use of time in schools, there would be no improvement in learning if teachers did not have adequate support to help them change their classroom teaching practices (lecture, Richmond, VA, 1997).

Other instructional issues that must be explored include teaching expectations in a larger block of time; that is, the encouragement of a higher level of creativity from teachers and students, and quality achievement from both teachers and students. Preparation of teachers to engage in team teaching and interdisciplinary lessons is also a high priority.

Curriculum should drive the schedule rather than the schedule dictating the curriculum and the method of delivery.

If teachers and students are to be successful using the block schedule format to increase student achievement, teachers must re-think how they plan lessons. The use of allocated instructional time, what happens in the classroom, and how extended time beyond the classroom is used must be given serious consideration.

PLANNING FOR CHANGE IN CLASSROOM INSTRUCTION

Planning for classroom instruction is critical during the initial year of implementing the block schedule. Teachers no longer plan for one class period at a time. They look at long-term planning and determine instructional objectives they want to accomplish over a semester of instruction.

Change is not easy, nor does it occur without planning. If successful change is to occur, steps that lead to change must be identified using a team approach. Karen Collins chaired the mathematics department at Atlee High School and was one of the most verbal supporters of the block schedule

---

CASE IN POINT

As a teacher of English, Tom had the opportunity to experience firsthand that lessons could be completed in one session. In one block of instructional time, he was able to introduce a writing assignment and provide individualized instruction to each member of his class. Students were engaged in pre-writing activities and completed the first draft of a writing assignment during the one block of instructional time (1 hour and 47 minutes). These students were able to produce a higher quality final draft because they had time to synthesize and apply theory. This gave them a more thorough understanding of their assignment. As students and teachers adjusted to the longer block of time, Tom observed higher quality final products. He is convinced that when time is used efficiently, the longer block of time results in more opportunities for learning and teaching.

from the beginning of the change process. After six years of teaching in the block schedule, she told Tom that she would not continue to teach if she had to return to a traditional 55-minute period format. From the very beginning of the implementation process, she sought new ways to make instruction exciting and rewarding for students. She also knew that for this to happen for all students, teachers must be successful. As chairperson of the mathematics department, she set out to model ways that make it possible for this to happen. She developed a framework for instructional change that we have expanded and present as a tool for working with faculty. Much of this information, with the exception of the content of the lesson plans, can be adapted to meet the needs of any content area.

A CLOSER LOOK AT CHANGING INSTRUCTIONAL PRACTICES

As teachers begin planning for block instruction, either individually or in teams, a number of approaches or strategies can be used to stimulate thinking about best practices. Using the framework presented, we will briefly comment on the components of this framework to help establish a baseline of understanding about the complexity of change in the classroom and to ensure clarity of the concepts used in the framework. Again, principals may use this information to guide staff development they conduct with the faculty or share the information with department chairs or team leaders who can work with small groups of teachers.

WHAT DO I CHANGE? PLANNING

Teachers should re-think the traditional way of planning for delivery of instruction in the classroom. They can begin with a mini needs assessment of their practice, determining what has worked particularly well over the years and what no longer works well. They should think about the topics or lessons they would like to use but have been unable to include due to a lack of time or depending on

FIGURE 52
Instructional Change Framework

WHAT do I change?	...and HOW do I change it?
■ Planning • Identify concepts and merge concepts • Plan in units (not topics) • Integrate technology and manipulatives into instruction • Develop productive cooperative learning strategies	**■ Planning** • Start slowly and build up to an integration of all the ideas • Plan together; divide tasks among subject leaders • Organize supplementary materials
■ Classroom Environment • Focus on student-centered learning • Create atmosphere of inquiry and investigation • Encourage cooperation among students • Provide immediate feedback to students	**■ Classroom Environment** • Don't teach too much • Give lots of wait/think time • Conduct discovery activities
■ Assignments/Homework • Focus on quality, not quantity • Develop investigative, not repetitive, assignments	**■ Assignments/Homework** • Allow for practice and feedback in class; not homework time • Take the time to explain all parts of an assignment
■ Assessment and Evaluation • Implement assessment procedures that measure student learning in the way it was taught • Review student performance to determine how block is working	**■ Assessment and Evaluation** • Develop rubrics for portfolio or other multiple criteria assessments • Modify the instructional process to maximize learning in your classroom

teacher delivery of instruction rather than experiential learning by students. Teachers should ask themselves: "What topics could I combine under some big idea or major concept area that would enrich the students' curriculum while allowing them to see a more integrated view of learning and their world?"

Concept mergers. By merging concepts, teachers begin to teach how concepts interrelate rather than attempting to teach one single concept. Students can experience learning that will help to internalize concepts and show how they interrelate with each other. As students understand a concept and the set of similar properties or attributes that make up the concept, the teacher has the opportunity to provide learning activities that move up Bloom's Taxonomy. Students can not only apply what they are learning to different situations, they can also cross disciplines and see the value of their learning in a larger context. It is critical for students to understand the academic knowledge base associated with the concept if they are to achieve success in understanding and applying the concept, but critical thinking skills develop as students are asked to use information in ways other than procedural thinking. Merging concepts, therefore, helps the teacher broaden the curriculum that can be covered by compacting the way information is presented and taught. In addition, merging concepts benefits students by helping them see knowledge in a context larger than a single lesson.

Units, not topics. Planning to teach units rather than topics will be a major change for some teachers. In some cases, this means looking at different instructional materials and how these materials are presented by the teacher. The idea of starting at Chapter One of the text on the first day of school and ending with the last page of the last chapter in the text on the last instructional day of school will need to be reviewed. Teaching units to cover concepts will require teachers to draw materials from a variety of resources and to present these materials in ways that will give students an opportunity to understand the depth of the concept, not just the superficial nature of the topic. Again: It is critical to understand expectations as they are related to academic achievement.

If teachers have difficulty thinking in terms of units, we suggest two things. One: If you know a strong elementary teacher (who can relate to secondary teachers) who is experienced in unit planning and delivery, ask him/her to develop a short presentation for faculty leaders. What comes naturally to many elementary teachers is less comfortable to secondary teachers, but the methodology can be shared and learned.

Two: If you as the leader would rather work directly with teachers (or use an outside consultant) to develop these skills, you may choose to develop a workshop on concept identification and integration. In a two-hour period you can work teachers through the thinking required to initially understand concept identification. Ongoing staff development on the topic would be highly appropriate if you sense a lack of responsiveness by teachers or the need for further training on this topic.

Integration of technology and manipulatives. Given the large blocks of time that teachers have to utilize materials, the use of technology as an integrated teaching/learning tool will enable students and teachers to access hardware and software that support the content areas. Additionally, students will be able to explore opportunities that will translate to continued academic learning (formal education/training) or job-related skills. Students will have the opportunity in one class period to complete technology-related assignments that previously were time prohibitive. Similarly, teachers can plan activities with learning manipulatives that encourage student exploration but require time to use. As teachers begin seeing the classroom as a laboratory of learning that extends beyond the blackboard and overhead projector to include scientific probes, graphing calculators, Internet searches, and computer simulations to engage students in research and projects, time becomes the facilitator of learning.

The use of both technology and manipulatives will assist the teacher in making the transition from a teaching style dominated by lecture to a more balanced teaching style that will be compatible with the varied learning styles of students. This does not translate to less rigorous demands upon students. This change provides an opportunity for a more active student learning environment that can lead to challenging content, demanding learning activities, and higher student achievement.

Effective cooperative learning strategies. Teachers may want to be cautious in using cooperative learning strategies as a part of their teaching strategies. Cooperative learning is just one strategy that can be used successfully in a longer block of time. But without appropriate training it can be misused and is deemed ineffective by some administrators and parents. In many situations that we have observed, teachers use cooperative learning as the only instructional strategy during a class period, or they believe they have to use cooperative learning if they are on a block schedule.

We suggest that cooperative learning be one component of your staff development plan that looks at a number of teaching methods and pedagogies. Help teachers understand why cooperative learning is good to use, and help them understand when and how to use it. Learning in groups is highly beneficial to learning, and learning to work together in a noncompetitive environment is a job-entry skill highly valued by employers. Our caution is that we have seen cooperative learning done poorly and become misused. Therefore, we suggest that you offer support and reinforcement during the first months of implementation.

WHAT DO I CHANGE? CLASSROOM ENVIRONMENT

Classroom teaching must change from teacher-centered to one that uses the teacher to focus on the student. However, you may choose not to use this particular language, because some teachers become offended when it is suggested that their present methodologies focus more on them than on their students. Just help teachers understand the difference—that learning in the 90-minute block must include activities with high student interaction. Teachers should provide opportunities that support an atmosphere of inquiry and investigation, allowing students to feel comfortable taking risks and making mistakes as they apply academic knowledge in ways that encourage creativity and independent thinking. This environment encourages learning and problem solving. The length of the block allows teachers greater opportunity to give individual feedback to students on daily assignments and long-term projects, building a climate of responsiveness and concern while pushing expectations to a higher level.

Teacher/Student-centered classroom. Strategies are developed to create a student/teacher-centered classroom and not a teacher-centered classroom. Teaching strategies are designed to focus on actively involving students in the learning process. The teacher will consider changing roles and become a facilitator of instruction as well as a disseminator of knowledge.

In simpler language, the teacher must continue to convey expertise in the content area and serve as an authority on much of what is taught. But the reality of today's world is that no one individual can know everything that is available to students, even in Biology I, U.S. History, or Automotive Technology. The teacher must be able to help students learn how to access information and how to continue learning beyond the classroom. Teachers must be comfortable with the role of facilitator—one who helps others with the process of learning. They can best do this by modeling the lifelong learning process to their students and by utilizing activities that actively engage students in thinking and producing.

Atmosphere of inquiry and investigation. This strategy promotes creativity within the classroom. Teachers allow students an opportunity to ask questions and investigate all possibilities that allow them to make constructive decisions regarding teacher-assigned tasks.

Cooperation between students–students and teachers–students. Another strategy that we observed and many teachers indicated as useful in teaching in the block schedule format, is fostering a climate of cooperation. Because of the length of time in the block, students have opportunities to become partners in learning. They know that it is acceptable to work with other students and that this is perceived as a positive learning experience to help gain a more thorough or different understanding of a concept. Teachers also indicated that peer pressure from other students to participate in an orderly and productive manner had a positive impact on the behavior of some students in the classroom.

Years ago, a colleague of Yvonne's told her that teachers operate on a game plan that has existed for decades—one that is built on the premise that the teacher has the information that the student needs, and that the teacher will not share that information unless the student can figure out what it is—sort of a keep-away game. We challenge students to determine what information that we teach is really important and will therefore show up on the next test. If the student is able to sort through the textbooks and lectures and homework and find the magic answers, s/he not only learns what is considered important by the teacher but she gets a good grade as well.

We're not so cynical about instruction, but we do believe that in today's world of high academic standards for all students, it is imperative that teachers view learning as a cooperative venture between them and students. Creating a climate that fosters cooperation between teacher and learner can only help students understand the importance of their coursework and the value of the learning activities we oversee.

Immediate feedback. Teachers have an opportunity in the larger blocks of time to respond to student questions and give immediate feedback that is needed for a student to gain an understanding of a concept and move forward with an application. As teachers we sometimes have only one

window of opportunity to reach a student. If we do not take advantage of the open window, it may never again be available. If classrooms are designed to become teacher/student-centered learning environments, and if students are allowed to explore all of the possibilities as they inquire, there is a chance

---

CASE IN POINT

A parent, a teacher, and a student were having difficulty agreeing on the student's expected level of achievement in a science course. Tom, the principal, requested a conference with all involved. As they waded through the reasons for low achievement, Tom asked the student for his thoughts. He gave an answer that teachers, parents, and administrators have heard more times than they would care to count. "I don't always understand what she is talking about." The response from the teacher and the parent came almost simultaneously: "Why don't you ask?" We all know the answer. "She won't let us interrupt, and she doesn't provide opportunities to ask questions."

The student shared the same story that we have all heard many times: He was afraid to ask questions. Students in this teacher's classes never had an opportunity to become involved in the discovery of what science is about. They sat and listened for 107 minutes every other day and eventually all curiosity faded because there was no chance for inquiry.

The teacher knew she had a reputation for not allowing students to ask questions or participate in learning. Together Tom and she put in place a plan of improvement that would allow the teacher an opportunity to participate in staff development that would provide her with strategies to encourage student inquiry and investigation. After a year of teaching under this revised plan, there was a dramatic difference in her teaching strategies as well as in her attitude toward teaching.

How can we expect a student to investigate and inquire if s/he is not allowed to ask questions? How else does a student become a lifelong learner?

that we will see a revitalization of creativity and excitement in both teachers and students.

Sometimes it appears to us that teachers miss opportunities to work with students and provide the kind of feedback that supports learning. When 15 minutes of the block is used for guided practice, it should be guided by the teacher. While teachers want to build independence among students, they also should take advantage of every moment they have to observe students in tasks and stop them when their process is faulty. Homework should be used to build skills around what is shown to work. Guided practice should be used to help students master the process initially, receiving feedback throughout to ensure that the process is understood and can be repeated flawlessly.

WHAT DO I CHANGE? HOMEWORK/CLASSROOM ASSIGNMENTS

Recently Tom was working with a group of teachers in a school that was considering the implementation of block scheduling. A veteran math teacher asked him a question that we hear frequently from seminar participants. "How am I going to give the same amount of homework in 90 days as I have given in 180 days?" Tom's response was to address this as an issue of assigning quality homework that extends class activities.

The issue of homework has in some instances become a major barrier to block scheduling. An action team should make appropriate decisions about this issue based on the needs of your school or school district. There should be consensus among the faculty and administration about homework and whether teachers may use part of the block instructional period for it. When principals complain about teachers using 20 to 30 minutes of instructional time for homework, we rarely find that they have articulated their concern to the faculty.

Quality not quantity. Guide teachers to look at the quality of homework they give and not at how much homework they assign. Quality will increase as the nature of homework assignments changes from reinforcement exercises to investigative or creative assignments that will expand the student's understanding of base academic knowledge.

CASE IN POINT

Many of the teachers in a large urban school district were concerned about students not completing their homework or failing to turn in any homework assignments. During a workshop on block scheduling, we began to search for the cause of the problem. As we discussed the issues surrounding the problem, it became apparent that many students did not live in an environment that was conducive to doing homework. After deciding that assigning homework every night might not be the answer to reinforcing daily instruction, we moved to developing other instructional strategies that would support the regular classroom instruction. The teachers determined that when homework was assigned, it would be "quality homework."

When is homework a tool for reinforcement, and when is it a barrier to student success?

Investigative not repetitive. Outside-of-class assignments should be new experiences for students instead of a repetition of the day's activities. If the instructional objective for homework is to provide practice or reinforcement of previously introduced skills, find creative ways for students to practice or reinforce a particular skill. Consider the following example that Tom used in his English class. When making homework assignments related to writing mechanics, he assigned students the task of searching printed materials such as newspapers or popular teen magazines for mistakes in the use of mechanics (or any other mistakes they could find). This activity was in lieu of assigning repetitive sentences from the text that required students to identify the mistakes. Thus, they had to explore and investigate other options that were related to real-world issues.

WHAT DO I CHANGE? ASSESSMENT AND EVALUATION

Measure student learning as it was taught. Sometimes it is not clear that a change in instructional methodology requires a change in assessment practices. Why? Because the two should match.

When teachers focus on low-level, factual acquisition, it is appropriate to ask students to demonstrate mastery on paper-and-pencil tests. As teachers move up Bloom's Taxonomy and include activities that require synthesizing information from multiple sources and evaluating products constructed, different assessment procedures are appropriate. Similarly, as students are asked to give oral presentations on research conducted or to use technology as a part of an assignment, it only makes sense to look at multiple criteria for assessment.

For years, elementary teachers have developed portfolios of student work that demonstrated the level of proficiency matched to a grade. These portfolios have now become more sophisticated as software allows teachers to keep them on disk, scanning in documents that can be viewed on the computer and kept forever. Most secondary teachers have not utilized portfolios to document student performance. They are most frequently found in English and vocational/technical classrooms. The use of portfolios is one option for a more comprehensive assessment of student performance.

A second option for creating assessments that match instruction is to develop rubrics or other lists of multiple criteria. Yvonne has found that while many secondary teachers have not been trained in the use of a rubric, after being given a model, teachers can develop these easily. For example, use the notion of a cooperative group doing a project together. What would be the skills, concepts, and content that should be developed during the project? A teacher can list these usually with no difficulty and then merely needs to assign weights to each. For example, perhaps 50 points would be given for the final paper, 25 points for an oral presentation, 10 points for group interaction skills, 10 points for the use of technology, and 5 points for a personal interview. The 50 points for the paper could be divided into the specifics the teacher felt were important: references, content specificity, style of writing, grammar, etc.

Teachers who work together on interdisciplinary projects or joint assignments can develop two rubrics—one for each class assigning a grade.

CHANGING INSTRUCTION IN THE CLASSROOM

The idea of changing instruction in the classroom seems simple to the noneducator: use a different textbook or implement a different approach or adopt higher standards or give more difficult tests or allocate more time for learning. However, changing instruction is complex. In fact, each of these ideas for change can work when it is used in conjunction with other changes in the instructional process. To say that many educators do not understand the learning process is not an indictment of their craft but more the reality of the limited education they receive before entering the classroom. Unlike other professionals who complete internships or craftsmen who are apprenticed, teachers have little opportunity to learn from master teachers before being

---

CASE IN POINT

Yvonne has visited schools on block schedules in several states. She has observed many classrooms in which the last 20 to 30 minutes were used for homework assignments. A few teachers used the beginning of class for homework catch-up. She has served with teams of educators who visited these schools expecting to see great things happening with block scheduling, but tended to focus on the time they viewed as lost to homework.

In one school, teachers bragged about using the time this way, believing the block schedule provided the time needed for homework that students were previously not completing out of school. These teachers also talked about not having enough time to complete the content required by the curriculum. Principals expressed great concern that class time was being used for homework when they had expected to see students working on challenging projects. In this school, teachers were generally teaching the same amount of time they did in the traditional schedule, using instructional time for homework. They couldn't complete the curriculum in the shorter time frame. They continued their previous methodologies and didn't utilize the longer time frame to challenge students in high-level activities.

Determining what is appropriate as in-class activities should be a faculty decision. If time for homework is to be given during the instructional block, teachers and administrators must be aware of the price being paid and balance activities to ensure that the curriculum is taught, standards are met, and students are actively engaged.

---

expected to perform as one. Their background in curriculum and instruction usually includes no more than the minimal amount required for graduation from teacher training institutions. As principal and change agent, you may find it helpful to share a model or description of the teaching-learning process with faculty to help them understand the importance of looking at all components when changing to a block schedule.

Over the past several years, Yvonne has developed the flowchart description of the learning process in Figure 53, which she has used with teachers. Teachers in workshops have said that this model is helpful for them to understand the big picture of the process they are trying to improve.

How do I change . . . planning?

Start slowly and build. To some change agents, this advice sounds pedestrian. Many leaders enjoy the role of change agent because they like to move ahead quickly. While we also like to help schools meet goals and take on challenges, our experience shows us that the task of trying to implement all of these changes at once will be too cumbersome. Divide tasks among subject area leaders. Empower these teacher-leaders to develop strategies that will ensure the success of change. Teachers as instructional leaders in schools have much to offer. We make this suggestion after personally experiencing successful change in suburban and rural high schools using teachers as leaders. They can move mountains that administrators must tunnel through.

Start slowly and build up to an integration of all ideas. It is a major mistake to attempt to change all instructional strategies at once. It can be an overwhelming experience and can create a climate that will frustrate teachers and thus minimize the chance of success. Try a few new instructional strategies initially and add to the instructional menu as you become accustomed to the new time allocation. Where should you begin? Identify an area of need but one in which you can be assured of success. Any new initiative must have a few victories early on to gain credibility with both the staff and the public.

Plan together. If there is to be successful change in the use of instructional time, it is important

FIGURE 53
Continuous Learning

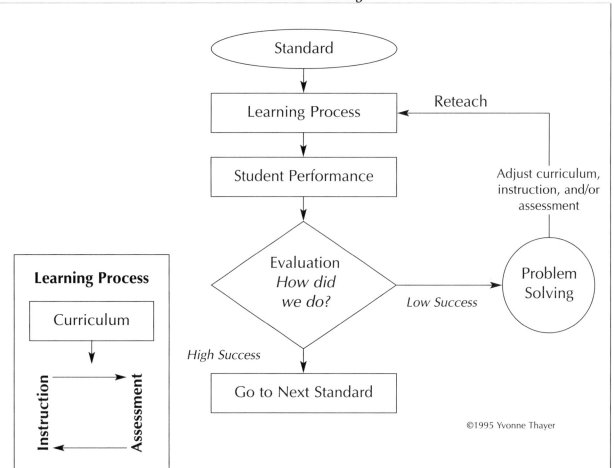

©1995 Yvonne Thayer

Continuous Learning begins with the identification of the Standard that the teacher is working toward. The Standard probably has several benchmarks that will be used to determine the objective(s) for the class. Understanding the Standard, the teacher implements the Learning Process, which is composed of the curriculum, instruction, and assessment. The curriculum is chosen to teach to the Standard. Instruction and student assessment are cyclical—each determining the other. That is, if a teacher knows that the student will be assessed in a certain way, the teaching methodology should match. If pedagogy drives the process, the assessment should be appropriate for the teaching-learning process. At the conclusion of the Learning Process, the teacher examines some type of student performance that indicates how well the student attained the objective or met the benchmark. This performance can be taken from an assessment or it can be a separate measure. This information answers the question, "How did we do?" It gives the teacher a way of evaluating the overall program. The teacher determines if the class did well enough to move on to the next standard or if reteaching is indicated. If low performance (that is, lower than what is acceptable in your school) calls for continued instruction, the teacher must enter into a problem-solving phase to know what to do next. Is the problem with the curriculum (choice of materials and content), the methodology (how material taught), or the assessment (how performance was measured)? Appropriate adjustments to the Learning Process should be made before reteaching and following the process again.

that all players participate in the process. This means making each team member a part of the change. This team approach will lend itself to providing a supportive climate, and the chances of success will be optimized. We recommend that initially instructional teams be divided into two team classifications. One team operates as a cross-functioning instructional team that considers issues related to all areas of the school course of studies. (This team can function as the school improvement team.) The second team operates as a content team dealing with issues that are related to specific content areas; i.e.: a math team, English team, fine arts team, or technical arts team. Other support personnel such as administrators, guidance counselors, and media center specialists also will participate as members of the team.

Divide tasks among content leaders. If tasks are divided among different groups, the chance of the task being completed successfully is higher. Rather than requiring the entire faculty to be responsible for change throughout the school, assign tasks to instructional leaders such as department chairs, instructional team leaders, or lead teachers.

Organize supplementary materials. During the start-up phase of block scheduling, as teachers plan differently for the use of time in classrooms, it is helpful for them to have teaching materials that aid or supplement regular curriculum materials. Being able to access auxiliary materials eliminates apprehension and makes it easier for teachers to plan activities they have previously not used. Supplementary materials can be collected by teachers, media center specialists, teacher aides, or other support persons. It would be a particularly good gesture for central office supervisors to assist, as it would indicate to teachers that the move to block scheduling is supported by all of the administration and is important.

HOW DO I CHANGE . . . CLASSROOM ENVIRONMENT?

On a survey administered at Atlee, both students and teachers identified lecturing as the most common form of instruction. On the same survey students identified lecturing as the least popular learning strategy. If we are going to teach using different strategies, then we need to redefine our definition of "good" teaching and include active learning as a more frequently used teaching strategy. Redefining effective teaching strategies will provide direction in methodology and content that educators can use more effectively. Some simple strategies that might replace lecture and change the way we currently teach in the classroom are suggested here.

Don't teach too much. Allow students the opportunity to be active partners in the classroom experience. We argue that students will learn if teachers allow them to explore and investigate on their own. Lecturing is definitely needed as a classroom strategy, but it is only one strategy to provide learning opportunities for students. Allow students the opportunity to be teachers as well by using strategies such as Anna Marie Palinzcar's Reciprocal Teaching. We as teachers should change roles with students on occasion and become the learner.

Ask a lot of direct and indirect questions. Ask students a lot of questions, not just one. Ask questions in many different ways. Students sometimes fail to answer questions because they don't understand what the question is. Try allowing each student in the class to ask you one question about the lecture that you have just completed. Are

---

CASE IN POINT

The math department at Atlee High School met on a weekly basis to seek new ways to support each other during the implementation of the block schedule. Each teacher provided direction and offered suggestions for effective teaching strategies of a particular content area. The assigned teacher would collect as much information as possible on best teaching practices. They shared these strategies at their working lunch. Teachers made copies of lectures and shared practices that were successful in the classroom. As one teacher put it, "We would survive together or perish as individuals!" The math department became known as risk takers at Atlee. They became leaders in innovative ways of teaching in the block as student achievement in math increased.

all of their questions clear, or in some instances do you need to ask them to rephrase their question?

Give students "wait/think time." Ask questions to assess what students know, not to see how quickly they can respond. Based on what we know about learning, students need time to process a question in order to provide a complete response. Student responses might come in different forms. Responses might include an outright answer to the question, a request for clarification, or silence that means that the student is processing information in order to provide a response. In any case, allow students time to respond. After all, it takes a computer some time to process the input and provide a response, and some computers need more time to provide information than others. It depends on the computer's capacity.

Also, keep in mind that some people need to process information verbally while others process internally. That is why you may find the same students quickly responding to questions or talking a lot in class. Others are saying little, yet you know they have something to say. Give introverted thinkers time to talk internally before expecting them to volunteer answers.

Conduct discovery activities. Conducting investigative activities is an opportunity for teachers to allow students to become actively involved in the learning process. Many times this type of teaching strategy will require more planning, but it will keep students engaged in a longer block of time. The strategy might be as short as a ten-minute activity or it might exceed 30 minutes. It might include individual, small-team, or whole class activities. Cooperative learning is highly useful in discovery activities. In his English class, Tom would provide each study group with copies of newspapers as the basis of a scavenger hunt. He usually rewarded the group(s) that successfully completed the hunt, and many times the hunt was related to the homework assignment or the next class assignment.

How do I change . . . homework/ classroom assignments?

Allow time for practice and feedback in the classroom. Because the present use of time in school is so fragmented, students rarely have opportunities to practice new assignments, ask questions to clarify new concepts, or receive teacher feedback in one class period. Students need to understand a concept or skill before they are asked to use the concept or skill. How many times have we as teachers made an assignment just as the bell rings and the students head out the door? Longer blocks of time will allow teachers to discuss possible solutions to homework problems and refer students to examples from class when making assignments.

Take time to explain all parts of the assignment. We suggest that one of the primary reasons that students do not complete homework assignments is that they do not understand the assignment, or they do not have a base knowledge of information upon which to complete the assignment. In either case, students become frustrated with the assignment, and either older siblings or parents end up completing the assignment or it is not completed at all. One parent informed Tom: "I am not in the business of doing my child's homework. She needs to understand what she is to do before she comes home from school." Whether we agree with this philosophy or not, she has a good point about her child understanding what she is supposed to do. With a longer block of time, teachers can provide students with clear directions and confirm that students understand the assignment before they leave the class. We are not suggesting that large amounts of class instructional time be allowed for students to complete homework assignments. Be very selective in how you use allocated instructional time for homework.

How do I change . . . Assessment and Evaluation?

Develop rubrics or other multiple criteria assessments. We believe that almost any instructional process can be improved when teachers work together as a team. Although teachers can certainly develop criteria for assessments individually, we suggest beginning by working together. If all of the senior English teachers sit down together to talk about the assessment criteria for the senior projects or all of the science teachers work together to establish the criteria for the Junior Academy of Science research projects, the task becomes easier and the criteria will be more comprehensive. Remember, the purpose of using a rubric is not to make the assessment process more difficult but to better assess all of the skills or components of the assignment you have given.

Modify the instructional process to maximize learning. All teachers want to be successful and want their students to learn. Some teachers do a good job of monitoring their results and adjusting the learning process when students are not learning. Now is the time for all teachers to use the information they have to ensure that all students are successful. The current national emphasis on testing and performance makes monitoring for success extremely important.

Teachers can begin by reviewing unit tests and conducting an item analysis. If they find that a concept, skill, or important content area yielded poor results on the assessment, now is the time to reteach. The block schedule gives you the time to work a mini unit or skill review into the 90-minute time period. It is easy to place a 10-minute review at the beginning of the day or use it as a transition when moving from one major activity to another.

Teachers on a block schedule inevitably make decisions about what is important to teach and what needs to be emphasized. Using the data collected from assessments and grade reporting periods,

teacher teams can now discuss curriculum issues and make these decisions in an informed manner.

Curriculum drives the schedule

Block scheduling allows curriculum developers to design a curriculum that places emphasis on the development of concepts and thinking skills. This design allows teachers to emphasize instruction driven by critical thinking, problem solving, and thus a deeper understanding of concepts and major ideas that cross curriculum areas.

More time for creativity for students and teachers

The larger block of time provides an opportunity for teachers and students to become more creative and develop a sense of a learning community in the classroom. Active student participation in the classroom and less teacher lecturing is a role change for students and teachers. Students become active participants in the instructional process as less emphasis

---

CASE IN POINT

Identify and assign individuals within a department or instructional unit the responsibility of collecting supplementary materials for a particular subject area. In the history/social studies content areas, one teacher might be assigned to collect supplementary materials for geography, another U.S. history, another government, another world history, another sociology, and yet another psychology. In English, one might collect information on units related to Elizabethan English, one on American literature, another on writing or the use of a particular writing process being used in the school, and still another in mechanics and grammar by level of the English course (i.e.: ninth-grade English). Special content areas in mathematics would include areas such as algebra, calculus, and geometry. Other content areas could act accordingly. Not only do departments develop interesting collections of support materials by working together on this task; they begin talking about what is happening in each course and articulating the curriculum informally.

is placed on teaching and more emphasis is placed on learning. This collaborative role has not always been the case in the classroom and may take some adjustment for both teachers and students. The roles have changed, and the question is: Do the participants know how to handle these new roles?

HOW DOES INSTRUCTION DIFFER FOR TEACHERS?

Less teacher lecture and more student participation will dominate the new look in the classroom as teachers move to make the learning experience for students more productive. Consider the following plans that might be used to balance teacher-student ownership in a new-look classroom. The emphasis is on the process, not the content, in these activities. The operational words for these activities are "teacher-led" and "student-led." The amount of time assigned to the activities will vary depending on the objectives for the class and the climate of a particular class.

The amount of time spent on each activity will vary based on individual teachers. We recommend that at least a portion of allocated instructional time be student led. Teachers would then serve as facilitators, providing direction that leads to a rigorous academic learning experience.

The suggested lesson plan does not address student projects and research assignments. Obviously, on some days a large portion of the instructional block will be devoted to individual student work. While teachers should always avoid "study halls" during precious instructional time, it is appropriate to give students time to work individually and in teams on research projects that require technology and/or library access as well as group interaction time.

Greater flexibility to team teach, allow interdisciplinary learning, and plan provides a climate that encourages teachers to share teaching strategies. Some of these strategies will be successful, and some will need additional development before being used by teachers. If some strategies do not work, it will be necessary for teachers to adjust their plans. Teaching methodologies can be learned and should be practiced, so there is no reason for a teacher to give up after trying something new and not being

satisfied with the results. Coaching by peers or other support may be required. Longer instructional periods allow greater flexibility to provide assistance to teachers. The longer block provides time to observe others who are using the block successfully.

USE OF THE SCHEDULE TO SOLVE INSTRUCTIONAL PROBLEMS

Based on the number of high school teachers that we have observed teaching during our careers, we know educators rely too heavily on the lecture model of teaching. When collecting data for his dissertation, "Classroom Behaviors of Secondary Teachers," Tom found that lecturing consumed most of the allocated instructional time. Throughout his administrative career, Tom has attempted to find strategies to help change instructional behaviors of secondary teachers. Providing longer blocks of time is a proven strategy that will encourage teachers to select a variety of teaching strategies to help them motivate students to learn and achieve at a higher level. Many of the following issues can be resolved by using the scheduling process efficiently and effectively.

CASE IN POINT

Near the end of the first semester of each school year, Tom identified teachers who were experiencing difficulties teaching in the longer block schedule. This was done through self-identification or recommendations from instructional staff leaders or other administrative staff. A plan of improvement was developed for the teacher. This plan included observation of teachers who had been identified as successful teachers. These observations could be done during the teacher's planning block or duty block. Because these blocks were approximately one hour and 45 minutes long, a teacher could complete an assigned duty during the first 50 minutes and then make a pre-arranged observation of another teacher during the last part of the class. The same procedure was followed during a planning period. This proved to be a strategy that was non-threatening and very beneficial to teachers who participated.

FIGURE 54
Lesson Plan Components for One Class Period

Teacher-Led Activities: Summary of previous class meeting should include the main points covered in the last class. Next steps include an explanation of how the previous lesson relates to what will be addressed in today's lesson.

Teacher-Led Activities: Introduce concept(s) for today. Teacher will lecture, and students will take notes. Identify the objectives and expectations for students during this block. Make sure students know where they are going and how they are going to get there.

Student-Led Activities: Response by individuals and groups; interaction between students, who will dominate this portion of the block. Interaction could be in response to teacher-led portion of the class, homework, small-group discussion, as well as individual student-initiated discussion on related concepts.

Student-Led Activities: Individual students, groups, and teacher share information and partic-ipate in discussion. Writing assignments (regardless of course students enrolled in) can be used as a tool to allow students an opportunity to develop thoughts and questions and to formulate responses/answers. Writing will also give teachers feedback on the success of the lesson or on how well a student might be doing in the class.

Student-Led Activities: Student and teacher discussion of major concepts. Teacher checks for depth of understanding of concepts by listening to student-led discussion as well as using writing assignments to check for students' level of understanding.

Teacher-Led Activities: Summary of concepts. Teacher analyzes progress of class and gives new assignment for next class meeting. Students are allowed time to practice new assignments before class is dismissed. Teacher provides directed instruction with an emphasis on checking for understanding of assignment.

Wasted time. When educators and critics of education raise the issue of time in schools—asking for longer days and extended years—we should not respond to them by determining if we need longer days and longer school years. We should address the situation as it is currently and seek to improve academic achievement. If we need to change the way we use time, then let's do it.

One of the measurable objectives that we hoped to accomplish when we made the decision to implement the block schedule at Atlee was to increase the amount of instructional time in a single block. The following opportunities are just a few that provide increased instructional time when teaching in the block schedule.

- Valuable time lost in passing, starting, and stopping class is limited to three/four class changes instead of the traditional six/seven class changes.

- Start-up and clean-up times are reduced, particularly in subjects that have labs.

- Record-keeping issues are lessened with fewer class meetings.

- Both teachers and students must manage time efficiently.

- Differing time formats can be used to meet instructional needs of students.

- Needs of special students can be met during the regular class block.

ALIGNING CURRICULUM, INSTRUCTION, AND ASSESSMENT WITH DESIRED RESULTS

Perhaps one of the most penetrating effects of block scheduling is the impact on curriculum and its alignment with instructional objectives and course offerings available to students. With the block schedule format in mind, consider the following questions as they relate to curriculum, instruction, and courses available to students:

- Does the schedule allow for curriculum and instructional strategies that meet the high academic performance standards that are expected of students regardless of their learning styles or career paths?

- Does the schedule allow for teaching strategies that accomplish the stated objectives of the curriculum?

- Does the schedule facilitate an appropriate curriculum audit format that would meet stated curriculum objectives and academic expectations?

Climate. Consider the impact of block scheduling on the following characteristics that contribute to the climate in schools that are currently using a six- or seven-period day schedule.

- Teachers must change their mindset five to six times a day depending on the number of classes they teach within the current school schedule. This creates a higher emotional demand of servicing 125 to 150 students daily and a stressful situation for many teachers as well as students.

- Students must also deal with emotional demands of meeting the requirements of six or seven different teachers and courses daily.

Based on our observation and reports from schools that have implemented the block schedule, fewer class changes appear to improve school climate, discipline, and cleanliness of the physical plant. We also have observed that in a block schedule, teachers worked together more. This creates a healthier and more inviting school climate, one in which a sense of school community and personal responsibility exist.

DAILY PLANNING

Because of the increase in allocated instructional time, daily planning is critical to success. The lack of planning can mean a waste of instructional time, and thus one of the major goals for implementing the block schedule format will likely not be met. When planning for instruction in the block schedule, teachers should look at possible instructional options that are available to be used in a longer block of time as well as options that will meet the instructional objectives of the class.

SUGGESTIONS FOR INSTRUCTIONAL PLANNING IN ALL CLASSES

Planning appropriate, meaningful, and constructive uses of time will provide many opportunities for success for both students and teachers. Make sure that the classroom management/delivery system is firmly in place from the first day of instruction. Rethink the various processes that you use to conduct business in the classroom on a day-to-day basis. Explore positive teaching opportunities that are currently being used. Build on these instructional strategies to provide even more positive learning experiences for students. Plan, plan, plan!

Consider these suggestions when planning a class for the longer block of time.

■ Develop plans for the year or semester, rather than on a day-to-day basis or on a weekly timeline. These long-term plans can be broken into smaller units of planning such as by semester, by grading periods, or even by smaller units of planning such as units/themes. Flexibility is the key. Adjust plans as necessary.

■ Plans for a longer block of time should include opportunities for extended learning. They should use a variety of teaching strategies such as discussion of a concept, analysis of the concept, and an eventual debate regarding the important points of the concept. Through careful planning, all of these strategies can be used in one block of time.

■ Laboratory sessions in science, computer applications, vocational/technical areas, journalism, art, music, drama, and physical education allow more opportunities to engage students. Many laboratory assignments, from pre-lab lecture to discussion of findings, can be completed in one block.

■ The use of instructional technology as a teaching/learning tool will be enhanced with careful planning. Increased instructional time will allow opportunities for students and teachers to take advantage of available computer lab time as well as to use instructional technology as a tool for enhancing interdisciplinary studies in all curricular areas.

■ Through careful planning, a single lesson plan can include the introduction of new information required to understand a concept, the application of the information regarding the concept, and analysis and evaluation of the concept.

■ If you are using a semester block schedule, think in terms of 45 lessons per term, not five per week, to cover the prescribed (yearly) curriculum.

■ Teachers who are currently teaching in the block schedule format report that it is difficult to use lesson plans or combinations of lesson plans that have been used previously in shorter blocks of time. They have reorganized many of the "good pieces" of previous lesson plans into new units of instruction.

■ Make any adjustments to your long-term plans at least two weeks in advance. It is important to look ahead and plan as the situation requires. Always think ahead.

■ Be time and task conscious in your planning. Use a time management plan when planning and teaching in each block. (See Figure 56.)

■ Vary your instructional approaches during the course of each block. Consider using a minimum of three instructional strategies for each block. These strategies should include a combination of hands-on, group activities as well as self-directed learning and traditional methods, such as lecture, discussion, and drill/repetition. Check with colleagues for other suggested strategies that they have used successfully.

■ Invite colleagues to participate in planning with you by initiating team teaching, interdisciplinary programs, and actually exchanging classes to share an area of expertise. Examples include:

• A chemistry teacher and a horticulture teacher exchange classes to teach units stressing the importance of how a working knowledge of chemistry relates to success in the horticultural industry.

• English teachers work together as a team to share their areas of expertise. An English teacher who is an expert in the mechanics of writing would teach a unit of mechanics to students in one class while another teacher who has expertise in Elizabethan literature would teach a unit to another class. At the end of the units, the teachers would return to their original classes.

■ Teach more than one traditional lesson per class. Think in terms of multiple lessons in which you might devote one daily lesson to process skills, one lesson to content/curriculum, and another lesson to your personal goals for the students' learning.

■ Consider building each lesson around a theme. Explore your theme from varying perspectives and approaches as you cover the required content. Use a thematic approach to liven up your anticipatory set.

■ Include in each lesson a product-oriented activity. Avoid using simple practice exercises, but strive to have students implement what they have learned by engaging in more hands-on learning and assigning more related projects.

■ Build in daily checks for learning and lesson closure. End class with review of the day's topic and/or an assessment session that could include questions and an oral or written review of material covered in class. Consider using the last five minutes to reinforce student use of the assignment books and thoroughly explain your expectations for the homework assignment. Whatever you do, make sure that students know the expectations for the next class. Use instructional time to communicate these expectations to students.

■ Design homework so that it is used not only as a practice activity but also as the necessary foundation for the next lesson. Avoid having students do homework during allocated instructional time, except when it is a part of the pre-determined objective as identified in lesson plans.

■ Use "open-ended" closure with your lessons. Leave your students "hanging" and use homework assignments to answer the questions with which you leave them.

■ Consider having students do directed silent reading in class. Follow up this strategy by conducting a question-and-answer session or by having students answer written questions on assigned readings. (This is not to suggest that students would read material in class that should be assigned as out-of-class reading. Nor are we suggesting that teachers should routinely use end-of-chapter questions to fill time in the block.)

■ Do more in-class writing. This is worth repeating: *Do more in-class writing.* Students can pre-write, write, edit in groups, and revise in one block. They have time to critique other students' papers, and they can work one on one with the teacher if they are having particular problems with the assignment or the writing process. Writing reflects a student's thinking, and it is a critical skill that is under-utilized in high school classrooms.

■ Use appropriate cooperative learning strategies. Put your students in groups for 20 to 30 minutes to help break the monotony and provide them opportunities to become actively engaged in learning. Provide individual think time to prepare for the next learning experience in the classroom. Some teachers have students select names for their groups and academically challenge other groups. Change groups often. Students can be grouped according to ability (great for standard students) or by personality (seems to work well with advanced students).

Through organization, careful planning, efficient use of instructional time, and the use of a variety of instructional materials and activities suitable for longer blocks of time, teachers will better accommodate the different learning styles of all students. And teachers will become better teachers.

SAMPLE LESSON PLANS FOR ORGANIZING AND TEACHING IN THE BLOCK

The more we learn about block scheduling, the more we realize how critical planning and staff development are to the success of restructured instructional time. One of the most popular items that we share when working with teachers on block scheduling is sample lesson plans. Teachers inform us that these examples give them confidence and relieve anxiety about planning for the first few weeks. They have been tested and can serve as a road map. The following guidelines and plans are designed to be used in longer blocks of time and have all been developed and used by teachers on block schedules. (They also are great resources to use in staff development.)

■ The process of designing block lessons

We provide three types of lessons to guide planning. First is a simple, three-step model that can be used to help teachers initially. Second, we offer a collection of lesson outlines that show how teachers are dividing time in the 90-minute block. Finally, Tom talks about how he planned in the block, and we show several detailed lessons that are good models.

STEP 1: Understanding the Methodology Framework (STIR© 1996—A Teaching Method that Works in the Block Schedule). Karen Flowe is chair of the English department at Gloucester High School in Gloucester, Virginia. A master teacher, Karen was instrumental in guiding teachers through the change process that helped them adjust to the block schedule while implementing a number of innovative practices. Karen found that if she prepared her lessons around a simple three-step process, which she called STIR—**St**imulation-**I**nvolvement-**R**esponse—the lessons would include a variety of learning activities and yet be manageable.

Stimulation	10–20 minutes
Involvement	50–60 minutes
Response	10–20 minutes

The first 10 to 20 minutes of the block are spent stimulating the curiosity of the students. The stimulation activity varies to fit the lesson. The majority of the time is designed for active learning. As Karen puts it:

A mood thermometer, a watchful eye on success rates, and a constant check of the big picture are probably your best tools for making the choices for you and your stu-

■ Become organized very quickly.

■ Never spend an entire block on one activity.

■ Be ready to "change direction" if a certain activity is not working.

■ Spend a little time at either the beginning or the end of class and initiate a "chat" with your students as you reinforce academic expectations. Some of our teachers have remarked that they feel the extra time gives them a chance to get to know their students' learning styles and are thus able to teach them more effectively. (Tom found this to be helpful when class was "dragging" and needed a change in direction. He just asked students what he could do to move the class forward, and they told him!)

■ Some teachers in the ninth- and tenth-grade classes find that giving a short break in the middle of the block helps their students' attention span. The eleventh and twelfth graders do not seem to have a problem if the class moves smoothly.

■ It is very important to do lesson plans by the week(s) instead of by the day.

■ Be sure that you thoroughly explain and put in writing your policy for missed class work or tests. This can be a real problem, since students will take advantage of extra time to complete their assignments. It is also more difficult for teachers to remember who is absent on a particular day if you are using the alternating day block.

■ Don't panic! Remember that this concept is as new to the students as it is to teachers. As a teacher, you will be very surprised at how quickly students and teachers get used to this schedule.

dents. Teaching is more art than craft, and no two years, courses, or even classes are the same. There is no "right" way, even though there are many "wrong" ways. If it works well, do it!

The 10 to 20 minutes of **R**esponse, or reflection, are Karen's "key to block scheduling success." This concluding activity reinforces the day's learning and helps the students understand the value of the activities experienced. Developing the **R**esponse activity also helps the teacher focus on what the big idea or key learning for the day should be. It brings into focus the whole lesson and helps transition to the next topic.

This model provides one way of looking at how time should be structured in a 90-minute block. While the use of time on any one day may vary, initially it is important to get an overview perspective of how time should be used to engage students effectively and involve them in their learning. After

thinking about how to stimulate, involve, and secure responses from students, the next step is to allocate time to various lesson components.

STEP 2: Understanding How to Manage Time. When Tom was teaching on the block schedule, he developed three lesson frameworks that are helpful as we begin looking at lesson designs. (See Figure 56.) Although generic, it is easy for teachers to use these to think about how they could implement something similar in their classrooms, because all teachers lecture, use videos, and test.

While these designs are self-explanatory, just a few comments are in order. Experienced teachers have indicated that they give tests at different times on a block schedule. Some find that they prefer to give a test at the beginning of the period and move on to a new topic following the test. This may be particularly helpful in providing extra time for students who require a modified testing situation. These teachers believe students come ready to test and think it is better to administer it early in the period. Other teachers tell us that they find it is better to give the test later in the block so that the test ends at the conclusion of the period. When to give a test and other decisions must be made on the basis of individual classroom situations.

Over the years, teachers have become accustomed to showing videos during the standard 50-minute class and then waiting until the next day to discuss the importance of the video. It may be necessary to talk with teachers about debriefing after videos to ensure that they use the video effectively and tie it to the instructional unit.

Now let's look at more lesson plans. (See Figures 57 through 63.) Look at how the following teachers are using time. The lessons in this section are from teachers at Gloucester High School in Gloucester, Virginia, who have been working with the block schedule since 1993.

The first (Figure 57) is from Lora Price, former chair of the foreign language department and currently an educational technology specialist for the school.

Lora notes that if computer access is available within the classroom, try to work in an all-class instructional session at the beginning of the period. While the teacher continues with the regular lesson and practice, individual or paired students can rotate to the computer and use it throughout the period.

She gives two other suggestions. First, at every class meeting, try to ensure practice and development of each of the four skills related to the current structure being taught (listening, speaking, reading, and writing). Include culture as the fifth component. Doing so naturally breaks up the longer period of time. Second, use a variety of activities and games to reinforce vocabulary and develop mnemonic devices to help students with recall. "It's difficult to create in a language if one has no vocabulary," she says.

Jo Anne Coogan, a French teacher, also believes that all aspects of language learning should occur during the 90-minute block at each class meeting, as she demonstrates in Figure 58.

English teacher Melissa Baldwin demonstrates in Figure 59 how reading, writing, lecturing, and discussion can be combined in one lesson to introduce a novel study.

FIGURE 56
Lesson Plan Frameworks

Class with Lecture

5 min.	Introductory remarks/lesson preparation
30 min.	Group activity (questions/selected reading)
25 min.	Discussion of outcomes, products (class)
20 min.	Lecture (culmination)
10 min.	Review/closure

Class with Video

5 min.	Introductory remarks/lesson preparation
45 min.	Video with activity sheet
10 min.	Review of activity sheet/video
25 min.	Selected reading—Pair-Share activity
5 min.	Review/closure

Class with Test

5 min.	Test directions
50 min.	Test (students complete + or -10 min.)
15 min.	Debrief/introduce new unit
15 min.	Selected reading/group discussion
5 min.	Review/closure

Sheila Austin chairs the science department and incorporates games into her program. She suggests that teachers use a kitchen timer to help students keep track of their time and become used to working in a limited time period. Students become aware of the need to stay on task, but they also know that all lessons are subject to time alterations depending on the group's needs. Her Biology I lesson (see Figure 60 (a)) uses small groups and a video to begin exploring the topic of study. Award-winning teacher Carolyn Smith also teaches biology courses and submitted a lesson from an Advanced Placement course (see Figure 60 (b)).

Figure 61 shows how Jim Eccelston moves from one day to the next in the study of legislative districting while teaching on the alternate day 90-minute block.

Before leaving Gloucester, David Sutton taught mathematics and was a member of several math teams. The four teachers who taught Algebra II planned together weekly for about 30 minutes, coordinating what they were teaching, how they would teach and assess progress, and what level of mastery they would require before moving to another topic (see Figure 62).

FIGURE 57
Spanish Lesson Plans

SPANISH I

10 min.	Complete & review activity/attendance/return tests
15–20 min.	Presentation of new chapter vocabulary
10–15 min.	Practice reading aloud in groups
15–20 min.	Bingo game or other vocabulary game
10–15 min.	Listening comprehension practice
20 min.	Writing practice with worksheet, workbook, or text activities (individual or paired)
3 min.	Closure and assignment

SPANISH IV

10–15 min.	Complete & review activity/attendance
15 min.	Review homework from previous class
15 min.	Listening comprehension practice
20 min.	Project work (collaboration on joint project)
15 min.	Instructional presentation
15 min.	Guided practice
2 min.	Closure

FIGURE 58
French Lesson Plan

FRENCH III

10 min.	Students write three sentences from words provided/Show answers on transparency/Pass out film worksheets
5 min.	Answer questions about worksheet
15 min.	Show 10 min. of film, stopping to answer questions
15 min.	Review verb endings/Conjugate on paper/Put correct answers on board
15 min.	Correct homework from last class
20 min.	Present new lesson/Listen to tape of dialogue/Students practice with partners
10 min.	Comprehension written activity in text Hand out crossword puzzle of new vocabulary for homework

The final lesson outline comes from two health and physical education professors at Western Carolina University. David Claxton and James Bryant have assisted teachers as they consider the advantages of block scheduling in physical educa-

FIGURE 59
English Lesson Plan

ENGLISH 10

10 min.	Students read recent article on Bradbury's themes & predictions; teacher distributes *Fahrenheit 451*
10 min.	Prewriting: Journal responses to article
5–10 min.	Discussion of article
30 min.	Oral reading of Bradbury's "The Pedestrian" (text)
10 min.	Mini-lecture linking short story to novel's themes
15 min.	Students begin reading novel/Teacher checks vocabulary study notes
5–10 min.	Poll students to see who found cryptic reference to short story's protagonist/Remind students of reading goal for next class

tion classes. They developed a sample schedule for a 90-minute class (see Figure 63).

What do these lesson outlines tell us? First, successful teachers on a block schedule do not lecture for the 90-minute class. Further, they do not use the class as a study hall. They may ask students to read passages or work problems as guided practice, but the activities are supervised and are a part of the overall structure of the lesson. Additionally, teachers plan activities in 10- to 20-minute blocks of time. There is movement throughout the 90 minutes as lessons progress, and students are involved in several activities. Finally, these lessons show that students are working in small groups and are involved in activities that go beyond notetaking.

You can cover a lot of material by standing in front of a class and talking about a subject. You can cover a lot of material by handing students study sheets to memorize for tests. But if you want students to develop a knowledge base of concepts and skills that can be used to analyze new material, solve problems, and look at situations critically, teachers must engage students in learning and allow them to apply what they are learning in contexts that make sense to adolescents.

STEP 3: Thinking and Teaching in Units of Study (See chart on page 174). When preparing a lesson plan or unit, Tom divided the task into an

FIGURE 60
Biology Lesson Plans

(a) BIOLOGY I

5 min.	Students read "scenario" handout and complete activity
10 min.	Mini-lesson on types of viruses, structures, effects on organisms
15 min.	Students in small groups: brainstorm and answer questions related to scenario handout
10 min.	Teams' spokespersons record explanations for problem on whiteboard; recorders compile data for groups
5 min.	Class votes on most plausible explanation
18 min.	Video: Documentary on outbreak of viral infection from Centers for Disease Control and Prevention
7 min.	Class discussion relating video to problem in scenario
20 min.	Group work: Each team generates a research proposal for further study presented in scenario (experimental design)
5 min.	Proposals submitted/Summary/Closure Anticipatory activity for next class using proposals

(b) AP BIOLOGY

INTRODUCTION OF NEW CONCEPTS: 10 MINUTES

10 min.	Teacher introduces "biome" and teams' assignments made to determine previously learned material/Students brainstorm biome characteristics while teacher checks for homework and tardies

TEAM ACTIVITY—POWER THINKING: 45 MINUTES

20 min.	Teams complete activity classifying characteristics of biomes
10 min.	Teams evaluate other teams' work and reach consensus Teacher feedback as needed
10 min.	Students refer to text to evaluate accuracy of teams' work
5 min.	Students summarize major concepts

INDIVIDUAL REINFORCEMENT: 35 MINUTES

35 min.	Writing assignment

CLOSURE: 5 MINUTES

5 min.	Writing submitted Summary by teacher

FIGURE 61
Government Lesson Plans

U.S. GOVERNMENT—Day 1

3 min.	Administrative tasks
10 min.	Students copy vocabulary—congressional apportionment topics
8 min.	Discuss vocabulary
10 min.	Demonstration of formula for apportioning congressional districts/Student practice
20 min.	Practice sheet: Using math skills, students apportion representatives
5 min.	Summary
10 min.	Transition: Use of newly apportioned districts to draw district boundaries
10 min.	Demonstration: Why and how to gerrymander districts
10 min.	Student practice worksheet
5 min.	Summary
4 min.	Assign homework

U.S. GOVERNMENT—Day 2

3 min.	Administrative tasks
5 min.	Review previous lesson (two days earlier)
15 min.	Show congressional districts on overhead: Non-gerrymandered, gerrymandered, editorial cartoons
5 min.	Discussion
5 min.	Conclude gerrymandering by showing Virginia districts
20 min.	Activity: Students complete maps of Virginia districts
5 min.	Discuss Virginia districts noting district students live in
25 min.	Students work in groups to answer questions about Virginia congressional districts
10 min.	Discussion: Proposed bills, congressional guideline policies under consideration this session
2 min.	Close lesson

FIGURE 62
Algebra II Lesson Plan

ALGEBRA II

10 min.	Focus activity from the board that reviews a recent class topic; hand out past assignments
10 min.	Review answers to the Focus activity and discuss next help session, next test, next progress report, etc.
10 min.	Review answers to last homework or Turn-In assignment. Students work at board to explain procedure and answer other students' questions.
20 min.	Present new material. Several examples are illustrated using the overhead. Questioning occurs throughout the presentation.
20 min.	Group work: About 1 out of every 3 blocks sees students doing group work. *(Some teachers assign a grade for this work, others do not.)*
15 min.	Turn-In: This takes the place of the conventional quiz. It consists of 5/6 questions related to the material discussed. Students use notes, focuses, homework, or the textbook to complete the graded assignment. The class average serves as a benchmark. The Turn-In is popular with students and it gives the teacher immediate feedback as to what should be covered more thoroughly in the next class period(s). Students realize when they are getting behind and can make plans to get additional help right away.
10 min.	Homework assignment/Closure/ Student questions

---

informal road map of major highways. The highways were: **objectives, time, materials,** and **strategies/activities.** He followed these major highways as he planned throughout the year. It was a way to sort and select as he planned and added new strategies, changed time elements, found new materials that might fit into the expansion of a new section of the highway, or added and deleted objectives that were not in tune with the curriculum.

As the principal of the school, Tom had the opportunity to teach one block of English each year.

FIGURE 63
Physical Education Lesson Plan

PHYSICAL EDUCATION

5 min.	Dress out and roll call
5 min.	Stretching/Warm-up
20 min.	Cardiovascular or strength fitness routine
10 min.	Lesson (fitness concepts, game rules and strategies, ethical considerations)
30 min.	Skill practice/Skill testing/Scrimmage/ Game
10 min.	Wrap-up/Debriefing: What did you learn? What key skill elements do you remember? Did you and your classmates work and play fairly?
10 min.	Dress for next class

Because they used an alternating day (A-B) schedule, he was only committed to teaching three days on A week and two days on B week. The unit on Searching for Self-Identity (below) is one that Tom taught following the principle that concepts must be taught in blocks, not chapters or single literary works.

There are many activities that can be used to meet the objectives of this unit and to introduce each of the works that will be presented. In this section, only a few examples of how to expand activities to be taught in a longer block of time are shared. Teachers can add, delete, and adjust accordingly. Every teacher has his/her own creative flair used to maintain interest in a particular classroom or school. Each activity is tied to an objective for the unit.

UNIT: SEARCHING FOR SELF-IDENTITY

Instructional Team: English

Course: AP English Literature

Performance Objective(s):

- To expose students to works that are part of the recommended list of literary works for the Advanced Placement course. Students will identify and distinguish differences of the major concepts of each work as related to the principal players and be able to summarize these concepts with support from these literary works.

- To expose students daily to "word builders" related to vocabulary found on previous AP examinations as well as teacher-identified vocabulary. There are many strategies that can be used to incorporate "word builders" into the daily lesson plans. Tom used the following strategies to teach "word builders":

– Incorporate assigned words into assigned writings, use them in presentations to the class, and ask students to identify the words and how they had been used in the assigned writings

– Give daily quizzes by simply requiring students to identify words, use synonyms, etc., to replace words in paragraphs, verbal exercises, etc.; require students to create their own definition of the word

• To identify, categorize, explain, and correct certain problem areas in writing that will be identified as the unit unfolds.

THINKING AND TEACHING IN UNITS OF STUDY

Objectives—State objective(s) and how these objectives are aligned with the curriculum used in your school. It is important that the objectives match the school curriculum and that teachers continue to build on knowledge previously learned by students. All content areas make up the students' knowledge base and contribute to prior knowledge in your subject area.

Time—Estimate the amount of time that you have for the block (90–110 minutes) and plan strategies based on a predetermined amount of time for each strategy. Adjust accordingly.

Materials Needed for the Unit—List materials that are available as well as materials that will be gathered from other sources.

Strategies/Activities—List activities in the most appropriate sequence that provide the needed structure and flexibility for your class:

• Teacher-led activity
• Student-led activity
• Small group activity
• Large group activity (whole class)
• Individual student activity

• To develop a clearer appraisal of oneself in preparation for career choices by identifying discriminating characteristics of the major characters of great works of literature, with emphasis on justifying the role of the female player as the principal character in each work studied.

• To provide students with opportunities to learn about a variety of career options that will assist them in making discriminating career choices.

• To provide students opportunities to continue to develop present computer skills as well as to develop new research-related skills that will assist in developing higher-level thinking and problem-solving skills.

Underlying Objectives

Underlying objectives are identified in each lesson plan. They usually have to do with teaching analytical/critical thinking skills, problem-solving skills, and higher order thinking skills. These objectives can be many and varied depending on the needs of students and the teacher's philosophy about teaching these particular skills.

The chart on page 175 might be used to simplify the problem-solving process. If it is possible to provide each student a disk with the chart's format, this problem-solving process could become a part of problem solving in each class. A separate sheet of instructions should be provided.

Assignments that Require Students to Use the Problem-Solving Chart

• Identify and state a common problem that exists in the relationships of Willie and Linda, Macbeth and Lady Macbeth, Torvald and Nora, Othello and Desdemona, and Tea Cake and Janie.

• Analyze the problem that you have identified.

• Generate and analyze possible solution(s) for the stated problem

• Select, present, and defend a solution to your audience (class peers and teacher).

• Evaluate how the solution might be implemented, and identify additional issues that could arise from the implementation.

PROBLEM SOLVING CHART

What is/are the problem(s) to be solved?	Identify problem(s): The primary problem(s) is/are _____
What is/are cause of problem(s)?	Analyze reason(s) for problem: The primary reason(s) for the problem is/are _____
What is/are possible solution(s)?	Generate solution(s) for problem: The following option(s) is/are solution(s) to the problem _____
Defend your solution(s).	Select/defend solutions: This/ These option(s) are best because _____
Predict what will happen once your option(s) is/are applied.	Implement solution: The following will happen as a result(s) of implementing my solution _____

Assessment of Student Progress

Many teachers have a favorite method for identifying the progress of students. Regardless of the method, it is extremely important to have a system in place to assess students who are instructed on the larger block of time. Instruction moves at a faster pace, and students may need to be evaluated more frequently. When considering a long unit of study, determine specific strategies to assess student progress, and pace the unit within the timeline you have established, because this is only one unit you will be teaching during the year or semester. Be sure to share your evaluation criteria with your students. The following are some of the criteria Tom used and shared with his students. They contributed ideas as to what needed to be measured and how.

- Observation of student participation in class activities, writing, oral communication, class participation, and team participation.

- Evaluation of assigned papers and projects.

- Assessment of every homework assignment with feedback. If you are going to give it, use it.

- Daily assessment of vocabulary builders.

- Written examination on teacher-presented information as well as on information assigned as student responsibility.

- Final examination on the total unit based on information covered and presented.

Of course, there are many standardized tests as well as teacher-made evaluation instruments that may be used.

Instructional Activities

Instructional activities will be assigned for each block based on the progress of the unit and the teacher's preferred teaching methodologies for a particular objective. These activities can be assigned to as many blocks as necessary to meet the needs of the students. Tom addressed the following needs before beginning a unit.

Materials, Audiovisual, Computer/ Technology Equipment

- Schedule computer time in labs and the resource center for research purposes.

- Acquire floppy disks.

- Write a description of each principal male and female character to give to each student.

- Acquire copies of the following literary works to be used for this unit:
  Macbeth, William Shakespeare
  A Doll's House, Henrik Ibsen
  Othello, William Shakespeare
  Death of a Salesman, Arthur Miller
  Their Eyes Were Watching God, Zola Hurston

NOTE: There will be other materials needed that are identified as the unit unfolds. In some instances, Tom chose to use Ethan Frome *in place of or in addition to the previously mentioned selections.*

Time: 110 minutes per block for 12 blocks

Strategies/Activities

DAY 1

The first day of the new unit is critical to the teacher and the students. What happens during this first class will determine the success or failure of the unit. Tom's first day of this unit went something like this:

Introduction—Use Entire Block: Invited a recognized local female professional (medical doctor) to describe to the class her journey to the pinnacle of her profession. Provided ample time for the guest to interact with students and answer questions. Asked her to explain at length the apprehensions/barriers relative to math and science she identified when she was approximately the students' age and how she justified choosing her profession after assessing these barriers. Also asked her to construct any strategies to support her choice once she had identified such obstacles. Provided the entire block for this visit; discovered that guest lecturers are more willing to adjust their schedules and make an effort to visit a class when you can share with them the objectives of the unit, allowing the guests a meaningful amount of time to spend sharing their experiences with students as well as time to interact by answering questions and asking questions of students. At the end of the block, Tom explained the objective(s) of the unit with students (large group activity), reminded them of their first reading assignment, and provided opportunities for questions to related assignments.

DAY 2

- **20 min.** Introduce the unit by providing each student with a brief written description of the major male player (Willie, Macbeth, Torvald, Othello, and Tea Cake) and major female player (Linda, Lady Macbeth, Nora, Desdemona, and Janie) of each work they will be studying. Students read, paying particular attention to characteristics and physical descriptions.

- **15 min.** Convene in study groups and discuss the similarities and differences of each player and what role each player might play if they were all characters in the same novel (small group activity). Teacher should share some samples of characterization with students.

- **15 min.** Students will discuss the findings of their analyses with the class (large group activity).

- **20 min.** Teacher introduces the novellate assignment as a class project. Timeline is developed by students and teacher (large group teacher-led activity).

- **30 min.** Teacher and students will brainstorm a plot for the novellate and determine which principal player of the works will play which character in the novellate. Then teacher and students will determine which study group develops which character (large group). Instructions for the process should be pre-developed by the teacher and distributed at this time.

- **10 min.** Close the lesson. Remind students that the reading of the first work *(Death of a Salesman)* is due for the next block.

NOTE: Tom found that Death of a Salesman *is the most "user friendly" selection. You might choose to assign it as the first reading assignment.*

DAYS 3 & 4

In some situations, Tom plans for two blocks. This is because there is much information to present and many activities that must be completed to assess a student's progress. This also allows some flexibility in moving ahead or slowing the pace, based on the results of student assessment.

Lesson plans for days 3 and 4 will be modified accordingly. The teacher will divide activities and strategies according to the progress of the class, but the goal is to meet the objectives identified for two blocks of time. Remember: You are on a planned timeline to complete the unit. Although you may be flexible in presenting materials within the blocks of time identified for the unit, there is a deadline for completion of the total unit.

- **10 min.** Give five-question quiz on first assigned reading and discuss objectives for today's block (large group activity). Check answers by using an activity that will allow all students to respond. This will give the teacher a feel for the readiness of the class to move ahead or a chance to re-evaluate what must be done to prepare the class to move ahead.

- **15 min.** Allow students to meet in study groups to work on class project. This will provide time to check for student understanding and to check attendance as you move throughout the class without wasting valuable instructional time for bookkeeping activities.

- **20 min.** Students and teachers will discuss vocabulary assignments as related to standardized test samples. Students will suggest creative ways to expand vocabularies. A list of these strategies will be compiled and shared with other classes in the English department. Other classes will add to the list. All students will be encouraged to use all identified vocabulary words in their project assignments. (Students will be awarded special credit if they use all assigned vocabulary words in their final individual project.)

- **20 min.** Students will participate in a large group discussion of *Death of a Salesman,* paying special attention to the strengths and weakness of the personalities of Willie and Linda. This will provide students a model to use when they summarize their readings of the other works in the unit. Specific questions that will challenge students are designed by the teacher.

- **30 min.** Students will convene in study groups, analyze the characteristics of each character, select the principal player that they consider to be the strongest, and make their case before the class (small group and large group activity). Using information from this activity, the plot will be set and study groups will have their assigned chapter for the novelette.

NOTE: The next two activities will be completed in the computer lab or using classroom computers.

- **40 min.** Students will solve problems by composing an essay (using at least five vocabulary words from vocabulary assignment) that describes in detail how the use of technology

(Internet, World Wide Web) might have helped Willie be successful in both his professional and personal life. Students pay particular attention to the parallel of their lives with that of the Loman (Willie and Linda's) family. Based on their knowledge of modern technology and their understanding of Willie's professional responsibilities, would they choose a similar profession? Why? Why not? Make a case using the problem-solving chart.

During this writing activity, the teacher has individual conferences with students to discuss the assignment, paying particular attention to the use of the steps in the writing process. Tom pays particular attention to individual writing problems as he evaluates the papers and holds individual conferences. Generally, it will take parts of two blocks to hold individual conferences. If a particular student is having major writing problems in areas such as mechanics, grammar, or style, Tom will request that s/he meet with him before or after school.

- **70 min.** Invite a highly successful marketing representative to address the class and explain:

  - the part that technology plays in his/her profession

  - what his/her professional goals were/are

  - how a sales professional's career can lead to the corporate level of management within the organization

  - how the perception of sales/marketing professionals has changed over the years

  - the similarities and differences of his/her profession with that of Willie's (will need to provide a summary of *Death of a Salesman* to the guest speaker if s/he is not familiar with the work)

  - how s/he might relate to Willie's behaviors because of stress-related problems caused by the demands of the position

- **15 min.** Bring closure to *Death of a Salesman* by assigning a "take-home test" that generates a comprehensive analysis which summarizes support for choosing a sales career as a profession, with specific written objectives for the test given to the students. Use this test as a learning/teaching tool. Require students to document research such as a salesperson's average income (including bonuses), the percentage of females who move into managerial positions, average number of nights away from home because of job related responsibilities, etc. Encourage investigation of marketing positions in math, science, and medical related professions. Information could be gathered by interviewing a marketing representative (should not include retail sales).

NOTE: Tom used the following timeline for the 90-minute block with modifications depending on the pace of previous lessons. Because of the length of the block, this allowed some time for discretionary purposes. In the sample lesson plans he used the total of 110 minutes because he followed a very structured timeline during the block.

10 min. Introductory remarks and review

20 min. Group activity

10 min. Class discussion and feedback

15 min. Lecture, teacher input

35 min. Writing assignment and individualized instruction as needed; rough draft of assignment expected at the conclusion of the block

20 min. Review and closure: assignments for the complete unit made; questions related to the assignment answered; students reminded of the assignment for the next block. *(As a rule, Tom did not allow students more than 10 minutes to work on the next block assignment.)*

- No basal text was used for this unit. The unit was designed to introduce students to recent works used in the Advanced Placement examinations.

- The unit was designed to be completed in a 12-block cycle.

- We used an alternating day block schedule, which gave students 12 blocks to complete the unit. This allowed for:

  - 1 block to introduce the unit

  - 2 blocks for each assigned work

  - 1 day for concluding and reporting-out related assignments

- Instructional pacing will depend on the ability of students.

- Planning for this unit must be done at the beginning of the school term or in time to gather the literary works needed for the unit.

- Remember: Planning, organization, and the efficient use of time will increase the time that you have for instructional purposes.

Sharing lesson plans will provide examples of the flexibility that a longer block of time provides for using a variety of teaching strategies. It will also point out the importance of planning, and the efficient use of time by teachers and students.

(See accompanying CD for a lesson plan for a unit on Sherlock Holmes, English.)

■ Mathemmatics suggestions and lesson plans

Mathematics teachers can work together to insure a smooth transition to block scheduling by sharing lesson plans, articulating course goals, and developing unit approaches to courses of study. We appreciate the following suggestions for mathematics teachers provided by Karen Collins, a former mathematics teacher at Atlee High School and curently a math teacher at Green Hope High School in Morrisville, North Carolina. The following section is identified for use in math department/classes but can be easily adjusted for use in any content area.

■ Acquiring materials for your department

Manipulatives:

- Divide the tasks among your department members by subject (such as Algebra I, Algebra II, calculus, etc.) and find a storage place in your resource room for these materials.

- If you have limited funding, when purchasing certain materials that will be used by various members of the department, buy overhead models **only**; other materials will be made from poster board or construction paper. Laminate a class set of materials OR cut overhead models from blank colored transparencies.

- A roll of bulletin board paper or butcher paper of newsprint can be purchased at a minimum cost. This can be used for many hands-on activities. Check with your local newspaper printing company; sometimes they will give away the ends of the rolls of newsprint.

- Acquire puzzles and appropriate commercial activities that provide opportunities to develop creative problem-solving skills. Subscribe to *Games Magazine* or buy different puzzle books from the newsstand. Make 10 copies of the puzzles that you see as being the most useful in the classroom and have them laminated. Store in resource notebooks (with the solutions).

Technology:

- Purchase only one overhead graphing calculator of each style. Different calculators have different functions. It is productive for students to have access to different models that will provide different demonstrations.

- Set up one computer, with LCD panel already connected, on a cart that can be moved from room to room if computers are not in each classroom.

- Develop partnerships with the Parent Teacher Student Association (PTSA) to purchase a certain type of graphing calculator in bulk quantities and sell them to students at cost or no more than one dollar over cost. This benefits students as well as PTSAs. Other schools, community organizations, or businesses can be used as partners in this type of venture, if PTSA is not available.

- Request from different graphing calculator companies a loaner classroom set of certain calculators. Many companies will pay for shipping

to and from your school, and will allow loans for approximately two weeks.

- At Atlee High School, we had a student/parent orientation each year before school started. The purpose was to allow students and parents to collect books, check out lockers, meet teachers, collect student schedules for the coming session, pay fees, look into student organizations, etc. The math department set up a booth to demonstrate overhead graphing calculators. We gave parents and students flyers with descriptions of different calculators, their features, approximate cost, and suggestions where to purchase calculators for the best price. (This works great!)

(See accompanying CD for math activity ideas to use in the block.)

■ Mathematics lesson plans

Once a pool of various teaching strategies and materials is in place, the next step is to develop lesson plans. A generic lesson plan model, revised to incorporate time constraints, is the first step in developing a detailed lesson plan. Teachers adapted the following model for their particular use.

Any Math Class

20–30 mins: Go over homework

- (Study teams were identified at the beginning of the school term or semester.) Allow student study teams to take five minutes to check their homework and compare results. Each group chooses two problems that the team feels that they need to see worked to solution. Other groups will work problems if they have correctly solved the particular problem, or the teacher will work the identified problem.

- If students have questions, they make a list and choose one or two problems to solve completely. Then, select a third problem from the list. The teacher starts solving the problem, but the class completes the problem. Next step: the class will work the remainder of the problems on the list. Students who successfully complete the assignment serve as homework assistants and help others during this time as they continue through the learning process.

20–30 min: Quiz on previous class topics

- Group quizzes can be effective, if they are not used too often and if they are used for an assessment rather than in a negative instructional activity. It is helpful to initiate the following accountability measures. This will make the activity meaningful to students.

  - Students will do two to four problems together in teams.

  - Students will do two to four similar problems individually.

  - Combine the team and individual work for one quiz grade.

20–30 mins: Introduction of new material

- Do **not** tell students which chapter or how many sections of the book you are going to cover in class that day. Simply introduce the concept you would like students to learn. Combine sections in your text that can be used to tie the concept together. These sections will come from different chapters. Sometimes you can lead into the next concept from a discussion of a more difficult homework problem than was assigned the previous class.

- Do **not** rework the examples from the book. My students know that when they leave my classroom at the end of the block, they will have three examples of each type of problem. This is also great preparation for homework assignments.

  Three examples:

  - **Example 1:** The first example is taken from the book. We read this example in class and answer student questions.

  - **Example 2:** The alternate example is taken from the teacher's book. The teacher completes this problem, step-by-step, in class.

  - **Example 3:** A similar problem is selected from the assignment section from which students have worked selected problems in class.

This use of the discovery method provides the opportunity to use the "easy" parts of the assignment section for practice and then assign the "medium" to "hard" problems for homework. Many students will begin to ask you to let them try one before you work an example for them. They also enjoy working solutions before the class on overheads, on the chalkboard, etc.

10–15 mins: Manipulative/Game/Activity

An alternative to giving a quiz to check for understanding is for study teams to do an activity or give a challenge problem with rewards for teams who finish first, second, or third.

10 mins: Closure

When I make a homework assignment, it often covers several pages, sometimes from various chapters in the text, so I take the time during class and require all students to turn to each page and read over all the instructions. I will clarify questions and point out which problems are similar to specific examples worked in class. Sometimes, we may see a particularly challenging problem and take a minute to discuss possible approaches. In a lower-level math class, this makes all the difference for student success.

■ **Unit planning**

The following is a plan for a unit for Algebra I using different information from different chapters of Sobel, Maletski, and Lerner's Algebra I (1985), published by Harper and Row.

Algebra I Unit Planning

Chapter 6 from **Algebra I**

6.1— Factoring Positive Integers

6.2—Factoring & Dividing Monomials

6.3—Common Monomial Factors

6.4—Factoring by Grouping

6.5—Difference of Two Squares

6.6—Trinomial Squares

6.7—Factoring $x^2 + bx + c$

6.8—Factoring $ax^2 + bx + c$

6.9—More Factoring of Polynomials

6.10—Solving Equations by Factoring

6.11—Problem Solving using Factoring

Teachers note: *all 2s in Chapter 12 are squares*

Each daily objective depends on the pacing of the instruction by the teacher and the identified curriculum objectives.

Day 1: Many students have practiced factor trees, so a brief review of 6.1 will suffice. Approach 6.2 and 6.3 together. Introduce 6.4 as an extension of 6.3.

Day 2: More work on 6.4. Quiz. Introduce 6.7 and 6.8; 6.6 will automatically be covered in this process. Teach ONE procedure that works for all trinomials.

Day 3: More work on trinomials. Include an activity here and/or visit the computer lab if available. Also include some trinomials that **do not** factor. If you have access to IBM Toolkit or some similar software, it will factor and students can visit the lab to check work they completed in class. This also provides an opportunity to check students' understanding of the pattern for trinomial squares.

Day 4: Quick Review. Quiz. Introduce 6.4 with the middle term as zero so students can use the same method they learned on Day 2. Give them opportunities to see and discuss the pattern.

Day 5: Begin 6.9, which pulls all the skills together. This is a great review for this entire chapter.

Day 6: Review before test. This is one of the many advantages of block scheduling. Teachers indicated to me that when they had time to review extensively with students before testing, in general, students scored higher on the test. Give the test and provide time in your lesson plan to post-teach test. This will also allow time for students to evaluate the test that they have just completed. During this review, students should provide feedback on strategies that will make future tests more useful and student friendly.

Day 7: Introduce 6.10. Students will use Graphing Calculators to graph the quadratics. How will that help them? It helps them **trace** on calculators. Compare the answers when the quadratics were factored. How about the quads that did **not** factor? What do their graphs look like?

Day 8: Use information from 12.2, 12.3, and 12.4 to discuss the shape of the graphs of quadratics. What does the constant do? What does the middle term do? What about both together? What about quadratics that don't factor but **do** have x-intercepts?

Day 9: Introduce 12.6. Do not complete the square for them in class. Explore using the formula in a variety of ways:

- by calculator only

- without the assistance of a calculator

- by using a combination of both methods

Investigate when/where/how the formula "messes up." Check your ideas by looking at 12.7.

Day 10: Bring closure to the unit by looking at application problems from 6.10, 6.11, and 12.8.

Of course, lesson plans for each day of the unit are developed according to activities and teaching strategies that each teacher would choose based on teaching style and student learning styles. Having time to adjust teaching styles to meet student learning styles is another advantage of block scheduling.

(See accompanying CD for an example of a daily lesson plan for Algebra I or Algebra II.)

One of the many advantages of block scheduling is the amount of time that a teacher has to use strategies that provide hands-on activities for students. A good example of a field study lesson plan for geometry classes can be found on the accompanying CD.

The math department at Gloucester High School developed a pacing guide for the year's Algebra I study that helped them plan effectively to maximize class time. On the following page is their map that guides the year's work.

Pacing Guide

Unit 1   *Introduction to Algebra*   7 days
Addition, subtraction, multiplication,
    and division of rational numbers
Order of operations
Evaluation of expressions
Addition and subtraction of matrices
Scalar multiplication
Properties of real numbers

Unit 2   *Linear Equations*   8 days
Solving linear equations
Using formulas
Estimating and computing square roots

Unit 3   *Linear Word Problems*   14 days
Writing word phrases and sentences
Solving word problems

Unit 4   *Inequalities*   7 days
Writing word phrases and sentences
Solving inequalities

Unit 5   *Ratio, Proportion, and Percent* 3 days
Expressing ratios
Solving problems involving ratios
Solving problems using proportions
Working with percents and decimals
Solving problems involving percents

Unit 6   *Polynomials*   11 days
Addition, subtraction, multiplication,
    and division with monomial divisors
Application of the laws of exponents
    (scientific notation)

Unit 7   *Factoring*   9 days
Factorization of first and second
    degree binomials and trinomials
    in one or two variables

Solving quadratic equations
Solving rational equations

Unit 8   *Graphing Linear Equations*   10 days
Plotting ordered pairs
Graphing (using charts slope-intercept,
    x- and y-intercepts)
Writing equations of a line
Solving direct variations
Determining functions
Determining domain and range of
    a function

Unit 9   *Systems of Equations*   8 days
Solving by graphing, substitution,
    and linear combinations
Solving problems with two variables

Unit 10 *Statistics*   3 days
Analyzing graphs and organizing
    data
Mean, median, range, and mode
Frequency tables
Stem and leaf plots
Box-and-whisker plots
Measuring central tendency
Writing the equation of best fit when
    given a set of data points

Unit 11 *Intro to Radicals*   2 days
Simplifying products and quotients
    of radicals
Addition and subtraction of radicals

82 teaching days, 1 first day of school, 4 exam review days, and 3 exam days = 90 days

---

TEACHING MUSIC IN THE BLOCK

One issue that is perhaps contested more than any other issue related to time, sequencing, and learning in the block schedule format is the music program. Some music teachers feel that that the 4x4 block schedule has done irreversible damage to their program, usually through lack of sequencing. They have seen some of their best musicians drop music after the first semester block to pad their transcripts with courses that college and university admissions directors look at favorably for admission. On the other hand, some music teachers have also praised the 4x4 and indicated that the number of students participating in the music program is increasing and that their music programs are thriving in competitions.

Administrators are continuing to look at ways to schedule classes so that students in music, as well as students in all programs, achieve at a higher level.

There are many combinations of schedules being used to schedule music and other courses that need special consideration. We have received minimum negative feedback related to the alternating day (A-B) block schedule because each music course was scheduled for the entire year. The music teachers at Atlee High School, James Dalton, and George Saddler, shared the following suggestions with us.

■ **General concerns of music teachers about block scheduling concerns**

- What am I going to do with 45 to 50 students for 90 minutes?

- How is my teaching going to be affected?

- How is my program going to be affected?

■ **Advantages**

- Longer rehearsal time—less wasted time in an instructional period.

- Can accomplish many tasks in one class (review previous class work, change task completely, bring closure).

- Get to know students better, especially the quiet ones and troubled students.

- Advanced classes provide opportunities for sectionals.

■ **Disadvantages**

- Advanced planning required to prepare for instructing students for longer blocks of time.

- Interruptions of daily instructional time creates problems, especially when rehearsing for performances.

- Must plan extra rehearsals to match alternating days if using the alternating (A-B) schedule.

- Use of planning time must become more efficient and productive.

- Keeping students in music program after the first semester if using a semester (4x4) schedule.

- Can no longer depend on traditional teaching strategies; must find new strategies or ways to build on and expand existing strategies.

- Must be more prepared and plan for the more efficient use of time; must find ways to provide individualized instruction to exceptional students as well as students that need help to move to another level.

- Must find ways to keep students who choose to be involved in music throughout the school year if on the 4x4 schedule.

■ **Use of instructional time for band**

8:30–8:40—Prepare
8:40–9:00—Warm-up and tune, circle of 4ths and scales
9:00–9:30—First piece: work a small section with possible expansion
9:30–10:00—Second piece: same as above
10:00–10:20—Sight reading and closure

■ **Use of instructional time for chorus**

10:30–10:50—Warm-up exercises, rhythmic reading or exercises, and work on group problems identified during warm-up
10:50–11:45—Introduce new material or most difficult sections of pieces, usually two to three pieces, depending on group's success
11:45–12:05—Review previously used material
12:05–12:15—Review and closure

- Some days, other activities are substituted, such as sight reading, theory, and choreography.

- From time to time, rearrange sequence of activities to avoid monotony.

After a year on the alternating day (A-B) block schedule, the number of students in music programs at Atlee High School continued to increase, and an additional music teacher was added to meet instructional needs. If administrators, music teachers, students, and parents work together, music programs can be successful when using the alternating day (A-B) schedule, the 4x4, a combination of the two, or a traditional 55-minute block. The question is: Which one is most effective for the school or the program and will provide the best possibilities for instruction and success for students?

We have attempted to address only a few of the instructional issues that teachers will need to consider as they prepare for block scheduling. Other issues have not been addressed, and new issues arise daily as teachers, administrators, students, and parents look at educational reform practices that are best for students in their attempt to succeed at a higher level of achievement.

SPECIAL EDUCATION

Although we are not aware of any specific issues that teachers of students with disabilities have expressed about working in a block schedule, Yvonne heard a few parents of special education students express concern that the block of instructional time was too long for their children. We believe that these concerns can be addressed in Individualized Educational Programs (IEPs), but we understand that teachers of students with disabilities—like all high school teachers—must adjust their teaching to the 90-minute block. The success that many teachers of students with disabilities were having in self-contained classrooms was one of the reasons that Tom considered moving to longer blocks of time for all students.

(See accompanying CD for an algebra activity used with learning disabled students in a block schedule.)

TEACHER ISSUES

Helping teachers learn to plan is a critical issue that is often ignored when preparing for block scheduling. Formal and informal feedback indicates that this is one of the most important components to the success of block scheduling.

Regardless of the type of block schedule format used, planning for instructional changes has been a consistent concern among administrators and teachers.

PLANNING FOR INSTRUCTION

■ Plan in advance and plan units instead of on a day-to-day basis. If you can't plan for the semester or the year, plan at least two weeks in advance. Always plan more instructional activities than you need because in many instances, you will be able to cover more content than originally planned. If you are using an alternating day

schedule, be aware of blocks that will not meet because of school breaks, holidays, or special assemblies, and any special accommodations that need to be made because of these breaks. A yearly calendar should be distributed to all customers of a school indicating which block meets on which day throughout the year. If the schedule you use is a 4x4, the yearly calendar is not an issue.

■ Plan your class instruction around a time management system (see Figure 56). Allow activities for each unit of time and adjust only if there is an instructional reason for adjusting.

■ If you are on an alternating schedule (A-B), plan to adjust homework assignments, because you will only see students every other day. It is helpful if the assignment can be divided into two parts: One part assigned one night, and the second part assigned the next night. This will provide a daily reinforcement that may be needed for some classes, such as foreign languages. If you are on a semester schedule, remember that you will be covering twice as much material in a single block. Design homework so that it serves not only as a practice activity but also as the knowledge foundation for the next class. Avoid having students do homework during class time. Utilize "open-ended" closure with your lessons. Leave your students "hanging," and use homework assignments to answer the questions you leave them with. Using class time for homework assignments can be very tempting when you have not prepared enough material for a block, but it can also be devastating to the students in class. Avoid using large pieces of time in the teaching block for homework. Both parents and students will share their feelings about this practice with the principal or division superintendent, and their opinions are generally negative.

■ Have objective(s) visible for all students to see when entering the classroom. It will signal to students that class is in session from the time they enter the room.

■ Vary instructional approaches and never attempt to use a single teaching strategy for the entire block. Plans for instruction should include opportunities for students to use reading, writing, speaking, and listening skills. These skills should be incorporated into all lesson plans. Consider implementing strategies such as cooperative learning and student self-directed learning along with traditional lecture/discussion or drill/repetition. Have optional strategies ready if prepared methods are not successful.

■ Use appropriate cooperative learning as only one strategy during any one block. Cooperative learning is a good match for the value-added time available because of the block schedule. Group work provides opportunities for students to think, listen, and interact to issues related to instruction in the class. Teams should be changed frequently. Students should be placed in teams according to ability (mix and match students with varying abilities as well as with similar abilities) or by varying characteristics.

■ Consider having a product evolve from each lesson plan. Avoid using simple practice exercises. Provide opportunities for students to apply the knowledge they have learned. Consider planning each block with a theme as the focus for the day. Explore your theme from varying perspectives as you cover the content. Use a thematic approach to liven up your anticipatory set.

■ Regardless of the content you teach, provide opportunities for student writing. Students are able to complete several steps of the writing process in one block, and there is time for peer interaction. Also, students can work one on one with the teacher if they have special problems. Meet with English teachers in the school for assistance if you are not familiar with the writing process. (The writing process could be a focus of staff development for the entire school year.) Explore strategies that include teaming with teachers for writing assignments and peer coaching in writing teams. This is an excellent way to use the larger pieces of time in a more productive learning experience for students.

■ Provide student opportunities to read silently in class with follow-up strategies that include a question-and-answer session. Conclude with a writing activity related to the reading assignment.

■ Use multimedia teaching tools to support other teaching strategies. These tools include: video- and audiotapes, transparencies, maps, computers, CD-ROMs, interactive CDs, graphing calculators, and scientific probes. These tools should become a part of the daily instructional plan.

■ If you are on an alternating day schedule, a review is very important at the beginning of the class. This review should be limited to three to five minutes.

■ Provide opportunities for students to exhibit learned or prior knowledge. This will provide checks and balances for learning so that you, as a teacher, can increase the pace or re-teach if necessary. (See Continuous Learning model in Figure 53.) End class with a review of new concepts that will signify closure for the class.

CASE IN POINT

While visiting an English teacher's classroom, Tom observed the following strategy being used with her students. Before class began, she wrote a sentence on the overhead projector for students to diagram the moment they entered the classroom. As students entered the room, they immediately went about the task of diagramming the sentence, and the teacher went about the task of assisting them with their assignment. As each student entered the room s/he became involved in the same process before the tardy bell rang to officially begin class. Although the teacher did not teach a unit on diagramming, she informed Tom that they did one sentence during each class throughout the year. She acknowledged that it was a strategy that served two purposes. The first, to get students immediately on task, and the second, as a way to teach what she considered a boring concept in as painless a method as possible. They both appeared to work, and the climate for the class was set.

Consider using the last five minutes to reinforce student use of the time management/assignment books, and make sure that students clearly understand expectations for the homework assignment and for the next class meeting.

■ If necessary, provide a short break when transitioning from one activity to another. This appears to be very successful in maintaining the attention of younger secondary students (ninth and tenth graders) and is especially effective at the beginning of the year, when students are becoming accustomed to the longer block of time. Older students (eleventh and twelfth graders) do not appear to have problems, if teaching strategies are varied and are designed to engage students in learning.

■ Strategies for testing should be given careful consideration. Unless students are taking a comprehensive examination, the full block will not be used. With a longer block of time, an effective teaching strategy is to review materials before

testing. Provide opportunities for students to ask questions and interact with the teacher and other students before testing.

NOTE: *It is important to note that rearranging time will require student testing/assessment to be reconsidered, because classes meet fewer times in a grading period.*

■ Think in terms of covering multiple lessons or concepts during a longer block rather than teaching one lesson or one chapter from the text. Think in terms of how you might consolidate several single lessons into one longer block, including process skills, content, and goals rather than breaking them down into what you would normally teach in one traditional class period. Consider a different configuration for reorganizing your previous lesson plans into concepts that would be covered in units of instruction rather than a single lesson.

■ If your class make-up policy is different from the school's policy or has been revised to meet your expectations when moving to a block, make sure that you provide it to students in writing. Clarify your expectations of this policy as it relates to make-up work on a regular basis. Remember: Students are on a fast track, and one missed class can have a negative impact on student performance.

■ Keep accurate records. You are covering twice as much material and moving twice as fast. Keep records of what you did or did not cover in a particular block. This might be more important if you are using the alternating day block format because of the lapse of time between classes.

■ Again: Because the use of time is so important, be prepared for class. Have all technical equipment and handouts ready and in place before class begins. This will save instructional time.

■ Always be over prepared. Have a "bag" of instructional activities ready that will relate to the daily plan for class. Regardless of how carefully you plan, there will be times when you complete plans for the day prior to the end of the block. Utilizing instructional activities from the "bag" can transform additional time into valuable instructional time. An assessment activity is a good teaching tool to insert at the end of a class. It not only provides information on what students did or did not learn, it also provides information that will allow for more effective planning for the next block. These types of activities will eliminate any "down time."

■ Be flexible with time and be willing to adjust as needed. A flexible classroom structure will allow for teacher and student creativity. As a teacher, Tom found the flexible use of time to be a valuable tool that allowed him to implement different teaching strategies that meet the needs of students with different learning styles.

■ Plans for each block should include legitimate "movement" activities. If possible, during each class meeting, plan some type of activity to allow for legitimate movement, such as student presentations, legitimate talking, group work, etc.

■ When an opportunity arises, spend some time talking with students. Teachers have indicated that this helps them get to know students and their individual learning styles better and therefore provides a vehicle to establish a positive rapport between teacher and student. When students encounter learning difficulties, it is easier to work with students you know well.

■ Explore opportunities that provide different learning experiences for your students. Consider team teaching for a unit—changing classes with a teacher who has the expertise in a particular area for one block or a series of blocks. Cooperative teaching is dependent on the length and topic of the unit.

■ Be patient. The block scheduling concept is as new and different to the student as it is to you. You will be surprised how quickly you and the students will adjust to it.

LOOKING BACK . . .

Instructional leaders and teachers must become creative in an attempt to provide a more efficient use of instructional time to improve student achievement. Be prepared and plan, plan, plan! Be a risk taker, and use a variety of strategies in challenging your students to achieve above minimum standards. Instructional strategies are limited only by the imagination of the teacher, but much can be learned by working with colleagues.

There are good models for planning lessons, and teachers who have worked on a block schedule will share almost anything you need. But remember: There is no magic formula for designing plans for instruction, just as there is no one methodology that will work every day. The strategies that teachers are using in 90-minute periods have been around a long time. Teachers are finding that having longer blocks of time encourages them to use methods they previously didn't try. While some practices like small grouping strategies and cooperative learning match good pedagogy for adolescent learners, the strategies themselves are not new. Good questioning strategies, Socratic teaching, and project learning have been encouraged for many years. Now that teachers have time to use a variety of approaches, they are willing to experiment.

CASE IN POINT

When analyzing student grades, Tom observed that a particular math teacher's students' grades were much lower in one class than the other four classes that she taught. This inconsistency was even more puzzling because students were heterogeneously grouped in each of her five classes. When this pattern continued over several grading periods, Tom asked the teacher for an explanation. She stated that the class where performance was poor was an Algebra II class taught in a single block that met for 55 minutes each day. She taught the other four Algebra II classes in a longer block (1:45 minutes), and these students appeared to be performing at a higher achievement level. Upon analysis of teaching strategies, the only apparent difference was that she provided a significant review period for students in the longer block of time. She felt that she could not spare the time in the shorter block of time, so she was not providing an opportunity for those students to review on the day the test was administered.

This is what block scheduling is about: finding the best approaches to instruction that maximize student learning. We believe that this is best accomplished in the classroom where there is enough time to explore topics in depth and involve students in their own learning. ❏

Chapter 9 Appendix on CD

❏ Instructional Change Framework

- Lesson Plan Components for One-Class Period (word version)
  - Teacher Tips for Dealing with Block Scheduling in All Classes (word version)
  - The Process of Designing Block Lessons (word version)
  - Sample Lesson Outlines
  - Sample Lesson and Unit Plans

How Does Staff Development Lead to Improved Instruction?

*T*o live in a quantum world, to weave here and there with ease and grace, we will need to change what we do. We will need to stop describing tasks and instead facilitate process. We will need to become savvy about how to build relationships, how to nurture growing, evolving things. All of us will need better skills in listening, communicating, and facilitating groups, because these are the talents that build strong relationships. It is well known that the era of the rugged individual has been replaced by the era of the team player. But this is only the beginning. . . . More and more relationships are in store for us . . .

—Margaret Wheatley, 1992

LOOKING AHEAD IN THIS CHAPTER . . .

We in education spend valuable resources designing new programs, developing new curriculums, inventing better methodologies, and creating appropriate assessments in our quest to improve schools. Yet, we often forget that the key to better instruction is the classroom teacher. Without education and training, anything "new and improved" has little chance of making a difference in classrooms.

Block scheduling requires a commitment to ongoing staff development. Those schools that have been highly successful with their alternative schedules have involved teachers in professional activities that allowed them to grow into the new schedule and new way of teaching. Principals of those schools understood that this effort would take several years and could not be viewed as a one-shot approach at change.

This chapter invites principals and teachers to plan activities that will encompass new teaching strategies, classroom management, using small groups for learning, and articulating curriculum in a number of delivery formats. While we know that some schools allocate more time for staff training than other schools do, we suggest that it is time to view staff development as an intricate part of the school improvement effort, connecting each in-service activity to a school improvement goal.

PLANNING AND IMPLEMENTING STAFF DEVELOPMENT

From the beginning of our work with block scheduling, we have emphasized the importance of education and teacher training if block scheduling is to be successful. The effort must be a grassroots initiative, and funding for training must be available. All partners must understand the possibilities offered by a change in the use of time (education), and they must become skilled in practices that will enhance the chance of success of the modified schedule (training). Peters (1987, p. 504) ratifies the urgency and importance of training in the following statement: "Make strategic planning an exclusive 'bottom up' activity, with two-thirds of the content focusing on skill capability rather than the prediction of the future."

His statement sums up the critical urgency and necessity of training for all partners if block scheduling is to be successful in your school. There must be a philosophical as well as financial commitment to the project. If we put in place a system to support our people, then we have the capacity to adjust when there is a need. Deming believed that no more than 15 percent of an organization's problems were due to problems with people. If we believe in this rule, we should focus on putting processes in place that work well to maintain a smooth functioning system, and develop a support system that will "fix" the 15 percent of problems caused by people. In schools, many of these people problems can be attributed to a lack of adequate training. If we believe that people problems can be solved, and we have the resources to address the problems, we can expect positive change.

Based on our experiences, ongoing staff development is perhaps the most critical piece of implementing the block schedule. When we are approached by administrators who indicate they are having trouble with block scheduling, our first question is: Have teachers changed the way they teach? If not, you can expect a problem, but the problem is not the schedule. The problem is lack of training for teachers who are continuing to do business as usual.

The importance of staff development is also supported in the literature previously cited in this book. There is also a strong feeling from some of the principal players involved in innovative scheduling that it is critical to conduct staff development during, as well as after, the implementation of block scheduling. Tanner (1996) points out that "the change in teaching that occurs as a result of the extended time [in the classroom] is the true means of reaching the goals and objectives around which the schedule is built." Tanner notes that ". . . successful change involves learning to do something new." She notes that for teachers involved in block scheduling, "'something new' may be learning new instructional strategies and for others it may be adapting instructional practices to 'fit' the newly developed time periods" (p. 34). Block scheduling literature supports the need for teacher training (Canady & Rettig, 1995; Shortt & Thayer, 1995), and the need for staff development is reinforced when connected to change (Thayer, 1996). Based on supporting literature, Tanner (1996, p. 46) indicates that the 1990s will be identified as a period of high school reform. If we have learned lessons from the past, these reform efforts will only be meaningful and successful if they have been made with meaningful input from those closest to the reform effort and if the needs of those closest to the reform effort are met.

Additional thoughts on training abound from the private sector. As proponents of Total Quality practices in schools, we believe it is helpful to look at how businesses are changing their organizational cultures by educating employees about Quality principles and training them in the use of Quality tools. Juran (1989, p. 329) states:

> The basic purpose of training should be to secure a *change in behavior*: to carry out an improvement project, to replan some existing plan, or to evaluate process capability for some ongoing operation. The purpose of the training should be to assist the participants in making the change in behavior. It is usually feasible to design the training in ways that provide the participants with means of applying the training to actual job situations.

Juran (1989) relates training to Quality and discusses the various levels of training through a multidimensional approach. One dimension is concerned with fundamental concepts, a second with the hierarchical level of the trainees, a third with various organizational functions, and a fourth with the numerous tools and techniques used in work processes. In the face of this multidimensional content, the organization must establish a training curriculum. This curriculum is a collection of training courses, which can meet the training needs for all of the dimensions.

These dimensions can be translated to the world of educational change. Dimensions one and two would be an understanding of the change concept, and the block schedule in particular, by all customers and change agents. The quality of the schedule and how it relates to carrying out the school's mission as it relates to quality instruction is also included in these dimensions. The third dimension relates to the tools such as teaching strategies, resources, and materials that lead to the success of teaching in the block. The final dimension is the recognition of the needs of internal customers and developing a curriculum that will meet the training needs of all school folks—the student to the principal—involved in the change process. Curriculum is critical as a road map when providing direction for student success and achievement. Why not a curriculum for teachers? It surely is something that educators are familiar with, and it could lead the reform movement to recognize the importance of training for all stakeholders.

Let us state at this point that we believe the change agent—the principal—has a responsibility to plan development experiences for all staff early in the change process. We also believe that while generally staff development should be nonmandatory, there may be some experiences—some training—that may be required for all teachers. For example, at Gloucester High School all teachers were required to participate in two days of Quality training. They were given a choice of dates, and they were given staff development credit for license renewal, but everyone had to participate in training that laid the foundation for teamwork. If the planning team feels strongly that all teachers should have a background in a topic or skill, and if the principal is going to support the use of that skill in the classroom, it is only right to deliver training to everyone.

We believe organizations are developmental. That is, teachers work together to move schools to different levels of maturity. When schools have teams that function autonomously, they move toward becoming learning organizations. Senge (1990) says that a learning organization is "an organization that is continually expanding its capacity to create its future" (p. 14). It is characterized by high-functioning teams that enter into judgment-suspended dialogue for decision making. Block (1993, 1996) suggests that as teams truly become functional, the staff development emphasis should be shifted from training to learning, giving the learners the choice for their personal development agenda.

We agree. We would like to see all schools becoming learning organizations—ones in which administrators, teachers, parents, and students learn together and create the changes needed to improve the school continually. You can move your faculty in that direction by initiating effective teams. As faculty understand more and more about using time differently and begin working together in teams, they should identify their needs and plan their own staff development (or seek help from those with expertise in staff development). What we are proposing in this chapter is that there are topics and activities for staff development that are highly appropriate for the principal to consider during the early phases of block scheduling planning. While it is always appropriate to ask teachers what they want and need, they may not be able to articulate what they need. For example, in 1981 few teachers knew that they would be required to use computer technology in their teaching, so they didn't ask for in-service programs in hardware and software. Today, they are very specific about what they need to keep updated with computer utilization. When teachers see themselves on a road that is being shaped in front of them as they walk it, it is unproductive to ask them which fork to take. The principal's job is to serve as the guide. As the road becomes clearer, and teachers are willing to move ahead of the guide to forge new pathways, then they are able to identify the tools they need.

TOPICS FOR TRAINING

A broad planning matrix to provide training services for customers of block scheduling might look something like Figure 64.

This chart, although not comprehensive, is designed to help the school leadership begin thinking about training needs. Each school will have its unique set of circumstances and must add, delete, or adjust accordingly.

We have discovered that as soon as you mention block scheduling, the first questions to arise are related to the issue of training. Questions such as: Should training be voluntary or mandatory? If voluntary, should the participants be compensated? Who should participate? Should administrators be included?

To answer these questions, we offer the following research support. Juran (1989) suggests that upper managers should be the first to receive training for change. The reason for this is obvious, because managers—principals—must provide the leadership and need to know as much as possible as they begin influencing change. Peters (1987, p. 75) says that everyone in the company should be trained. "Instruct everyone . . . Some train only first-line supervisors. This is a serious mistake. The chairman of the board should take the course. . . . More important, every person in the company should be extensively trained."

In fact, if the purpose of creative scheduling is to use human resources more efficiently, then training is a must. The training plan must go beyond the search for short-term results and concentrate on long-term results. If we emphasize short-term results, then we are defeating an attempt to maintain constancy of purpose, one of Deming's principles for quality improvement. He (1982, p. 53) states that in fact "the greatest waste in America is failure to use the abilities of people." The only way this will change is to train our people so that they can use their abilities. Training is not the solution to all of the issues related to block scheduling, but if the organization has good people who are willing to become better by improving with training, the chances of the success of the block scheduling will improve. "What an organization needs is not just good people; it needs people that are improving with education" (Deming, 1982, p. 86).

Creating a climate of confidence and risk taking is very important when implementing the block schedule format. Teachers must feel that it is acceptable to experiment and experience failures, to learn from experience and move to the next level. Staff development should provide teachers with the skills that are needed to develop confidence that will allow a level of comfort with experimenting and risk taking. This will also require a change on the part of the principal. Principals must be flexible and encourage teachers to experiment with new strategies that will result in teacher and student success. Planning and staff development will enable faculty members to become involved in an extensive change process with courage to alter the very structure of an institution that has changed very little in the past century.

A concern that we often hear from principals is that they do not have time for staff development. They also contend that many teachers do not want to stay after school, and even when they do, the afternoons are not the most productive time of the day to offer staff development. Other principals cite union contracts that prohibit additional time for staff development without compensation, which many schools cannot provide. But we suggest that with a thorough analysis of allocated instruction time and creative use of human resources and time, many administrators will find time to provide staff development opportunities for teachers during the identified teacher school day or during other times that are convenient for both teachers and administrators.

The areas in which teachers have most often expressed to us a need for staff development include the following:

- **Instructional strategies**—How do teachers use skills such as questioning techniques, direct instruction, and problem solving to improve the use of instructional time? What hands-on activities, manipulatives, and student projects should be included in instruction? Should they concentrate on developing interdisciplinary activities or joint projects with other teachers?

- **Empowerment**—How do teachers provide opportunities for students to become self-directed learners, so that they buy into the learning process? How do teachers become the decision makers related to matters in which they are the stakeholders—especially when refining systems that relate to the organization of curriculum and instruction, and the use of time within the school?

- **Proactive decision making**—How do teachers use proactive decision-making skills to eliminate potential classroom management problems, such as inappropriate student behavior, student or teacher organization problems, time management concerns?

- **Discovery learning**—How do students learn by using the discovery process? What kind of inquiry model is most appropriate for adolescents?

FIGURE 64
Training Matrix

MODULES	STUDENTS	PROFESSIONAL STAFF	SUPPORT STAFF	COMMUNITY PARTNERS
		Teachers, Guidance, Support Staff, Central Office, Administrators, Board Members	Custodial Services, Food Services, Bus Drivers, Nurses, Aides, Volunteers	Parents, Community, Social Services, Feeder Schools, Professional Organizations, PTA, Special Interest Groups, Professional Community, Business/ Employers
Awareness of Change	✔	✔	✔	✔
Concept Level		✔	✔	✔
Organizational Functions	✔	✔	✔	✔
*Cooperative Learning	✔	✔		✔
*Time Management	✔	✔		
*Instructional Strategies		✔		
*Planning	✔	✔	✔	✔
*Discovery Learning	✔	✔		
*Teaching Strategies	✔	✔		
*Organizational Skills	✔	✔		
*Integration of Technology	✔	✔		
*Learning Styles	✔	✔		
*Alternative Strategies for Remediation		✔		

*Components of organizational function

- **Time management**—How can teachers divide the class period into manageable pieces of time that will provide opportunities for positive learning and teaching experiences?

- **Field trips**—How can teachers prepare effective field trips as a part of the learning experience? Will the block schedule impact field trips positively or negatively?

- **Classroom management**—How do teachers manage materials for longer blocks of time? How do they manage students who have shorter attention spans? How can they plan and manage paperwork if the schedule is an alternating block? How can they adjust to the management of the planning cycle for longer blocks of time?

- **Organization**—How do teachers organize classrooms that permit multiple teaching strategies and learning activities? How do teachers organize student teams? How do they organize the classroom for student projects and research?

- **Student-to-student information sharing**—How do teachers manage students so that they can work together effectively in teams of two?

- **Teacher information sharing**—Can systems be established for sharing of information between teachers on a daily or weekly basis? What kind of support system is best for teachers?

- **Individualized instruction**—How can teachers use individualized instruction more effectively in a larger block of time?

- **Expanded use of technology**—How do teachers identify and use the most recent technology as a teaching and learning tool? Can technology be used effectively in each block of instruction?

- **Teaching models**—How do teachers become familiar with various teaching models, and how do they implement these models? Do some models require larger blocks of time?

- **Cooperative learning techniques**—How and when do teachers use cooperative learning in the classroom? Should everyone use cooperative learning? Why do some parents object to cooperative learning?

- **Team teaching**—How can longer blocks of time be used to develop opportunities for teachers to collaborate and develop team teaching opportunities? How should team teaching be organized (e.g.: two teachers share same students, two teachers exchange students, two teachers exchange to teach a unit, etc.)?

- **Interdisciplinary teaching**—How can opportunities be designed to encourage both interdisciplinary and major concept teaching?

- **Balancing teaching strategies in the block**—How do teachers balance a variety of teaching strategies to provide learning opportunities for students with different learning styles? How much small-group work is enough, and how much lecturing is acceptable? How much lab or experiential learning should be planned?

- **Understanding change**—How can teachers help all stakeholders understand the process of change? Is it OK to tell parents that the change to block scheduling may require some adjustment for all who are involved?

- **Skills in facilities use**—How do teachers re-engineer the traditional classroom layout to maximize instruction?

- **Skills in collegial dialogue**—How can teachers interact with colleagues on a regular basis? How can human resources and time be organized to provide opportunities for positive dialogue between colleagues that will allow for exchange of ideas and the development of a support system?

- **Teaching students with different abilities that share the same classroom**—How can teachers teach students with different abilities who share the same classroom? Which skills are effective for which students? How can students with different abilities be grouped within the same classrooms? Can teachers implement the block schedule while attempting to eliminate academic tracking in the school?

- **Conflict resolution**—How can teachers mediate conflicts that arise in the classroom during the increased block of time?

- **Test-taking strategies**—How do teachers identify the best strategies for assessing learning objectives designed for students in a larger piece of time? How do teachers match assessment to the instructional methodology?

- **Intervention strategies**—What teaching or behavior modification strategies should be used when students are not meeting performance or behavior expectations within the classroom?

- **Alternative education**—How can the block schedule provide alternative education opportunities for students that do not "fit" into the regular school day?

- **Alternative strategies for remediation**—How does a teacher plan a class that will pro-

---

CASE IN POINT

Look beyond the way business has always been done. Through a creative look at scheduling, possibilities abound. Assume that a school is using a 75-15-75-15 block schedule format. It does not matter whether you use an alternating day (A-B) or a semester 4x4, but we must look at the long-term possibilities.

The first 75 days are used for the first semester. The first 15-day period is used for remediation, acceleration, community volunteer work, special projects for both teachers and students, fine arts tours, extended field trips, etc. By teaming teachers and using other innovative ways of scheduling, the possibility of freeing approximately one-fourth of your faculty for 7.5 days is increased. During the next 7.5 days of the 15 days, an additional one-fourth can be freed by switching assignments or using other sound instructional practices and strategies that are congruent with the curriculum.

The second 15 days would be broken into the same time frame. Teachers without teaching responsibilities for the 7.5 days will be involved in planned teacher training. By the end of the year, each teacher in the school should have a minimum of 7.5 days of planned teacher training. Of course, there are many combinations that this format can take—but a team must be willing to take risks and let the creative juices flow.

---

vide opportunities to look at the learning styles of unsuccessful students and re-teach material when necessary? What types of extra-help opportunities are available for students who need extra time for mastery?

- **Strategies for acceleration**—What strategies should teachers use for students who understand concepts more in depth and faster than other students (i.e.: gifted students)?

- **Critical thinking**—How do teachers plan activities that will allow active student participation and enhance a student's ability to analyze and provide critical insight into concepts?

- **Pacing**—How do teachers pace content to cover adequately the curriculum and learning objectives planned for students?

- **Long-term planning**—How do teachers plan for the entire course rather than for one lesson at a time?

Perhaps the question asked most often is: "If you were planning a workshop or staff development inservice for block scheduling before you implemented the schedule, what would you offer?" Our answer usually is that we would assess the needs of the faculty and base the contents of the workshop on the identified needs. When pushed by colleagues to make a suggestion, we offer the Five-Day Teacher Training Plan on pages 198–199 for their consideration.

A SECOND OPINION ON STAFF DEVELOPMENT

One of the pioneers in block scheduling, Dr. Marian B. Stephens, former principal of Osburn High School in Manassas, Virginia, implemented block

scheduling there in 1992. Since then, she has done presentations and conducted staff development for teachers and administrators throughout the country. Dr. Stephens uses the staff development model presented here in Figure 65. The issues that she addresses during these presentations are primarily for teachers and are drawn from her own experiences as well as from those of her staff and from research. She begins the training process by sharing with the participants the paradigm shift that occurs as the change is made to block scheduling.

Dr. Stephens then goes on to include the following topics in her training program:

- Principles of Instruction for a 90-Minute Block

- Structuring Sequences of Activities Within the Block

- Components of a Lesson Design

- Principles of Active Learning

- Assessment

She concludes her training by asking teachers to consider the question, Am I a thinking teacher? (see Figure 66.) We include it because we think it has real value as you challenge teachers to change their classroom practices.

PRINCIPLES OF ADULT EDUCATION FOR PRINCIPALS TO FOLLOW WHEN PLANNING STAFF DEVELOPMENT

While public school educators are well trained in the development of children and the teaching methodologies that are successful with students of various ages, most educators know little about adult education. Even staff developers, whose work is directed toward adult education, commonly have very little preparation in the principles and practices of adult education. We devote the next section of this chapter to the topic of adult education because we want to provide assistance to leaders so that they may be successful in their efforts to provide appropriate staff development for block scheduling.

Most principals are aware of the environmental arrangements that create a good atmosphere for learning, such things as a comfortable room, breaks and refreshments during meetings, and activities that involve participants. Other guidelines for practice may not be as well defined. What do researchers in adult education advise?

One adult educator who is well known in the staff development literature is Malcolm Knowles. Knowles is recognized for his work in andragogy, the pedagogy of adult education. Knowles' work became known in the 1970s with the publication of *The Modern Practice of Adult Education* (1970, 1980 revised). In this landmark book, he states that andragogy is premised on four assumptions about the characteristics of adult learners that are different from the assumptions of traditional pedagogy:

1. As individuals mature, their self-concept moves from one of being a dependent personality toward being a self-directed human being.

2. As individuals mature, they accumulate a growing reservoir of experience that becomes an increasingly rich resource for learning.

3. As individuals mature, their readiness to learn becomes oriented increasingly to the developmental tasks of their social roles.

4. As individuals mature, their time perspective changes from one of "postpones application of knowledge" to "immediacy of application" and accordingly, their orientation toward learning

shifts from one of "subject-centeredness" to one of "performance-centeredness."

Knowles' work is helpful in understanding that adults should be involved in setting their own agendas for learning. His work points out that teachers want staff development highly related to their work—thus, the common need teachers have to take something home with them that they can implement in the classroom immediately. He recognizes that teachers bring a wealth of experiences from many contexts to the learning experience. Their background and prior experiences should not only be recognized; the various contexts should be used to build the new learning experience.

A principal planning staff development should:

- Include teachers in the planning process, asking them to help identify topics, suggest times for training, set goals for staff development, help identify trainers, etc.

- Use the varied backgrounds of the teachers in the development activities. For example, ask

(Coninued on page 200)

CASE IN POINT

The second year Gloucester High School was on the A-B block, Yvonne was approached by a senior who wanted to rearrange his schedule so that he could devote time to developing his computer programming skills—his planned career path. The student needed English and government for graduation, wanted to continue band, and was enrolled in AP Calculus. These four courses were scheduled on A days, and B days were free for him to work all day in the Smart (computer technology) Lab. The student maintained this schedule all year, developing an independent study project that concluded with a graphing program for the calculus classes to use.

The student found that the six-hour day was perfect for studying new computer languages, writing programs, and troubleshooting. He contributed more hours at school and at home for this project than any other student taking independent study.

OBJECTIVES

■ To provide information to teachers relative to block scheduling that will increase their comfort level and educate them on planning issues

■ To develop skills in planning for the block time frame

PRODUCTS

Lesson plans for one unit of study

DAYS 1 and 2

Consider issues that teachers need to address in order to design lesson plans that will provide effective instructional practices for teachers teaching in a 90-plus-minute block of time. Issues that need to be addressed before designing lesson plans include the following:

• Teaching concepts instead of chapters

• Planning for the length of the class/year/semester depending on the block schedule format that your school has chosen

• Time management in the classroom

• Methods for recognizing individual differences in learning and identifying appropriate instructional strategies

• Methods for providing a variety of strategies that include active student participation

• Strategies for integrating technology and community resources into the daily teaching and learning process

• Defining the role of a teacher in a block scheduling concept: a disseminator of information as well as a facilitator of learning

• Developing a support system for teachers

A successful teacher with experience in teaching in the block schedule serves as the facilitator of this teacher-training program.

After teachers become familiar with the previously addressed issues, all teachers analyze exemplary lesson plans proven to be effective in the block schedule format. Teachers give consideration to how the previously mentioned issues have been embedded in the exemplary lesson plans.

The last half of the second day is used for all participants to individually practice designing lesson plans for the increased block of time.

DAY 3

Day three is dedicated to cooperative learning and reviewing other models and strategies that are effective in longer class periods. This will provide teachers an opportunity to learn strategies that will help them implement the lesson plans they will be designing the last two days of the seminar. Additional training on cooperative learning can be planned during time allocated for staff training during the school year.

No teacher masters a teaching method in one introductory lesson. Therefore, staff development must continue to provide opportunities for teachers to learn and practice methods with which they are unfamiliar. The district's staff development coordinator or instructional supervisor should help secure resources for training in the following:

> Information Processing Models
>> David Ausubel's Advance Organizer Model
>> Richard Suchman's Inquiry Training Model
>> Joan Fulton's Conceptual Development Model

Social Models

Donald Oliver and James Shaver's Socratic Dialogue (Jurisprudential Model)

Simulations, Games, Role Playing

Nondirective Models

Johnson & Johnson's Cooperative Learning

Student Team Learning (Johns Hopkins)

Product-Oriented Strategies

Project-Based Learning

Joint Projects (among two or more classes)

Senior Projects

Independent Study and Research

NOTE: *Schools that provide technological resources in classrooms (that is, multiple computers per classroom and/or multimedia retrieval systems) or offer state-of-the-art computer labs that are highly accessible to teachers should also offer training in inquiry approaches that utilize technology. Examples of this kind of teaching/learning that is facilitated with longer periods of time for exploration and experimentation can be found in the science modules being developed on CD-ROM by the Institute for Connecting Science Research to the Classroom, College of Human Resources and Education, Virginia Tech. Contact Dr. Joy Colbert, Director.*

DAYS 4 & 5

The final days of training focus on the completion of a project that includes:

- Unit and classroom instructional plans for the first unit to be taught during the upcoming school year.

- An assessment plan used by the teacher to determine both teacher and student progress. This plan should be designed to assess progress on a weekly basis.

- Pacing guides for courses that will help teachers keep on track to complete the stated objectives for the course.

All teachers will work in content-area teams to develop these products; i.e.: English teachers, math teachers, social studies teachers, science teachers, music teachers, physical education teachers, vocational education teachers, etc.

Of the three products, the lesson plans require the most attention. If adjustments need to be made because of time constraints, we recommend that only a working draft be developed for the assessment and pacing product. These can be fully developed as the year progresses.

Follow-up sessions in areas where teachers feel most uncomfortable should be the topic of planned staff development throughout the school year, which should lead to a long-term staff development plan. Other topics for staff development might include sessions on additional cooperative learning strategies, teacher grading practices that support student learning, seminar teaching, and classroom management for teachers and students.

trade and industrial teachers to share how they have taught in a block format in past years, or ask experienced teachers to share with less experienced teachers methodologies they know but have not had time to use in class.

• Recognize that teachers have a limited tolerance for theory and want to see the immediate application of training topics for their classroom.

Principals have indicated a concern about motivating teachers to want to learn about block scheduling or to learn new methods for teaching in a longer block. Some folks rely on A.H. Maslow's hierarchy of human needs (1954)—indicating that if teachers don't adjust to the block schedule, their survival needs will be challenged! We prefer to look at the work of Raymond Wlodkowski, who included in his *Enhancing Adult Motivation to Learn* (1990, pp. 68-69) six motivational strategies that can be helpful to the principal:

1. Positively confront the possible erroneous beliefs, expectations, and assumptions that may underlie a negative attitude.

2. Reduce or remove components of the learning environment that lead to failure or fear.

3. Whenever possible, make learner reaction and involvement essential parts of the learning process; that is, problem solving, games, role playing, simulation, and so forth.

4. Use a cooperative goal structure to maximize learner involvement and sharing.

5. Provide consistent feedback regarding mastery of learning.

6. When learning has natural consequences, allow them to be congruently evident.

Wlodkowski's strategies are applicable to block scheduling preparation. This chapter cannot address motivation as well as Wlodkowski does, so we recommend that principals read his work. We encourage principals to pay particular attention to his first motivational strategy, which deals with assumptions and beliefs that teachers may bring to staff development. Teachers' beliefs and assumptions create the principles that guide their thinking about schools, teaching, and learning. These principles also bind the culture of the school together. Since the move to block scheduling is part of a change effort, block scheduling challenges the culture of the school. The principal must understand

FIGURE 65
Changing Methods for Block Scheduling

METHODS	OLD WAY OF DOING BUSINESS	NEW WAY OF DOING BUSINESS
Curriculum	Content-based	Skill, Process, Product
Role of teacher	Teacher-centered	Teacher/Student Centered
Assessment	Consists mostly of tests and quizzes	Varied
Methodology	Dominated by lecture	Multi-modal
Instructional tools	Textbook-based	Various modes of technology
Mode of learning	Factual	Thematic
Products	One right answer	Alternatives
Instructional results	Memorization for test	Learning how to think and application

FIGURE 66
Am I a Thinking Teacher?

- Do I frequently ask students open-ended questions, questions with more than one answer?

- Do I ask a variety of questions at all levels of thinking?

- Do I ever ask questions with unknown or indefinite answers?

- Do I frequently encourage students to seek alternative answers?

- Do I encourage students to give reasons for their statements, defend their ideas, support their opinions with evidence, or respond to each other's ideas?

- Do I use subject matter as a source from which students generate their own questions or problems? Do we then seriously consider those questions?

- Do I allow "wait-time" after I ask a question to encourage careful consideration and thought?

- Do I monitor my responses to students' answers?

- Do I answer my own questions?

- Do I create an open environment in my classroom that encourages initiative, independence, and originality?

- Do I encourage student production that requires a higher level of thought, namely analysis, synthesis, and evaluation?

- Do I utilize a seating arrangement in discussions that encourages student-to-student interaction?

- Do I encourage students to see connections, to relate subject matter to experiences/ideas in other subjects or in their personal lives?

- Do I stress HOW to think rather than WHAT to think?

- Are the students in my classroom actively involved or passively present but mentally absent?

---

the current culture of the school—the beliefs and assumptions of teachers—to create a climate for change. The principal must understand teachers' beliefs and must encourage them to voice these beliefs.

As beliefs are voiced and erroneous statements are made, the principal can challenge the assumptions that teachers hold. Challenging assumptions is a key step in educating adults, but it takes skill and confidence. Sometimes skilled facilitators can best lead teachers through this critical thinking process. We recommend that those leaders interested in learning more about how to challenge assumptions and engage teachers in critical dialogue should read the work of Stephen Brookfield, especially *The Skillful Teacher* (1989). Additional information on integrating critical reflection into staff development programs can be found in the work of Hillkirk, Tome, and Wandress (1989). Their list of suggestions to facilitate the integration of reflection includes teacher writing, discussion, facilitator-led questions that encourage future thinking, and quick

responses to suggestions for program improvement that are an outcome of the reflection process.

As a staff development program is designed, school principals should remember another principle of adult education: Mutual respect between the learner and teacher. "One of the most daunting and difficult (but essential) tasks of the facilitator . . . is . . . to assist in the development of a group culture in which adults can feel free to challenge one another. . . ." (Brookfield, 1986, pp. 13–14). The kind of mutual respect that Brookfield cites refers to respect for what one brings to the learning situation as well as who one is. He states that a fundamental feature of effective facilitation is making participants feel that they are valued as unique individuals deserving of respect (pp. 12-13). Brookfield talks about this principle of practice in terms of respect for participants' uniqueness, self-worth, and separateness. But this principle serves the learning process in a way that goes beyond respect in and of itself. Brookfield is interested in developing a climate for learning, or a culture for behaving, that encourages critical reflection and the challenging of ideas and attitudes (p. 13). Critical reflection is achieved by examining underlying assumptions adult learners hold and making the learners aware of their assumptions.

Mutual respect is vital to participants' open discussion and effective participatory learning exercises, lest intimidation and censure impact the situation. The role of the facilitator becomes one of developing the group culture for learning, encouraging honesty and openness, and dealing with the realities of prejudice and differing values or beliefs.

As a principal, you cannot demand mutual respect in learning situations. However, you can create an atmosphere in which mutual respect will be valued and encouraged. It may be helpful for you to discuss the concept of mutual respect with instructors or facilitators who will be working with your teachers. Ice-breaking activities, meeting guidelines, and training parameters can reflect a commitment to mutual respect. Even attitudes toward license renewal points or other "rewards" for staff development represent an understanding of the learner. Additionally, the principal planning the education for teachers and the facilitator leading the event can build mutual respect if they remember that each learner comes to the event with a slightly unique context for learning. Recognizing contextual differences in a positive way—honoring diversity—may enhance mutual respect.

Demonstrating mutual respect as teachers' assumptions are identified and challenged is the initial step in *double-loop learning*, a concept from organizational development developed by Argyris and Schön (1978). Double-loop learning is the notion of "workers" becoming aware of the underlying norms, objectives, or assumptions of a process; reflecting upon them; and then advocating change. Schön (1987) proposes to adult educators that professional practice, such as teaching, may depend less on rigid decision-making models, than on the capacity to reflect before taking action, in cases where established theories do not apply. He argues that reflection-in-action emerges within a teacher's activities of teaching; that is, actions and responses to actions are closely intertwined in the process of reframing new meanings in theory and new strategies for practice (Russell & Munby, 1991).

Implementing a block schedule as part of a school improvement initiative calls for reframing a teacher's view of schooling and is a paradigm change for all but the visionary. Helping teachers get to the level of professionalism where their decision making is driven by what is best for the customers of the school rather than what is most comfortable for them is an outcome that is possible with double-loop learning. This means that teachers will inevitably ask "why?" when they are changing what they are doing—but that is good. We should all be prepared to address why we are doing what we are doing in the education of our youth.

To summarize this section on adult education, we encourage principals to practice the following:

- Think of staff development as an ongoing process that will always be a part of teacher development and school improvement. Plan staff development activities for block scheduling for several years. During the planning process, offer opportunities on a regular basis. During this time period, plan activities for the first year of implementation.

- Involve teachers in the planning of staff development. A staff development design team is ideal. It is very helpful to have at least one teacher who becomes a staff development specialist and who understands adult education. Provide release time for this person to plan and deliver training throughout the school year.

  - Ask teachers what they want and need. Recognize that they may not know what they need during the first year or so. Provide the leadership needed to guide them.

  - Involve teachers in identifying trainers and facilitators. Let them plan agendas and give input to instructors. Also involve them in designing the evaluation of staff development.

- Recognize as you plan any activity that teachers bring varied backgrounds and experiences to staff development sessions. Connect the new learnings—the new emphasis—to their experiences. Give them an opportunity to share "where they are coming from."

- Ensure that any instructors or facilitators show respect to the faculty and do not make them feel inadequate, unaware, or ignorant. We believe there is no place for instructors with massive egos who have something to prove to the teachers. Instructors must be seen as colleagues and should behave as such. While they must be highly competent, they cannot talk down to the teachers.

- Develop activities that encourage teachers to talk about their beliefs. Use activities (and the skills of a good facilitator) to challenge old practices and assumptions that are preventing the faculty from seeing the possibilities of the block schedule.

  - Let teachers air their concerns and doubts. Accept what they say without critical comment (even if this is hard for you to do!).

  - Talk with teachers using "why" and "what if" questions to help them think reflectively.

  - Show teachers alternate ways of doing things, of seeing possibilities, of making something happen. Create an atmosphere of critical reflection that challenges thinking in a psychologically safe environment. Help teachers see there is more than one way to do something, including teaching high school.

  - Build on critical reflection from staff development activity to activity, so that over a period of time, teachers begin viewing all decisions in their classrooms with a critical eye.

- Remember you have two goals with staff development: education and training. First, you must educate the faculty regarding the need for and mechanics of block scheduling. After you have successfully created a new mindset—convinced teachers that block scheduling can improve student achievement—then you work on the skill development that is needed. Training relates to skills (methodologies and management).

- Give teachers time to change, but provide a structure through which the change can occur. Offer staff development activities that place teachers in small groups so that they can discuss and think about the changes that are proposed. Give them the opportunity to talk about professional matters in a psychologically safe environment while stretching them to consider new behaviors in the classroom.

UNENCUMBERED PLANNING EACH DAY

Thoughtful administrators can find unencumbered planning time for teachers each day regardless of the time framework being used. When using a 4x4 block, a daily unencumbered planning period is not usually an issue. Neither should it be when using the A-B schedule. On alternating days when a teacher has only a duty period scheduled (assuming that teachers are responsible for teaching five blocks every two days and have an unencumbered planning period and a duty period assigned), s/he could be responsible for duty half of the block and have planning time the remaining 50 percent of the block. This time should be exempt from the mundane housekeeping chores such as administrative paperwork, non-productive meetings, supervisory tasks, or other non-value added activities. This additional time should be used to enhance teaching skills or to provide leadership that will impact student performance through collaboration, experimentation of various teaching and learning strategies, and dialogue among all players. Teachers can be divided into action teams based on the block of unencumbered time that they share. We recommend that these action teams be designed as interdisciplinary, cross-functional teams. Teams can use shared planning time in a variety of ways.

■ Team teachers should work together to plan and evaluate student work.

■ Alternative student assessment, interdisciplinary instructional planning, and team teaching should be a focus for action teams.

■ Teacher mentors of gifted and talented students can plan strategies for extended instructional activities and evaluation plans for student performance.

■ An action team can plan strategies for engagement of the total school community in the implementation of the school's long-term plan for academic excellence (that may include high expectations, individualized instruction for all students, and development of a vision for academic success for the students of the school).

- Teacher action teams working together to raise expectations and levels of student performance should be a priority.

- Teachers working in total departmental efforts to improve and/or develop curriculum—including the use of instructional technology—will provide support for the total school staff.

- An action team to develop a student-teacher mentor program will develop positive rapport with students involved in the program.

FEWER CLASSES AND STUDENTS PER DAY

Teachers will be more effective in evaluation of student needs, progress, and achievement when responsible for fewer students each day. With fewer classes and fewer students per day, teachers are able to focus more on the individual needs of students. This provides time to use a variety of effective teaching strategies.

CONTACT HOURS REMAIN THE SAME

Depending on the block format implemented, the yearly instructional time should remain the same or increase. Instructional contact time will decrease only if additional classes are offered and the length of the school day or the school year is not extended. Although student contact hours might slightly decline with some schedules, the amount of instructional time actually increases because of the reduction in class changes, class start-up, and class closure time.

TEACHER AS A PROVIDER OF KNOWLEDGE AND FACILITATOR

Perhaps the most significant impact that the block schedule will have on many teachers is the role change from that of providing knowledge to that of providing knowledge and facilitating learning. This will provide a format of opportunities for teachers to become actively involved in the learning process. Teachers will have the opportunity to emphasize

critical thinking, problem solving, and analytical skills. Effective strategies to teach these skills will allow for active student involvement in the learning process rather than becoming passive consumers of information.

Teachers and students will need to develop new time management skills or refine previously used time management skills to be adapted to block scheduling. The efficient use of time is critical if allocated instructional time is to be optimized.

AUDIT AND REVISE CURRICULUM AS NECESSARY

One of the most common mistakes that we observe when schools are transitioning to the block schedule format is a lack of curriculum review by teachers. Most teachers tend to double-up previously developed lesson plans; that is, teaching two lesson plans that had been developed for a 55-minute period in one block. For many classrooms, it becomes **more** of the **same** because teaching strategies do not change.

As curriculum becomes a focus of the change process, consider the following four focus areas.

- Align curriculum with standards and rigorous academic expectations so that there is a balance between content and understanding of concepts.

- Connect teaching content with concepts or ideas.

- Change the role of the student from a passive consumer of information to that of an active participant in the learning process.

- Enhance problem solving by constructing student learning assignments that call for the use of critical thinking skills. This can be accomplished through classroom assignments or can be included in homework assignments that will ensure a more meaningful use of extended classroom time. This also provides an opportunity for critical thinking skills to be developed by being embedded in the teaching process rather than taught as a separate skill.

It is critical for teachers to be aware of the issues that will face them as they change to a different schedule format. Those mentioned here are just a few. The list can be as extensive and detailed as any school district may feel necessary. The issues that we have listed are intended to bring an awareness to all customers that positive change does not occur in isolation of leadership. All customers must be aware of their roles in the change process.

CHANGE FOR STUDENTS

Block scheduling provides many opportunities for students. It provides a chance to increase expectations to a more rigorous educational program as well as opportunities for students to become more responsible for learning and social behaviors. It is important to provide "staff development" for students as well. Consider the following training issues for students.

■ Students must adjust to becoming active participants in the learning process rather than the traditional passive consumer of information.

■ Students must adjust

• to using independent time within the classroom in a productive manner

• to processing more information and concepts in longer periods of time

• to meeting in class less often

• to managing study time out of class because they will be covering more content in a shorter period of time

■ Students are more accountable for learning and management of their time and social behaviors.

■ Students will be asked to work in teams, work independently, and be a productive unit of the total class.

Although the responsibilities of students become greater, there is an opportunity for students to be more successful and excel academically in an attempt to increase academic achievement. Consider the impact that block scheduling has on the following student indicators for academic success.

■ **Student choices.** As school divisions and other governing agencies call for an increase in expectations, students will have to make selections that they have not previously made. Just because stu-

CASE IN POINT

During a staff development workshop for block scheduling, a teacher asked Tom what to do with a double block of time. He assured Tom that he already had problems motivating students for 55 minutes. Attempting to understand his teaching style, Tom asked him what he did in a 55-minute block of time. His response: "Show a film." Tom's question to the teacher: "What strategies would you use to expand this activity?" His response: "Show two films." While this may sound funny, showing two films in the place of one does not provide a richer and more beneficial learning experience for students. Whether it is two films or two of anything else, multiplying the traditional activity by two is not what we are after in block scheduling. Our goal for block scheduling harbors around increased academic expectations for students, so our expectations for ways of delivering instruction should also change.

dents have opportunities to select more course offerings does not mean that they can or should take all additional offerings. It means that sometimes students will need to make hard decisions concerning classes they choose to enroll in as part of their course of study. It has not been many years ago that high schools were offering only five class periods per day. Then there were six, then seven, and then eight. Generally, the one piece of the school day and course offerings that has remained constant throughout has been time. We are offering students many more courses, but students must make choices when there are conflicts. These choices should be based on students' career plans. Sometimes this means a student will need to make a choice between taking an Advanced Placement course and taking a music class. Both of these courses are very important for a student receiving a "well-rounded" education. But sometimes a choice must be made because schools cannot be all things to all people. There are limits to services that schools can offer their customers.

■ **Dropouts.** We discovered that the block schedule format provided administrators and coun-

Visitors from several school districts were visiting Atlee, and they were questioning students about the block schedule. One of the visitors asked Michael about his attendance. His response was that his attendance was better because he knew that if he missed one class it was the equivalent of two classes, and it would be more difficult to make up the work. Michael, a member of the basketball team, also shared with the visitors that in the past after getting home late from a basketball game he would "sleep in" and miss the entire day or report to school late. "Now I drag myself out of bed and get to school on time."

selors opportunities to be flexible in their approach to scheduling. The schedule could be tailored to the needs of students. The last two years that Tom served as principal of Atlee High School, there was not a single dropout. We have documented many case studies regarding the flexibility of block scheduling related to potential dropouts. Several have been referred to in this book.

■ **Tardies.** It is safe to assume that because of the reduction in the number of times classes are changed during the day, there is less opportunity for students to be tardy for class.

■ **Transfers.** If a student is transferring to a school with a different schedule format than the schedule format of the sending school, it is important that the student take responsibility with support from the receiving school counselor to determine the options that are available in the new school. Students will need to adjust to different teaching/learning styles until they are "worked" into the scheduling cycle of the receiving school.

■ **Inclusion of all students.** Because of the large block of time that the block schedule format offers, teachers have the opportunity to provide more individual instruction for students. Block scheduling also provides a more friendly format

for heterogeneous grouping and inclusion of all students in a collegial learning climate.

■ **Attendance.** Based on data that Tom collected while principal, student attendance increased each year. Attendance will not just increase because you implement block scheduling. It does, however, allow school personnel flexible situations to schedule at-risk students so that they will be in attendance.

■ **Make-up work.** Make-up work becomes more critical because of the amount of class time a student misses when out of school only one day. The more the student misses, the more critical make-up work becomes. If a school is on a semester block schedule format and a student misses five days, this will be equivalent to 10 days under the single-day schedule. Students must take the responsibility for make-up work because it is so critical. They must become familiar with the policy of the school or teacher for making up work, and be responsible for following the policy.

■ **Time management skills.** The way a student uses time becomes critical because one of the goals of block scheduling is to use time more efficiently. Students must prepare for longer classes and must have a plan for use of time in class and time used for preparing for class. Many schools have developed student planning agendas. These planning agendas can be developed by a school, or a school can select a commercial model. One of the most commonly used student planning agendas is available through Premier. Since there were none available commercially the first year Atlee implemented block scheduling, students and faculty developed one for use at the school.

■ **More credits earned upon graduation.** Depending on the scheduling format, students have an opportunity to earn additional credits for graduation. Some school districts are increasing the number of credits required of students for graduation. In some instances, the increase in credits is implemented so that students will stay in school and take advantage of the additional course offerings rather than leaving school earlier in the day or graduating early. Students will need to take the responsibility of long-term planning based on career goals.

- **Fewer classes each day**. Students will have fewer classes each day regardless of the block schedule model. Therefore, they will be able to concentrate on fewer subjects each day and have a more in-depth understanding of concepts. Students are also accountable for more coverage of curriculum in a shorter period of time. Fewer classes also mean fewer tests or tests given more frequently, and homework assignments may increase in quantity and importance.

- **Active classroom participation.** Students will need to adjust from being passive consumers of knowledge to active participants in the learning process. Their focus should become one of learning and not just of graduating from high school.

- **Accountability.** Students will have the opportunity to take responsibility for their own learning process because they will become actively involved as partners with teachers in the learning process. This should send a clear message that learning is the "business/job" of students.

- **Requirements for graduation.** In some cases, requirements for graduation might be affected. This depends on the requirements of the local school district and the type of block schedule that a school implements. There are some concerns by administrators that students will not willingly take advantage of additional course offerings. We have reports of school districts that have increased graduation requirements. This action will, in effect, force students to take advantage of additional course offerings.

- **Extra- and co-curricular activities.** Again, because of the pace of the class, the management of time before, during, or after school is critical. This might cause some students to have to make choices regarding the number and type of extra- and co-curricular activities that they participate in. We scheduled 30 minutes each Friday for stu-

---

CASE IN POINT

A student came to Tom concerned that she was not "learning as much as she should be learning." She was an excellent student and informed him that she was not concerned about grades. She had confidence that because of her grade point average, her standardized test scores, and her school-community activities, she could get into the university of her choice (which she did). Her concern was that a particular teacher's expectations were not high enough. The teacher did not use the time in class in a very productive manner. It appeared that he was giving lots of busy work after the first 30 minutes of the block. He was allowing the last 30 minutes of the block for homework/study hall. She needed the knowledge that he could offer her. She had taken responsibility for her learning. Tom realized that she was an exception, but this is a goal that all students can strive for.

---

dents to participate in co-curricular activities. The number of students participating in these activities increased each year.

We recommend that a section of each student class at the beginning of the school term be dedicated to providing "student development" for students who are new to the block scheduling format. Further, some of the issues previously addressed should be the content of the "student development" series. It is important to train all customers affected by the process.

LOOKING BACK . . .

As we stated at the beginning of this chapter, addressing organizational, instructional, teacher, and student issues appropriately and in a timely manner will enhance the success of the schedule format that you have chosen. If these issues are addressed and a contingency plan for unexpected issues is in place, a win-win situation is created for all customers.   ❑

> ### *Chapter 10 Appendix on CD*
> ❑ Training Plan for Switch to Block Scheduling
>   - Suggested 5-day Training Plan for Teachers
>   - Changing Methods for Block Scheduling
>   - Am I a Thinking Teacher?
>   - Training Matrix

How Do We Build a Master Schedule?

*W*e must first construct a roadmap that will assure us the fastest and
most expedient route to our destination.

—Tom Shortt

LOOKING AHEAD IN THIS CHAPTER . . .

If a master schedule is to be completed in a timely
fashion, perhaps one of the first activities that you as
the change agent will conduct is the organization of
an action team whose goal it is to develop a time line.
Remember: one of the principles of a good team
membership is that all customers be represented on
the team. If an action team is assigned this project,
considerations must be given to all of the issues
needed to be addressed when building a master
schedule. In this particular instance, the issue is to
develop a time line for study and implementation of
block scheduling as well as a time line for building the
master schedule. The two factions cannot operate
independently and must be addressed by the team
during the planning process. Juran (1992) refers to
the Quality Planning Process as "the activity of
developing the products and processes required to
meet customers' needs." The steps Juran suggests

(pp. 14 & 15) are universal for organizations and we
think can be interpreted for schools as follows:

- Establish quality goals using the school planning
  team and input from all customers.

- Identify the customers—those who will be impacted by the efforts to meet the goals: students,
  teachers, parents, and the business community.

- Determine the customers' needs using action
  teams to coordinate surveys, interviews, and
  informal feedback from customers.

- Develop product features that are student- and
  teacher-friendly and that respond to customers'
  needs.

- Develop processes that are able to produce these
  product features. Utilize time lines and processes
  that facilitate the work of the school improvement and action teams.

- Establish process controls and transfer the resulting plans to the school improvement team, action team, or to any individual or teams involved in the development and implementation process.

We recommend that these principles of process be followed when designing a master schedule.

CONSIDERATIONS PRIOR TO BUILDING THE TIME LINE FOR IMPLEMENTING A BLOCK SCHEDULE AND A MASTER SCHEDULE

Prior to the school planning team establishing a time line, all pieces of the process must be considered. That is, look at all of the steps needed to complete the project and then "back" the time line into the process. Certain responsibilities must be assigned to action teams, such as:

■ Implementing a block schedule

- Reviewing and gathering research/literature
- Designing and selecting surveys to be used to collect data
- Selecting schools with comparable schedules to visit
- Engaging public relations/communications activities
- Selecting block schedule models
- Identifying all customers who will be impacted so that they will not be excluded from the process
- Reviewing staff development needs of the faculty

■ Building a master schedule

- Reviewing previous scheduling process
- Reviewing current course offerings
- Reviewing number of students dropping previous classes and why
- Reviewing new policies related to schedules, offerings, and increase in student requirements for graduation, etc.
- Reviewing each course offering and number of students previously taking the course to make

recommendations to administration concerning the relevance of the class for the coming year.

TIME LINE CONSIDERATIONS FOR BUILDING A MASTER SCHEDULE

The following dates should be considered when developing your time line.

- Beginning of next school term
- "Drop-dead" date for setting schedules irreversible before the next school term
- Final changes of schedules (add/drop)
- Schedules delivered to faculty and students
- Computer run—This is very important if schedules are run on shared computer time and equipment at an external location.
- Matrix of class enrollment and recommendations by teachers/department teams
- Student selection of courses from class offerings; advisement with parents

SHARING TIME LINES WITH CUSTOMERS

Time lines should be distributed to all customers and posted to keep everyone advised of the progress of the process. We recommend that monthly checks of the progress be made available to all customers by mailings and postings in appropriate locations throughout the school building and the community. Be creative in how you distribute this information or any other information needed by both external and internal customers.

The following time line might be considered for a two-year study of block scheduling and the implementation process. It can be adjusted to meet any particular situation.

TIME LINE FOR IMPLEMENTING BLOCK SCHEDULING

Consider the time line outlined in Figure 67, which would be appropriate for a two-school-year (a 21-month) study of block scheduling before implementation. Before pursuing the issue of changing to a block schedule (or any other major change), discuss the issue with the superintendent so that s/he will have information to share with the local school board or other interested customers. We recommend meeting with him or her or the designee on a monthly basis to keep top leadership informed.

ASSUMPTIONS

- The study team has been meeting on a regular basis.

- The public relations action team has designed and will carry out a plan to keep all customers informed during the process.

- Teachers will continue to visit schools, attend conferences, and participate in staff development activities during the process.

- The school improvement team will continue to meet as needed.

- Action teams will continue to meet as needed.

- Activities scheduled in the same month will be arranged so that all participants will have opportunities to participate in all activities that they desire.

- This time line is not inclusive and may be adjusted to meet a particular school's need.

A note of caution: Based on our work with schools implementing block scheduling, many schools have studied the block too long. This has resulted in confusing the staff and focusing on the negatives of block scheduling rather than the positives. We suggest looking at the level of support you have for block scheduling and then determining the time line for studying the block concept. Many schools that we have worked with, which have successfully implemented block scheduling, studied and planned for the process in a year or less.

If you choose to use the 21-month study, follow the following process. If you choose to use the 12-month process, simply adjust by beginning with the 12th month and adjusting components of the process as necessary.

This brief matrix can serve as a road map as you move into the process. It can be adjusted to meet individual needs of a school. Action teams can be convened to serve any purpose related to the process. Many action teams can operate simultane-

---

CASE IN POINT

Tom received a call from a key instructional leader in a school district who wanted to know the State Department of Education's position on certain types of block scheduling. After posing her questions, she told him how excited the school community was about changing to a block scheduling format for the next school year. A few months later, we read a newspaper article that said that the local school board had voted not to allow the school to implement the block schedule. Tom called the key instructional leader and asked why the school board had not approved the proposed schedule. The answer was simple: all but one of the steps had been taken in the process to gain support for the block schedule. The local school board had not been informed until they had been asked to approve the schedule. They expressed concern that a major change initiative was happening in a school for which they were responsible. Why had they not been informed of this change? The system had failed.

---

ously. The school improvement team will serve as the steering team for the process.

BLOCK SCHEDULE IMPLEMENTATION: WHAT HAPPENS AND WHEN

November—At the beginning of the process, 21 months or so before implementation, convene the school improvement team to identify a vision statement and goals that will address the structure of the school day. This vision statement, which should be developed during the first meeting, and goals should be a part of the strategic plan for a school. The following vision statement and goals suggest that which your team may be thinking about at this stage of implementation.

VISION STATEMENT

To **develop collaboratively** a schedule that emphasizes flexibility, thus allowing all students to maximize their academic experience and to pursue their scholastic and extracurricular interests.

GOALS

■ To identify the study of the use of allocated instructional time as a goal for the coming school year.

■ To design—or collect previously designed—surveys that match our school's needs and administer those surveys to students, teachers, and parents to determine if the school community perceives a need to explore innovative scheduling that will provide opportunities for more productive and efficient use of the school day for teachers and students. (See accompanying CD for sample surveys.)

■ To interview faculty by department, to assess the needs of each content area in relation to time. (See interview forms on accompanying CD.)

■ To visit other schools using innovative scheduling techniques, and gather information that will be helpful when making an informed decision.

■ To identify the strengths and weaknesses of the current instructional day schedule and identify alternatives that might better meet the needs of students.

■ To consider only options that will raise academic achievement and increase more rigorous learning opportunities for all students.

■ To provide opportunities for students, teachers, and parents to express their concerns and provide appropriate responses to their questions.

■ To provide opportunities for faculty to participate in appropriate staff development activities.

■ To provide opportunities for community orientation that include special programs for students and parents.

■ To establish an action team to facilitate the development of a master schedule based on recommendations of the school improvement team.

■ To design a system to evaluate any needed change to the block schedule concept at the end of the first year of implementation and make changes based on these responses as a never-ending improvement process.

FIGURE 67
21-Month Matrix for Block

BEG. DATE	STRATEGY(IES)	RESPONSIBILITY	CLOSURE DATE
Nov. **Year 1**	Convene school improvement team (SIT)	Principal	Ongoing
Dec. **Year 1**	Visit blocked schools	Data collection action team chair	Sept. **Year 1**
Dec./Feb. **Year 1**	Collect data to determine if change is needed	Data collection action team chair	Feb. **Year 1**
Mar. **Year 1**	Recommendation by SIT made to principal	SIT chair	Mar. **Year 1**
Mar. **Year 1**	Decision to move forward or abandon concept	Principal	Apr. **Year 1**
Apr. **Year 1**	Develop rationale for change	Action team	May **Year 1**
May **Year 1**	Educate customers	Action team	Ongoing
July/Aug. **Year 1**	Share information with feeder schools	Principal	Ongoing

FIGURE 67 (Continued)
21-Month Matrix for Block

BEG. DATE	STRATEGY(IES)	RESPONSIBILITY	CLOSURE DATE
Sept. **Year 2**	SIT identifies issues that need addressing by action team	SIT chair	Ongoing
Oct. **Year 2**	Design strategies for visitation teams to visit blocked schools	Data collection action team chair	Ongoing
Nov. **Year 2**	Action team shares information collected on first visit to block schools	Data collection action team chair	Nov. **Year 2**
Dec. **Year 2**	All action teams make final presentation to SIT	Action team chair	Jan. **Year 2**
Jan. **Year 2**	Seek final approval from school board	Selected members of SIT and the principal	Jan. **Year 2**
Feb. **Year 2**	Continue to collect data, train faculty, and visit blocked schools	Action team chair	Ongoing
Mar. **Year 2**	Continue education for customers, especially student and parent base	Action team chair	Ongoing
Mar. **Year 2**	Build master schedule	Principal/Designee	May **Year 2**
Apr. **Year 2**	Continue scheduling process	Principal/Designee	June **Year 2**
May **Year 2**	Initial master schedule shared with faculty for feedback	Principal/Designee	May **Year 2**
June **Year 2**	Faculty/student schedules distributed prior to summer break	Principal/Designee	June **Year 2**
July/Aug. **Year 2**	Ongoing training	Action team chair	Ongoing
Aug **Year 2**	Plan "Back-to-School" week	Action team chair	Aug. **Year 2**
Aug. **Year 2**	Implement/Celebrate	All customers	Aug. **Year 2**
Oct. **Year 2**	Preliminary evaluation	Evaluation design action team chair	Ongoing
Ongoing	Plan/Do/Study/Act	Principal	Ongoing

December—Year 1

■ Select a scout team (small team of four or five members) consisting of the principal, central office personnel, faculty, and a non-educator(s) from the school improvement team to visit both schools that have implemented a block schedule and conferences where information on the block scheduling concept is being presented.

■ Mail surveys to collect data, if this is a selected strategy.

December–February—Year 1

■ Visit schools, participate in conferences, and collect preliminary data.

■ Prepare report for the full school improvement team.

February (last week of the month)—Year 1

Present findings to the school improvement team.

March—Year 1

School improvement team decides whether to move forward with exploring the block scheduling concept or to make recommendations to delay or even abandon the project.

April—Year 1

■ Develop the rationale for change. The following is an example of such a rationale.

The school improvement team anticipates that the block schedule format will provide an effective framework for opportunities for teachers to deliver a more in-depth curriculum. With the increased increments of instructional time, teachers will develop teaching strategies that will provide opportunities for students to become active learners and partners in the learning process. These activities will provide opportunities for students to develop critical thinking skills, as well as to provide a forum for practice and application of these skills. We anticipate that block scheduling will offer opportunities for students to learn and teachers to teach. As Tom Peters (1987) says, "If it ain't broke, you just haven't looked hard enough. Fix it anyway!"

■ Identify goals that are measurable.

■ Design a time line.

May—Year 1

■ Provide an opportunity for faculty and staff to hear a person(s) with expertise in block scheduling discuss the strengths and opportunities it provides.

■ Identify schools that closely match the demographics of your school and make initial contact for possible visitations for the following school year. This might also be the time to ask if the other school is providing any summer staff development in which members of your staff could participate.

■ Schedule a visit to a matched school (a school on a block schedule similar to the school studying the block). This visit should be by selected faculty members and students to make initial contacts. The faculty members should be department heads, team leaders, and informal faculty leaders.

■ Plan quality summer staff development opportunities that can be used in any schedule format (e.g.: time management, conflict resolution, teaching/learning models, critical thinking skills, strategies that will provide opportunities for application of knowledge, and the use of technology as a teaching tool.

July-August—Year 2

■ Share with principals of feeder schools (middle schools that feed students into your school) the plan for block scheduling, and design a plan for keeping the communication among the schools updated and ongoing.

■ Continue staff development that will enhance the performance of teachers in any schedule format, with emphasis on making real-world applications and teaching through concepts.

September—Year 2

■ School improvement team meets to identify issues that will need addressing by action teams.

■ Assign action teams to address issues that have surfaced during the study. This does not mean that other issues will not surface, but there will probably be issues that need resolution by this point in the journey. We recommend developing a policy action team to address issues that are related to policy, such as: attendance, tardies, lesson plans, teacher evaluation for the first year of the implementation process, in-school/out-of-school suspension, grading periods, testing, and examinations. Other action teams could address the use of audio/visual and technical equipment, use of rest-room facilities, staff development, scheduling, curriculum development/audit, lunch schedules, co-/extracurricular activities, transfer students, sharing programs with schools located on another campus (such as a vo-tech center or magnet schools for gifted students, as well as two different schools on two different schedules sharing the same personnel), Advanced Placement, and special student populations. A public relations action team should have been formed somewhere near the very beginning of the process. This team is responsible for providing means of disseminating this information on an ongoing basis.

October—Year 2

■ Members of the school improvement team visit previously identified school to observe block scheduling in operation.

■ Members of the school improvement team visit the second identified school to observe block scheduling in operation.

■ Members of the team visit a third school using a different type of block scheduling than the two schools previously visited.

■ Faculty discussion should address various scheduling options observed in other schools, as well as the major pros and cons of the respective block schedule concept.

■ The team should review and discuss scheduling options/issues with faculty, parents, teachers, students, guidance counselors, administrators, school board, students, feeder schools, and the school community. The planning of these community meetings and formats for discussion are the responsibility of the public relations action team.

November—Year 2

■ Teams meet to share information collected on visits.

■ Action teams meet during November to collect data and prepare reports to the school improvement team.

■ Teachers and students from matched schools visit the planning school and make presentations to faculty-selected students, staff, and interested parents.

December—Year 2

■ Action teams make final presentation of assigned components to school improvement team for consideration before deciding which block schedule is identified as the best match with the school.

■ After an analysis of all collected data/information and in consideration of all customer input, the school improvement team makes a decision.

■ School improvement team makes a recommendation to the administration.

■ School improvement team presents recommendation to faculty.

■ If a faculty vote is to be taken, it should be scheduled within a week after the presentation to the full faculty.

■ Present findings and recommendations to the local school board for consideration. The presentation to the school board should include the goals for change, what you hope to achieve through change, additional costs (if any), benefits to students, problems that you anticipate may be encountered, plan for public relations, plans for training teachers, and other "hot-button" issues that you have encountered. You may choose to have parents, faculty, and students as a part of the team that presents to the school board. Request a specific time in January for the school board's final decision.

■ Meet with students by grade to provide information about how the block schedule will affect them. Allow time for questions and answers. We recommend that these meetings be completed before winter break.

January—Year 2

Seek final action from the local school board by the board's January meeting.

February—Year 2

■ Action from this point forward is based on the assumption that the local school board has approved the implementation of the block scheduling format. Of course, the first order of business for the school study committee would be to provide any additional feedback or information that the superintendent or local board might request.

■ Continue to conduct on-site school visitations. Selected teachers, guidance counselors, students and parents will continue to visit and observe schools that have implemented the block schedule format.

■ Principal and teacher representatives of the school improvement team meet with department heads to provide information, answer questions, and receive feedback. This should be an ongoing process. Provide information on block scheduling that has been gathered from visits, conferences, and publications. Scheduling issues and major areas of concern should be addressed. Department chairs are directed to share information with departmental faculties.

■ General faculty meeting for informational purposes and to answer questions should be scheduled on a weekly basis from this point froward.

March—Year 2

■ STUDENT information forums. We recommend that these forums be conducted in small groups. Issues such as scheduling and other concerns that students have generated since the previous meeting need to be addressed. These could be held before school, during lunch and/or study halls, after school, or in evening seminars. The purpose of choosing these times is to avoid interrupting academic instructional time. You may have an action team to plan these seminars and schedule them as necessary.

■ FACULTY information forums. These forums update teachers on the status of the block sched-

ule and should be scheduled at appropriate times during planning or duty periods, or at staff meetings.

■ PARENT/STUDENT information forums. We recommend that these be the first in a series of public forums for sharing information and responding to questions that the community at large might have. These forums should be conducted at various times during the day, evening, and week so that as many people as possible have an opportunity to attend. Schedule these forums at school, public buildings, at manufacturing facilities, or places where parents work, if possible, to share the good news and answer questions. The better informed the school community, the better the chances of success. We also recommend that these forums be continued throughout the months of April, May, and June and, to a lesser degree, in August.

■ Designing a plan for developing the **master schedule.** This should include recommendations from all action teams and any additional information previously gathered by any customers who want to contribute. This process should be ongoing until the schedule has been completed and distributed to faculty and students. As a part of the time line, all schedules for the next term should be available to students and faculty before the end of the current school year.

April—Year 2

■ The major thrust in April will be working with student and faculty schedules.

■ PARENT/STUDENT information forums for students with special needs. These forums are targeted for a special audience, and the groups are generally small in numbers. These groups might include students such as those with learning disabilities, gifted students, and students with physical disabilities.

■ Continue to provide frameworks for students, teachers, parents, and the school community in general to discuss issues related to the block schedule.

May—Year 2

■ Initial faculty schedules should be shared with faculty for feedback (preferably during the first week of May).

■ Master schedule finalized and distributed to teachers.

June—Year 2

Student schedules should be distributed to students before they leave for summer break. We recommend that these schedules include only the course and the time of each block and not the assigned teacher.

June, July, and August—Year 2

■ Ongoing staff development opportunities for all faculty and staff are held.

■ STUDENT/PARENT information forums. These forums should be scheduled a minimum of two times a month. This will serve transfer students and their parents in addition to parents who did not participate in the initial communication process. Parents will become more concerned about the new school schedule as time approaches for the opening of school.

■ Notify teachers of schedule changes that are made after the master schedule is distributed. This is critical because planning for teaching in larger blocks of time requires more time.

August—Year 2

Plan a "Back-to-School" week for information sharing. Parent, teacher, and student organizations can assist in planning this activity. Consider the following format.

PURPOSE: To inform students and parents about block scheduling.

TIME REQUIREMENT: Four days (This activity could be spread over a two-week period.)

TIME: 4:00 p.m.–8:00 p.m. Also offer sessions in the morning, from 8:00 a.m. to noon, to serve parents who work in the evening.

- Monday: Seniors
- Tuesday: Juniors
- Wednesday: Sophomores
- Thursday: Freshmen

ACTIVITIES: Schedule forums every 30 minutes to provide information and answer questions for parents and students.

- Collect fees
- Distribute books
- Provide students and parents an opportunity to go through their actual schedule, with time abbreviated. If teachers are not available to be in the classroom during the mock schedule for students, members of parent-teacher or student organizations or other support groups might be available to assist.
- Provide booster groups and student clubs an opportunity to participate by having an information booth for parents and students about their group and activities they are planning for the school year.
- Meet with the leadership team of the school to address any last-minute issues and to put in place a system to assist students on the first day of school.

August–September—Year 2

Celebrate! Implement the schedule.

October—Year 2

Begin the preliminary evaluation—and remember that evaluation should be a never-ending process. We suggest that you start the evaluation process as soon as possible so that all customers will know you are serious about the long-term commitment to block scheduling and refinement of the schedule based on input from all customers. The operation of the schedule and consequent changes in the school are evaluated to determine if they are in line conceptually with the local school division policies.

HOW DO YOU BUILD A MASTER SCHEDULE?

The purpose of this discussion is to provide direction that will assemble a pool of data used to build the master schedule. We have discussed many of the pieces of building a master schedule, but you may wonder what a master schedule looks like once it is completed. This section will provide various examples of schedules that have taken the collected data and implemented it into a framework of a master schedule for a school. These schedules are presented by departments; by alphabetical order of the last name of teachers (although we use numbers to represent the teachers); alternating day (A-B); semester (4x4); and embedded schedules for several purposes, including serving special-needs students, International Baccalaureate, and an intersession. Building a schedule depends on the block scheduling format that will be implemented. If the schedule format is an alternating day or semester schedule, the process will not be drastically different from the process used to develop a traditional schedule.

There are certain assumptions that must be made at this point. The first assumption is that a scheduling process will be in place with a pre-planned time line that acts as a road map for scheduling. The second assumption is that there is an action team in place to guide the scheduling process.

The first step in the process of building the master schedule is to look at the key issues that will impact students. Look at the issues that impact students regardless of the type of block scheduling format that is implemented, such as the following.

■ **Balanced schedule.** Careful consideration must be given to students' needs when planning their schedule for the semester or year. If the schedule is a semester or alternating day, schedulers must consider the difficulty level of the courses students take. The schedule should be balanced so that students will not have all difficult courses one semester and courses that are not so difficult the next semester. For example, should a student take Advanced Placement English, AP calculus, physics, and Russian V the first semester and music, art, work study, and AP government the second semester? Would we be setting up a student for failure without giving consideration for balance in the schedule? A similar situation occurs with the alternating day (A-B) schedule. It is possible for a student to have AP English, AP

Calculus, Japanese IV (as a singleton taken for a single period each day of the school year) and AP Physics on A day and art, music, drama, and Japanese IV on B day. Again, we must ask the question: Are we making it difficult for the student to balance the course load and be successful?

■ **Early release.** Because the schedule is flexible and students have different options such as earning more credits or scheduling their classes earlier in the day, will students be provided the opportunity to leave school after taking a certain number of classes and before the school day is officially over? Similar situations occur when implementing the semester block. Because students have an option to take more classes during the school year, many complete the required number of credits for graduation before their senior year. The same issues emerge. Some school districts in various states have increased the number of units required for graduation. Thus, students are taking more classes and earning more credit. But for the schools that have not increased the number of graduation requirements, the issues are present and must be dealt with. If, in fact, policy-making

---

CASE IN POINT

The leadership team at Atlee High School met with the Parent-Teacher Organization during the summer before students arrived for the new term. The purpose of this meeting was to put in place a system that would assist students and faculty who needed direction in interpreting block schedules or finding classrooms. The plan was to place key personnel in strategic locations throughout the building and be available to anyone who was on an endless journey of finding lockers and classrooms on the first day of school. The first day finally arrived. As students and teachers made their way to their first block, the leadership was ready. Although we were prepared to assist as needed, the only service we provided that morning was to help two teachers who could not figure out whether it was an A day or a B day. At 8:35 a.m., all halls were empty. Not bad, for an 8:30 a.m. class start!

agencies do require an increase in graduation requirements, the semester schedule is a way to increase the number of classes that a student may take.

■ **Sharing specialty schools (technical, gifted, magnet).** Consideration must be given to students who are enrolled in the home school as well as the alternative or specialty school program, because many times these schools are on different bell schedules. Accommodations must be considered for these students.

■ **Students with special or unique learning styles.** These students include those with learning disabilities, gifted learners, and students with physical handicaps that impact their learning styles. How do these students fit into the new schedule configuration? Decisions must be made regarding the impact that the new schedule will have on them. Will this type of schedule allow opportunities for inclusion of some or all students?

SCHEDULING ISSUES WITH THE 4x4

There are many issues that will be unique to your school. You will identify and address many of these issues as you work through the process. The following issues are of concern for schools that have chosen a semester (4x4) schedule—a schedule that has no embedded classes and which offers all classes for one semester only.

■ **Sequencing of certain courses.** Decisions must be made regarding when classes will be offered and when students are allowed to take certain classes.

■ **Extracurricular eligibility.** Will the new schedule translate into credits required for extracurricular activity participation? This is especially critical to athletic participation or activities that are governed by state associations that have certain requirements such as number of classes that a student must be enrolled in each year or semester. We find that the policy-making bodies that govern these rules are very cooperative in the flexibility they provide for students participating in extra- and co-curricular activities.

CASE IN POINT

In the school where Tom served as principal, the official school day was from 8:25 a.m. to 3:30 p.m. On day A, a student could take two classes and be through by 12:10 p.m. On day B, the same student could take two different classes and still be finished by 12:10 p.m. Thus, s/he could earn four Carnegie units in two days and finish each day by midday. The question: Do we provide these students an opportunity to leave, if they choose not to take additional classes? If there are state or local school board policies that prohibit students from leaving before the official school day is over, what do these students do? Study halls, electives, excuses each day to "check out," increased graduation requirements—all enter into this decision. Make a decision relating to these issues before scheduling students. We did not make that decision before we scheduled students the first year in the block schedule format, and we spent the next year dealing with students on a regular basis who wanted to leave school before the official school day was over. Seniors had permission to leave after completing five and a half hours of instruction per day. Of course, this was a policy that our local school board had put in place long before block scheduling had been implemented in our school. The bottom line: Check out these issues *before* scheduling.

■ **Advanced Placement.** Decisions will need to be made about how many AP courses students will have the opportunity to take in a semester and during which semester they will be taught. We suggest that you review the most recent research that addresses the performance of students in various schedules, including how students perform if they complete an AP course a semester prior to the test. Many schools have addressed this issue by scheduling students in creative ways, such as scheduling companion classes that will prepare students for the Advanced Placement Exam over a year's time (e.g.: AP English semester one and another course—creative writing, study of the novel, or study of British literature—semester two).

Long-term planning means success for students. Long-term planning is critical to the success of the student and block scheduling. It is important that students look at their schedules over a four-year period of time, a four-year high school plan. Course sequencing and the possibility of some classes being offered on a limited basis during the four-year span drive decisions related to both required and elective courses.

STUDENT PLANNING IN THE 4X4 BLOCK

Students should plan for their entire high school experience early in the cycle—eighth grade is ideal. This process must include the student, parent/guardian/student advocate, counselor, and teachers. A tentative plan mapping the direction of academic and career preparation should be in place. There are always reasons that we can think of not to plan for long-term success of the student, but none of these arguments is defensible. The success of our students should be our top priority on paper, and we should have a personnel commitment to see this through.

Figure 68 is an example of what a four-year plan might look like.

COMBINATIONS

There are many combinations of academic plans that students might use when planning a career. The

FIGURE 68
Student Career Success Plan for Grades 9–12

GRADE 9

TIME	SEMESTER 1	SEMESTER 2
8:30–10:00	Course 1 World History	Course 5 French 2
10:05–11:35	Course 2 Health/P.E. 9	Course 6 Fine Arts
12:15–1:45	Course 3 Lunch 11:35–12:10 Geometry	Course 7 Lunch 11:35–12:10 Earth Science
1:50–3:20	Course 4 English 9	Course 8 Journalism/ Creative Writing

GRADE 10

TIME	SEMESTER 1	SEMESTER 2
8:30–10:00	Course 1 Computer Systems	Course 5 French 3
10:05–11:35	Course 2 Health/P.E. 10	Course 6 Fine Arts
12:15–1:45	Course 3 Lunch 11:35–12:10 Algebra 3/Trigonometry	Course 7 Lunch 11:35–12:10 Biology
1:50–3:20	Course 4 English 10	Course 8 Journalism 2/Yearbook

FIGURE 68 (Continued)
Student Career Success Plan for Grades 9–12

GRADE 11

TIME	SEMESTER 1	SEMESTER 2
8:30–10:00	Course 1 Adv. Technology (CAD)	Course 5 French 4
10:05–11:35	Course 2 English 11	Course 6 Biology 2
12:15–1:45	Course 3 Lunch 11:35–12:10 AP Chemistry	Course 7 Lunch 11:35–12:10 Chemical Concepts/ AP Review*
1:50–3:20	Course 4 AP U.S. History	Course 8 Leaders in U.S. History/ AP Review*

* Companion course for AP (if student takes AP, s/he must take companion course)

GRADE 12

TIME	SEMESTER 1	SEMESTER 2
8:30–10:00	Course 1 Psychology	Course 5 U.S. Government
10:05–11:35	Course 2 AP English	Course 6 Novel/AP Review*
12:15–1:45	Course 3 Lunch 11:35–12:10 Physics	Course 7 Lunch 11:35–12:10 Calculus
1:50–3:20	Course 4 Fine Arts	Course 8 Economics

* Companion course for AP (if student takes AP, s/he must take companion course) critical issue is that each student should have in place a plan for success before entering any schedule or program of studies. It is even more important with the 4x4 or an eight-block alternate day, as these schedules offer so many options. Time management and course management becomes critical to all players involved in directing the students' four-year plan. Of course, the student and his/her parents should be most accountable for tracking the success plan.

■ **Special interest courses.** Students that have special interests in certain courses will need special advisement by the counselor or teachers.

■ **Standardized testing.** In some states, end-of-course testing or testing of state standards is required in all schools. These tests are given at the end of the term in which the course is offered, which may be interpreted to mean early spring. The reason given for testing in early spring is that local school districts want the results returned before school is out for the year. These results are used to drive staff development and curriculum reform, which in many school districts is planned for the summer, and to use in determining promotion/retention for some students.

CASE IN POINT

If a student elects to take French I the first semester of his/her ninth-grade year, when will the student be offered the opportunity to take French II? Will s/he have the option of taking the course the next semester or the next school year? Is this a student decision, or is it an administrative decision? Yvonne worked with one high school that made the decision during the planning year to offer students the second year of a language the semester immediately following the first-year course. This was especially important for the students taking their first year of foreign language in the middle school. We recommend that this decision be made and students be informed before students begin the scheduling process, as these decisions may have some impact on decisions related to college preparation.

■ **Teacher issues.** In some instances, teacher issues are similar to student issues and are just as important in positioning teachers for success when using the block schedule format. As with students, you will discover certain issues that are unique to your school when scheduling faculty for teaching assignments in the block; these issues should be addressed as such. In nine years of working with the block schedule, we have never witnessed two schools with the same problems as they implement the block schedule.

■ **Balance of teaching assignments.** Consider the course load of the teacher for each day on the alternating day (A-B) block and each semester, if on a semester block. Avoid assigning teachers all difficult classes on one day or in one semester, and study halls and duty assignments on the alternating day or semester. There are some exceptions.

■ **Number of class preparations.** The number of class preparations should be minimized. As they prepare to teach differently in the block, teachers need to concentrate on lesson design and pedagogy—not on several different courses with different content. Perhaps one of the greatest boosts we could give teachers is to minimize the number of preparations they have so they can prepare one or two courses really well.

BUILDING A MASTER SCHEDULE WITH ACCOMMODATING TIME LINE

Much of the same process used to make a recommendation for implementing a block schedule will be used to build the master schedule.

The master schedule action team takes the lead in this process. The chair of this team should be the person in your school who is responsible for building the master schedule and scheduling the students. This could be the principal, guidance counselor, or student personnel coordinator.

Tom discovered that perhaps the most important change in the way he did business during his tenure as a secondary school administrator using block scheduling was to include as many customers in the planning and implementation process of a project as possible. He found that this process accomplished two objectives. First, he had many different viewpoints from which to gather data. Second, there was ownership and greater success in the projects in which customers participated. He never ignored or backed away from a question, and he always gave the best and most straightforward answer. If he could not answer a question, he responded to the customer as soon as he could find the appropriate information. We are convinced that the reason Tom had few problems with the block scheduling process was that he involved customers and kept them informed.

Building a master schedule should be no different. Customers—both internal and external—should be involved in the process. This gives the school community ownership and allows parents to become involved in activities that have a meaningful impact on all students.

BUILDING THE ALTERNATING (A-B) DAY SCHEDULE

When building a block schedule, the first activity that we completed was the time line for the scheduling process. We developed the time line as we would

if we were developing any yearlong schedule. If you have a schedule time line in place, chances are that you may need to make only minor adjustments or no adjustments at all. Specific dates of each month can be added to this time line based on the school-year time line. Ours looked like the matrix on page 224.

The following information is a description of the matrix in more detail.

AUGUST—Review scheduling process that has just been completed, while problem areas are fresh in your mind, and make appropriate notes for changes. This process should include all team members involved in the scheduling process. If a decision is being made regarding new scheduling software, now is the time to explore software options.

SEPTEMBER–OCTOBER—Review course offerings for the next year. Input should be gathered from your school improvement team, students, parents, department chairs, and members of the central office support staff.

NOVEMBER—If new offerings are to be added to the course of study for students, appropriate activities and decisions should be completed to meet local and state policy regarding the offering of new courses.

DECEMBER—Begin the process of informing all customers of the change in the course-offering process. Schedule curriculum fairs, orientation of the registration process, and course offerings for eighth-grade students from feeder schools. Have orientation for students and parents who will be involved in specialty courses and programs such as dual enrollment (courses that are offered for high school and college credit), students with disabilities, gifted students, Advanced Placement courses, International Baccalaureate program of studies, schools off campus (such as magnet schools, vocational-technical centers, and other situations that are unique to your school district. Present course offerings focusing on core courses needed by specific students and new or different course offerings to all students through classroom guidance.

JANUARY–MARCH—Meet with students to finalize course selections.

FEBRUARY—Complete rough draft of master schedule (estimated number of course selections

AUG	Review the scheduling process recently completed
SEPT–OCT	Review and make necessary changes in course offerings
NOV	Add new course offerings to course of studies
DEC	Share information with customers
JAN–MAR	Finalize student course selections
FEB	Complete rough draft of master schedule
MAR–APR	Construct master schedule
MAR	Run course tallies
APRIL	Distribute verification sheets to students
MAY	Distribute initial drafts of course assignments and course requests to faculty and students
JUNE	Distribute final shcedules to students with announced dates for student changes prior to the opening of school
AUG	Stabilize schedule and begin cycle again

based on previous years of student selections). Teachers' names should not be used in the draft schedule, but rather blocks and courses projected. A trial computer run of the schedule should be conducted to discover logistical and instructional concerns prior to implementation. Instructional departments will make suggestions for teaching assignments for the coming year.

MARCH–APRIL—Construct master schedule.

MARCH—Run course tallies and finalize courses and number of sections of courses to be offered. Department heads are given the number of sections and courses and recommendations for staffing. Departments make adjustments to rough draft and submit final draft to principal.

APRIL—Distribute verification sheets to students. Course selections are verified by students. Adjustments are made to master schedule, and student course-request conflicts are resolved.

MAY—Faculty and students receive initial draft of course assignments and course requests for the coming year.

JUNE—Final schedules are distributed to students, and a two-week period is set for student schedule changes. This will eliminate interruptions of instructional time when school starts that occur when students want schedule changes.

AUGUST—Stabilize schedules and begin process again.

The time line above can be adjusted as necessary. With the use of software, scheduling is becoming less complicated and can be done more quickly. Therefore, you may be able to adjust this time line to accomplish your goals more quickly. Our recommendation is to complete the master schedule so that students leave school in the spring with a schedule for the fall.

The alternating day (A-B) schedule is actually just rearranging the traditional bell schedule to use allocated instructional time more efficiently to provide larger blocks of time for teaching and learning. The scheduling process is simple. Follow the same procedure as scheduling for a seven-period day, and then combine single periods into double blocks. For example, period 1 on a seven-period day becomes block one on Monday, Wednesday, and Friday of A week; period 2 becomes block one on Tuesday and Thursday of A week. Period 3 becomes block two on

Monday, Wednesday, and Friday of A week; period 4 becomes block two on Tuesday and Thursday of A week. Period 5, a singleton, becomes block three and meets each day of the week for a shorter block of time, usually 55 minutes. Period 7 becomes block four on Monday, Wednesday, and Friday of A week; and period six becomes block four on Tuesday and Thursday of A week. For B week, the blocks are reversed and the cycle begins again. This schedule was developed in this manner to keep it as simple as possible and to provide equitable time for all classes.

BALANCED STUDENT SCHEDULE

The schedules in Figures 69 and 70 are actual student schedules that show a balance of scheduling so that students are provided opportunities for success. It is also important to note that students are scheduled in a first-year foreign language in the embedded singleton (block III)—one way that the issue of continuity in a skills-based class can be addressed. It is important to consider what classes are scheduled in block III.

Figure 71 is a schedule addressing co-op students who are off grounds for part of the day.

During B week, students will take Monday, Wednesday, and Friday classes on Thursday and Friday. Tuesday and Thursday classes will be taken on Monday, Wednesday, and Friday.

CASE IN POINT

If a student has a special interest in music and wants to take music courses throughout high school as electives, the student should be informed that s/he could accumulate a total of eight credits in music over a four-year period. If a student only wants to take music the first semester of each year, and if there is a policy in the music department that the student must take performance courses (such as band) each semester, then the student and his or her parents must be informed of this policy or any other policy that restricts which courses s/he can or cannot take. This has been an issue in schools in which we have worked, as music directors attempted to keep talented students in the music program throughout the year.

OFF-GROUNDS SCHEDULE THAT DEALS WITH CLASSES AWAY FROM SCHOOL GROUNDS

The schedule in Figure 72 will clarify many of the concerns related to off-campus classes for students that attend an off-grounds program such as a technical school, a magnet school, vocational center, etc., for part of the day.

During B week, only block IV would change for this student. U.S. History is taken on Tuesday and Thursday; and English on Monday, Wednesday and Friday.

BALANCED SCHEDULE FOR TEACHERS

The teacher schedule in Figure 73 was built based on the assumptions that:

- There are seven blocks in the school day and school year.

- Teachers are responsible for five teaching blocks.

CASE IN POINT

After completing a very successful all-day Saturday fund-raising project at his school, Tom was discussing the day's events with the parent of one of his students. During the discussion, the parent asked Tom a question that he had been asked many times: "Why are parents not involved in meaningful school activities?" The parent went on to say that the only time the school called on parents was to raise money, serve as chaperones, or serve on clean-up detail. He assured Tom that he thought this was important and he was willing to do these tasks, but he would like to serve on a team that was involved in what he called the "meat-and-potato" decisions. He explained that he meant work on curriculum, or scheduling the use of time, finding mentors, and apprenticeships, etc.

There is no task that you will undertake that is more "meat and potatoes" than building the master schedule for any scheduling configuration. *Involve your community.*

FIGURE 69
Student Schedule

Alternating Day (A-B) Block: A Week

BLOCK	MONDAY	TUESDAY	WEDNESDAY	THURSDAY	FRIDAY
I	Period 1	Period 2	Period 1	Period 2	Period 1
II	Period 3	Period 4	Period 3	Period 4	Period 3
III	Period 5	Period 5	Period 5	Period 5	Period 5
IV	Period 7	Period 6	Period 7	Period 6	Period 7

B Week

BLOCK	MONDAY	TUESDAY	WEDNESDAY	THURSDAY	FRIDAY
I	Period 2	Period 1	Period 2	Period 1	Period 2
II	Period 4	Period 3	Period 4	Period 3	Period 4
III	Period 5	Period 5	Period 5	Period 5	Period 5
IV	Period 6	Period 7	Period 6	Period 7	Period 6

FIGURE 70
Actual Student Schedule

Alternating Day (A-B) Block: A Week

BLOCK	MONDAY	TUESDAY	WEDNESDAY	THURSDAY	FRIDAY
I	AP English	Government	AP English	Government	AP English
II	Music	AP Calculus	Music	AP Calculus	Music
III	French IV	French IV	French IV	French IV	French IV
IV	Physics	Business Law	Physics	Business Law	Physics

B Week

BLOCK	MONDAY	TUESDAY	WEDNESDAY	THURSDAY	FRIDAY
I	Government	AP English	Government	AP English	Government
II	AP Calculus	Music	AP Calculus	Music	AP Calculus
III	French IV	French IV	French IV	French IV	French IV
IV	Business Law	Physics	Business Law	Physics	Business Law

FIGURE 71
Co-op Student Schedule

A Week

BLOCK	MONDAY Periods (1-3-5-7)	TUESDAY Periods (2-4-5-6)	WEDNESDAY. Periods (1-3-5-7)	THURSDAY Periods (2-4-5-6)	FRIDAY Periods (1-3-5-7)
I	English	History	English	History	English
II	Horticulture III	Geometry	Horticulture III	Geometry	Horticulture III
III	Co-op Release	Co-op Release	Co-op Release	Co-op Release	Co-op Release
IV	Co-op Release	Co-op Release	Co-op Release	Co-op Release	Co-op Release

FIGURE 72
Off-Grounds School Schedule

A Week

BLOCK	MONDAY	TUESDAY	WED	THURSDAY	FRIDAY
I	Tech. Building	Tech. Building	Tech. Building	Tech. Building	Tech. Building
II	Tech. Building	Tech. Building	Tech. Building	Tech. Building	Tech. Building
(Home School) III	Geometry	Geometry	Geometry	Geometry	Geometry
(Home School) IV	History	English 11	History	English 11	History

- Teachers are responsible for one duty/planning block.

- Teachers are assigned to one unencumbered planning block.

When building the schedule, we took into consideration daily teaching load, difficulty of course load, and number of class preparations.

Figure 74 is a small part of an actual alternating day (A-B) master schedule that Tom's leadership team built from the ground each year. (See accompanying CD for the schedule in its entirety.) Their philosophy was for the schedule to match the needs of students—not to fit students into the quirks of a schedule!

The alternating day (A-B) block schedule is just one of the alternatives that a school community has to use instructional time in a creative manner. The intent of restructuring school time is to allow more opportunities to raise the expectation bar for student success.

BUILDING A SEMESTER BLOCK SCHEDULE

Assumptions—Because of the many variables that each school must consider when building a master schedule, there are assumptions that we have made for the semester schedule in Figure 75.

- Courses and sections are not designed for repeats but are designed for students who need courses to move ahead in their planned course of study.

- All courses are available both semesters, if needed, and based on numbers who enroll.

- Students register for all courses for both semesters that follow in the spring of each year. Adjustments are made for only seniors that need courses to graduate. This is usually for seniors

FIGURE 73
Teacher Schedule

Alternating Day (A-B) Block: A Week

BLOCK	MONDAY	TUESDAY	WEDNESDAY	THURSDAY	FRIDAY
I	AP Calculus	Algebra I	AP Calculus	Algebra I	AP Calculus
I	Plan	Calculus	Plan	Calculus	Plan
III	Algebra I	Algebra I	Algebra I	Algebra I	Algebra I
IV	Calculus	Duty/Plan	Calculus	Duty/Plan	Calculus

B Week

BLOCK	MONDAY	TUESDAY	WEDNESDAY	THURSDAY	FRIDAY
I	Algebra I	AP Calculus	Algebra I	AP Calculus	Algebra I
II	Calculus	Planning	Calculus	Planning	Calculus
III	Algebra I	Algebra I	Algebra I	Algebra I	Algebra I
IV	Duty/Plan*	Calculus	Duty/Plan	Calculus	Duty/Plan

Planning blocks and duty blocks can be divided during any one period so that a teacher is assured of a planning block each day and a duty period on alternating days. We were able to provide teachers with a full planning block on days scheduled for planning blocks, and on days scheduled for duty blocks, we split the duty period into two blocks of equal time. The teacher was assigned non-teaching responsibilities half of the block and had the other half of the block for planning. Assuming that the block is a minimum of 90 minutes, this would equate to 135 minutes of planning over a two-day cycle. Some teachers who had duty the same block made their own rules. One would serve the duty for the entire block for a day or a week and then the next day or week that teacher would have the entire duty block for planning, and the other teacher would take the duty the entire block. Various arrangements can be made, if teachers are teamed for duty blocks.

who have failed a required course and who need to repeat to graduate. The only other exception for a change of schedule is for students who fail a pre-requisite the first term and cannot move to the next level.

- A student at any grade level may repeat a course, if teacher, counselor, and parents agree that this is the best course of action for the student.

- The same scheduling time line can be used for the semester schedule with one exception: adjustments must be made to certain students' schedules at the end of the first semester (e.g.: seniors who have failed required courses or other unique situations that the school has iden-

tified before the school year begins). We recommend that copies of the original schedule be distributed at the beginning of the second semester. Common sense allows us to assume that many students may not have in their possession the original copy issued in the fall.

QUESTIONS

When building a semester block schedule, several questions must be answered, and decisions must be made before the scheduling process is started. The issues that need to be addressed include the following:

- Do students sign up for classes for both semesters at the beginning of the year?

FIGURE 74
Master Schedule for Alternating Day (A-B) Block

BLOCK	EARLY MORNING	BLOCK I	BLOCK I	BLOCK II	BLOCK II	BLOCK III	BLOCK IV	BLOCK IV
PERIOD	O	1**	2*	3**	4*	5***	6*	7**
ENG. DEPT	XXXXX	XXXXX	XXXXX	XXXXX	XXXXX	XXXXX	XXXXX	XXXXX
Teach E1	English 12	English 11	Duty/Plan	English 12 Dual Enrollment	English 11	English 12	Plan	
Teach E2	Eng. 12 AP	Plan	Eng. 12	Eng. 12 AP	Eng. 12	Duty/Plan	English 12	
Teach E3		Plan	English 9	English 9	English 9	Journalism I	Journalism I	Duty/Plan
Teach E4		English 9	English 9	English 9	English 9	Dept.	Plan	English 9
Teach E5		English 9	Creative Writing	Duty/Plan	Plan	English 9	English 9	English 9
Teach E6		Eng. 12	Eng. 10	Eng. 12 AP	Eng. 12 AP	Duty/Plan	Plan	Eng. 12 AP
Teach E7	English 11	Plan	Drama II	English 11	Duty/Plan	English 11	English 11	
Teach E8		English 10	Plan	Duty/Plan	English 10	English 10	English 10	English 10
Teach E9		English 9	English 10	Journalism I	Plan	Duty	English 9	English 9
Teach E10	Eng. Dual Enrollment	Plan	Drama I	Drama I	English 9	English 9	Duty/Plan	
Teach E11		English 10	ITL Duty	ITL	English 10	Plan	English 10	English 10
Teach E12		Plan	Duty/Plan	English 10	Novel	English 10	English 11	English 11
Teach E13		Journalism/ Yearbook II	Journalism 1	Journalism/ Yearbook III	Journalism/ Yearbook II	English 11	Plan	Duty/Plan/ Yearbook
Teach E14		*Elective Comp.	Elective	Duty/Plan	Basic Comp.	Basic Comp.	Plan	Elective
Teach E15	English 12	English 11	English 11	Basic Comp.	English 11	SCA	Plan	

* Periods 2, 4, 5, and 6 meet on Tuesday and Thursday.
** Periods 1, 3, 5 and 7 meet on Monday, Wednesday, and Friday.
*** Period 5 is embedded and meets each day for the entire school year.

ITL—Instructional Team Leader
SCA—Student Council Association (sponsor)

FIGURE 75
Student Schedule—Semester Block Schedule

Semester I

BLOCK	MONDAY	TUESDAY	WEDNESDAY	THURSDAY	FRIDAY
I	Marching Band	Marching Band	Marching Band	Marching Band	Marching Band
II	Accounting	Accounting	Accounting	Accounting	Accounting
III	AP English Creative Writing	AP English Creative Writing	AP English Creative Writing	AP English Creative Writing	AP English Creative Writing
IV	AP Physics	AP Physics	AP Physics	AP Physics	AP Physics

Semester II

BLOCK	MONDAY	TUESDAY	WEDNESDAY	THURSDAY	FRIDAY
I	Jazz/Ensem. Orchestra	Jazz/Ensem. Orchestra	Jazz/Ensem. Orchestra	Jazz/Ensem. Orchestra	Jazz/Ensem. Orchestra
II	Government	Government	Government	Government	Government
III	AP English/ Creative Writing	AP English/ Creative Writing	AP English/ Creative Writing	AP English/ Creative Writing	AP English/ Creative Writing
IV	AP Phys. Review	Early Release	AP Phys. Review	Early Release	Early Release

- Do students have a choice as to which semester they can take a class?

- What semester will Advanced Placement classes be taught?

- How many AP courses can a student take?

- Will students be required to take certain courses for both semesters (e.g.: music)?

- Will there be combination courses (e.g.: AP English and creative writing) that will last for both semesters with a weight for two credits?

- What courses will require sequencing consideration, and will students be informed that sequencing will immediately be scheduled for the next semester?

- Under what circumstances will the school offer students the opportunity to repeat courses for remediation purposes? Each semester? Each year?

- Will there be embedded courses in the schedule?

These are not the only issues that must be addressed, but they provide an opportunity for the schedule builders to use their problem-solving skills. You will discover other questions that are unique to your school as you move forward with the process.

A SCHEDULE FOR BALANCING THE STUDENT LOAD EACH SEMESTER

The following student schedule takes into account the balance necessary for opportunities for student success, including course sequencing and concerns about Advanced Placement courses. Some students will attempt to take too many courses with high academic rigor in one semester. Each student should choose courses based on the expectations (difficulty level) of the course, the amount of time s/he will spend with extra- or co-curricular activities, jobs, and other obligations, as well as other uses of time that the student has beyond the instructional school day. There will be other issues that are unique to your school, such as travel time between home and school. Don't let these issues stop students from taking the most challenging and rigorous courses that they can successfully manage.

Students would receive two credits for the English/creative writing course, but it would be two full semesters in length. This would keep students engaged in an English course until the Advanced Placement exam is given.

For students to continue to be involved in music for the entire school year, those taking marching band the first semester will take jazz ensemble or orchestra during the second semester. It is possible to schedule half of the students for 45 minutes of jazz ensemble and the other half for orchestra, and then switch for the second 45 minutes.

Any day/s of the week can be used for review for the AP Physics examination. The closer to the examination time, the more frequent the review would be. Students do not receive credit for the review course, however. A teacher could be assigned to review for AP exams as a duty period.

The teacher schedule in Figure 76 was built with the assumption that the teacher is responsible for three teaching blocks and one planning block each semester over the year. The second semester schedule could mirror the first-semester schedule, or teaching assignments could be totally different—as long as the teacher is certified to teach the assigned courses.

The information in the matrix on page 233 is a small part of the master schedule for teachers. (See accompanying CD for complete semester master schedule.)

BUILDING AN EMBEDDED IB MASTER SCHEDULE

As we look to the future of scheduling and accountability for higher academic expectations, administrators are again challenged to do more with time and human resources. Perhaps one of the most demanding academic courses of studies with which we are familiar is the International Baccalaureate (IB) program of studies. We find that more and more schools are exploring the possibilities of what the IB program has to offer beyond other educational options. Many administrators who are considering implementing block scheduling ask: How

---

CASE IN POINT

A member of the math faculty at Atlee High School taught three classes on Monday, Wednesday, and Friday with a planning block daily. Each instructional block as well as the planning block was 107 minutes long. During B week, she taught two 107-minute blocks and was assigned a duty/planning block during block I, which was also 107 minutes. She was assigned a duty of student make-up test coordinator during the first half of her duty block, and the second half was for planning. Therefore, she was getting approximately 160 minutes of planning every two days, or an average of approximately 80 minutes daily, which is an average increase of approximately 30 minutes each day over the traditional 50-minute planning time each day.

The amount of time allocated for planning would be based on allocated time for instruction, planning, and personnel in each school situation.

---

does block scheduling impact IB offerings? We suggest that block scheduling would offer an advantage to students enrolled in IB courses or in the IB Diploma program. If you are familiar with the IB course of studies, you know that the expectations for students are conducive to utilizing longer blocks of instructional time.

The course offerings are primarily the same. The difference is the creative use of the allocated instructional time to provide different course offerings and opportunities for students. This can all be accomplished within the time limitations of the instructional day.

STILL UNCOMFORTABLE WITH THE ALTERNATING DAY (A-B) OR SEMESTER (4X4) BLOCK?

Recently while we were working with a principal of a high school, he discussed his need to meet the educational needs of his students, his school board, and his superintendent. Having a reputation of being a very effective but conservative principal, he and a

FIGURE 76
Semester Block—Teacher Schedule

Semester I

BLOCK	MONDAY	TUESDAY	WEDNESDAY	THURSDAY	FRIDAY
I	AP English	AP English	AP English	AP English	AP English
II	Plan	Plan	Plan	Plan	Plan
Study Block	Composition Tutoring	Composition Tutoring	Composition Tutoring	Composition Tutoring	Composition Tutoring
III	English 12	English 12	English 12	English 12	English 12
IV	English 9	English 9	English 9	English 9	English 9

Semester II

BLOCK	MON	TUES	WED	THURS	FRI
I	AP English	AP English	AP English	AP English	AP English
II	English 12	English 12	English 12	English 12	English 12
Study Block	AP Eng. Review	AP Eng. Review	AP Eng. Review	AP Eng. Review	AP Eng. Review
III	English 12	English 12	English 12	English 12	English 12
IV	Plan	Plan	Plan	Plan	Plan

very mature staff were not ready to take on a full block schedule. As we discussed the situation, it was evident that the only solution to his current dilemma was a rearrangement of instructional time. With his state's emphasis on the four core areas of English, mathematics, science, and social studies, the principal felt it was important to put more emphasis on these subject areas during the school day. The question was: How do you add 10 additional instructional minutes to each of the identified core classes?

There were several limitations that he had to address.

- 140 hours of allocated instructional time are required for each of the core courses to issue a Carnegie unit.

- The school day or school year could not be extended to schedule the additional time.

- The current schedule was a traditional seven-period, single-period day.

- Students would need 23 Carnegie units for a regular diploma and 27 for an advanced diploma.

- Physical constraints of the building required three lunch blocks.

- An award-winning fine arts programs with very vocal support of parents was in place.

- It was necessary to continue to offer classes on a daily schedule for the entire school year.

- A strong vocational program was in place.

- The transportation system (bus routes) was driven by elementary, middle, and secondary school connections.

- The existing school-day structure—8:14 a.m. until 2:56 p.m.—provided time limitations.

We worked on a different schedule that was based on some "new" assumptions. The new schedule assessed teaching assignments and considered assigning some teachers more minutes "teaching"

English Department Semester I				X	English Department Semester II			
BLOCK 1	**BLOCK 2**	**BLOCK 3**	**BLOCK 4**	**X**	**BLOCK 1**	**BLOCK 2**	**BLOCK 3**	**BLOCK 4**
AP Eng.	Eng. 12	Plan	Eng. 12	X	Novel*	Plan	Eng. 12	Eng. 12
Eng. 11	Eng. 11	Eng. 11	Plan	X	Eng. 11	Eng. 11	Duty	Plan
Eng. 10	Plan	Eng. 10	Eng. 10	X	Eng. 10	Plan	Eng. 10	Eng. 10
Plan	Eng. 10	Eng. 10	Eng. 10	X	Plan	Eng. 9	Eng. 10	Eng. 9
Eng./Soc. St. 11/12	Academic Counseling	Eng./Soc. St. 11/12	Plan	X	Plan	Academic Counseling	Eng./Soc. St. 11/12	Eng. 10
Eng. 12	Plan	Eng. 11	Eng. 11	X	Plan	Eng. 11	Eng. 12 Dual Enroll.	Eng. 11
Eng. 9	Plan	Yearbook I	Eng. 9	X	Yearbook I	Plan	Duty	Journ. I
Plan	Journ. II	Yearbook II	Duty	X	Yearbook II	Duty	Journ. II	Plan
Eng. 9	Eng. 9	Plan	Creative Writing*	X	Plan	Eng. 9	Duty	AP Eng.
Eng. 12	Plan	Eng. 12	Eng. 12	X	Plan	Eng. 12	Eng. 12	Eng. 12
Eng. 9	Eng. 9	Eng. 9	Plan	X	Eng. 9	Plan	Eng. 9	Eng. 9
Plan	Eng. 12	Eng. 12	Eng. 12	X	Eng. 12	Eng. 12	Eng. 12	Plan
SAT Prep	Eng. 11	Plan	Eng. 11	X	Eng. 10	Eng. 10	Eng. 11	Plan
Eng. 10	Eng. 10	Plan	Eng. 10	X	Plan	Eng. 11	Eng. 11	Eng. 11

*Indicates companion course for AP course and is required to be taken with an AP course. If a student signs up for an AP course, s/he must take the companion course.

than others. Those with fewer teaching minutes could be given greater non-teaching responsibilities. Features of the new schedule included:

- An opportunity to enroll in four core classes per day

- An opportunity to enroll in three electives each day

- An opportunity for seven Carnegie units per year

- Three core classes will meet for 58 minutes per day.

- One core class will be split because of lunch and will meet for a total of 57 minutes each day.

- Non-core classes will meet for 38 minutes each day. Non-traditional time will be used to ensure instructional objectives are met, as follows.

  - Music—Before- and after-school rehearsal/practice for competition, performance, independent practice, and composition, etc.

  - Art—Use of non-traditional school time for exhibits, continuation of projects, before- and after-school work, independent study/projects, etc.

  - Physical education—Utilize time spent in interscholastic athletic competition, cheerleader, organized activities, or independent

FIGURE 77
Schedule with Time Emphasis on Identified Core Courses

Student schedule with 4 core and 3 electives and lunch 5A

PERIOD	MONDAY	TUESDAY	WEDNESDAY	THURSDAY	FRIDAY
1 8:14–9:12	core	core	core	core	core
2 9:16–10:14	core	core	core	core	core
3 10:20–10:58	elect	elect	elect	elect	elect
4 11:02–11:40	elect	elect	elect	elect	elect
5 11:44–12:41	core	core	core	core	core
6 12:45–1:12	lunch	lunch	lunch	lunch	lunch
7 1:16–2:14	core	core	core	core	core
8 2:18–2:56	elect	elect	elect	elect	elect

teams/events not associated with the school (such as gymnastic training, dance, soccer, golf), independent studies, etc.

– Vocational education—Actual application of skills in part-time, job-related activities associated or not associated with the curriculum, preparation for contests, independent projects, actual time related to competition, before- and after-school related activities.

• Students enrolled in morning classes will complete the first period at the home school, periods 2 and 3 at the vo-tech school, core-course periods 5 and 6 and an elective period 7 at the home school.

• Students enrolled in afternoon vo-tech school will complete periods 1 and 2, 4A or 5 with elective periods 3 and 4. Vo-tech periods are scheduled for periods 6 and 7.

• Students not enrolled in vo-tech school have an opportunity to enroll in the following combinations.

– four core courses and three electives

– three core courses and four electives

– two core courses and six electives

• Other uses of the short block include:

– identify and re-engage students who need additional time to be successful in core classes required for graduation, work-related skills, performing skills, etc.

– tutoring

– review for standardized tests, etc.

– activity period for non-related or co-curricular activities (pep rallies, pictures, assembly, etc.)

– make-up work

After much conversation and thought and examination of various options with the schedule, a special schedule was recommended that met the needs of the school to emphasis core academic areas. A portion of the schedule is outlined in Figure 77. (See accompanying CD for the schedule in its entirety.)

As we have stated many times throughout this book: You should use scheduling and the creative use of instructional time as a problem-solving tool. Do not fail to design an evaluation plan for this or any schedule that you decide to implement.

LOOKING BACK . . .

Principals have been working with the instructional day time frame for years. We are beginning to use time in more creative ways as we demonstrate a commitment to higher expectations for students. It is critical to use time in the most efficient way in order to provide students every possible opportunity to be successful. It is just as important to provide teachers the same opportunities. This process begins with a plan for building the schedule. All of the elements of a schedule must be considered before developing such a plan. This plan must be updated each year and should reflect the needs of the students, not the physical facilities or athletic schedules or other non-instructional variables. Once all issues are considered by the action team assigned the task, careful planning must be completed as you listen to all customers affected by the process.

A time line for scheduling the students as well as for building the schedule is critical. Be sure to communicate the time line and the progress of the task to all customers. Be sure to make the process, not the time line, flexible in order to meet the needs of students. This is what we are about. This is our job. ❑

Chapter 11 Appendix on CD

❑ Plans for Block Scheduling

- Student Planning in the 4x4 Block—includes all four success plans (word version)
  - Success plan for Grade 9 (word version)
  - Success plan for Grade 10 (word version)
  - Success plan for Grade 11 (word version)
  - Success plan for Grade 12 (word version)
- 21-month Matrix for Block Scheduling (word version)

How Do We Measure Our Progress?

*A*ccountability demands that a high school have a set of objectives and assess and report the extent to which they are met. The purpose of this accountability is to ensure that teaching and learning serve the needs of student to the fullest extent.

—from *Breaking Ranks: Changing an American Institution*

LOOKING AHEAD IN THIS CHAPTER . . .

One of the greatest challenges to a school leader is determining how well the staff, faculty, and community are meeting the goals and objectives of the school. In our experience, we have found that many school administrators have difficulty effectively measuring school progress because of lack of time and expertise, or because they simply do not consider it a priority. In many instances, principals are not aware of the amount of information that is available for taking a snapshot of the effectiveness of their school. Because of recent calls for accountability of schools nationwide, there is perhaps not a building principal in any public school throughout our country who is not looking at ways for more effectively restructuring his or her school in order to improve student achievement. We have observed schools that make data-driven decisions regarding reform, and there is much data available in a school that can be used to make decisions. Although a school usually has a file of norm-referenced test results that can be analyzed, successful principals utilize other information available in their schools that indicates progress toward previously determined goals. These data can be studied and displayed in a format that allows the principal, teacher leaders, staff, students, and community members to see what is happening in a school. School faculties and stakeholders can determine how well schools are making progress toward goals by examining student and teacher attendance, dropout rates, grading period results, tardies and absences, discipline issues, lunch participation, and teacher contacts with parents. A school is full of information that—gathered properly, displayed in a manner that is understandable, and studied carefully—can help school leaders know the next steps needed in a process of continuous improvement. Of course, the key to success in reform is to determine what needs to be changed in a school. Schools committed to improving services to current and future customers must first identify what needs to be changed. Next, in order to sustain systemic change, schools must identify existing data and determine other data needs before they will understand what should be changed to meet customer needs.

This chapter will focus on the importance of measurement in schools. School leaders who have developed a sound plan for alternative scheduling must take the time to determine what should be measured when planning for the new schedule. **Determining what should be measured is the key to monitoring for success.** Monitoring the processes within a school is one way a principal in a school or a teacher in a classroom can "fix" problems that impede progress, thereby preventing errors in the future. Monitoring for success empowers the principal or the teacher. Reviewing data gives us the knowledge to say with authority that we know why something is not working: We have data that show us. Or we can say proudly that we know why our school is getting better: We have data that point to success.

DEFINITIONS OF MEASUREMENT TERMS

So that we are all on common ground, we must define what we mean when we talk about measurements. Clarification of the issues could perhaps be the first step to the success of the project. Therefore, we will use the following definitions as we work through this chapter on measurement.

■ **Assessment** is the process of giving value to something. In schools we assess how students are doing in a unit of study or what progress they are making in learning a skill. We assess how well teachers teach or how successful the basketball coach is. Assessments often have value attached to them that are interpreted as grades or ratings. If a student makes 85 percent on a test, we assume that there is 15 percent of the information from the unit of study that the student was unable to demonstrate on the test. That is an

assessment of the student's performance. It doesn't tell the whole story, but a good assessment is very helpful in developing a bigger picture.

■ **Evaluation** is the process of judging the worth of programs, initiatives, and improvement efforts. Evaluation requires collecting, analyzing, and interpreting information that can be used for program improvement and organizational development. Evaluation is bigger than assessment but may include the information gathered on various forms of assessment. It drives continuous improvement if the information gathered is used well and serves as the basis for accountability. For example, if a faculty reviews data that show unacceptable performance after a unit of study, the faculty can use the data to guide a problem-solving process in which they determine if the problem is attributed to the curriculum, the instructional process, or the method of assessment. Then the faculty knows what to change and can begin the reteaching process. Although teachers are responsible for teaching the unit of study and acquiring a level of mastery, the evaluation process permits an informed interpretation of what happened and why it happened.

■ **Measurement** is the process of determining the progress toward a goal or objective, which can be described by criteria. It is a way of gauging progress. Measurement looks at capacity and doesn't place value on actions, behavior, or events. It is the reporting of data objectively—without value and without accountability.

■ **Unit of Measure** refers to the part of the organization whose process is measured.

A WORD OF CAUTION: HARD AND SOFT DATA

There are other baseline data that can be used. When using data, we have found that certain data tend to be more accurate predictors of how successful a change is. These data are usually derived from standardized tests such as Advanced Placement examinations, national normed tests, and norm-referenced tests. We refer to these as hard data, and they give one indication of how a reform is working.

Other data that have variables which cannot be controlled or accounted for, we call soft data. These data consist of teacher-assigned grades, perceptions of change without supporting data, number of students on the honor roll, and grade point averages. When using these types of data, we offer a word of caution. Many educators have found that when a school focuses on a particular change, the results are initially positive. For example, if a principal announces to the faculty at the beginning of the term that the focus for the year will be to increase the number of students on the academic honor roll, the number of students on the honor roll will more than likely increase. Our caution is using these measurements in the short run to determine the success of the block schedule. Track the data over a long period of time to determine patterns of performance. Short-term success may not always indicate the realization of long-term goals and rewards. Of course, more credibility would be given to the data if multiple measures were used to verify the outcome. Multiple measures might include an increase in the number of students on the honor roll, an increase in grade point average, and an increase in student achievement on standardized test scores.

A WELL-DESIGNED ASSESSMENT SYSTEM

If an organization wishes to experience success, it must have guiding principles that provide direction as well as integrity to the assessment process. Designing an assessment system for an organization is more complex than throwing together a few surveys and reporting the perceptions collected from the data to customers. Before the assessment system can be designed, principals need to consider initially what training should be provided to all school personnel to help them understand the assessment system, the process for collecting data, the skills for interpreting data, and the skills for reporting data. Principals should also consider other variables, such as undistorted collection of primary information, straightforward measurement of priorities, and a feeling of urgency and improvement (Peters, 1987).

When designing the format for the assessment, the principal should seek guidance and support from persons with expertise who are not members of the formal organization. If financial resources are not available to bring in an outside expert to assist with this phase of the process development, perhaps there are experienced principals available outside the building or other knowledgeable individuals that understand the process and are willing to help. Perhaps a principal from another area school who has successfully completed a similar process and understands what you are doing will be willing to review your plans. You could also take advantage of members of your school community, such as central office staff and parents with related expertise, for this assistance. Remember to focus the acquisition of information on your school goals, not the goals of another principal or non-school manager. These resources help us collect information and provide direction.

If the focus of the change process is block scheduling, the content of the assessment must relate to block scheduling. Collecting data will go beyond asking the question, "Do you like block scheduling?" Assessment will help you set your course of action. It will help you determine the success, the failure, or barriers that need to be altered as you implement the process. The assessment will help determine if you are making progress on critical indicators of success.

Assessments can be designed in various ways. It is probably best to think of this assessment as one that will have both quantitative and qualitative information to study, analyze, and report. As Tom Peters points out, quantitative data, such as listening, is very important—especially listening to the external customer. And there are many opportunities for listening to external customers: extracurricular activities such as sporting events, visual arts exhibits, and performances by members of your performing arts programs; academic recognition programs; PTA meetings; as well as the mall or the grocery store. You can informally collect data in the schools by listening as you visit teacher work areas; engage in informal conversations with students, teachers, custodians, food service personnel, and bus drivers; review issues in faculty meetings; and listen to requests at budget time. Although the data-gathering process may not be recognized as being the most scientific method available, it can be very important in helping you to respond in a reasonable and timely manner to your customers. In many instances, this type of data is as important as other "hard" data you will collect, and it tells the story of block scheduling that you can't determine from the numbers.

Involving everyone in the process of assessment will help ensure that you are hearing from all who are being impacted by the change within the school. And it will give customers the voice that they need, especially when you report data that indicate there are major issues that must be addressed.

REVIEW THE CHANGE PROCESS

Let's look at the process of changing to a new schedule as we have discussed the process to this point. We have provided a great deal of information and offered a number of options in the preceding chapters. We can review what we have done by organizing the steps of change around Deming's planning cycle discussed earlier: Plan, Do, Study, Act.

PLAN—The first step in the planning cycle provides the opportunity to think about what needs to change and how a change will improve the school. In order to do this, we must have data that will provide direction as we move to make plans for changing to the block schedule. If we are already using the block schedule, data must be available to effect necessary changes that will make the schedule more conducive to meeting the academic needs of our students.

The major actions we discussed earlier are:

- Convene a restructuring team that represents all customers (school improvement team).

- Explore restructuring possibilities that can increase student achievement **based on previously collected data.**

- Determine the focus of the restructuring efforts by establishing **measurable goals and objectives.**

- **Gather information/data on the focus areas.**

- Assess potential impact of change on each aspect of the school instructional community.

- Build the schedule.

- Provide opportunities for staff development.

DO—The action phase of the cycle allows us to implement new ideas by creating new processes, new ways of operating the school. These include:

- Implement the schedule.

- Identify key strategies for success and how these strategies can be measured by collecting **appropriate data.**

- Adjust instructional strategies.

- Continue in-service opportunities for teachers/staff by **using appropriate data** to determine what is needed.

- Provide time for dialogue among school leaders, teachers, and impacted customers to collect **informal data.**

- **Collect initial data** (e.g.: student attendance, student achievement, and discipline referrals).

STUDY—This is a very important part of the cycle. Deming originally called this step CHECK because the purpose was to check on the system to see how it was functioning. He changed the term to STUDY because it better reflects what the leader is doing—s/he is studying **data** that reflect how processes are working and is using this knowledge **to make decisions** about process improvement. This phase of the cycle depends on **good measurement.** Specific actions that occur in this phase are:

- Study other identified components (data) of restructuring that might be helpful in reaching goals. Examples of other initiatives include curriculum alignment and integration, cooperative instructional strategies, instructional department reorganization, special education inclusion in general education, and new attendance policies.

- Monitor outcomes by using appropriate data.

- Increase use of available technology in the evaluation process.

ACT—The fourth step is logical. After putting a plan into action and studying its effectiveness by using **appropriate data,** develop ways, if needed, to improve the process. Correct components of the schedule that don't work well or modify the schedule based on the **analysis of data,** to meet customer needs. Action may be needed on support components. For example, if after studying relevant data, you determine that staff development priorities should be rethought or changed based on these data, an appropriate action would be to develop a modified plan for staff development.

The major action for this step is to modify or adjust the schedule as necessary. None of these steps should be taken without considering the assessment process that must be built into the system. It is critical to determine how the assessment piece of the change process will fit into the total process.

THE BENEFITS OF MEASUREMENT

After following the steps of the Plan-Do-Study-Act cycle, putting a new schedule in place to improve the functioning of the school, and establishing an appropriate support system, expect to see several positive changes.

■ Teachers will be more effective in the evaluation of student needs, progress, and achievement. With fewer classes and fewer students per day, a teacher is able to focus more on individual students.

■ There will be expanded time and opportunities for various instructional curricular designs and opportunities for interdisciplinary education.

■ A healthier and more inviting school climate will exist, one in which the school community shares values that are guided by respect for others and personal responsibility, accountability, and integrity among all members of the school community.

■ Students will be able to focus on fewer subjects per day/semester, thereby gaining a greater depth of knowledge or understanding of content.

FORMATIVE ASSESSMENT

It is important to assess where we are in the process from time to time. We must constantly refer to our roadmap (plan) to keep in touch with where we are and where we are going. By monitoring, assessing, and adapting this model, we can extract the most creative and productive use of time. It is unlikely, however, that a school will continue to improve if

measurement does not become an important part of program evaluation.

As educators search for new and different ways to raise the bar for academic achievement, they try many reforms. For each of these reforms, a system for measuring success must be designed and implemented. To give further credibility to reform, a reporting system must be designed to share results of the change with customers. Block scheduling results can be seen in many ways, but ultimately they must correlate with student achievement. Progress must be reported regularly. In the National Association of Secondary School Principals' report "Breaking Ranks: Changing an American Institution," the Commission recommends assessment and accountability measures as follows (p. 53).

■ The high school will assess the academic progress of students in a variety of ways so that a clear and valid picture emerges of what they know and are able to do.

■ High schools will guarantee that students can meet performance standards in entry-level jobs. Recent graduates who fail to meet these basic standards will have the opportunity to return to school for additional studies.

■ Each high school will report annually to the community, disclosing schoolwide assessment results and other pertinent information.

■ At least once every five years, each high school will convene a broad-based external panel to offer a public description of the school, a requirement that could be met in conjunction with the evaluation of state, regional, and other accrediting groups.

DATABASE OF INFORMATION

In order to meet the demands of our customers, principals must begin immediately to establish a database of information that can be used as an indicator of success. This database, as defined by Juran (1992, p. 407), "is a body of information derived from prior cycles of activity, and organized to aid in the conduct of future cycles. . . . A good database is a major resource for planners." The database could include the specific information the community is seeking. We have found that policymakers and parents want information on standardized testing, student attendance, number of students in special programs and their performance, SAT performance, scores from Advanced Placement and International Baccalaureate tests, number of students enrolled in college-level courses, number of incidents of violence, dropout rate, and percentage of students earning advanced diplomas. This information can easily be placed in a database that is updated throughout the year(s) as new information is available.

ACCOUNTABILITY

It is evident from recent literature that accountability is an issue that the school administrator will need to address now and in the near future (Watts, Gaines, & Creech, 1998). If accountability is demanded, then quantifiable data must be collected,

analyzed, and reported to the customers who are the policymakers within the local and state governing agency.

WHAT GETS MEASURED GETS DONE

In *Thriving on Chaos*, Peters lists attributes of a quality[1] revolution in organizations. He states that quality is measured, and that "what gets measured gets done." Measurement is the heart of any improvement process. "If something cannot be measured, it cannot be improved" (Peters, 1987, p. 74). This summarizes nicely what must be done when leading a school through a reform effort. Reform can be simple—as simple as changing the way allocated instructional time in your school is measured. Or it can be more complex. But whether simple or complex, change is driven by a good measurement system that provides constant feedback to the school leadership. Data derived from measuring that which is important keeps the vision of the school in focus, keeps the goals targeted, and is a constant reminder of what is important in a school.

Peters has a good message for educational leaders as well as the business community. His work supports the leader who is attempting to bring about reform in a way that not only makes sense but also will get results. There are three messages that we find constant throughout his writing and speaking which are tied to measurement:

LISTEN TO ALL CUSTOMERS.

MEASURE WHAT'S IMPORTANT.

KEEP ALL CUSTOMERS INFORMED THROUGHOUT THE PROCESS.

Since the purpose of this chapter is to look at measuring what we do—specifically identified, measurable goals—we will focus on the second message to support the importance of measuring quality of services offered to the customers of our school.

---

[1] Quality, as we use it in this book, refers to meeting customer requirements as they relate to various outputs or products of a system. Therefore, a quality report card would meet the needs of parents and students; a quality vocational program would meet industry standards; a quality school would meet the expectations of students, parents, community members, employers, higher education, and other stakeholders.

Collecting data can be a meaningless task unless it has a credible use. In addition, the data must be clean, error free, and viewed as credible. How do we give credibility to what we measure?

Peters (1987, p. 60) contends that part of the answer may be to quantify everything you measure. "I offer one last demanding piece of advice: Quantify. I am attempting to quantify almost everything. It can be done, no matter how apparently qualitative the attribute." This will bring credibility to the data, and as we have found, it is difficult for your customers to argue with quantified data collected from systems that provide opportunities for continuous improvement. Further, quantified data will make your case when change is desired. As educators, we are often accused of measuring success or lack of success based upon what we feel or what we perceive. If we are to change this perception, we must collect meaningful data that translate into usable information to improve the things we do right. These data can also be used to right the things we do wrong. All of this is in the name of providing better opportunities for student success. These data should be quantified so that we can build on the past and the present.

Peters expresses some very definite opinions about measuring what is important. His first advice on measurement is to "Keep it simple (and visible)." While we always want to hear good news, it is much more impressive if we can see it, visualize it. That means translating data to charts and graphs. You may remember Ross Perot, when running for president in 1992, talking to millions of Americans on television with his graphs by his side. He used his experience in business of graphing information to help explain his message. Principals must also initiate similar practices. Just as a picture conveys a meaning different from a written document, a graph translates data visually into where we have been and where we may be going. It helps us identify weaknesses or problems we need to address. It also tells our story when things are going well.

Figure 78 is the report card that Patricia Griffin, the principal of Princess Anne High School in Virginia Beach, Virginia, shared with her customers.

Quite often when speaking to educators, we refer to management experts Peters, Juran, and Deming. Generally the majority of our audiences are familiar with these experts. They also know that their work has been done in the private sector. Usually, at some time during our presentation, we are asked: "What does this have to do with education? These people are dealing with products and services, while we are dealing with students." Tom has been known to reply: "Motivation is the key to what we do and what leaders in the private sector do. Industry managers motivate workers to assess what they do, change the way they do it, and find ways to measure it through empowerment of the worker. Do we not do the same? If not, shouldn't we be doing it?" We should provide a climate that is conducive to motivating teachers to perform at a high level, which will lead to the motivation of students and to higher academic achievement that will provide us with measurable data.

Deming addresses the issue of where the public sector fits into the revolution of leadership and

CASE IN POINT

In 1995, the Virginia State Board of Education adopted rigorous Standards of Learning in English, history/social sciences, mathematics, and science. The Board called for implementation of these content standards in the Commonwealth's public schools. To make the Standards meaningful, the Virginia General Assembly provided the fiscal resources needed to design assessment that would measure student achievement. Further, school accreditation and student graduation are tied to the results of this assessment. A report card was also designed to provide parents and community members an annual progress report of how well schools are doing on the Standards of Learning tests as well as other measurable data. Other states such as Kentucky, North Carolina, Texas, Florida, Maryland, and cities such as Chicago are also measuring the results of student achievement and reporting to parents. Although some educators object to this type of accountability, these actions demonstrate a clear message: The general public has certain expectations of educators and wants them to share the results of these expectations.

CASE IN POINT

One summer afternoon, Tom's secretary entered his office and informed him that there were parents waiting to talk with him. Being responsive to his customers, Tom immediately greeted the parents and welcomed them to the school. They explained that they had recently found out they were being relocated to the area because of the father's job, and they were shopping for a school for their son and daughter. The son was a third-year high school student, and the daughter was a first-year high school student. The parents had done their homework and were very knowledgeable about the operation of schools. They asked questions related to student achievement, school climate (safety, discipline, suspensions, and expulsions), percent of students who graduated, and number of students who continued their formal education. After completing their questions, they informed Tom that they had been shopping at many public and private schools throughout the region. They also informed him that each principal they had "interviewed" had given them similar answers. They wanted to know how this school was different. Tom informed them that he was not competing with other schools but that he could verify the information that he was sharing with them. Tom provided them with a copy of his school-community report card and left them with additional data to ponder. Approximately 30 minutes later, they asked him to come into the conference room where they had retreated to look at the data. They were duly impressed and informed Tom that none of the other principals had chosen to share this information with them.

We don't know if other principals had data available that they could have shared with these parents. We do know that later that summer, the school gained two students who were honor students and outstanding athletes (and who had very supportive parents).

---

reorganization in his landmark book, *Out of the Crisis*. He writes (p. xi),

> This book makes no distinction between manufacturing and service industries. The service industries include government service, among which are education and the mail. All industries, manufacturing and service, are subject to the same principles of management.

Peters talks about "building systems for a world turned upside down." If you think the block schedule affects your world this way, or if you recognize that change in general calls for a different way of operating, the guidance Peters gives for building systems in organizations is useful. Let's look at each of his guiding principles and how they relate to measuring the success of block scheduling.

Measure what's important.

Revamp the chief control tools.

Decentralize information, authority, and strategic planning.

Set conservative goals.

Demand total integrity.

Let's look at each component of his system and think about situations in education where each can be applied.

MEASURE WHAT'S IMPORTANT

Peters's guiding premise is to measure what's important. Educators are becoming more accountable for student performance and the school climate that supports or impedes optimum student performance. What you and your customers decide is important should be measured. If the data collected and analyzed determines that the system is not working, and if you do not correct the problem area within the system, you are ignoring the needs of your customers (students, parents, etc.). As Peters (p. 235) points out, the customer's perceptions are what counts. So, how are you going to know what you are accountable for, if you do not seek your customers' input and if you do not measure that which customers perceive is important?

Lew Young, editor in chief of *Business Week,* contends that perhaps

> . . . the most important management fundamental that is being ignored today is staying close to the customer to satisfy his needs and anticipate his wants. In too many companies, the customer has become a bloody nuisance whose unpredictable behavior damages carefully made strategic plans, whose activities mess up computer operations, and who stubbornly insists that purchased products should work (Peters & Waterman, 1982, p. 156).

Perhaps his statement also applies to educators. Often, we see our customers as more of a nuisance than a helping hand.

We believe it is critical for educators to measure what's important and share the findings. If the news is good, you can celebrate. If the results are disappointing, use them as benchmarks against which you measure success in the future. To **measure what's important** consider the following:

- **Match measurements to the goals of the school.** If your objectives for meeting your goals are not measurable, revise them so that they are measurable. Here is an example of an objective that can be measured: "So that student achievement will increase, reduce the number of student absences as measured by the monthly student attendance rate." The measurable results should indicate increased student attendance and increased student achievement, because we know from the literature that the more students are exposed to information the more they learn.

- **Match measurement to the objectives of block scheduling.** Schools change schedules for a reason. Measure the indicators that will tell you if you are reaching your expectations. If you hoped for higher academic achievement in English, monitor the success rate of students at the conclusion of each grading period, the percentage of students in AP courses and the percentages scoring at 3 or higher on the AP examination, *(Continued on page 249)*

FIGURE 78
Staff Development Data for Implementation of Princess Anne High School's Strategic Plan

6,574 hours of staff development have been attended by the faculty and staff of Princess Anne High School from 1993 to date in 1997.

INITIAL RESEARCH PHASE OF IMPLEMENTATION OF BLOCK SCHEDULING

TITLE	DATE	NUMBER ATTENDING	HOURS PER PERSON	TOTAL HOURS
Flexible Scheduling	Ongoing	25	4	100
Research	Jan. implementation	48	6	288
Video: Creative Scheduling		5	8	40
Visitation—Atlee, Franklin		11	7	77
Interdisciplinary Planning	11/19/93	4	3	12
Special Education Conference	11/19/93	27	6	162
Facilities Review: Action Team	11/19/93	7	8	56
Mini Conference: Discussions on block scheduling with representatives of 14 content areas of Franklin High School	2/4/94	152	4	608
Lesson Plans for the Block: "A Generic Model Lesson Plan to Use in Formatting Lesson Plans for Use in a 90-Minute Teaching Block"	4/11/94	82	1	82
"Teaching in the Block" "Teaching Reading in the Content Areas"	7/5/94	120	3	360
"How to Conduct Effective Classroom Discussion Involving the Active Participation of All Students"	7/14 & 15/94 8/8–11/94	14 63	7 5	98 315
"Designing Successful Lessons for the 90-Minute Block"	8/2, 8–10/94	11	7	77

Average Number of Teachers Participating Per Title 94.8
Possible Faculty/Staff Attendance 131
Average Total Participation Per Title 72%

OBJECTIVE 1: Provide a more disciplined and safe learning environment in the school

TITLE	DATE	NUMBER ATTENDING	HOURS PER PERSON	TOTAL HOURS
Study Blocks: Brainstorming Session Collegial Session	11/18/94	43	1	43
Strategic Plan: Action Team Meetings	11/18/94	149	1	149
Discipline: Expectations, Empowerment, Expertise	2 sessions, 11/21/96	47	1	47
"Multi-Culturalism"	11/5/96	149	5	745

Average Number of Teachers Participating Per Title 107.75
Possible Faculty/Staff Attendance 149
Average Total Participation Per Title 72%

OBJECTIVE 2: Promote the infusion of technology into the mainstream of the environment

TITLE	DATE	NUMBER ATTENDING	HOURS PER PERSON	TOTAL HOURS
Gradebook: Mac	11/19/93	22	1	22
Gradebook Plus (Mac & IBM)	11/18/94	48	1	48
"How to Use Virginia Pen"	4 & 5/94	24	2	48
Gradebook (Mac or IBM)	4/94	12	1	12
"How to Use the Internet"	4/23/95	23	2	46
"How to Use Virginia Pen"	9/94 & 5/95	22	2	44
Gradebook	5/95	9	1	9
"How to Use the Internet"—Basic sponsored by Webcity (PIE)	3/3/97	16	2	32
"How to Use the Internet"—Beginner	3/4/97	16	2	32
"How to Use the Internet"—Beginner	3/5/97	16	2	32
"How to Use the Internet"—Intermediate	3/6/97	16	2	32
"How to Use the Internet"—Advanced	3/7/97	16	2	32
"How to Use the Internet"	To Be Announced			
"Acceptable Use Policy for the Internet"	To Be Announced			
"How to Incorporate the Internet into Your Content Area"	To Be Announced			
"How to Research a Topic on the Internet"	To Be Announced			
"How to Use GroupWise E-Mail Client"	To Be Announced			

Average Number of Teachers Participating Per Title   **80**
Possible Faculty/Staff Attendance   **149**
Average Total Participation Per Title   **54%**

OBJECTIVE 3: Refine and promote academic excellence

TITLE	DATE	NUMBER ATTENDING	HOURS PER PERSON	TOTAL HOURS
11 International Baccalaureate Program Visitations to Various School Systems	Throughout 94-97	28	6	168
IB Teacher Workshops	Throughout 94-95	40	5	200
Inclusion Classes	2/4/94	21	1	21
NCAA Clearinghouse Procedures	2/4/94	14	1	14
Preview: *Schindler's List*	2/4/94	32	2	64
CEC Special Ed Spring Institute	4/11/94	27	6	162
Cooperative Learning	4/11/94	112	6	672
"How to Form Inclusion Classes"	4/11/94	15	1	15
Portfolio Workshop	4/11/94	2	6	12
Videotape: "The Tie-In Series"	To Be Announced			
Peer Coaching	To Be Announced			

Average Number of Teachers Participating Per Title   **41.5**
Possible Faculty/Staff Attendance   **149**
Average Total Participation Per Title   **57%**

OBJECTIVE 4: Continue to monitor and refine block scheduling in order to improve the delivery of the curriculum and increase student achievement

TITLE	DATE	NUMBER ATTENDING	HOURS PER PERSON	TOTAL HOURS
PAR Lesson Plan Framework Content Area Presentations	11/18/94	122	1	122
Content Area Sharing/Planning Time	11/18/94	122	1	122
"The At-Risk Phenomenon" Graduate Course	2 & 3/94	20	30	600
"New Kids on the Block"	8/95	12	1	12
Inspirational Speaker	8/95	149	1	149
"Mathematics Citywide"	4/24/95	17	3	51
"CLOZE: How to Assess Students' Reading Levels in All Content Areas"	11/18/94	40	1	40
PAR Teaching Strategies: 3-Column Notetaking, GIST, and Questioning Strategies	2/96	25	1	25
"New Kids on the Block"	5/96	12	1	12
Lunch and Learn: Teaching Strategies for Extended Classes—Health and Physical Education	11/19 & 26/96	20	4	80
Lunch and Learn: Teaching Strategies for Extended Classes—Science and Work & Family Studies	12/3/96	17	2	34
Lunch and Learn: Teaching Strategies for Extended Classes—Business, Tech. Ed. & Marketing	12/4/96	15	2	30
Lunch and Learn: Teaching Strategies for Extended Classes—Social Studies	12/10/96	21	2	42
Lunch and Learn: Teaching Strategies for Extended Classes—English	12/11/96	21	2	42
Lunch and Learn: Teaching Strategies for Extended Classes—Special Education	12/12/96	12	2	24
Lunch and Learn: Teaching Strategies for Extended Classes—Math	1/8/97	16	2	32
Lunch and Learn: Teaching Strategies for Extended Classes—Fine Arts	1/13/97	8	2	16
Lunch and Learn: Teaching Strategies for Extended Classes—Foreign Languages	1/14/97	11	2	22

Average Number of Teachers Participating Per Title   132
Possible Faculty/Staff Attendance   136
Average Total Participation Per Title   97%

and scores on standardized and norm-referenced tests. If one of your reasons for moving to block scheduling is to increase student attendance, measure attendance rates each month.

- **Measure indicators of success that are defined by customers.** Parents want safe schools, so measure incidents of violence and numbers of suspensions based on the actual number of suspensions monthly. Community members ask about SAT scores, so keep a log of those scores over an identified period of time that will show patterns of (hopefully) increased scores.

REVAMP THE CHIEF CONTROL TOOLS

The next step in building monitoring systems is to **revamp the chief control tools**. Peters' message is to *share information with everyone—* this means on a regular basis. We concur but acknowledge that it takes a confident leader to share information. Those school "leaders" who still think they influence people by withholding information have not experienced the benefits of working with empowered subordinates. In fact, teachers and support staff remain subordinates only on the organizational chart. In reality when people share information and work together to make decisions that can and will be measured, there is no "boss" and "subordinate" but rather a team of people with different assignments working toward the same goal. Collecting data does very little to improve a situation that has gone astray if the information is not shared. This is critical when making data-based as well as research-based decisions.

We are very much aware that educators must respect confidentiality, sensitive policies, and laws, and that they might not be free to share related information. However, there is much information that can be shared with internal and external customers. Examples include composite standardized test scores at the national, state, and district levels; honors received by students and teachers; numbers and causes of expulsions and suspensions; student and teacher attendance; condition of the school facilities; and the school budget. What can be shared depends on local, state, and federal policies.

Make sure you are aware of what information you can share based on your local policies.

When the building leader shares information with staff and empowers staff to make "real" decisions based on that information, staff members become the owners of the process. If there are problems with the process or the results of decisions made based on the data shared by the building administrators, the identified issue becomes a "we" issue and not a "they" issue. Consider the Case in Point on page 250.

In order to revamp the chief control tools:

- Examine how data-related information is shared throughout the school. Develop a strategy for sharing information that will expand the locus of control (without jeopardizing confidentiality).

- Create a communications action team that can assist the school administration with the flow of information based on collected data.

DECENTRALIZE INFORMATION, AUTHORITY, AND STRATEGIC PLANNING

The third step in Peters's system is to decentralize information, authority, and strategic planning. Many educators do not have a system for collecting data or a system for sharing data, but we believe it is critical that we collect data and design systems for sharing data. Sharing information often quiets critics of change. If these critics have information that is factual, then they have only facts to report—not gossip, not half-truths, or perceptions—just accurate information that you have provided.

Providing customers with accurate information is a perceived source of power for the customer. Providing information is also very useful when attempting to build a relationship with customers, especially when tending to damage control. It can signal the beginning of a relationship built on integrity if the school leader trusts teachers, parents, and community members to know the whole story of an event.

Empowering decision makers is meaningless if we do not provide them with information that gives them the opportunity to be successful. If the delegation of authority is not accompanied with appropriate information, then why delegate? We would argue that a project is, in fact, doomed from the beginning if information does not flow to all of the people involved in it. We think that, without adequate information, it is improbable that any project will bear fruit. People who have information can't ignore the responsibilities.

Involving customers in the strategic planning process without adequate information is like sending someone on a long road trip without a map. The traveler may eventually arrive at his destination after many delays, but wouldn't it have been more efficient to provide a map? And then there are those folks who take another trek and never get to the destination. Providing information is the customer's road map. Planning has become too important in the reform process for school administrators to do it alone.

■ Sharing information and responsibility

When decentralizing the control systems of an organization, the key to managing an organization is working with people and understanding their basic needs. Common sense tells us that being valued as a part of the decision-making process is one of those needs. After all, people closest to the daily operation of a school and those who work directly with students are the people that we need in the information-gathering and decision-making processes. Based on our experiences, access to both money and information yields power. Whether the power is great or small, a sense of power felt by stakeholders who didn't feel that they previously had influence pushes them to look at change differently and to support that which they are involved in initiating. Decentralizing control is like a grass-roots initiative: Those who are empowered must be ready for the responsibility, and they must be given the tools needed to make effective decisions that must be data driven.

How often have teachers, students, and parents in your school had the opportunity to be a part of the process for planning and control of the money

Empowering staff was also important to Yvonne. As one means of encouraging faculty to work together in teams, Yvonne initiated a minigrants program. She had developed these programs previously and found that they encouraged teachers to generate new ideas in the classroom. She allocated monies from different program areas to fund an initiative that would put instructional dollars in the hands of teachers for them to use in ways they thought best.

After developing the guidelines for the minigrant program, two of her central office staff visited schools to tell teachers about the program and the opportunity they had to get money for team projects. The high school faculty that had begun the block schedule and the faculties of the middle schools that were working in teams latched on to the notion of minigrants and took great advantage of the opportunity. Elementary teachers who were working in traditional, isolated environments were highly suspicious. Some said they didn't believe the central office would really give them money for innovative projects. And they didn't understand why they would have to be accountable for the way the money was spent.

During the first year, more than 60 projects were funded at $600 each. The skeptics became believers, and minigrants have become a way of life in the school system. Yvonne learned that teachers have to be ready for empowerment—you can't give it to them; they must reach out and take it. She also learned that as you share your data with the public—in this case, describing the projects and how the money was used to improve instruction—people in the school system would come forward to make contributions to the program.

that accompanies related decisions? Money is power, and decision makers closest to the issues should have the responsibility and the power that accompanies the responsibility. **Fiscal authority and data must be shared with decision makers.** Of course, this authority and money must be shared within the parameters and polices of the school and the local school district.

■ Measurement systems must be built into customer-based planning

As stated throughout this book and in this chapter, it is critical to include your customers in the process of planning for block scheduling. Also include your customers in the larger strategic planning initiative that is part of your school improvement plan and the plan of your school district. Move the delegation of responsibility of planning from the central administration to those who are on the front line. This process gives ownership, and this ownership will likely create a positive situation for all involved.

As you think about planning and the measurement involved, consider who knows more about what needs to be measured. Isn't it those people on

the front line and the receivers of the service? Traditionally managers have done the planning. Even when representatives of various role groups participated in the process, decisions were left to managers. We should reconsider the traditional strategic planning process (designed by top-level management) and seek a process that has high involvement and leads the school forward. Peters (p. 510) contends that a good strategic planning process not only gets everyone involved, but it also is "perpetually fresh" and requires "vigorous debate." In order to **decentralize information, authority, and strategic planning,** the following must be done.

- Maximize the power of the school improvement team to have access to data and fiscal resources.

- Develop action teams to design and carry out the work of the school improvement team.

- Create team leaders who will facilitate the information flow throughout the school.

- Utilize newsletters, local cable TV, and community/civic groups as vehicles for information flow.

- Involve all staff—including support staff—in important data-driven decisions.

- Develop the strategic planning process by departments, teams, or schools within the school and provide appropriate data for decision making.

SET CONSERVATIVE GOALS

Over the past century many educators have been reluctant to change systems or processes that have established a climate of security and comfort. Now that our paradigm has evolved and we see a need for reform in schools, we must move cautiously. We are not saying that we shouldn't move—because we must—but we should use good judgment as we invest our resources in new efforts. Setting conservative goals with conservative financial investments can bring teachers and administrators into new decision-making roles, if the decision-making process is built on a system of integrity. The attractiveness of such a process is that the system honors all players, and administrators' ideas as well as teachers' ideas can be rejected or adopted. Giving teachers an education in the management of resources and a voice in decision making elevates their status—they begin to think like a board of directors that has broad responsibility for an organization. They can remain creative and generate wonderful ideas for the school, but they will ground their ideas to the resources available.

In order to set conservative goals:

- Prioritize what is really important to the life of the school in all areas as measured by specific data.

- Identify what is critical to school reform that requires resources based on data.

- Set goals that can be reached within a year's timeline.

- Set a manageable number of goals that can be measured.

DEMAND TOTAL INTEGRITY

Is it possible to establish trust in today's workplace? Have the role of teacher unions and the aggressive action of parents colored our thinking about the relationships in the school building? It is not only possible; it is also necessary to establish trust in schools. One way that we can bring integrity and trust to an organization is to share the responsibility of developing new ways of working with and involving all members of the organization. This creates ownership of the mission and goals of the school—and ownership, we have found, provides greater opportunities for success. We believe that the success of block scheduling in many schools has been the result of a system that establishes ownership and trust. Think of other successful initiatives. Didn't the leadership provide a climate of trust that supported the staff's ability to try something new, maybe fail at part of it, fix it, and keep working to make things better?

Why do we talk about systems, involvement and empowerment of customers, and the work of Peters, Deming, and Juran in this chapter? The work that we have done in school improvement is based on a belief that systems theory explains how schools operate, that everything we do ultimately must satisfy

---

CASE IN POINT

Based on our experiences working with block schedule reform, one of the top five reasons for not implementing the block schedule is the concern that additional funding is needed. Rather than setting modest goals for fiscal support, many school administrators have included other financial needs to implement under the name of block scheduling (e.g.: they wanted to add additional courses to the course of studies anyway). If you are incorporating other goals with the implementation of a new schedule, maintain credibility to the process and state this as a goal up front. Consider the financial situation within your particular arena and request accordingly. At the same time, be sure that you seek adequate funding to cover needed components to allow opportunities for success. If you are moving from a traditional six-period day to a block schedule, there is a chance that you will need additional funding to hire more faculty, more classroom space if you are expanding course offerings, and more and better class resources and equipment. Do not seek fewer funds than you will need.

---

the customers' requirements, and that these three management experts provide excellent guidance for building a quality organization based on data-driven decisions. The systems suggested by these experts help us facilitate measurement, document progress, and establish credibility. If you still are unsure about measurement, ask yourself these questions:

- If you do not measure what is important to the customer, why measure at all?

- If you do not listen to customers and collect data, how will you know what is important to measure?

- If you do not have systems in place, how will you collect and distribute data to customers?

- If you do not empower customers to become a part of the process by sharing data, how do you establish trust and integrity with internal and external customers?

WHERE DO WE BEGIN WHEN IMPLEMENTING A MEASUREMENT SYSTEM?

As in any assessment process, certain questions must be answered by the person(s) responsible for the assessment before the system can be designed effectively. In our experience, we have found that there are seven basic questions that must be answered before the process can be developed. They are:

1. What are the identified measurable goals of the school? In other words: What do we want to measure?

2. What data do we currently have available?

3. What data do we need?

4. Is it possible to collect the data that we need but don't have?

5. What data collection process do we have in place or will we put in place?

6. Do we have a system in place to analyze the data that will be useful? Do we have a system in place to analyze the data so that we can make data-driven decisions?

7. Do we have a process in place for sharing the data with all of our impacted customers?

CASE IN POINT

While working with a principal who was implementing the 4x4 block scheduling, Tom was asked by the principal to help with an unusual situation—a surplus of instructional personnel. As he talked with the principal about this unusual situation (most schools do not have ample teachers to teach the students they have enrolled), the principal informed Tom that his school had experienced a decline in enrollment and that eventually he would need to eliminate some positions. Tom asked if he needed to consider this information as he planned the type of block schedule that he wanted to implement. The principal insisted that the schedule that was recommended by the staff allowed many of his faculty members to teach two classes, have a planning block, and a duty block each semester—an arrangement that would help sell the notion of block scheduling. But would their schedule, Tom asked, be the same the following year, when the principal would have to eliminate some of his staff?

The schedule was a big hit with the faculty the first year. But the year that the staff was downsized and most of the faculty had to teach three classes per semester, the school began to struggle with the block schedule concept. Although the schedule is still in place at that school, the principal is no longer there, many key instructional personnel have also left, and the school is struggling with the block schedule. We would suggest that this was not what we mean when we discuss integrity. Had the principal shared all information that he had with the staff in the beginning, would they have made the same choice regarding the type of schedule that was best for the school?

It is improbable that all schools have the answers to all of these questions. We have found that some schools have some pieces of the process in place, but seldom do we find that all schools have all of the pieces in place. Each school is different and has different goals, different data needs, and of course different resources for collecting data and analyzing them. Therefore, schools will need to chart their own course of action for data collection, analysis, and change.

Perhaps you are one of the schools that has all pieces of a system in place for receiving customer input, collecting data, and distributing information. If not, Peters gives a general format that might serve as direction for designing such systems. We suggest that, if possible, you should start from the first step of the process and put in place all pieces that would bring about continuous improvement. Involve all customers in the process from the beginning.

The most important function of the leader is to insist that what is being measured is that which is happening in the trenches of the school. That includes instruction, building maintenance, transportation, food service, as well as community issues. Correlating these measurements with student achievement will generate results of interest to all customers. Many of our external customers have a tendency to track only those issues that impact them. This may mean that they do not understand what is happening in the "trenches" of the school and how what happens impacts what they are measuring.

DEFINING GOALS AND OBJECTIVES THAT CAN BE MEASURED

When a team determines the goals or objectives that are the target for data collection and measurement, these identified goals must also be defined. Juran (1992) defines a goal as "an aimed-at target—an achievement toward which effort is expanded" (p. 27). He also suggests that "[p]roduct features and failure rates are largely determined during planning for quality" (p. 25). So, if the design for implementing block scheduling and the associated measurement process is not quality, then the product—the new schedule—will not have the same chance for success as a schedule designed with quality in mind.

A common mistake of those designing a measuring process is to make the unit of measure too broad. The definition of the unit of measure is critical to your school. It must be defined in terms that relate to your customers. According to Juran (1992, pp. 124-5), the ideal unit of measure is understandable, applies broadly, is conducive to uniform interpretation, is economic to apply, and is compatible with existing designs. We can translate that definition to mean the following for us in schools.

The unit of measure:

- Must have a standardized meaning for all customers regardless of level.

- Must consider local dialects and jargon if the measurements are to be used with customers that are external. (Educators are considered notorious users of unfriendly jargon.)

- Must be friendly to avoid creating a climate of mistrust.

- Should allow us to compare our findings with other schools of similar demographics.

- Should allow us to concentrate our improvement efforts (e.g.: on the building, climate, math, science, cafeteria, transportation, or communications).

- Should be standard enough for broad-based interpretation (e.g.: Does "advanced courses" mean the same to each school with which you will be comparing your data?).

- Must yield advantages that add value to the system, making it cost effective.

- May be utilized with existing measurement systems in place (e.g.: If you want to add teacher absentees to your measurement system, is there a system in place that would allow this addition without designing a new system for measurement or disrupting the entire measurement system?)

MEASUREMENT OF THE MANY IMPACTS OF BLOCK SCHEDULING

As the issues of block scheduling are continually debated, it is obvious, in our opinion, that many educators are looking for immediate results. Those who support the concept are looking for positive results, and those who are opposed expect to produce negative findings. There are some immediate results that appear to be a result of block scheduling (e.g.: reduced discipline referrals). But the fact is, we are still collecting data that will provide us information on the success or failure of block scheduling. There are many reasons that educators have shifted their allocated instructional time to a block scheduling format, but the compelling reason should be to improve student achievement. To determine the impact of block scheduling on student achievement will require long-term data collection and an assessment process that will identify the true worth of block scheduling. At this point in the short history of block scheduling, we would argue that there are too many decisions, both positive and negative, being made or avoided relative to the education of students without sufficient data.

It is important to monitor the effects of the longer blocks of time on both teaching and learning as block scheduling evolves. This will allow the collection of data that permits us to make appropriate decisions regarding the scheduling of time in the school day that will be most beneficial to our students. As identified behaviors that affect student learning and teacher behaviors are monitored and assessed, we will continue to make appropriate changes and move forward as we seek the most productive ways of providing learning opportunities for students. Changes and adjustments will be made to ensure success for both teachers and students.

BASELINE DATA

As we have stated, it is critical to your success to collect baseline data. For our purposes, we will define baseline data as the initial data collected for determining a base by which to measure all other related data subsequently collected to determine the success of identified measurable goals and objectives.

Baseline data will be determined by the measurable goals that you identify. Each goal identified should be correlated to student achievement. Even if one of the goals does not appear to correlate with student achievement, it is critical to tie it to another goal that will support student achievement. For example, if an identified goal is to measure school climate, then support this goal with research/literature that links positive school climate with increased student achievement. These data can be measured at different intervals throughout the school term. Intervals might include weekly, monthly, end-of-grading periods, biannually, or at the end of the school term. Using data for analysis may be driven by when the data are available. You can look at student participation in the lunch program monthly, but you can only review performance on the Advanced Placement exams annually.

Some of the available data we have found in schools that we have worked with include the following.

- Various indicators of student achievement (local, state, or national standardized test scores for all students as well as special populations of students; honor roll; grade point average)

- Financial data

- Dropout rates

- Student/staff attendance

- Out-of-school/in-school suspensions

- Discipline referrals

- Incidences of violence (safety issues)

- Graduation rates

- Mobility of student population

- Local, state, and federal mandates that impact decisions

- Number of faculty, staff, and support staff

- Student-teacher ratios

- Disabled student population and requirements

- Socioeconomic status of community and students

- School demographics, such as urban, suburban, rural

- Student demographics, such as ethnicity, gender, speakers of English as a second language, number of free/reduced-lunch eligible students

- Faculty/administrator experience level

- Organizational structure of the school

- School funding

- Number of students participating in breakfast/lunch programs

- Number of students continuing formal education after high school

- Participation of parents in school activities, such as volunteer programs, PTA, extracurricular activities

- Parent education levels

IDENTIFYING MEASURABLE GOALS AND COLLECTING BASELINE DATA

As we begin to look at what we measure and identify the system by which we measure, we must remember that reform and the measurement of quality outcomes is a long-term process and that "Quality improvement is a never-ending journey. ... Each day, each product or service is getting relatively better or relatively worse, but it never stands still" (Peters, p. 80). A variety of data sources is used in an evaluation plan to provide a comprehensive picture of the program and to inform a variety of audiences. Because the types of data are varied and the audiences diverse, it is critical to identify measurable goals before implementing a block schedule. Identifying goals should be one of the first activities in the process. What goals are important to identify in order for you to determine the effects of block scheduling on student achievement? Once the measurable goals are identified, what next?

We suggest that you collect baseline data for the areas we discuss in the following case study. We have found that these are the areas that connect to student achievement and are being monitored to determine the success of block scheduling in many schools. Additionally, these areas generate data in which many of our external customers have a great deal of interest. This list is not exhaustive but is a manageable number with which to begin, and it represents highly critical areas of the school. As you can see, the areas in which we need to connect data are embedded in the measurable goals.

ESTABLISHING BASELINE DATA AND DISPLAYING IT

When Tom was principal at Atlee High School in Hanover County, Virginia, he led his staff through the process of goal setting. The part of the process that was new for them was thinking about collecting data that would give them true measures of effectiveness and learning how to display the data. As the faculty considered the block schedule for Atlee High School, the first question they asked was, "What measurable goals are we trying to reach that would make a measurable impact on student achievement?" After many community meetings, listening to customer input, and considering impact data, such as increase of fiscal responsibility, size of the teaching staff, needs of the students, and how this was all related to student achievement, the faculty defined several measurable goals. Tom determined the data that would be needed to monitor actions being taken to meet those goals. Throughout the year, data were collected and displayed in formats that were easily understood by Tom and his faculty.

The goals for Atlee High School are listed below. Following each goal statement are examples of the kinds of data displays that principals can use to measure goal achievement.

■ Goals for Atlee High School

GOAL 1—Students' academic achievement will increase annually, as measured by standardized tests scores, improved grade point average (GPA), increased number of students receiving academic monograms (letters), and the number of students entering and successfully competing in state or national academic competition (e.g.: science fairs, National Merit Scholarship finals, etc.). These data will also be analyzed based on a narrower variance in pupil achievement when data disaggregates (based on sex and ethnic backgrounds and special student populations) are compared with non-disaggregated group(s).

The following graphs (Figures 79–93) indicate how data related to this goal can be reported after being collected. We have found that the visual representation of the data in graph form has been highly effective when working with the faculty, school boards, parents, and other stakeholders. Additionally, it helps the school leadership understand what is happening in the school. While there are countless ways to display data and many sources of information, we offer a few examples of graphs that administrators and teachers can use to monitor that which has been identified as important in the school.

The three graphs in Figures 79, 80, and 81 are representations of data that can be created for each department in the school. Similar graphs can be constructed for teams, such career cluster teams, a ninth-grade team, or a school-within-a-school, as well as for the school as a whole (see Figure 82). It is very easy to compare results among departments and teams using these graphs. The purpose of comparing results is to recognize success and identify problem areas. It is not to reprimand individuals or to make quick judgments. Performance data should be viewed longitudinally. However, if the leader is monitoring results regularly, s/he will immediately spot an occurrence that is unusual or points to something being out of control. This is part of the value of regularly gathering and displaying data for decision making.

You can choose the type of graph to construct. For some data the circle graph is appropriate because you can compare a part to the whole. The

FIGURE 79
Grade Distributions

English Department—1st Semester

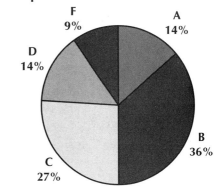

FIGURE 80
Grade Distributions

Vocational Department—1st Semester

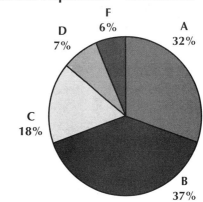

FIGURE 81
Grade Distributions

Special Education Department—1st Semester

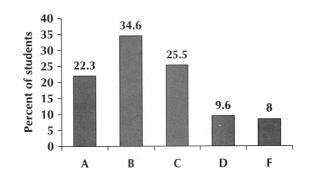

column graph used in Figure 81 is easy to read and can evoke discussion about normal distributions (bell curve).

The principal and faculty can use the information displayed in Figure 83 to initiate a discussion of possible problems, such as high failure rates in some courses, teacher expectations for performance, student motivation, and content alignment. When considering the data in Figure 83, Tom and the staff at Atlee found that the grade point average in social studies (2.5) was not consistent with the result of standardized test scores. Standardized test scores for social studies students were generally the lowest scores in the school. An analysis of the data might indicate that there is a problem with curriculum alignment or perhaps grade inflation.

Figure 84 shows us that this school's performance did not reflect a normal, bell curve distribution. As the goal of this school was to achieve high performance by expecting all students to excel, how would you interpret this graph to your faculty?

Figure 85 is a bar graph that compares the grade point averages (GPAs) of the students taught by each teacher in his or her course. When Tom used a chart like this one, he made one bar graph that showed all of the teachers' GPAs. Use this graph to look for inconsistencies in classroom performance. While you wouldn't share this information publicly, it could be very useful as you deal with parental requests for students being placed with a certain teacher or being removed from a teacher's class. As you view these data over time, would not this information help you determine whether the block schedule is working for or against students? Figure 86 will help you discern if teachers and students are performing differently throughout the day. Also, you can compare singleton classes to blocks. Keep in mind which classes are singletons and what level of students are in singletons, as well as the number of singletons you have compared to block classes.

Figure 87 shows how school leaders can view the performance of departments within the school. If you anticipate a problem in your curriculum, this information can be helpful.

For those schools planning to implement a singleton period (the traditional 50-minute period) as a

FIGURE 83
Grade Point Averages

1st Semester

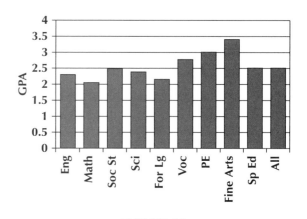

FIGURE 82
Grade Distributions

All Classes—1st Semester

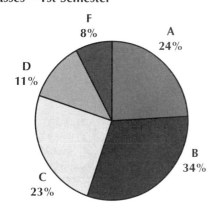

FIGURE 84
Grade Distribution

All Classes—1st Semester

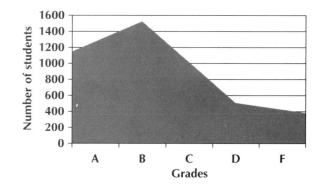

part of the new block schedule, it may be useful to prepare graphs of performance by subject area of singleton classes and blocked classes. You can prepare graphs that show grade point averages (as in Figure 88) or grade distribution by percent of letter grades (as in Figure 89).

SAT scores are one indication of student performance that stakeholders often request. A component of accountability systems in some states, SAT and PSAT average scores should be examined annually by the school leadership as a measure of quality. It is valuable to benchmark school scores against those of the state and the nation on these tests. (See Figures 90 and 91.)

In addition to maintaining records of student performance on these tests, it is helpful to note the number of students taking the tests annually. For example, if the number of students taking the SAT increases as greater numbers of students anticipate going to college, it is important to use this information to explain your SAT performance outcome—whether it decreases, increases, or is stable—compared with the performance of a smaller group of students.

In addition to collecting and displaying the information shown in Figures 79–91, principals may choose to monitor participation on the honor roll by semester, comparing grade levels, departments, or

FIGURE 85
Grade Point Averages by Teachers

First 10 of 76 Teachers—1st Semester

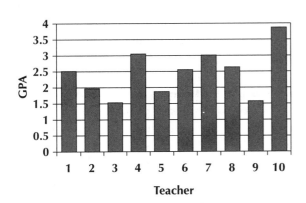

FIGURE 86
Grade Point Averages by AM–PM Blocks

1st Semester

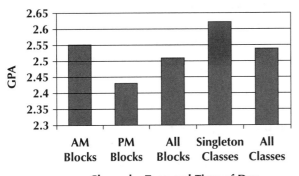

FIGURE 87
Grade Point Averages of Block Classes

1st Semester

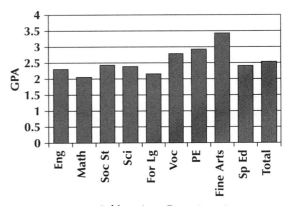

FIGURE 88
Grade Point Averages of Singleton Classes

1st Semester

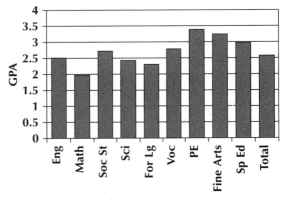

FIGURE 89
Distribution of Letter Grades

By AM and PM Block—1st Semester

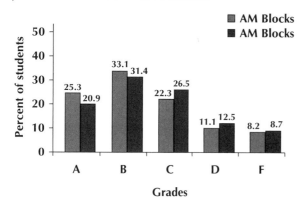

FIGURE 90
SAT Profile

School, State, and National Scores

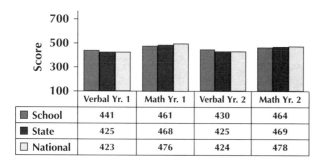

	Verbal Yr. 1	Math Yr. 1	Verbal Yr. 2	Math Yr. 2
■ School	441	461	430	464
■ State	425	468	425	469
☐ National	423	476	424	478

SAT Area of Testing by Year

FIGURE 91
PSAT Profile

Year 1, Year 2, Year 3

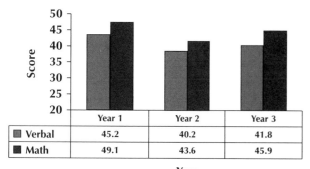

	Year 1	Year 2	Year 3
■ Verbal	45.2	40.2	41.8
■ Math	49.1	43.6	45.9

Year

teams. Similarly, student performance on exams can be monitored. Just remember: you can collect different kinds of data depending on what your goals are, and the data should be displayed so that school leaders, faculty members, and stakeholders can understand what the numbers mean over a period of time.

GOAL 2—More students will enroll in Advanced Placement and dual college credit courses annually, as measured by the number of students enrolled in these classes. Data will also be disaggregated by the number of students scoring a 3 or above on the Advanced Placement examination and the number of students scoring B or higher on the dual college credit courses. Data will also be disaggregated by ethnicity and socioeconomic status.

GOAL 3—More students will continue their formal education after graduating from high school, as measured by the annual number of students entering institutes of higher education. These data will be disaggregated by the number of students entering four-year colleges and universities, entering two-year colleges, and entering technical training schools. Figures 92 and 93 provide the exact data needed to measure progress toward Goal 3.

GOAL 4—Students will receive successful job counseling and placement services, as measured annually by the number of students who are successfully placed in jobs and entering college upon graduation from high school. These data will be disaggregated by the number of students being accepted at major colleges and universities, and the number being accepted at the first college of their choice when considering qualifications of the student.

GOAL 5—Achievement and success of special student populations in high school and the workplace will increase annually, as measured by the number of special student population receiving regular or advanced diplomas, transitioned into academic or training courses, and placed in appropriate work-related jobs upon completion of their education at Atlee High School. These data will be disaggregated by the type of the special student population. (See Figure 94.)

Figure 94 provides part of the information needed to evaluate Goal 5. What else would a principal need to report on progress toward this goal

FIGURE 92
Graduate Profile

Type of Diploma

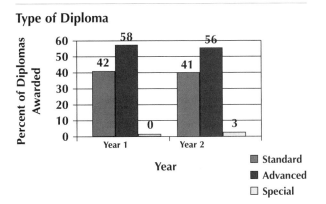

FIGURE 94
Grade Distribution

Special Education—1st Semester

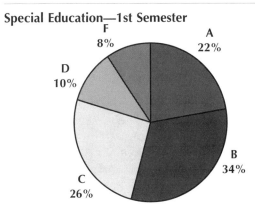

FIGURE 93
Graduate Profile

Post Graduate Plans

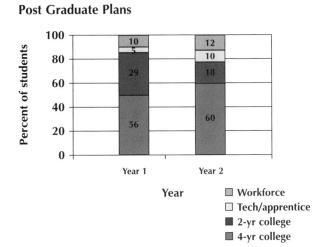

who need remediation courses when entering colleges or universities. These data will also be disaggregated by ethnicity.

GOAL 7—Dropout rates for students will be lower than the previous year, as measured by the official enrollment count on monthly and annual bases. (See Figure 95.)

In Figure 95, the school leader can monitor student attendance and the dropout rate on a regular basis. It is easy to keep this information in a database, update it monthly, and prepare graphs, such as this one, for monthly distribution. We recommend keeping these charts in a notebook or file—electronic or hard copy—for easy access by the principal.

GOAL 8—Student attendance will increase from the previous year, as measured by the official attendance data on monthly and annual

statement? Information should be kept on the type of diploma issued to students with disabilities and post-secondary plans/placements for special students. For special students in work-based programs during high school, it would be helpful to report their progress at the work setting. Federal requirements now call for schools to assess the progress of special students with standardized instruments, making it possible to monitor academic progress in an objective way.

GOAL 6—Fewer students will need remediation from the previous year, as measured by the number of students that are successful at completing and passing all courses the first time they take the course and the number of students

FIGURE 95
Student Attendance and Dropout Percentages

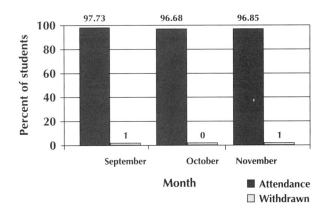

bases. (See Figure 96.) **Student tardies will decrease,** as measured by official tardy data on monthly and annual bases. (See Figure 97.)

There are advantages to monitoring student attendance and tardies on a monthly basis. Comparing data from year to year allows the leadership to make determinations about what is "normal" attendance for the school population. When a bar takes a dip or rises very quickly and then drops, it indicates that something special has occurred (e.g.: a flu epidemic or a special attempt to improve attendance).

GOAL 9—Faculty attendance will increase from the previous year, as measured by the official attendance data on monthly and annual bases.

Figure 98 provides a line graph of the first semester attendance of a school's faculty. The graph can be expanded to include attendance over several years for a longitudinal perspective. Dips in attendance (e.g.: October) should raise questions, such as:

• Were more teachers than usual sick during the month?

• How many teachers took personal leave during the month?

• Were teachers out of class due to staff development activities?

GOAL 10—Discipline referrals will decrease from the previous year, as measured by the number of referrals to the administrative offices. These data will be disaggregated based on ethnicity and socioeconomic status, as well as type of discipline issues, such as incidences of violence and non-violence.

There are many categories of information a principal can collect related to discipline. Figures 99 through 105 are examples of some of the categories that principals have found helpful. During this period of increased concern over school safety and security, and considering the report of many principals that discipline referrals decrease on a block schedule, the maintenance of data related to discipline referrals will be important.

GOAL 11—Graduation rates for students will increase annually, as measured by the number of students who enrolled in the school in the ninth grade, completed four years of coursework, and graduated after completing diploma requirements.

FIGURE 96
Student Attendance

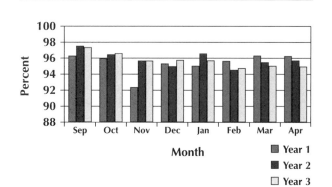

FIGURE 97
Student Tardies

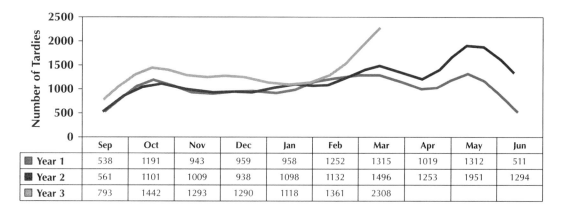

	Sep	Oct	Nov	Dec	Jan	Feb	Mar	Apr	May	Jun
Year 1	538	1191	943	959	958	1252	1315	1019	1312	511
Year 2	561	1101	1009	938	1098	1132	1496	1253	1951	1294
Year 3	793	1442	1293	1290	1118	1361	2308			

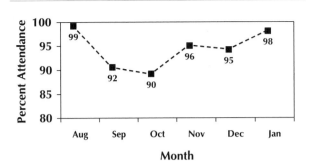

FIGURE 98
Teacher Attendance

FIGURE 99
Cumulative Discipline Referrals

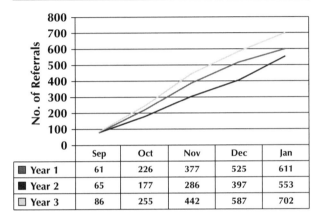

	Sep	Oct	Nov	Dec	Jan
■ Year 1	61	226	377	525	611
■ Year 2	65	177	286	397	553
□ Year 3	86	255	442	587	702

Although these were the initial goals and reasons for implementing block scheduling at Atlee High School, other measurable goals were added later. Data drove the decision to make adjustments. Data were collected to provide information on the following topics.

- **Perceived school climate,** as measured by results of a school/community sub-survey.

- **Community involvement,** as measured by the actual number of volunteer hours logged by parents and other community stakeholders.

- **Students enrolled in upper-level math and science classes,** as measured by the increase in numbers of students enrolled in these classes over a period of time to determine a pattern.

- **Students enrolled in other electives such as music, art, technology programs, Advanced Placement and dual credit courses,** as measured by the number of students enrolled in these courses over a period of identified years that will denote a trend. These data will also help with staffing priorities.

- **Change of teacher classroom behaviors,** as indicated by identified teaching strategies that can be observed by the administrative staff and measured by teacher and student observations and surveys.

- **Number of teachers/staff members who were involved in meaningful teacher training,** as measured by quality training initiative.

As block scheduling evolves, it is important to monitor the effects of the longer blocks of time on both teaching and learning. Identified behaviors that affect student learning and teacher behaviors need to be monitored and assessed. Changes and adjustments should be made to ensure success for both teachers and students.

There are many identifiable goals that are unique to each school community. We suggest that you include the measurable objectives that are

FIGURE 100
Weekly Discipline Referrals

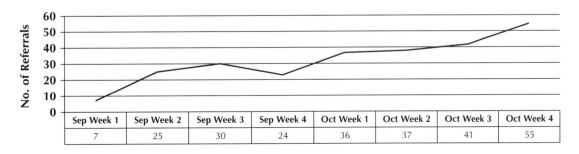

Sep Week 1	Sep Week 2	Sep Week 3	Sep Week 4	Oct Week 1	Oct Week 2	Oct Week 3	Oct Week 4
7	25	30	24	36	37	41	55

FIGURE 101
Discipline Study, Sep–Mar

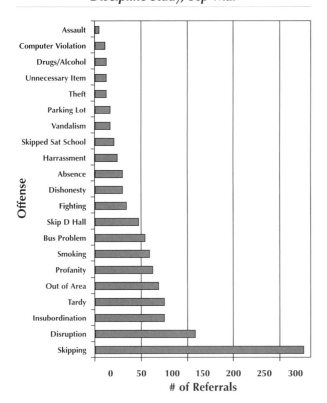

FIGURE 102
Discipline Outcomes

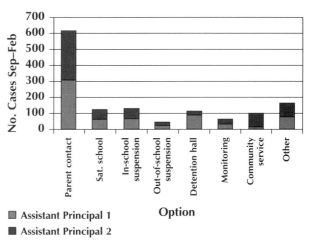

FIGURE 103
Discipline Referrals by Day

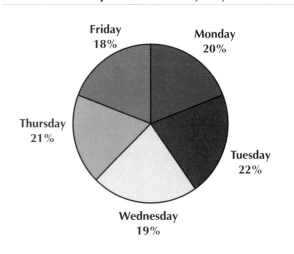

FIGURE 104
Discipline Referrals by Grade Level

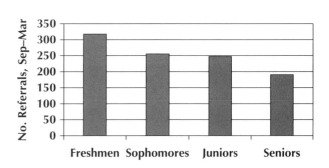

meaningful to your community in your plan for data collection. Goals can be modified as appropriate. One word of caution: Remember that successful change is not a quick fix. You can add or delete goals as often as needed. Also remember that if goals are measurable, the data can be disaggregated based on any number of variables.

Once data are collected and analyzed, how do you translate them into a format that is clear, jargon-free, and understandable by customers? At Atlee, Tom used a number of methods, but perhaps the most successful method was to present data in graphs and charts.

There were other pieces of data—difficult to collect but needed if the staff was going to monitor the success of the schedule—that the leadership at Atlee considered critical as they implemented block scheduling. Since there were few schools that had implemented block scheduling in 1991–92, out of necessity Tom and his staff had to be creative and design some of their own instruments for measuring goals or objectives.

FIGURE 105
Saturday School Utilization

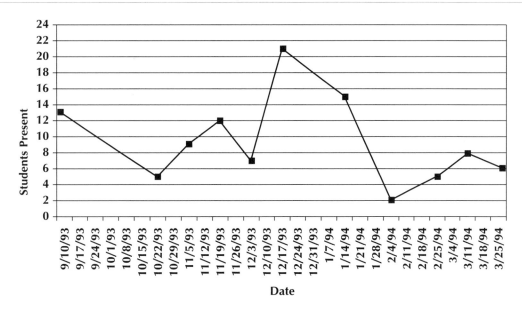

The school community felt that it was critical to have a positive school climate if students were going to achieve at the expected levels. Therefore, an early task was to identify an action team to design a survey that could be used to collect data from students, parents, faculty, and staff as well as other members of the community. It was first necessary to identify information that was needed. There are many surveys that can be used, but the ones on pages 266–267 are examples of Atlee's initial attempt to design meaningful surveys to collect the data that we needed to make appropriate decisions.

Atlee's leadership wanted to know how teachers, students, and parents perceived the new block scheduling, and they wanted to know if teachers were using different teaching strategies as perceived by students and parents. They decided to take an approach to collecting data that was not limited to surveying; they used the random sampling interview method for gathering the initial data. Fifteen team members were trained to interview teachers, students, and parents. The data were collected and analyzed by central office personnel in the school district.

INTRODUCTION TO SURVEY

The first year both of our schools were on a block schedule, we gathered information from teachers,

students, and parents to get a reading for how the block scheduling was working and being perceived. Surveys and interviews were conducted in May. In Gloucester, Virginia, we used the parent organization to administer our instrument to a sample of parents to foster a sense of openness and objectivity. As leaders, we were interested not only in gathering data for continuous improvement but also in responding to requests for information from parents and school board members.

In this section, we share the instruments used by Atlee High School. The first research instruments were simple survey questions that asked the respondents to mark either YES or NO to the given statement. The findings of the survey follow the instruments.

FOLLOW-UP SURVEY

After analyzing the data from the first survey and putting action teams in place to recommend strategies for implementing recommendations, additional data were gathered at the end of the first semester of the second year of block scheduling.

We sampled students, teachers, and parents at random but asked open-ended questions rather than using a forced-choice response. The survey is presented with the responses by category.

TEACHER BLOCK SCHEDULING SURVEY QUESTIONS

Please respond either YES or NO to the statements below. Thank you for your time with this survey.

1. The double block of instructional time allows me to provide individual attention to students.

2. The double block of instructional time deters students' absences.

3. The double block of instructional time enhances student-teacher and student-student relationships.

4. The double block of instructional time enhances students' continuity of learning.

5. The double block of instructional time allows me to change my teaching strategies to meet the needs of students.

6. The double block of instructional time allows me to pace instruction to suit the learning styles of students.

7. The double block of instructional time allows me to vary activities and provide students with opportunities for instructional interaction, dialogue, and discussion.

8. The double block of instructional time facilitates the use of instructional resources such as guest speakers and community enrichment programs.

9. The double block of instructional time facilitates the use of computer labs, audio-visual aids, and multimedia technology systems.

10. The double block of instructional time creates additional needs for staff development opportunities.

STUDENT BLOCK SCHEDULING SURVEY QUESTIONS

Please respond either YES or NO to the statements below. Thank you for your time with this survey.

1. The double block of instructional time allows me to receive individual attention from my teacher.

2. The double block of instructional time focuses my attention on the importance of regular attendance.

3. The double block of instructional time enhances student-teacher and student-student relationships.

4. The double block of instructional time enhances students' continuity of learning.

5. The double block of instructional time allows teachers to use a variety of teaching strategies.

6. The double block of instructional time allows teachers to pace instruction to meet my needs or my learning style.

7. The double block of instructional time allows teachers to vary activities and provide students with opportunities for instructional interaction, dialogue, and discussion.

8. The double block of instructional time facilitates the use of instructional resources such as guest speakers and community enrichment programs.

9. The double block of instructional time facilitates the use of computer labs, audio-visual aids, and multimedia technology systems.

10. The double block of instructional time allows my teacher a more efficient use of class time.

PARENT BLOCK SCHEDULING SURVEY QUESTIONS

Please respond either YES or NO to the statements below. Thank you for your time with this survey.

1. The double block of instructional time allows teachers to provide my child with individual attention.

2. The double block of instructional time deters my child's being absent from school.

3. The double block of instructional time enhances student-teacher and student-student relationships.

4. The double block of instructional time enhances the continuity of learning for my child.

5. The double block of instructional time allows my child's teachers to change their teaching strategies.

6. The double block of instructional time allows teachers to pace instruction that meets the needs of my child.

7. The double block of instructional time allows my child's teachers to vary activities and provide student opportunities for instructional interaction, dialogue, and discussion.

8. The double block of instructional time enhances the education of my child because it facilitates the use of instructional resources, such as guest speakers and community enrichment programs.

9. The double block of instructional time enhances the education of my child because it facilitates the use of computer labs, audio-visual aids, and multimedia technology systems.

10. The double block of instructional time creates a need for additional staff development activities for my child's teachers.

SUMMARY OF SURVEY PROCESS

1. A majority of teachers, students, and parents responded positively to almost all of the statements presented.

2. A strong similarity resulted between the teachers' and parents' responses of "yes" to statements.

3. Students gave positive ratings to statements on a less frequent basis than teachers and parents.

4. Teachers gave the highest positive responses overall on the statements presented.

5. Students gave the lowest positive response to the following statement: *The double block of instructional time enhances students' continuity of learning.* (56.1% "yes" responses)

6. Teachers and parents gave the lowest positive responses to the same statement.

   Teachers: *The double block of instructional time deters students' absences.* (52.7% "yes" responses)

   Parents: *The double block of instructional time deters my child's absences.* (44.5% "yes" responses) Many parents noted that they had not had problems with their child's attendance before going to the block scheduling.

7. The following items received the highest positive ratings by teachers, students, and parents: *The double block of instructional time facilitates the use of computer labs, audio-visual aids, and multimedia technology systems.* (teachers—98.2%; students—83.2%; and parents—80% "yes" responses)

8. Parents also gave 80% "yes" responses to the following four statements:

   The double block of instructional time enhances student-teacher and student-student relationships.

   The double block of instructional time allows my child's teachers to change their teaching strategies and to suit the learning style of my child.

The double block of instructional time allows my child's teachers to pace instruction that meets the needs of my child.

The double block of instructional time allows my child's teachers to vary activities and provide opportunities for instructional interaction, dialogue, and discussion.

9. Teachers, students, and parents gave a 90% "yes" response to the following statement:

   The double block of instructional time creates a need for additional staff development opportunities for teachers.

10. There was no consistent pattern to comments from teachers about what they liked best and least about block scheduling. What they liked best ranged from the schedule allowing time for a variety of instructional activities to the time allowed for personal interaction. Teachers indicated that by having more personal interaction with students, they were able to get to know them and their learning styles better than before block scheduling. What they liked least about block scheduling ranged from students' lack of attention to the fourth block being too long.

11. The respondents cited what they liked best and least about block scheduling in the following phrases:

    Students: **BEST**—Not having all classes every day; longer time between classes to do homework; more time to complete lab work and use technology; more time to be creative; and more time to learn things in depth that I didn't understand before because I have time to ask the teacher questions. **LEAST**—sitting for long periods of time; lecturing by teachers, and boredom in some classes when teachers do not change teaching strategies during the class.

    Parents: **BEST**—Students have to prepare for only four classes per day rather than the traditional seven; more time is available for learning; chance for discussion and participation in the classroom. **LEAST**—some classes are too long and students get bored because teachers do not change teaching strategies.

    Results from the survey indicate that much progress has been made in implementing block scheduling during the first year. A good foundation has been established. Teachers, students, and parents seem to realize that block scheduling requires a different approach to teaching and learning, and that there is an increase in student responsibilities. It was interesting that teachers, students, and parents all rated the use of computer labs, audio-visual aids, and technology systems as having the highest level of benefits from the block scheduling format. It was also interesting to note that teachers, students, and parents recognized the need for teacher staff development.

RECOMMENDATIONS

1. Continue to provide staff development for teachers to develop skill in differentiating instruction; enhance intellectual and social growth; to increase continuity of learning; to provide a wide variety of activity-based learning opportunities; to promote student interaction in the classroom; and to integrate technology and community resources into the learning process.

2. Ask the instructional leadership team at Atlee to analyze the results of the survey and their own experiences in order to modify and refine the schedule and the instructional program to meet the needs of students.

3. Consider giving students orientation about the purpose of block scheduling and their responsibilities.

4. Request that periodic checks be made to determine what teachers, students, and parents think about how block scheduling is working for them.

5. Focus on student motivation and participation in interesting, challenging, and meaningful activities to increase student achievement and student confidence in achieving in rigorous academic classes.

SECOND BLOCK SCHEDULING SURVEY

QUESTION	RESPONDING GROUP	NUMBER	RESPONSES
What would you like to change about block scheduling?	Students	3 6 3 3 4 2	too long in class change/vary activities during class meet all classes on Friday have breaks during each block and a longer lunch break too much lecturing in math and history classes foreign language classes should meet during block three (55-minute singleton block that meets daily)
	Parents	14 2 2 1 1	nothing teachers use time more effectively change the 55-minute block to the longer blocks give short breaks during blocks advantage to some courses such as science, physical education, music; disadvantage to classes like history, foreign language
	Teachers	4 6 2 4 1 1 3	third block too short/eliminate (singleton of 55 minutes) nothing need more teacher planning time need to have training on motivational activities to use in the classroom more time between classes shorten activity period only certain classes should meet during the singleton (e.g.: first year of foreign language, Algebra I)
	Support Staff (includes food services staff, custodial staff, health support service, secretarial staff, etc.)	2 2 1 1 1	nothing eliminate the 55-minute block need a common study period for all students begin lunch a little earlier need a homeroom base
Have you been involved in a variety of classroom activities and had an opportunity to interact with other students?	Students	10 6 3 1 1	more activities (didn't identify) some classes use group work and allow creative thinking more cooperative learning too much time to "goof off" in labs
What instructional strategy does block scheduling provide opportunities for you to use?	Teachers	7 5 4 3 3 2 2 1 1 1	discovery learning—hands-on, labs time to integrate technology cooperative learning work more one-on-one with students group work field experiences allows time to complete units more thoroughly steps of the writing process completed in one block student-centered learning demonstrations, debates, discussion, critical thinking, and creativity

QUESTION	RESPONDING GROUP	NUMBER	RESPONSES
How has block scheduling affected behavior of students?	Students	11	fewer discipline problems/behavior better
		2	students get bored in some classes after a while, so they become rowdy
		2	no change
		1	more self-discipline
		1	behavior worse
		1	depends on how teacher conducts class—the more student involvement, less discipline problems
	Parents	7	positive/better/calmer
		5	no change
		3	less homework
		3	decrease in discipline problems
		1	students more self-controlled
	Teachers	9	improved/better
		4	no change
		2	no problems
		1	more difficulty with ninth graders
	Support Staff	5	improved/better/more controlled
		1	normal behavior
		1	when teachers use time effectively, improves; if not, gets worse
How has block scheduling affected learning outcomes of students?	Students	11	grades overall better/learned more
		3	no change
		2	chance to participate
		2	prepared for college
		1	bad year/bored because classes too long
	Parents	12	overall better
		4	no change
		2	chance to participate more
		1	course dependent and teacher dependent
		1	more in depth
	Teachers	7	improved/more understanding and learning
		3	no change
		2	expect more from students under new schedule
		2	less covered but more in-depth
		1	foreign language achieving less
Have you received individual attention and instruction suited to meet your needs?	Students	19	yes or most definitely/more time spent with student
		2	small-group discussions
		1	more classroom activities
How has block scheduling affected your child's attitude toward school and learning?	Parents	13	positive/more enjoyable
		4	no change
		2	closer relationship with teachers
		1	able to find friends and adjust easier

QUESTION	RESPONDING GROUP	NUMBER	RESPONSES
How has block scheduling affected relationships with students, teachers, administrators, and parents?	Students (with teachers and other students)	14 4 1	improved/better/stronger/closer no effect more time to talk/small groups
	Parents (with teachers)	12 5 2	positive/good/know teacher better no effect teachers know their students better
	Teachers (with students, student-student)	12 8 1	better (get to know students better/stronger bond/more support) no change more time to interact
	Support staff (with students, teachers, and administrators)	3 2 2 1 1	more accessible no effect calmer day students/teachers supportive makes job easier
How has communication been affected by block scheduling?	Students (with students, administrators, teachers)	15 5 5	improved/increased/more time to talk no effect student—part of the decision-making process
	Parents (with teachers, administrators)	10 7 2 1	no change positive effect/good no problem talk more
	Support staff	4 2 2 2 1	safer calmer/good fewer discipline problems sense of ownership/pride in school good behavior
What are the expectations for student achievement under the block-scheduling format?	Students	19 1	higher/tougher/expect more depends on teachers; some expect more, some less
	Parents	10 5 5 1	higher no change more time to get work done teacher dependent
	Teachers	10 3 1 1 1	higher no change better mastery/grades improved more learning through hands-on more in-depth learning

QUESTION	RESPONDING GROUP	NUMBER	RESPONSES
Do you perceive that your child has more opportunities to use technology for instruction under block scheduling? How was it used?	Parents	18 15 1 1 1 1 1	yes, definitely yes, computer labs yes, photography yes, business law yes, art yes, library yes, film making
Do you perceive that you have more opportunities to use technology for instruction under block scheduling? If so, in what ways?	Teachers	11 8 4 4 1	yes computer labs other labs located in classrooms throughout the building graphing calculators need training to use equipment
How has block scheduling affected your use of community resources and involvement of parents?	Teachers	6 3 2 2 1	improved /used more community resources volunteers increased this year no effect/need training call parents more guest speakers/use of business partnerships
What kinds of training or experiences would you like to have to improve your performance when teaching in the block schedule?	Support staff	6 2 2 1 1 1	computer training teacher advisory group workshop student assistance program for at-risk children information on what students want for meals at school more training on finance/record keeping training in remediation
What are your three top priorities for professional development activities?	Teachers	10 3 6 5 2 4 4 1 3 3 3 2 1 1 1 1 1 1	cooperative learning/collaborative learning use of technology more effective lesson plans differentiation in classroom opportunities to develop various teaching techniques student assessment strategies for motivating students organization of time in the classroom team teaching special education student inclusion develop new materials for classroom activities strategies and materials for Advanced Placement students advanced training in content areas how to group in the classroom improve understanding of high school student time for collaboration between different departments interdisciplinary teaching techniques attending professional conferences/seminars to improve teaching strategies

SUMMARY RESULTS OF SECOND SURVEY

Overall, results from the interview indicated that block scheduling has had a positive effect on expectations, student learning, school climate, student interaction with teachers, and communications. Refinement, staff development, and student involvement should further these gains in the future.

1. Many students indicated that the time in classes seemed too long and that activities should be more varied. Most parents indicated that not much needed to be changed about block scheduling. No common pattern emerged from teachers for changes, except that five of them felt that the last block of the day was too long.

2. Most students and teachers agreed that a variety of activities and opportunities for students to interact with others had been made available.

3. A majority of students, parents, and support staff indicated that block scheduling had affected student behavior in a positive manner and that student behavior had improved.

4. Most students indicated that under block scheduling their grades overall were better and they learned more. About half of the parents and teachers responded in the same manner.

5. Most students indicated that they had received individual attention and instruction suited to their educational needs.

6. Slightly more than half of the parents indicated that block scheduling had affected their children's attitude toward school and learning in a positive and more enjoyable way.

7. A majority of students, teachers, and support staff indicated that block scheduling had improved or made better relationships with students, teachers, administrators, and parents. A majority of parents indicated no effect.

8. A majority of students, teachers, and support staff indicated that communication had improved, increased, or was positive. Students made the most positive comments about this change. A majority of parents indicated no change.

9. Most students, teachers, parents, and support staff indicated that the school environment was positive, friendly, calm, and safe.

10. Students overwhelmingly indicated that there are higher expectations for student achievement under block scheduling. About one-half of teachers and parents agreed.

11. Most parents indicated that their children had more opportunities to use technology for instruction under block scheduling, with most naming computer labs as how technology was used.

12. A majority of the teachers indicated that they had more opportunities to use technology for instruction under block scheduling; however, not many details were given on how it was used.

13. Some teachers indicated they had used community resources, including guest speakers, volunteers, and groups.

14. No pattern emerged for training needed by support staff, except food services staff indicated a need for computer training.

15. No pattern emerged for professional development activities for teachers. The most frequently cited needs were cooperative learning, use of technology, differentiation in the class, effective lesson plans, student assessment, and opportunities to develop effective teaching strategies and student motivation.

RECOMMENDATIONS FROM SECOND SURVEY

1. Continue staff development to help teachers use the longer blocks of instruction to enhance the motivation, participation, and attention of students and to increase student achievement.

2. Analyze survey results and research successful practices from other schools using block scheduling to refine teaching practices.

3. Provide orientation for freshmen on expectations and responsibilities when using the block schedule.

4. Continue to enhance communications, positive and safe climate, and high expectations.

5. Increase greatly the use of technology in the learning process.

6. Use more community and world resources to provide outside expertise, applications for learning, and international dimensions to the curriculum.

7. Provide time for ongoing open forums and focus sessions for small groups of students, teachers, parents, and support staff to express concerns and share ideas about block scheduling.

PARENTS AND OTHER EXTERNAL CUSTOMERS

Although there are many ways to collect data from parents and other external customers, perhaps the most efficient data collection method is the use of well-constructed surveys. Generally, a well-constructed survey is an effective instrument when collecting certain types of information. If you are trying to determine the perceptions of parents concerning block scheduling, a survey administered in a timely manner can be very effective. If you choose to use a survey, be cautious about your timing for distribution. If you distribute surveys at a time when there is a controversy that might affect the results, note this situation when the data is analyzed.

These are some guidelines we follow when using surveys.

- Distribute surveys at the end of each semester in order to assess how parents perceive the block schedule in relation to their own child's performance and experiences.

- Select the optimum time to distribute the surveys. Don't distribute a survey on school safety immediately after a student has been arrested at school for possession of a gun on the school campus.

- Collect surveys in a timely manner.

- Analyze the surveys as soon as possible after they are returned.

- Share all results with all customers.

- Make sure the survey mirrors the information that you are interested in collecting.

ANALYSIS

So that analysis of the data is meaningful, before gathering data, it should be determined how the data will be used to make short- or long-term comparisons (e.g.: "Our assessment will examine the difference between spring data of the current school term and spring data of the next school term."). Once the data are collected, they should be distributed to the appropriate team(s), members of the school faculty and staff, or school community for analysis. Based on the results of the analysis, a plan of action should be put into place to address the identified deficiencies. Good news should drive a celebration.

CHANGE IS A SERIES OF NEVER-ENDING ASSESSMENT ACTIVITIES

As you analyze data, remember that assessment and refinement of plans are never ending. You will periodically re-sight your targets for improvement. The first critical steps include the following.

1. Baseline data should be identified once a decision is made to move to block scheduling. This includes existing information that will give a good picture of what your school is like before changing schedules. These data can include previous patterns of student performance on standardized test scores, attendance patterns, dropout patterns, etc.—the types of indicators discussed in this chapter.

2. The second step is to collect data provided during the early implementation level (first full year and a half after full implementation) to identify possible problems in the transition. (See Atlee's first and second surveys.)

3. The third step will assess the impact on how students and teachers regard the change. This can be collected with your second data collection.

Our decision at Atlee was to use a cumulative evaluation to cover a three-year period. The first year and a half, our goal was to provide the faculty, staff, and community with formative data that could be used to initiate change and refinement. The second year and a half emphasized summative results. A formative and summative evaluation process should give an adequate look at where you are and suggest possible changes needed. This does not mean that you stop collecting data and assessing changes made. It means that you are on your way to making the needed adjustments.

MEASURING OUR STUDENTS' PROGRESS ON THE BLOCK SCHEDULE

Since assessing the needs and outcomes of students and their adjustment to block scheduling is perhaps the most complex and complicated of our tasks, we should look at many variables before making broad judgments about block scheduling. Perhaps the most critical issue that we need to assess is how block scheduling is affecting student achievement.

Student achievement can be monitored in a variety of ways. We believe it is very valuable to monitor those students who score in the bottom quartile on standardized tests, whose grades reflect Ds or Fs, or who are identified as being at risk for a variety of reasons. All of these students who either are not successful with schoolwork or are in grave danger of dropping out of school or not attaining a standard diploma deserve our serious attention. Nothing could be more important as a test of the block schedule than to monitor these students' performances in the new structure.

The first task is to ask teachers to identify academically at-risk students early in the school term by reviewing information that is available at the school. This identification can also be accomplished by studying students' academic histories. Their progress should be monitored at a "quality check" meeting on at least a monthly basis. These checks could occur at regularly scheduled staff/stakeholder meetings (to avoid additional meetings) and would be considered an ongoing item on the agenda. In our experience, these checks have taken only minutes when participants used quality tools for conducting meetings. This process eliminates relying on summative types of data that become "old" in a short time (e.g.: end-of-semester or yearly grades).

Other data that can be used to assess student progress and plan for student instruction include the following.

- Statewide, basic competency/proficiency tests that focus on student achievement

- Summative or end-of-course tests. These tests are given at the end of the course and measure the proficiency level of the students' understanding of skills or content in a course. They are usually a series of common examinations based on established course curricula, and the results can be used to plan programs for students or staff development for teachers.

- Student enrollment and the results from the Advanced Placement program

- Results from college entrance examinations, including:

  Preliminary Scholastic Aptitude Test (PSAT)

  Scholastic Aptitude Test (SAT)

  American College Test (ACT)

- Grade distributions in various departments and comparison of schools not on block scheduling across the same school district.

- Grade distributions within departments. This offers teachers of the same course an opportunity to analyze why students earn Ds and Fs (such as incomplete homework) and develop a strategy for raising performance among those students.

An analysis can be made of student attendance and student dropout rates—additional data that point to school success. The same strategies for monitoring student achievement can be used to monitor these students' behaviors. Because of the formative nature of the assessment, we were able to identify causes that were related to high absentee rates for some students. The flexibility of the block scheduling allowed us to provide schedule changes for students who had legitimate needs for attending school on an irregular basis. In many instances, this action addressed the needs of the potential dropout. We were able to create student schedules that allowed those who were parents to continue their studies at school. These outcomes can be measured by the monthly and annual reports on dropouts and attendance.

A decrease in discipline referral should be one of the immediate positive results of block scheduling. We know from our own experiences that most discipline problems occur when students are unsupervised. With fewer class changes and fewer opportunities to be unsupervised, student opportunities for violating school discipline codes are decreased. As students become familiar with the block scheduling, they will find ways of "working the system," and there could be a resultant increase in negative classroom behavior. The chances of this occurring will be greatly reduced if teachers are aware of the teaching methodologies that should be used in a block schedule format—those that will maintain student interest while increasing motivation. Training teachers in conflict management will also assist them in handling problems that are generally referred to the administrative offices for resolution. One school faculty reported a 17 percent reduction in discipline referrals the first semester that block scheduling was implemented. The administration should measure the number of referrals to the administrative offices and the nature of the referrals. This information can be reviewed during the monthly quality check sessions, and special students can be given priority in the "fix-it" column.

HELPING TEACHERS DO THEIR PART

How do we get teachers to respond positively to using pedagogy that will be successful in the block schedule format? Based on our observations, **this is perhaps the major implementation problem schools have with block scheduling.** Many teachers that we have observed and data that we have collected support the notion that teachers have not changed teaching methods and continue to use the pedagogy they were trained to use in teacher training programs. In other words, they continue to use the methods that they used in the traditional block of time. Based on our data, many teachers still rely on lecturing as their most common form of teaching, even though good pedagogy for adolescents should be based on student involvement. We have found that lecturing is the strategy that many students identify as being least effective. Tom provided students with the opportunity to give feedback concerning instructional methods and techniques used by their teachers. This information was used to design staff development activities and was not used in any punitive way.

Other methods for providing feedback on what is happening in the classroom include the following.

- Creating pacing guides that offer faculty an opportunity to discuss curriculum pacing and classroom expectations.

- Reviewing lesson plans to make suggestions on using various teaching strategies in one block. Tom required his faculty to use at least three different teaching strategies during any one block.

- Listening informally to faculty, students, and parents. Always use sound judgment before acting on information received this way.

LOOKING BACK . . .

As we look to the future of block scheduling and the positive impact it has had on student learning and teaching during its birthing, we must remember that this is only one aspect of restructuring traditional schooling to meet the needs of 21st-century students.

We must continue to assess and improve the effects of time on teaching and learning. As we do this, we will improve curriculum design, eliminate ability grouping (or tracking), enhance staff development, institute self-governance, and promote self-directed learning.

Deming (1986, p. 19) indicates the success of systems is based on participation from all levels of the organization. "There is no substitute for teamwork and good leaders of teams to bring consistency of effort, along with knowledge." As we have pointed out consistently throughout this book, you should involve everyone—every stakeholder—who cares about the school, whether the viewpoint comes from a worker or consumer perspective. Do not forget postsecondary educators who receive your graduates. They have an important role in giving feedback about the success of our students after high school. They also, in many schools, partner to broker programs that help to build a seamless program with the high school.

Bottom line: Think democratically—involve everyone, listen to everyone, and share what you learn with everyone. ❏

Chapter 12 Appendix on CD

❏ Introduction to Survey Instruments

- Parent Survey (word version)
- Student Survey (word version)
- Teacher Survey (word version)

How Do We Prepare for Cyberschools and Virtual Learning Experiences?

*B*oth learners and teachers need more time—not to do more of the same, but to use all time in new, different, and better ways. The key to liberating learning lies in unlocking time.

—from *Prisoners of Time*

LOOKING AHEAD IN THIS CHAPTER . . .

If the use of flexible time is to have a positive impact on future efforts to restructure high schools, we must expand the vision of high schools and how time is viewed. It is time for educators to stop limiting their thinking about time for learning. As technology continues to develop, a critical eye must be given to the traditional high school, its efficiency and cost effectiveness in the emerging age of the virtual high school. The virtual high school: truly a paradigm shift.

In the past decade, we have begun using the term *paradigm* to describe a change in thinking. Indeed, it is that but much more. A paradigm is a worldview that reflects our assumptions and beliefs and colors how we take in new information. Your paradigm is the structure in which you put new information, the structure that sends the information to a specific place that makes sense for you. You can then deal with the information; draw conclusions about the information; reject or support subsequent corollaries, inferences, or deductions about the information; or totally ignore the information because your worldview has placed the information inside your structure in a way that is comfortable for you.

That is a paradigm: a structural way of viewing information. It is developed over time, and it is tied closely to your historical perspective on events. Your life experiences lead you to view the world in a particular way—a unique way from others—and it is very difficult for anyone to convince you that there is a better (or different) way of accomplishing a purpose. A paradigm is too complex to change easily, and it doesn't change because one piece of information discomfort. **A paradigm shift occurs after careful reflection upon many events, ideas, or circumstances that impact your**

thinking. A paradigm shift is the result of thinking critically about that which has occurred, that which is occurring, and that which is likely to occur in your world.

We propose a paradigm shift. We are using this chapter to conclude our discussion of changing how time is used in schools by examining several important factors impacting our nation's schools. These factors—sociological, political, cultural, economic, and technological—force a different look at schooling and call for a critical look at how schools must operate in the future to successfully serve various populations of students. By requesting a critical look, we are not saying that we want to criticize schools. On the contrary: based on our observations of schools throughout this country and other parts of the world, we believe that given the challenge of educating all children in a diverse society, the schools are responding to the challenge. We believe also that we must continue to look for ways that will allow us to continue to respond to these and additional challenges that we will face in the future. As educators, our current status leaves us at a fork in the road of education that allows us to examine several paths for the future. Schools can continue to function as they have, but we believe they will not be highly successful unless they respond appropriately to the external factors that impact the school on a daily basis. A response may be to restructure the school day and optimize the resources that we have to the fullest extent. The most basic resources at a principal's disposal are the physical facilities, time, and human resources. This may mean operating the school in the evening as well as during the day or teachers using flex scheduling to meet the needs of the students within the school. Another response may be to utilize mass media technology to allow students to learn at home as well as in school buildings or other locations.

There are many paths available. As a principal or teacher, your task is to find the critical path that will successfully lead your students. To do this, you must shift your thinking from school days of 8 hours to days of 24 hours; from 180 days a year to 365 days a year; from classrooms with desks, books, and teachers to classrooms with computers, video databases, and real-time video; from schools in a build-ing to schools in many locations throughout the world; from a curriculum that is managed by administrators and teachers to one that is limited only to the technological resources that are available; from students who come to school each day to students who meet together periodically. It is time to shift our thinking about what school is and how time is used to educate our children.

PREPARING FOR THE VIRTUAL SCHOOL

When Howard Rheingold published *Virtual Reality* in 1991, we were introduced to the notion of artificial worlds being created by technology, worlds that seemed far away from the classroom. Later, in *The Virtual Community,* Rheingold explored the possibilities of human development and community behavior given the accessibility of the Internet and other webs of information. Rheingold explains behavior in virtual communities (i.e.: personal relationships conducted via the Net) that sounds remarkably like behavior in high schools.

> People in virtual communities use words on screens to exchange pleasantries and argue, engage in intellectual discourse, conduct commerce, exchange knowledge, share emotional support plans, brainstorm, gossip, feud, fall in love, find friends and lose them, plan games, flirt, create a little high art and a lot of idle talk (Rheingold, 1993, p.3).

If Rheingold's description of the virtual community is accurate—and we couple that with an acknowledgment that CD-ROMs, videotapes, and the Internet provide greater access to information than any textbook—we must ask the question: what is the role of the high school as an institution during this time of instant access to information? Some educators are beginning to explore the notion of a virtual high school that exists for a student through technology rather than in a classroom. The idea suggests a new definition of "the school," a new role for teachers, and certainly a different way of looking at time for student learning.

While most of us feel removed from the challenge of a virtual high school, we acknowledge we are in the midst of change that is driven by technological innovation. A typical 50-minute period does not give either the teacher or the student enough time to prepare, explore, and follow up a lesson using a network, CD-ROM, or even a video. We want students to create meaning for themselves, and that requires more than merely watching a video or logging onto the Internet, and the block schedule provides more time for this kind of learning to occur. While technology makes information more readily available, it demands the time that is necessary to utilize the information effectively and creatively, especially for the student to go beyond the level of accessing knowledge for information alone.

But let's stretch our thinking beyond the advantages offered by 90-minute blocks of time, for these have limitations, too. Let's begin thinking about time for learning without bell schedules. Those students (and faculty) who regularly access the Internet will report large blocks of time spent in exploring, reading, printing, and using information found. Those who communicate via e-mail or in chat rooms are not restricted to the second period, Monday through Friday. Those who purchase a CD-ROM to learn Spanish (just think of the opportunities available to students of foreign language!) or purchase time over the Internet to learn a language are not restricted to 90 minutes a day during the first semester. Our technology has freed us from the restrictions of primarily acquiring information in the structured setting of school. He who has access to the technology has unlimited access to information. While thousands of books were available in libraries in the past, the quick response and entertaining format of our technological world attracts us in a different way to unlimited information. Additionally, the immediacy of Internet access provides information as it emerges. Just as we watched a war being fought in the Persian Gulf and Eastern Europe, we can experience space travel with astronauts and talk to scientists in labs as experiments are conducted.

Technology is only one field that is impacting education. The forces that drive change in our schools are the same forces that change our society. The broad areas used for strategic planning are one way to group these forces so that they can be examined individually and collectively, because it is clear that these forces interact in a system that reflects interdependencies impacting schools both positively and negatively. We see the major forces impacting schools today and in the future falling into these categories: sociological, political, cultural, economic, and technological advancements. An examination of each of these categories—past, present, and future—is necessary to identify the context in which schools of the early 21st century will operate.

AN EXTERNAL SCAN OF THE ENVIRONMENTAL FORCES REQUIRING SCHOOLS TO CHANGE

An examination of the environment that surrounds our schools begins with a look at the forces affecting schools over the last two decades. A brief analysis of the critical factors we have seen working in schools is summarized in Figure 106.

We do not claim to be comprehensive in our approach, nor are we saying that these are the only factors affecting how schools function. We believe the behaviors and actions of students and parents that are a result of the factors listed here are significant for most school administrators. Our projection of where these factors are leading schools is based solely on our global view of schooling. The point we want to make is that schools have changed over the last 20 years as a result of many things, and taken collectively, we see these factors evolving and having significant impact in the future.

A look at this chart and a synthesis of the information suggests that school leaders will face continuing challenges during the next decade. The source of the challenges—political, social, technological, etc.—may be insignificant in that leaders will be forced to address the challenges regardless of their source. We believe that these challenges and others yet to be revealed will force school leaders to think about their resources prudently. The use of time will continue to be an issue for high school teachers and students. We will think differently about how we are using time as we find solutions for the problems we face. As students' lives become more complex, as teachers' responsibilities widen, and as our community's expectations increase, we will look differently at the time that is available for teaching and learning.

(Continued on page 284)

FIGURE 106

External Scan of Environmental Forces Affecting Schools in the 1980s, 1990s and Present to 2005

FORCES	1980s	1990s	Present–2005
SOCIOLOGICAL	Permissive teen years; Concept of family redefined to include single parents; Alcohol/drug abuse by teens acknowledged; Families continue to lose contact with the school	Teenage pregnancy openly accepted and by choice; Violence in school; Weapons accessible; Increased suspensions/ expulsions; Rights of students and parents voiced; Special education services expanded; Family defined to include single parents by choice; Home schooling grows and is accepted as viable option; Charter schools provide options to parents; Important role of parent in a student's performance is recognized; Cybernet/Internet become acceptable delivery systems for students	Conservative attitude toward social issues; Unskilled workforce lacks opportunity to achieve "American Dream"; Definition of family continues to expand; Traditional family more involved in education; Schools without resources for technology widen gap between haves and have nots; Home schooling continues to grow with rights of home schoolers more liberally defined; Other alternative schooling choices such as school choice, charter schools, and school vouchers increase, as schools become more accountable; Schools transition into Community Learning Centers; Students act violently in schools; Numbers of students receiving alternative education increases largely because of acceptances of behaviors in community schools
POLITICAL	End of liberal social programs	Conservative policy makers voice concern about education; Higher standards and accountability required; Christian Right active in public education; Interest in privatization of public school, private education, charter schools, school choice, and vouchers	Continued conservative philosophy toward education; Support for choices for parents; Accountability efforts identify weak schools, putting greater political pressure on schools to make drastic changes; Return to traditional academic curriculum; Use of new delivery systems for instruction; Flexible use of time in school; Teachers continue to become more actively engaged in politics and policy making

FORCES	1980s	1990s	Present–2005
ECONOMIC	Reliance on three levels of government to fund education; Threat to America as leader in business and manufacturing as technological developments drive change; Low-skilled jobs go to third-world countries	Initiation of school-business partnerships; Employers voice concern about availability of a highly skilled workforce; Support for infrastructure for technology; School facilities and equipment need upgrading or replacing; Call for accountability of schools	Traditional business partnerships diminish; Business partnerships develop to include meaningful input and role; State and federal role in maintenance of school facilities begins; Growth of community-based resources and foundations to help support education; Technological accessibility widens gap between haves and have nots; Re-thinking compensations of educators necessary to channel best students into education career
TECHNOLOGICAL	Microcomputers, computer labs, and computer-assisted instruction begin in schools; VCRs used in classrooms	Integrated learning systems adopted; Desktop computers prevalent in classrooms; Technical courses include robotics; Internet connections develop; Graphing calculators and scientific probes are integrated into instructional programs; Textbook companies develop materials on CD-ROM; Distance learning widely accepted in higher education	Children grow up with facility for technology use; Laptops for students become accessible; Virtual schools become popular; New learning systems seen as viable alternative to traditional classwork
CULTURAL (School Culture)	School traditions are expanded to include minority groups in schools; More liberal acceptance of student behavior; Parents impact school policy and demand more input	Traditions change little; Negative social behavior, such as violence, impacts school events; Management of school shared by site-based teams	Traditions of school viewed as socializing force for students who spend minimal time in classrooms or are home schooled; Community develops strong role in school management, including assessment; Role of "teacher" expanded to include community mentors, members of business community, and people accessed through new learning systems

CREATIVE NEW SCHEDULES

In addition to the opportunities for students to learn through technology, students learn outside the classroom in mentoring and apprenticeship programs. Again, these programs require more than the traditional class period to provide authentic learning experiences in real-world settings. These programs are emerging for all students, those interested in technical careers and those pursuing an academic discipline (for example, high performing students may desire time for extended study in one subject or interest area). These students need the opportunity to expand their learning experiences beyond the regular classroom and to approach learning from a global perspective. We must never disengage students from being skilled in the basics of knowledge necessary for learning experiences, but we must allow them to use this basic knowledge in a more creative and challenging way than confining them to the school, the classroom, the state, or the nation as a learning laboratory. The student and the teacher, the administrator and the parent must look at learning as a global opportunity. If we are to educate our students to become the world leaders for the next millennium, we must think in terms of educating them beyond the classroom. We must think in terms of educating students in ways that impact their opportunities for successful and productive lives. These opportunities must provide other occasions for learning outside the local community, the state, the nation, and even beyond the global community into the universe. We must provide them the skills that will equip them to make the most of these opportunities.

As we continue to look at student needs, we must look at the most efficient way to utilize allocated instructional time without extending the school day or the school year, or using other options that are prohibitive because of a lack of funding. What are the creative ways of using time? How can we continue to manipulate the allocated time of the school day to provide services more efficiently for students? At Atlee High School in Hanover County, Virginia, the dropout rate for students in grades 9 through 12 during the 1992–93 and the 1993–94 school years was 0 percent. Success was attributed to a more flexible schedule that would meet the needs of students as the principle ingredient in successful school restructuring.

Creative use of instructional time allowed the faculty and staff to identify at-risk students and provide educational opportunities relevant to their needs. These alternative opportunities, while grounded in academic expectations, not only provided an appropriate program for students but also removed disruptive students from the classroom. This action allowed teachers to concentrate on teaching rather than on disciplinary issues that interfered with student learning in the classroom. Examples of alternative educational plans for students include completing academic courses off campus in a program that resembles adult education programs or integrating academics in a cottage industry operated by the students.

On the alternating day (A-B) schedule, identified at-risk students attend classes in the building on Monday, Wednesday, and Friday of A week and Tuesday and Thursday of B week. On the alternating days, these students are placed in co-op jobs or work-based training programs, mentorships, or apprenticeship programs. This plan has had a direct effect on attendance, discipline referrals, student achievement, and dropout rates because these were the accountability indicators written into the program. Identified students are given specific instructions on what they must do to maintain these accountability indicators to remain in the program. Students consider it a privilege, not a requirement, to be in this program. The use of technology in such an educational plan for students will make the learning opportunities of the students even more flexible. This can be accomplished by providing audio/video learning packets or Internet learning opportunities that are made available for students other than during the traditional school day. Again, providing learning opportunities for students beyond the microcosm that we know as the school building is the key to the future of schooling for some populations of students.

This plan could also be transferred to the 4x4 semester schedule by offering the same opportunities for either morning or afternoon schedules. Students would be allowed to take two academic courses in the morning or afternoon and would be involved in co-op training or work-based programs off school grounds during the afternoon or morning.

For students who are dealing with personal issues such as pregnancy or dysfunctional families that act as a barrier to a student's educational experience, the flexible use of allocated instructional time allows them an opportunity to attend classes at school on certain days (or part of the day) and leave the school grounds as needed to deal with these issues. For students who are parents and cannot afford full-time child care, creative alternative scheduling will give them the opportunity to attend school on alternating days to take required classes and leave school to attend to their responsibilities on off days.

Some school districts may require waivers from local school divisions, state agencies, or accreditation agencies in order to implement these types of schedules and opportunities for students. But policy makers must be reminded that we must change the way we do business if we are to meet the needs of students of today and the future. We should also remind them that many of the policies that are now in effect were written in a time when schools were not confronted with all of the issues that they now must deal with on a daily basis.

There are also many advantages for teachers and administrators when creative scheduling is implemented. Opportunities for more flexible scheduling and more efficient use of teacher time can be realized. If a teacher prefers flex scheduling to meet certain needs that s/he might have, there are many opportunities for the administration and faculty to join together in a partnership that would meet the needs of all of the educators and the students as well as a more efficient use of building and human resources. Teachers can still teach the same number of minutes as they would during the traditional teaching schedule.

Some teachers may prefer to teach in the evening rather than teaching a continuous school day. Teachers who wish to come in at the end of second block and teach two blocks in the afternoon could continue their contractual obligations after the traditional school day. They could teach students who work during the school day or who are failing and need tutoring after traditional school hours.

One way to use time differently is to help students plan schedules over a period of years that will provide a block of time in the senior year for special projects. In Gloucester High School, Gloucester County, Virginia, a senior student has been able to work solely on an independent study project on alternating days. Having met most course requirements, this student only needs to use the three blocks on A days (the A-B block schedule) for traditional courses, and he is able to work on a very sophisticated computer programming independent project on B days. Rather than taking additional electives on B days, he has six continuous hours of time to complete a project that is leading to an internship with a major software developer and is congruent with his career goals. The A-B schedule provides the large block of time that allows this student to work with his mentors and do research that is best facilitated when full days are available.

Perhaps a combination of scheduling options would meet the needs of students of the future. A schedule that would provide a daily 55-minute block of time for certain courses, such as music or first-year foreign language, would provide options that would be more appealing to students as well as meet the needs of other stakeholders. The larger blocks of time—whether on an alternating day or daily greater time block—would meet the needs of stakeholders who need the additional instructional time

---

CASE IN POINT

"Teresa" is a senior who needs two credits to graduate from high school. She has a small child and cannot afford child care. With assistance from the Parent/Teacher/Student Association, the school administration provides child care for two blocks a day, three days a week, during A week and two blocks a day two days a week during B week. Since the student is a senior and needs only English and government to graduate, she attends school two blocks a day on alternating days. For the 4x4 semester schedule, she could attend school five days a week for two blocks for one semester and still meet graduation requirements.

for completion of science labs, art labs, and short field trips.

At Atlee High School, students choose three classes per day of approximately 109 minutes and one class of approximately 55 minutes daily on the A-B schedule. This gives any student an opportunity to take a total of seven classes per year. If a student elects to take a 55-minute block each day or the 109-minute block every other day during the early morning block, s/he can earn a total of eight credits per year. This would lengthen the student's day by approximately 55 minutes. These opportunities could be offered without additional cost to the school or school district. It is just a matter of adjusting a teacher's teaching day so that s/he arrives earlier and leaves earlier than his or her colleagues. With this combination of scheduling, administrators could choose to schedule math, music, and other courses where sequencing is an issue during the 55-minute block of time that meets on a daily schedule for the duration of the school year.

A different configuration would possibly meet the needs of more stakeholders. This model includes a combination of a 75-day session, followed by a 30-day intersession, and concluding the 180-day year with a second 75-day session. The first 75-day session would provide an opportunity to take three or four Carnegie units, depending on the length of the school day. The 30-day intersession would provide an opportunity for in-depth experiences in a particular area of interest, an opportunity for a community service component, an extended field trip, an immersion in a foreign language at home or abroad, mentoring, and distance learning.

Another advantage that such a schedule offers is an opportunity for the student who needs remediation or acceleration. During the 30-day intersession, students who have not been successful in previous attempts in certain classes would have an opportunity to remediate in a maximum of two courses. For those students who want to accelerate or study a subject in depth, this schedule offers the opportunity to select one area they would choose to pursue. This would be an advantage to students who have been identified as gifted and who need additional time to explore areas of interest in-depth or pursue research over a meaningful period of time.

The final 75 days of the 180-day school year would be used to continue the courses that were started the first semester if the school is on the alternating day schedule, or elect four new courses if the school is on a semester schedule. If the 30-day intersession is placed at the end of the first 150 days, this format would allow students who were not successful during the first 150 days an opportunity to re-take certain courses. For those students for whom summer school is not an option, it would allow them to move forward with their class for the next school term. Hopefully this opportunity would allow at-risk students more time to increase their knowledge base so that they are successful and can apply these skills in a real-life environment. This configuration would be especially beneficial for seniors who have failed required courses, because it would provide them with an opportunity to re-take those classes and graduate.

In our experience, we have found that if teachers know that students have opportunities to make up course requirements for graduation or for moving to the next grade or course level, expectations are higher. More students re-take courses if teachers are even a little concerned about them not possessing the knowledge base needed to move to the next level. The bottom line is that the schedule works for the student, and the student is not the victim of the schedule.

CASE IN POINT

A teacher has pre-school children at home, but child care is not available until after classes have started. She may decide that she would like to have her planning or duty period during the first block of the day so that she can stay at home with the children until day care is available. Through an arrangement with the administration, her school day does not begin until the end of the first block. Her school day is extended beyond the normal school day, and the time missed in the morning is then transferred to the end of the day. Her duties, such as tutoring students or monitoring after-school detention, will be assigned at the end of the day.

CASE IN POINT

Students who fail English the first semester will re-take the first semester in the evening program while continuing the second semester during the regularly scheduled time of the school day. At the end of the school year, if the student successfully completes the first semester requirements for English, then the first semester's incomplete grade is replaced with the highest grade that the student earned in the evening program.

At W. Marshall Sellman School in Cincinnati, Ohio, principal David Stouffer implemented the 75-75-30 plan. After completing the first year of this plan, he reported that:

> . . . the program has been a tremendous success. As everyone knows, keeping students (and staff) excited about school at this time of the year is very difficult, but our last 30 days (with students taking classes they chose and teachers teaching subjects they chose to teach) has produced an excitement about school that is really positive. As one teacher said, "It's like the first day of school all over again."

Mr. Stouffer reported that teachers were taking risks in teaching their classes, trying innovative approaches in the classroom. As one teacher told Mr. Stouffer, "I should do more of this kind of teaching during the regular school year."

There are many variations on this configuration (see Figure 107) limited only by the imagination of the stakeholders.

THE RESOURCE OF TIME

As we look at the future of block scheduling and the effects that it has had on learning and teaching, we must remember that this is only one small part of restructuring that is taking place in the secondary schools of our nation. The use of time is but one resource that the principal can use as a catalyst for change. Time interacts with other features of the infrastructure of the school: climate, empowerment, governance, staff development, and technology. This infrastructure supports the work of the school to improve learning, provide appropriate curriculum, and utilize best practices for teaching. In the traditional school, time has driven the schedule and forced classes to adhere to time constraints, thereby encouraging teacher-directed lessons and discouraging highly interactive student learning. In the restructured school that uses a block schedule, time is a resource that creates additional learning opportunities for students and additional teaching opportunities for teachers.

A variety of options for using school time to enhance student learning will continue to emerge. If we recognize that courses need greater periods of time for student interaction and technological applications, why should we continue to dissect our school days into small chunks of time? As a national report stated, "Both learners and teachers need more time—not to do more of the same, but to use

FIGURE 107
Flexible Scheduling to meet the 180-Day School Year

5 Possible Configurations

Configuration I	75	30	75	**XXX**
Configuration II	75	15	75	15
Configuration III	15	75	75	15
Configuration IV	15	75	15	75
Configuration V	30	75	75	**XXX**

all time in new, different, and better ways. The key to liberating learning lies in unlocking time" (*Prisoners of Time*, p.10).

WHAT ARE THE BLOCK SCHEDULING ISSUES THAT MUST BE ADDRESSED TO ENSURE FUTURE SUCCESS?

After a decade of collecting data, visiting schools, working with teachers and administrators, we still are identifying certain issues that were commonly identified when block scheduling was first on the horizon of the reform movement in secondary education. Administrators have addressed many of the issues that initially plagued block scheduling, but the following issues continue to emerge as problem areas that must be addressed.[1] We would encourage teachers and administrators to consider technology and electronic delivery systems when looking at all of these issues.

Staff development—Educators must continue to focus on staff development for teachers. Although we have observed much effort being placed on teacher staff development, we continue to hear from teachers that more training is needed to be successful in the block schedule. Any major restructuring effort requires retraining of those impacted by the change. If block scheduling is to continue to provide unrestricted learning opportunities for students and teachers, opportunities must also be available to teachers to grow professionally and sharpen their teaching skills. In particular, with the emergence of technology, emphasis should be placed on training in its use as a teaching tool and as a tool for exploration and problem solving. As teachers are hired who grew-up with technology, the training emphasis can become more focused on innovative practices and cyberschooling.

Sequencing of certain subjects—There are still concerns about the issue of sequencing of certain classes in order to build upon previously learned knowledge. Most of these concerns are voiced by foreign language, algebra, and music

teachers. Principals should continue to familiarize themselves with current related literature on learning and cognition so that they can respond in an informed manner regarding short- and long-term memory and the need for daily learning activities. The research on the brain and learning that has emerged since the early 1980s is highly relevant to the decisions that will be made about learning environments of the future.

Transfer students—Although schools have always responded to students transferring from schools where course offerings were different or where more or fewer electives were offered, the variety of block schedules now being implemented exacerbates the transfer issue. If a student transfers to a school that is on a different schedule than the sending school, how does this affect the quality of the educational program that the receiving school offers the student? Specifically: any transfer involving the semester block presents problems, depending on the time of year the student is moving into or out of the 4x4 block. There are fewer issues to deal with if a school is on the A-B block because of the yearlong format for classes.

As in the past, the principal should anticipate such difficulties and have in place a program of assistance that would support the transferring student as s/he makes adjustments to the new schedule. Support should be provided either to help a student catch up if the instructional pacing in the new school has been faster, or to assist a student enrolling in a new course at any time during the school year. This continues to be a major issue, as statewide testing becomes a major component of the accountability issue facing high schools.

Advanced placement course offerings/ international baccalaureate program offerings—AP courses continue to be popular among students. Faced with fierce competition for space in the top colleges and universities in the country, students are responding to higher expectations by enrolling in more AP classes. In addition, we are seeing an increase in the number of schools that are offering IB opportunities for students. The semester block schedule presents a challenge to the teacher and student of the AP course. Again, through careful planning, the principal can respond to this chal-

---

[1] For those interested in reviewing these early problems, please see our article, "A Vision for Block Scheduling: Where Are We and Where Are We Going?" in the December 1997 issue of the NASSP Bulletin.

lenge. It is critical that principals find ways to address the issue of "retention of information" when a student completes an AP course at the end of the fall semester but cannot take the AP examination until the conclusion of the second semester.

Instructional pacing —Two of the major staff development issues for teachers continue to be the pacing of instruction and curriculum alignment with adopted standards. Traditionally, teachers are accustomed to structuring lesson plans to be taught in a 45- to 55-minute block. Many are still looking for innovative methods to move from this practice. Teaching in a block scheduling environment requires that teachers adjust to teaching in longer blocks of time. This, in many instances, requires a change in teaching behaviors as well as a paradigm shift in attitudes. Teachers continue to report that pacing is a concern, even as they gain experience in teaching in the block schedule. Concerns are still expressed that teachers will not meet instructional objectives mandated by the curriculum and, in many instances, they will not cover objectives that will provide the basis for students to move to the next level of expectations.

Assessment—In addition to providing training and education to staff, the principal must continue to monitor the effects of the larger blocks of time on both teaching and learning through collecting data. Although a body of literature on block scheduling is emerging, there is still a need for additional data that will assist principals when refining schedules or validating the successes of block scheduling.

Time and learning—The issue of the amount of time that students need to learn a particular concept is one that educators must deal with as we look at the future of block scheduling. Does it take the same amount of time for every student to learn and retain the amount of information needed to move successfully to the next level of knowledge associated with a specific course? Perhaps analyzing the research on Opportunity to Learn is the next step educators need to make as we move into the next millennium of using instructional time more efficiently and more effectively.

LETTING THE STUDENT SHAPE THE FUTURE

The role of a leader has been defined in many ways by great scholars and effective leaders. We close this handbook by issuing a challenge to the leaders of our schools. If you are a teacher-leader—and all teachers should be—assess the needs of your students as our technological society evolves. What do students need to prepare for a complex life in an unpredictable world? How can you help them access the information, skills, and experiences that will teach them—help them learn—in the new millennium? What will the role of the teacher become? How will the resource of time be used most effectively to help our students become the best-educated students of the 21st century?

And to the principal . . . how is your role changing? What does it mean to be an instructional leader? How will you help your teachers meet the needs of all of your students? Where will your students find the resources that will educate them? How can you manipulate all of your resources—human, financial, and time—to provide the most flexible and most rewarding learning environment?

Will you be a principal of a cyberschool? Will your school day run around the clock? We do not know where technology is taking us, but we do know that the complexity of our society and the changing natures of our home and work environments will continue to challenge us as educators. Think about the time you have with your students, with your teachers, with your students' parents. What can you do to maximize the effectiveness of the time you are given?

How will you respond to the challenges of the next decade?   ❏

Chapter 13 Appendix on CD

❏ An External Scan of the Environment Requiring Schools
to Change

Argyris, C., and D. Schon. *Organizational Learning.* Reading, Mass.: Addison-Wesley, 1978.

Bennis, W. *On Becoming a Leader.* Reading, Mass.: Addison-Wesley Publishing Company, Inc., 1989.

Blai, B., Jr. "Educational Reform: It's About 'Time.'" *The Clearing House* (September 1986), 60, 38–40.

Blanchard, K., and P. Zigarmi and D. Zigarmi. *Leadership and the One-Minute Manager.* New York: William Morrow and Company, Inc., 1985.

Block, P. *Stewardship.* San Francisco: Berrett-Koehler Pubishers, 1993 and 1996.

Block Scheduled High School Achievement: Comparison of 1995 End-of-Course Test Scores for Blocked and Non-Blocked Schools. Raleigh, N.C.: North Carolina Department of Public Instruction, 1996.

Block Scheduling in North Carolina: Implementation, Teaching, and Impact Issues, 1997 Survey Results, Executive Summary. Raleigh N.C.: North Carolina Department of Public Instruction, 1997.

Bloom, B., and M. Englehart, E. Furst, W. Hill, and D. Krathwohl. *Taxonomy of Educational Objectives: The Classification of Educational Goals. Handbook I: Cognitive Domain.* New York: Longmans, Green, 1956.

Bottoms, G., and B. Creech. *Mathematics Performance of Career-Bound Students: Good News and Bad News from the 1996 High Schools that Work.* Atlanta, Ga.: Southern Regional Education Board, June 1997.

Breaking Ranks: Changing an American Institution. Reston, Va.: National Association of Secondary School Principals, 1996.

Brookfield, S.D. *The Skillful Teacher.* San Francisco: Jossey-Bass, 1989.

Brookfield, S.D. *Understanding and Facilitating Adult Learning.* San Francisco: Jossey-Bass, 1986.

Canady, R.L., and M.D. Rettig. *Block Scheduling: A Catalyst for Change in High Schools.* Princeton, N.J.: Eye on Education, 1995.

Carroll, J.B. "A Model for School Learning." *Teachers College Record* (1963), 64, 723–733.

Carroll, J.M. *The Copernican Plan Evaluated.* Topsfield, Mass.: Copernican Associates Ltd., 1994.

Carroll, J.M. *The Copernican Plan: Restructuring the American High School.* Andover, Mass.: The Regional Laboratory, 1989.

Carroll, J.M. "The Copernican Plan: Restructuring the American High School." *Phi Delta Kappan* (January 1990), 358–365.

Cawelti, G. *Effects of High School Restructuring: Ten Schools at Work.* Arlington, Va.: Educational Research Service, 1997.

Cawelti, G. *High School Restructuring: A National Study.* Arlington, Va.: Educational Research Service, 1994.

The College Board. *AP and January Examination.* Princeton, N.J.: Guidance, Access, and Assessment Services, September 1996.

Cooney, S. *Education's Weak Link: Student Performance in the Middle Grades.* Atlanta: Southern Regional Education Board, 1998.

Cuningham, R.D., and S.A. Nogle. "Implementing a Semesterized Block Schedule: Six Key Elements." *High School Magazine* (March–April 1996), 3:3, 28–33.

Deming, W.E. *Out of the Crisis,* 2nd Edition. Cambridge, Mass.: MIT Center for Advanced Engineering Study, 1982 and 1986.

Dempsey, R.A., and H.P. Traverso. *Scheduling the Secondary School*. Reston, Va.: National Association of Secondary School Principals, 1983.

Diggs, L. "Why Four Days a Week Makes Sense for Us." *School Administrator*—Online, March 1999. As accessed on the World Wide Web (http://www.aasa.org/SA/mar9902a.html), March 12, 1999.

Dragseth, K.A. "A Minneapolis Suburb Reaps Early Benefits from a Late Start." *School Administrator*—Online, March 1999. As accessed on the World Wide Web (http://www.aasa.org/SA/mar9901b.html), March 12, 1999.

Drucker, P.F. *The Changing World of the Executive*. New York: Truman Talley Books, 1982.

Drucker, P.F. *Managing for the Future: The 1990s and Beyond*. New York: Truman Talley Books/Dutton, 1992.

Fullan, M. "Notes from Keynote Address." American Society for Curriculum Development Conference, Williamsburg, Va., 1995.

Fullan, M., and A. Hargreaves. *What's Worth Fighting for in Your School*. New York: Teachers College, Columbia University, 1991 and 1996.

George, P.S., and W.M. Alexander. *The Exemplary Middle School*, 2nd Edition. Fort Worth: Harcourt Brace College Publishers, 1993.

Georgia Department of Education. Telephone conversation. Atlanta, Ga., 1999.

Goldberg, M. Lecture. Virginia Department of Education, Richmond, Va., 1997.

Goodlad, J.I. *A Place Called School: Prospects for the Future*. New York: McGraw Hill, 1984.

High Schools That Work Site Development Guide #5. Atlanta, Ga.: Southern Regional Education Board, 1994.

Hillkirk, K., and J. Tome and W. Wandress. "Integrating Reflection into Staff Development Programs." *Journal of Staff Development* (1989), 10:2, 54–58.

Jones, D.C. Personal conversation. Richmond, Va., July 3, 1999.

Juran, J.M. *Juran on Leadership for Quality*. New York: The Free Press, 1989.

Juran, J.M. *Juran on Quality by Design*. New York: The Free Press, 1992.

Karweit, N. *Time on Task: A Research Review* (Report No. 332). Baltimore, Md.: Center for Social Organization of Schools, Johns Hopkins University, 1983.

Kennedy, M. "Policy Issues in Teacher Education." *Phi Delta Kappan* (May 1991), 659–665.

Kentucky Department of Education. Telephone Conversation. Frankfort, Ky., 1999.

King, A.J.C., and J.L. Clements, J.G. Enns, J.W. Lockerbie, and W.K. Warren. *Semestering the Secondary School*. Toronto: Ontario Institute for Studies in Education, 1975.

King, A.J.C., and W.K. Warren, J. Moore, G. Bryans, and J. Pirie. *Approaches to Semestering*. Toronto: Ontario Institute for Studies in Education, 1977.

Knowles, M.S. *The Modern Practice of Adult Education* (Revised). Englewood Cliffs, N.J.: Prentice Hall Regents, 1970 and 1980.

Kramer, S.L. Unpublished research report used as basis for two articles in the *NASSP Bulletin* (February and March 1997), 1996.

Kramer, S.L. "What We Know about Block Scheduling and Its Effects on Math Instruction, Part I." *NASSP Bulletin* (February 1997), 81:586.

Kramer, S.L. "What We Know about Block Scheduling and Its Effects on Math Instruction, Part II." *NASSP Bulletin* (March 1997), 81:587, 69–82.

Ky.Re.Stat. *Alternative Use of School Time: The Kentucky Education Reform Act KRS 158.6451* (4), Frankfurt, Ky., 1990.

Levin, H.M. *About Time for Educational Reform.* (No. 83–A19. IFG0). Stanford, Calif.: Stanford University (1983), 29–30.

Manning, M.L., and R. Saddlemier. "Implementing Middle School Concepts into High Schools." *Clearing House* (July–August 1996), 69:6, 339–342.

Maslow, A. *Motivation and Personality.* New York: Harper and Row, 1954.

Mezirow, J. *Transformative Dimensions of Adult Learning.* San Francisco: Jossey-Bass, 1991.

Murphy, J. "Instructional Leadership: Focus on Time to Learn." *NASSP Bulletin* (March 1992), 19–25.

National Commission on Excellence in Education. *A Nation at Risk: The Imperative for Educational Reform.* Washington D.C.: U.S. Government Printing Office, 1983.

North Carolina Department of Public Instruction. Telephone conversation. Raleigh, N.C., 1999.

Peters, T.J. *Crazy Times Call for Crazy Organizations.* New York: Vintage Books, 1994.

Peters, T.J. *Liberation Management.* New York: Alfred A. Knopf, Inc., 1992.

Peters, T.J. *Thriving on Chaos.* New York: Alfred A. Knopf, Inc., 1987.

Peters, T.J., and N. Austin. *A Passion for Excellence: The Leadership Difference.* New York: Random House, 1985.

Peters, T.J., and R.H. Waterman. *In Search of Excellence.* New York: Harper & Row, 1982.

Prisoners of Time: Report of the National Education Commission on Time and Learning. Washington, D.C.: United States Printing Office, 1994.

Questline. International Insights. *Teaching Time: More Isn't Necessarily Better.* Organization for Economic Cooperation and Development (Date unknown).

Raphel, D., and M.W. Wahlstrom and L.D. McLean. "Debunking the Semestering Myth." *Canadian Journal of Education* (1986), 11:1, 36–52.

Rettig, M.J. *Memo to Friends: Study on Block Scheduling in North Carolina.* Harrisonburg, Va.: James Madison School of Educational Leadership, January 1997.

Rheingold, H. *The Virtual Community.* Reading, Mass.: Addison Wesley Publishing Company, 1993.

Rheingold, H. *Virtual Reality.* New York: Summit Books, 1991.

Ross, J.A. "An Evaluation of Timetable Innovation in Ontario," *Canadian Journal of Education* (1977), 3, 23–36.

Russell, T., and H. Munby. "The Role of Experience in Developing Teachers' Professional Knowledge" (pp. 164–187). In D.A. Schon (Ed.), *The Reflective Turn: Case Studies In and On Educational Practice.* New York: Teachers College, 1991.

Schoenstein, R. "The New School on the Block." *The Executive Educator* (August 1995), 17:8, 18–21.

Schon, D.A. *Educating the Reflective Practitioner.* San Francisco: Jossey Bass Publishers, 1987.

Schon, D.A. *The Reflective Practitioner.* New York: Basic Books, 1983.

Senge, P. *The Fifth Discipline: The Art & Practice of the Learning Organization.* New York: Doubleday Currency, 1990.

Shortt, T.L. *Block Scheduling Virginia: Implementation, Teaching and Impact Issues—An Executive Summary.* Richmond, Va.: Virginia Department of Education, 1999.

Shortt, T.L. "Teacher Classroom Behaviors and Their Effects on Student Achievement in Secondary Classrooms," an unpublished dissertation. Charlottesville, Va.: Curry School, University of Virginia, 1986.

Shortt, T.L., and Y.V. Thayer. "Block Scheduling Can Enhance School Climate." *Educational Leadership* (December/January 1998), 76–81.

Shortt, T.L., and Y.V. Thayer. "Vision for Block Scheduling: Where Are We Now and Where Are We Going?" *NASSP Bulletin* (December 1997), 81:593, 1–15.

Shortt, T.L., and Y.V. Thayer. "What Can We Expect to See in the Next Generation of Block Scheduling?" *NASSP Bulletin* (May 1995), 79:571, 53–62.

Shusterman, A. "Annenberg Institute for School Reform Releases First-ever Report on Public Engagement in Education." Personal correspondence via electronic mail list service. March 23, 1998.

Skrobarcek, S.A., and H-W.M. Chang, C. Thompson, J. Johnson, R. Atteberry, R. Westbrook, and A. Manus. "Collaboration for Instructional Improvement: Analyzing the Academic Impact of a Block Scheduling Plan." *NASSP Bulletin* (May 1997), 81:589, 104–111.

Smith, R., and W.J. Camara. *Block Schedules and Student Performance on AP Examinations.* Research Notes, RN-03, Office of Research and Development, The College Board, May 1998.

Stallings, J. "Allocated Academic Learning Time Revisited or Beyond Time on Task." *Educational Researcher* (1980), 9:11, 11–16.

Styles, K., and G. Cavanagh. "Seventy Minutes and What to Do with Them." *OSSTF Bulletin* (February 1974), 54, 51-54.

Survey Results, Block Scheduling in North Carolina: Implementation, Teaching, and Impact Issues—An Executive Summary. Raleigh, N.C.: North Carolina Department of Public Instruction, 1997.

Tanner, B. "Perceived Staff Development Needs of Teachers in High Schools with Block Schedules," an unpublished dissertation. Charlottesville, Va.: Curry School, University of Virginia, 1996.

Task Force on Education for Economic Growth. *Action for Excellence.* Denver, Colo.: Education Commission of the States, 1983.

Thayer, Y.V. "The Development of a Handbook for Virginia Public School Staff Developers on the Total Quality Process in Education," an unpublished dissertation. New York: Teachers College, Columbia University, 1996.

Third International Mathematics and Science Study (TIMSS), 1999. International Study Center. As accessed on the World Wide Web (http://www.csteep.bc.edu/timss), July 26, 1999.

Traverso, H.P. "Scheduling: From Micro to Macro." *The Practitioner* Published by NASSP (October 1991), 18:1, 1–8.

Traverso, H.R. *Instructional Leadership Handbook.* Reston, Va.: National Association of Secondary School Principals, 1984.

Visher, M.G., and D. Emanuel and P. Teitelbaum. *Key High School Reform Strategies.* Berkeley, Calif.: MPR Associates, Inc., 1999.

Wang, J. "Opportunity to Learn: The Impacts for Policy Implications." *Education Evaluation and Policy Analysis* (Fall 1998), 20:3, 137–156.

Watts, J.A., and G. Gaines and J. Creech. *Getting Results: A Fresh Look at School Accountability*. Atlanta: Southern Region Education Board, 1998.

Weatley, M.J. *Leadership and the New Science*. San Francisco: Berrett-Koehler Publishers, 1992.

Wiley, D., and A. Harnischferger. "Explosion of a Myth: Quality of Schooling and Exposure to Instruction, Major Educational Vehicles." *Educational Researcher* (April 1974), 9:11, 7–12.

Wlodkowski, R. *Enhancing Adult Motivation to Learn*. San Francisco: Jossey-Bass, 1990.

INSTRUCTIONS FOR USING THE ACCOMPANYING CD

The complete contents of the accompanying CD-ROM can be viewed through a Web browser such as Netscape® or Internet Explorer®. If you wish to print a page, select the Print command under the File menu, or click on the print button.

The content also is available for download in Microsoft® Word version 6.0 (Mac) and 95 (Win). By downloading files to your hard drive and open-ing them in Microsoft Word, you can edit and customize them for your own use.

Files that are available for download are linked directly off the CD. Click on a link that reads "download word document," and you will be prompted to save the file. Once you save it, you can open it in your word processor. ❏

CD-ROM

Printable, downloadable, and editable materials
html and Microsoft® Word documents
Netscape Navigator® for Windows® 95/98/NT and Mac OS®
Documents usable with Netscape® or Internet Explorer®
Macintosh® and Windows® compatible

TABLE OF CONTENTS: ACCOMPANYING CD

INSTRUCTIONS FOR USING THE ACCOMPANYING CD

CHAPTER 5 APPENDIX
Communications plan for implementing block scheduling
Menchville High School, Newport News, Virginia
> Informational Paper: New Kids on the Block (word version)
> Trifold Brochure: New Class on the Block (word version)

CHAPTER 6 APPENDIX
Surveys to assist in adoption decision
> Cover Letter to Principal (word version)
> Information-gathering Surveys
>> Administrator Survey (word version)
>> Descriptive Survey (word version)

CHAPTER 7 APPENDIX
Success Stories
> A Success Story from the Southeast: Using the Alternating Day (A-B) Block at Princess Anne High School, Virginia Beach, Virginia (word version)
> A Success Story from the North: Using the 4x4 Intensive Schedule at Hatboro-Horsham High School, Horsham, Pennsylvania
>> Success story (word version)
>> Regular Bell Schedule (word version)
>> Regular Bell Schedule with Minutes (word version)
>> A.M. Assembly Schedule (word version)
>> P.M. Assembly Schedule (word version)

CHAPTER 8 APPENDIX
Creative Scheduling at the Middle School Level
> Even- and Odd-day Schedules from Stonewall Jackson Middle School, Mechanicsville, Virginia
>> Sample Master Schedule for Even Days (Blocks 2/4/6/8)
>>> Grade 6 (word version)
>>> Grade 7 (word version)
>>> Grade 8 (word version)
>>> Content Area Teachers (word version)
>> Sample Master Schedule for Odd Days (Blocks 1/3/5/7)
>>> Grade 6 (word version)
>>> Grade 7 (word version)
>>> Grade 8 (word version)
>>> Content Area Teachers (word version)
> A Case Study of the Sellman 50-50-50-30 Block Schedule
>> Introduction to Case Study (word version)
>> Timeline (word version)

Materials and Forms from Sellman
 Parent Information Sheet (word version)
 Letter to Parents (word version)
 Registration Instructions (download word document)
 Registration Form (word version)
 Student Evaluation Form (word version)
 Parent Volunteer Form (word version)
 Teacher Evaluation Form (word version)
 Parent Evaluation Form (word version)
Evaluation Results
 Student Evaluation Results (word version)
 Teacher Evaluation Results (word version)
 Parent Evaluation Results (word version)
Course Offerings (word version)
Sample Schedules
 Traditional 90-90 Schedule (word version)
 The Sellman 75-75-30 Block Schedule (word version)
The Sellman 30-Day Intersession
 Introduction (word version)
 Teacher Schedule (word version)
 Student Schedule (word version)
Course Descriptions
 Language Arts (word version)
 Reading (word version)
 Math (word version)
 Science (word version)
 Social Studies (word version)
 Computers (word version)
 Art (word version)
 Physical Education (word version)
 Other Courses (word version)

CHAPTER 9 APPENDIX

Instructional Change Framework
 Lesson Plan Components for One-Class Period (word version)
 Teacher Tips for Dealing with Block Scheduling in All Classes (word version)
 The Process of Designing Block Lessons (word version)
 Sample Lesson Outlines
 Spanish (word version)
 French III (word version)
 English 10 (word version)
 Algebra II (word version)
 Social Studies (word version)
 Biology (word version)
 Physical Education (word version)
 Sample Lesson and Unit Plans
 English: Searching for Self-identity (word version)

English: *Sherlock Holmes* (word version)
Math: Activity Ideas for Block Periods (word version)
Math: Integrating Technology in Block Periods (word version)
Math: Generic Lesson Plan (word version)
Math: Generic Unit Plan (word version)
Math: Algebra I or II Lesson Plan (word version)
Math: Geometry Field Study Lesson Plan (word version)
Music: General Lesson Plan Help (word version)
Special Education: Algebra Football (word version)

CHAPTER 10 APPENDIX

Training Plan for Switch to Block Scheduling
   Suggested 5-day Training Plan for Teachers
   Changing Methods for Block Scheduling
   Am I a Thinking Teacher?
   Training Matrix

CHAPTER 11 APPENDIX

Plans for Block Scheduling
   Student Planning in the 4x4 Block—includes all four success plans (word version)
      Success plan for Grade 9 (word version)
      Success plan for Grade 10 (word version)
      Success plan for Grade 11 (word version)
      Success plan for Grade 12 (word version)
   21-month Matrix for Block Scheduling (word version)

CHAPTER 12 APPENDIX

Introduction to Survey Instruments
   Parent Survey (word version)
   Student Survey (word version)
   Teacher Survey (word version)

CHAPTER 13 APPENDIX

An External Scan of the Environment Requiring Schools to Change

ADDITIONAL MATERIALS

Master Schedule for Alternating Day (A-B) Block
   English (word version)
   Math (word version)
   Science (word version)
   Social Studies (word version)
   Foreign Language (word version)
   Business (word version)
   Special Education (word version)
   Physical Education (word version)
   Fine Arts (word version)
   Vocational Education (word version)

Schedule with Time Emphases on Identified Core Courses
  Student Schedule with 4 Core and 3 Electives and Lunch 5a (word version)
  Student Schedule with 4 Core and 3 Electives and Lunch 5b (word version)
  Student Schedule with 4 Core and 3 Electives and Lunch 5c (word version)
  Student Schedule with 2 Core and 4 Electives (word version)
  Student Schedule with 9 Electives (word version)
  A.M. Vo-Tech Student Schedule with 2 Core and 5 Electives (word version)
  P.M. Vo-Tech Student Schedule with 2 Core and 5 Electives (word version)
Survey Instruments
  Administrator Survey #1 (word version)
  Administrator Survey #2 (word version)
  General Survey (word version)
  Parent Survey #1 (word version)
  Parent Survey #2 (word version)
  Student Survey #1 (word version)
  Student Survey #2 (word version)
  Student Survey #2 results (word version)
  Teacher Survey #1(word version)
  Teacher Survey #2 (word version)
  Teacher Survey #3 (word version)
  Teacher Survey #4 (word version)
  Teacher Survey #5 (word version)

THE COMPLETE HANDBOOK OF BLOCK SCHEDULING BIBLIOGRAPHY